DEMOCRATIZING EDUCATION AND EDUCATING DEMOCRATIC CITIZENS

‖‖ ‖ ‖‖‖‖‖‖‖‖‖‖‖‖‖ ‖ ‖‖ ‖‖‖
I0028133

DEMOCRATIZING EDUCATION AND EDUCATING DEMOCRATIC CITIZENS

INTERNATIONAL AND HISTORICAL PERSPECTIVES

EDITED BY
LESLIE J. LIMAGE

Routledge
Taylor & Francis Group
NEW YORK AND LONDON

First published 2001 by Routledge Falmer

Published 2016 by
Routledge
711 Third Avenue,
New York, NY 10017, USA

Published by
Routledge
2 Park Square, Milton Park,
Abingdon, Oxfordshire OX14 4RN

First issued in paperback 2016

Routledge is an imprint of the Taylor and Francis Group, an informa business

Library of Congress Cataloging-in-Publication Data is available from the Library of Congress.
    Democratizing education and educating democratic citizens :
international and historical perspectives
/ edited by Leslie J. Limage
ISBN: 0-8153-3570-9
Includes bibliographical references.

Between the time of research and the date of publication, World Wide Web sites may unexpectedly close or change addresses. The web sites listed in the references of this encyclopedia are the most recent known to the publisher.

ISBN 13: 978-1-138-96739-7 (pbk)
ISBN 13: 978-0-8153-3570-2 (hbk)

In memory of Emerita Professor Susanne Shafer (1924–1997)
for her constant commitment to democracy and to individual and
collective responsibility for social justice through education

Contents

Series Editor's Foreword
Democracy Isn't What It Used to Be . . .
and Perhaps It Never Was

"Take education out of politics!" "Education should not be a political foot-ball!" "Keep politics out of the schools!" "Educators should not be political!" These and similar warnings have been sounded at various times in various societies. Such declarations, however, miss the point that education *is* political. Not only is education constituted by and constitutive of struggles over the distribution of symbolic and material resources, but education implies and confers structural and ideological power used to control the means of producing, reproducing, consuming, and accumulating symbolic and material resources (see Ginsburg 1995; Ginsburg and Lindsay 1995).

Political struggles about and through education occur in classrooms and nonformal education settings; school and university campuses; education systems; and local, national, and global communities. Different groups of students, educators, parents, business owners, organized labor leaders, government and international organization officials, and other worker-consumer citizens participate (actively or passively) in such political activity. These struggles not only shape educational policy and practice, but also are dialectically related to more general relations of power among social classes, racial/ ethnic groups, gender groups, nations, and regional/multinational blocs. Thus, the politics of education and the political work accomplished through education are ways in which existing social relations are reproduced, legitimated, challenged, or transformed.

The RoutledgeFalmer Studies in Education/Politics series includes books that examine how education has been political in different historical periods and local and national contexts. The focus is on what groups are involved in political struggles in, through, and about education; what material and symbolic resources are of concern; how ideological and structural powers are implicated; and what consequences result for the people directly involved and for social relations more generally.

The purpose of this series is to help educators and other people under-stand the nexus of education and politics and, beyond this, to facilitate their active involvement in politics of and through education. Thus, the questions are not whether education should be taken out of politics, whether politics should be kept out of schools, and whether educators should be apolitical, but rather toward what ends, by what means, and in whose interests educators and other worker-consumer citizens should engage in political work in and about education.

This volume, edited by Leslie J. Limage, is the sixth book in the Studies in Education/Politics series and addresses a central issue in educational poli-tics and political education: democracy.[1] The authors came together through Limage's leadership to honor Susanne Shafer, an esteemed colleague who died in March 1997. Shafer had a lifelong great concern about democracy and education, as is evident in her introduction to an issue of *European Education* that was published around the time of her death. Shafer wrote, "As democ-racy spread across from West to East in Europe, the need was recognized for carefully constructed programs of political, or civic, education that would prepare youth for thoughtful, active participation in democracy" (1997, p. 3).

Shafer's version of the story of the dynamics in Central and Eastern Europe is in line with a more general trend that Diamond and Plattner (1993) described as a "global resurgence of democracy." There is another version of the story, however, that at least some of the "socialist" experiments, includ-ing those in Europe (e.g., that in the German Democratic Republic, to which Shafer devoted particular scholarly attention) had some success in creating democratic political economies. The contrasting stories, of course, derive at least in part from different meanings of the term *democracy* (on this issue in relation to the two Germanies, see Chapter 3 by David Phillips and Chapter 4 by Robert F. Lawson). That Shafer and some of the contributors to this vol-ume did not always highlight the multiple meanings of *democracy* put them in good company, even in what has been called a postmodern world. For example, although Anderson (1990), whose book inspired the title I chose for this preface, provides a detailed examination of how developments in the postmodern era have led scholars to consider more and more ideas and beliefs as social constructions of reality (Berger and Luckmann 1967), he employs the concept of democracy in an unproblematic manner. For Anderson, the "dilemma of democracy" is not that there are alternative perspectives of what democracy is (a point emphasized by Limage in the Introduction), but that there are a variety of interpretations of the issues that are available to citizens within democracies. He views the dilemma as arising from the fact that "while governance issues grow ever more complex and information more copious, the systems of mass communication make it ever more possible for political operatives (left, right, and center) to distort this complexity—to reduce it down to simple stories most people can understand without too much trouble, and can believe as long as they don't take in too much information" (182).

Democratizing Education and Educating Democratic Citizens provides contrasting perspectives on what constitutes democracy. In Chapter 2, Val Rust and Lisa Laumann distinguish liberal views of democracy, focusing on participation in the political system (e.g., voting) and on socialist views of democracy, emphasizing control over and benefits derived from the economy. Similar distinctions between political and social rights and between procedural and substantive dimensions of democracy are made by Nelly Stromquist in Chapter 1 and by me in Chapter 9. Stromquist also argues for taking seriously the private sphere (particularly the gendered power relations, division of labor, and distribution of resources in the home and family) as well as the public sphere (e.g., in government institutions and workplaces), suggesting that the extent of democracy in one sphere affects the degree of democracy in the other. In my chapter, I stress the relevance of consumer as well as worker and citizen roles in any examination of the nature of human experience in democracies and other types of political economies, noting that consumers' collective action may shape the behavior of corporations and affect government policy (see Gilbert 1997), even while citizens' relationship with electoral politics may be more like that of isolated individual consumers.

These different conceptions of democracy are drawn upon, explicitly or implicitly, by Elizabeth Sherman Swing, who interprets the dynamics of school restructuring in the United States in Chapter 5, and by Hans Lingens, who discusses higher education system reform in Europe in Chapter 6. Varying conceptions of democracy also inform the present author's analyses of challenges encountered in efforts to prepare democratic citizens in societies in transition, such as Central and Eastern Europe (Chapter 8 by Wolfgang Mitter); in pluralistic societies, such as Israel (Chapter 11 by Yaacov Iram); in centralized, homogenizing societies, such as France (Chapter 12 by Limage); in multinational societies becoming part of the European Union, such as the United Kingdom (Chapter 13 by Margaret B. Sutherland); and in former British colonies recently reintegrated with China, such as Hong Kong (Chapter 14 by Lee Wing-on and Leung Sai-wing).

These authors help us understand the intended impact of societal-level structural changes as well as curricular and pedagogical reforms in educational institutions. Other authors provide us with insights into how individuals experience such dynamics. For example, Gerlind Schmidt (Chapter 7) illuminates how German and Russian pupils view their schools in a period of transition, while Norma Tarrow, Ratna Ghosh, and Aurora Elizondo (Chapter 10) report on the values held by teachers in Canada, Mexico, and the United States.

This edited volume thus helps us to understand the complexities of efforts to democratize education and to educate democratic citizens. Such complexities might discourage some people from active participation in education/politics. That democracy isn't what it used to be and perhaps it never was, however, should serve as a catalyst for our active involvement in education/politics. Otherwise we leave to others the task of socially constructing the meanings and practices of "democracy" in education and society.

Mark B. Ginsburg

NOTE

[1]There seems to be a resurgent interest, at least rhetorically, in democracy in relation to education. One indication of this is that even as I write this, hundreds of scholars, practitioners, and policy makers are participating in a "Global Education and Democracy" Forum, organized by the Improving Education Quality project funded by the U.S. Agency for International Development.

REFERENCES

Anderson, Walter. (1990). *Reality isn't what it used to be: Theatrical politics, ready-to-wear religion, global myths, primitive chic, and other wonders of the postmodern world.* San Francisco: HarperCollins.

Berger, Peter, and Thomas Luckmann. (1967). *The social construction of reality.* Garden City, NY: Doubleday.

Diamond, L., and M. Plattner. (1993). *The global resurgence of democracy.* Baltimore, MD: Johns Hopkins University Press.

Gilbert, Rob. (1997). "Issues for citizenship in a postmodern world." In Kerry Kennedy (ed.), *Citizenship education and the modern state*, 65–81. New York: Falmer Press.

Ginsburg, M. (ed.). (1995). *The politics of educators' work and lives.* New York: Garland.

Ginsburg, M., and B. Lindsay (eds.). (1995). *The political dimension in teacher education: Comparative perspectives on policy formation, socialization and society.* New York: Falmer Press.

Shafer, Suzanne. (1997). "Humanistic education." *European Education* 29(1): 3–5.

Introduction
Alternative Perspectives on Democracy and Education

This book provides international and historical perspectives on the political role of education. How educational institutions around the world are addressing or neglecting to address the changing contours of democracy and civics is a main theme running through each chapter. The international authors taking up this theme are honoring the professional and personal commitment of Professor Susanne Shafer, who passed away in 1997 after a career in social studies, foundations of education, and comparative education through which she tirelessly promoted social and civic commitment among youth in the United States and abroad, especially Germany.

The chapters offer a broad range of research approaches to emphasize the multidimensional understanding needed to address issues of democracy and civics at the beginning of the twenty-first century. Ethnographic studies follow political science or historical approaches to awareness raising and practical experience of defining democratic processes and social commitment at different times and places in the past fifty years. There are lessons to be learned by students of public policy in education and teachers and decision makers at all levels through the multiplicity of approaches and often rigorously tentative conclusions. A major lesson to be drawn from this volume is that democracy and civic commitment are moving targets over time and context. The challenges of defining these terms and recognizing that education is neither neutral nor separate from the polity appear as partial conclusions in each country or case study. While many social scientists and policy makers going back hundreds of years have recognized the nonneutrality of education, others have seen schools as places apart from the pressures of the outside world.

The contributors to this volume demonstrate that such a distance has never been a reality and indeed is not an option. The last quarter of the twentieth century saw a narrower range of political worldviews come to dominate, with the collapse of many socialist systems of government and the questioning of many mixed forms of social and market-oriented polities. This collapse of visions of socialist well-being has not necessarily led to more participatory or egalitarian forms of government and society. This book speaks directly to the complexity of this dilemma. Some authors present case studies on specific groups of students in societies in transition, while others document growing awareness of social consciousness among teachers in training. Other authors take a historic perspective regarding the distance between discourse concerning democracy and equity and their particular country's school system practice.

Another major trend at this turn of the century is the rediscovery of history. Professor Shafer devoted her own early professional career to the study of the denazification of the schools in Germany following World War II, and several authors address attempts made in contemporary times to unveil mythologies about resistance to the many forms of modern and historical fascism. Others show the role of international bodies that ostensibly were created to promote human rights and democracy but in fact reinforce their denial or their maintenance in gender-biased forms.

All of the authors have firsthand experience of the countries and school systems they analyze, and many are either national or longtime residents and researchers concerned with the country or regional context. Having an international group of authors ensures that no simple answers are offered across the board for all countries and all time periods. Each author invites a critical look at schooling and education in the broadest terms. What are the contours of democracy and civic participation at a given time and place? Who are the actors most likely to promote one form or another? Readers must find the answers to these questions by critically examining the individual case studies presented herein in light of their own experience and analysis.

In Chapter 1, Nelly P. Stromquist deconstructs and reframes the current limited concept of citizenship, pointing out that it is not easily accessible to women in their everyday lives. She explores feminist definitions of citizenship that recognize women's multiple tasks in society and received images of what women should be. These representations affect women's availability for political participation, as either voters or political representatives. Women's conditions in society also affect the areas for political action in which they have been allowed to act in the past and in which they tend to be interested.

International development agencies today seek to promote women's incorporation as citizens in the nation-state. Their efforts, which greatly influence governments in the developing countries, are stubbornly centered on formal, public political institutions and on voting practices, thus failing to address how microsocial spheres such as those of the home and the school shape attitudes and beliefs about citizenship. In so doing, these agencies are helping to solidify rather than transform conventional forms and visions of citizenship.

Considering alternative forms of citizenship involves serving adult women so that they can rediscover their identities and reflect on the problems of women, two prerequisites to their mobilizing around issues important to them. Domestic violence, control over their bodies, and sexual harassment become important content areas for adult education programs serving women. When properly addressed, these topics can lead to the empowerment of women along psychological, political, and economic dimensions. In this regard, adult education for women undertaken by feminist nongovernmental organizations is working with the expanded concept of "social citizenship." At present, nonformal education programs for women are playing a much more important role than formal education, because young children and adolescents in regular schooling are seldom allowed exposure to curricula that are socially transformative, and they have not accumulated the experience needed to recognize circumstances that constrain the exercising of citizenship prerogatives and responsibilities.

In Chapter 2, Val D. Rust and Lisa Laumann analyze the political dimension of comparative education as a field of study. From its very beginnings comparative education has exhibited a political dimension. The earliest scholars who identified themselves as comparative educators were committed to a specific political orientation. Friedrich Schneider found himself in the middle of radical political currents in the first half of twentieth-century Germany and, though his writings were framed in rather abstract terms, the underlying political message was clearly in favor of a more liberal, democratic educational form. Isaac Kandel was deeply committed to democratic citizenship and judged educational systems on the basis of the capacity to instill in the youth of the system a commitment to democracy. During the period of theoretical hegemony of the 1950s and 1960s, comparative education scholars joined with social scientists to advocate a distinct form of political development, which is best outlined as modernization theory. Underlying modernization was an assumption of democratic and liberal education and citizenship. During the period in which so-called conflict scholars challenged that hegemonic domination, a special kind of political orientation dominated the discourse. This was framed in terms of social justice, and advocates of conflict spoke out in favor of racial, ethnic, social class, and gender equity and against the dominant political and economic conditions, which were considered to be biased against social justice. And in more recent times, the field has been colored by advocates against the domination of positivism and objectivity in favor of more humanistic theoretical orientations.

David Phillips explores in Chapter 3 educational issues reaching into the past, present, and future in Germany. Faced with the problem of "reconstructing" educational provision in Germany after the end of WWII, the Allies attempted in various ways to democratize the education systems reestablished in the four Zones of Occupation. Forty-five years later, when the territory of the former German Democratic Republic was absorbed into the

Federal Republic, similar tasks of reconstruction became necessary. This chapter examines the parallels in the postwar and postunification conditions in Germany with respect to the shaping of the education system.

In Chapter 4, Robert F. Lawson begins with the assumptions about democracy shared in the 1964/1965 studies by Susanne Shafer and myself on post–World War II changes in German education. The postwar evolution of educational policy is discussed with reference to the political-educational influence of the respective military occupation authorities on zonal differences, which eventually crystallized as differences between the Federal Republic of Germany and the German Democratic Republic. This section of the chapter concludes with the cultural and structural results that made Unification politically feasible, if not unproblematic. In short, because of land autonomy and because the structural principles were not essentially different in the two Germanies, the difficulty of including a decommunized East German education was not insurmountable. Lawson considers that the persisting tensions are more than economic. They are the residual tensions of clashing beliefs about democracy, the fundamental theme of this book in all its facets. In the contemporary period we have come to understand better the sources of those tensions, and the application of that understanding to the transfer of democratic practices. With that understanding of the theoretical openness of democratic principles, Lawson holds that American educators can bring to other countries American principles, strategies, and mechanisms as only *one* source, offering a context of alternatives. Although the available research provides a more refined theoretical base, it appears that the current literature and the transfer practice ignore it. On the one hand the cultural literature ignores structural effects of different policies; on the other, the structural literature emphasizes the universal efficacy of democratic forms in the United States, without the modification warranted by the democratic debate in the United States or by the research on educational transfer. He concludes, therefore, that what we know has not critically affected our efforts to assist other nations with democratization in education. Drawing from the studies on educational relationships in postwar Germany, one might conclude, contrary to the naive optimism of the American mission and also to the pessimism with which German writers have often criticized the limitations of socioeducational reform, that the values of education in Germany should be viewed independently of Anglo-American images, and appreciated for their persistence through political aberrations.

In Chapter 5, Elizabeth Sherman Swing examines three transformations, or would-be transformations, of public schools in the United States: decentralization, the attempt to transform a number of large urban school districts into smaller entities; choice, the attempt to set up a market economy in education by redistributing public money in the form of vouchers that would be applied to payment of tuition to the school of choice; and charter schools, which receive public funds but run semiautonomously, free from state and local regulation. All three of these emerging structures have premises based on the expectation that they will bring about greater equity in public education. All three present politically charged issues. Decentralization, which was attempted in New York City after the school strikes of the late 1960s, has reemerged in controversial proposals for reform in other cities, such as Philadelphia. Choice, a divisive national and local issue, is a concept favored by conservatives but not by teacher unions, who fear loss of control, or by liberals, who foresee a First Amendment court case if public money is used for religious schools. Charter schools, parallel perhaps to grant-maintained schools in England, are of concern to those who see such schools as evidence that public education is no longer responsive to local control. This chapter examines these proposed reforms, the disparity between expectations and reality in each of them, and the relationship of this disparity to the illusive goal of equity in public education.

In Chapter 6, Hans Lingens takes a regional and system-wide view. Higher education institutions in Europe are undergoing changes in response to the challenges of an increasing number of students, shortage of resources, changing demands of society and business, the unification of Europe, and the incorporation of the Eastern European countries into the free world. Institutions of higher learning want more autonomy in governance and in the distribution of funds received from the various government agencies. They also have to compete for funds from nongovernmental sources to meet their obligations in research and teaching. In return they must respond to the needs of these groups, which are sponsored by industrial or business organizations. Lingens explores the current attempts of higher education institutions in various countries to cope with these challenges and tries to show the development of these institutions from institutions of learning and research for personal development to institutions of service to provide a highly qualified work force in the most efficient way.

In Chapter 7, Gerlind Schmidt touches on those who are rarely heard in debates about the meaning and purpose of schooling: the pupils and students. She sets the context in which both earlier Soviet and German education evolved in fairly specific but sometimes similar ways and then proceeds with the results of a study that show what upper secondary school pupils actually think about schooling and their lack of a participatory and democratic voice. Every two years since 1993, the youngsters of about thirty St. Petersburg schools have been asked identical questions before they left school, having obtained the certificate for access to higher education *(attestat zreosti)*. From a Western point of view, Schmidt looks at the conceptual framework of the study within a period of transition of educational research and praxis from its beginning in 1993 to 1998/1999. The study aims to help headmasters and teachers in their everyday work, as well as offer a new concept of school life.

Schmidt also examines the "philosophy of education," understood as an inter-action between teachers and pupils, and presents results for the main topics of the questionnaire (what school provides pupils for their future life, what sort of place it is for their well-being, and what they think about their teachers). Schmidt then interprets the findings by the Russian authors of the study. They investigated young people's ability to respond to the challenges of the rapid transition of society and the surrounding world while teachers, parents, and the school show a certain inertia. The chapter paves the way for further work toward hearing how young people view themselves and their relation to schooling and the constantly changing world around them.

Wolfgang Mitter moves in Chapter 8 from the particular to the regional and offers a theoretical attempt to look at radical transformation in society and hence education. Mitter maintains that education for democratic citizen-ship can be identified as a basic educational challenge in states of Central and Eastern Europe. Regardless of distinctive discrepancies among the individual states, the region as a whole appears to be moving in somewhat convergent paths according to his analysis of legal documents (laws, decrees, and curric-ula) and available empirical findings. These convergences can be subsumed in global trends characterized by globalization on the one hand and localiza-tion on the other. Both of them are rooted in pluridimensional flows and meet in the dialectic and contingent concepts of globalization (Roland Robertson) and second modernity (Ulrich Beck). Mitter sees the prospects for education for democratic citizenship as deeply constrained by this complexity. Like comparable regions, such as South Africa, Central and Eastern Europe is distinguished by the coincidence of these global trends with radical transfor-mation processes having their specific impacts on education for democratic citizenship.

In Chapter 9, Mark B. Ginsburg turns to an interdisciplinary approach based on theoretical discussion, history, and empirical study. His chapter draws on ethnographic field work conducted in a teacher education program in Xalapa, Veracruz, Mexico, to examine key issues related to functioning of democracies. First, in considering democracy, one can focus on procedures (e.g., voting) and/or one can adopt a substantive notion, attending to the degree to which material and symbolic resources are equally distributed. Sec-ond, there are different conceptions of citizenship associated with "public democracy" (following Rousseau) versus "privatized democracy" (following Locke), with only the former implying the need for vigilance and active participation by the general population. On the basis of his analysis of field notes, documents, and interviews, Ginsberg describes how many of the students in this program develop concerns about the lack of substantive democracy, becoming critics of the inequality of wealth and power in Mexico and the world system. At the same time, however, they become estranged from the collective organizations (e.g., political parties, unions, and social movements) and even individual elements (e.g., voting and lobbying) of procedural democracy through which they might seek to address such concerns, viewing them as necessarily part of the problem. Thus, most students conclude that passivity or individual ameliorative activity in schools, families, and communities is the only strategy to pursue in seeking to deal with the problems of unequal society. Moreover, those who are—or plan to be— involved in organized forms of political activity do so primarily because they (accurately) perceive that such associations help them gain and maintain employment. The students, perspectives, and strategies are shown to be in line not only with popular images of citizenship in Mexico, especially for women, but also with messages they encounter in the formal curriculum, and more so in the hidden curriculum, of their teacher education program.

Norma Tarrow, Ratna Ghosh, and Aurora Elizondo offer a trinational study in Chapter 10, in which they discuss the results of collaborative research carried out in the faculties of education at three universities: the Universidad Pedagogica Nacional in Mexico, McGill University in Canada, and California State University, Long Beach, in the United States. The rationale for the study emerged from the experiences of faculty and students in two student teacher programs run jointly by the California State University and the Universidad Pedagogica Nacional. Anecdotal evidence indicated that significant cultural differences existed between the students and faculty of the two institutions and these differences affected students' learning experience. Differences in values and teaching styles led to problems in communication, teaching, and learning. This finding led to the development of a research project on the teaching of values. To make the study more useful in terms of comparison, the researchers asked McGill University, an English institution in a French milieu, to join the team.

Data from two phases of the project are presented. In Phase 1, Tarrow et al. conducted interviews with faculty and students in the preservice teacher education program to identify the values these participants considered the most important in teacher education. These interviews allowed them to develop two instruments that were subsequently used in Phase 2. The data from Phase 2 provided further information on the values that participants considered important for teacher education, the values that are taught in the programs, the strategies used to teach those values, and the issues that cause value conflicts. Their most important instrument, the semantic net exercise, gave them precise information on what the values identified actually meant to the participants.

Yaacov Iram takes the reader to another region of the world and another theoretical approach to pluralism and democracy in Chapter 11. According to Iram, political scientists estimated that out of 130 independent states in 1990, 45.4 percent were democratic. However, in 1973, out of 122 *independent* states, only 24.6 percent (30 states) were democratic. Indeed, since 1974, there has been a growing tendency toward democratization not only in Europe, particularly in the former Eastern Bloc, but also in South America, Africa, and Asia. Most of the democratic states are divided into ethnic or national groups, and a secondary division might include religion, language, socioeconomic status, and political power. Democracies might be classified as liberal or consociational according to Lijphart (1977, 1994). Israel represents a unique blend of both types of democracies, as Iram explains. In pluralistic societies such as Israel, education for democracy means more than teaching about a political system or a form of government. Rather, it is a process that imparts a way of living and a belief in individual and group worth and rights and is guided by the practice of social equality and solidarity. It is also expected to impart cooperation out of mutual respect, tolerance, and diversity. Iram concludes with a presentation of various programs of education for democracy in Israel to cope with socioeconomic, political, ideological, and national divisions in Israeli society in the wake of the continuing tensions in the region. A special program of education to preservice teachers is analyzed.

In Chapter 12, I raise a series of questions that are increasingly, rather than decreasingly, at the forefront of attempts to understand how history is repeating itself nearly worldwide at the dawn of the twenty-first century. Questions raised about individual and collective responsibility in the midst of civil war, conflict, and institutional and societal violence in and around schools in France are largely left untouched by French schools. The role of schooling in France appears to be little affected by the major social issues that rock traditional views of the country as a society of "liberty, equality, and fraternity." Major debates at the highest levels of French government and teacher and student strikes variously address violence in society and schools through the most traditional of analyses. History was replayed in a more critical fashion through the showcase trial of Maurice Papon, a high-level civil servant during World War II, for crimes against humanity, stressing for the first time the notion of individual responsibility, and yet history instruction in schools is unaffected. With rising youth unemployment, increased restrictions on immigration and legalization of immigrations, a feeble effort has been launched to attack violence in schools as a palliative. In traditional fashion, the "difficult" population of minority/immigrant youth is identified as the problem, and the solution is essentially punitive.

Civics education in French schools has generally been reduced to a one-term study of the institutions of the Fifth Republic. I return to the origins of French state schooling in the debates of the French Revolution to provide some understanding of the distance between a possible practice of democracy in society at large and the rigidities of the school system. Individual responsibility and social commitment through democratic processes are defined in very particular ways. The roles of teachers, parents, students, and the community at large can be modified only if there is an understanding of the history of the dilemma of a mythical national unity amid tangible political, socioeconomic, cultural, and linguistic diversity.

Parallel challenges in the United Kingdom are discussed by Margaret B. Sutherland in Chapter 13. The development of education for citizenship in the United Kingdom shows the interaction and conflict of major principles, notably, the fear of totalitarian indoctrination and the traditional belief that "citizenship is caught, not taught." Although religious education and civic education are not coterminous, they do have some elements in common: consequently, recent changes in the teaching of religion in public schools have had largely unrecognized effects on the transmission of some principles of good citizenship. With recognition of the multicultural nature of the British population has come unwillingness to seem to impose any one religion and, correspondingly, some hesitation as to the definition of appropriate civic education.

Attempts to implement proposals for a centralized curriculum for England and Wales following the 1988 Education Reform Act illustrate the various underlying principles: they show tendencies to lip service only, followed by growing recognition of a need to define, and give importance to, civic education. Scottish curriculum development, thought to be less rigidly controlled, displays some similarities. Yet in the case of Northern Ireland, curriculum reform since 1989 has given clearer recognition to the need for action to protect community life in situations of divided loyalties. A transverse theme, Education for Mutual Understanding, has received considerable practical attention. But in all parts of the United Kingdom, alongside official provision of education, we find many examples of individual schools, organizations, and teachers actively providing education for citizenship. A similar coexistence of public and individual initiatives may be found for the more recently introduced concept of European citizenship. Questions concerning future developments remain: How effective are central prescriptions for teaching citizenship? How important are individual initiatives? Is the belief that the major factor is individuals' assimilation of the standards of the community in which they live still valid?

In Chapter 14, Lee Wing-on and Leung Sai-wing discuss restraints on civic education both during Hong Kong's colonial period and in the period after its incorporation with China. Analysis is based on curriculum development, public debates, and the findings from the first phase of the International Educational Achievement (IEA) Civic Education Study in Hong Kong. The analysis of curriculum development highlights the depoliticization characteristics in the two periods of time, even though there are increased curriculum elements in China. The analysis of public debate focuses on the dilemma between nationalistic and patriotic education and democracy and human rights education. The analysis of the IEA Civic Education Study focuses on the lack of civic education activities and the lack of discussion of politically sensitive issues as from the research findings. The overall discussion focuses on how a society's civic education is constrained by its political circumstances. In fact, Lee and Leung show that models of analysis adapted for one cultural or political context are not easily transferred to a very different reality. Thus, this concluding chapter serves as a lesson for comparativists at all levels: policy and practice can only be cautiously designed and implemented across countries. This theme runs through the entire book as the various authors explore the past and present, seeking ways for a future democratization of society through education.

No single definition or model has ever been adequate to provide nearly universal social and individual justice and well-being. Yet the label of democracy covers a multitude of contexts in which individual and collective responsibility and participation are actually severely curtailed or denied. By and large, schooling is still a place where learning the practice of democracy is the exception rather than the rule. This seems to be the case even in countries that consider themselves unequivocally democratic in their political processes. The chapters offer a wide range of analyses that are critical but not necessarily pessimistic. There is agreement that there is no peace without justice; no democracy without critical participation; and no freedom from violence, need, or injustice without young people's and adults' learning that all age, ethnic, religious, and gender identities must be heard.

PART I

Conceptualizing Democratization and Democratic Citizenship

CHAPTER 1

Reframing Citizenship
Women As Full Actors in the Nation-State

NELLY P. STROMQUIST

With the fall of communist regimes, democratic rule is now in vogue, and the expansion of citizen rights is seen as a vital concomitant. Diverse political actors have expressed renewed interest in women's citizenship. These include national governments, international development agencies, and, of course, women in the movement to advance the condition of women.

Feminist theory and action are subjecting citizenship to intense scrutiny, finding that, in the experience of women, many assumptions about the nature of the democratic state have not been supported. The state's allowing and participating in the current unequal differentiation between men and women in status and life chances indicates that historically the state has not been neutral and thus citizenship has in fact been gendered. This chapter has a threefold purpose: (1) to show the elements that feminist thought has identified as important to make citizenship a relevant and attainable concept for women; (2) to illustrate how international development agencies, through their work in developing countries, are contributing to a form of citizenship that is still insensitive to the major rights and freedoms women seek to have; and (3) to highlight several political and educational initiatives underway to make citizenship a reality for most women.

PREVAILING IMAGES OF WOMEN AND POLITICS

Through a multiplicity of messages, rules, and norms codified into laws and cultural practices, most women are inducted into the service of others and into supportive activities. Changes after World War II and further transformations stemming from the contemporary women's movement since the 1970s have increased women's presence in the labor force, in more advanced levels of education, and in better economic positions. Women have also gained better legal treatment in such issues as inheritance rights, family disputes, credit access, and marital violence. Yet, despite some undeniable gains, women continue to face an existence in which motherhood is the main criterion by which a woman's measure of fulfillment and success is defined.

The construction of motherhood involves removing women from conflict, personal ambition, and public exposure. The social imagery is complex and variegated, with many forms and expressions depending on social class, ethnicity, culture, and historical moment. Yet, the end result is quite similar for most women. As mothers, women are represented as being outside the political process.[1] The political process, in turn, is constructed as involving primarily public institutions and decision making among formal organizations.[2]

In the ordinary world, women face societal arrangements that place obstacles in the way of their becoming full citizens. First the social definition of women as primarily mothers requires that they be devoted to their children and husband. Complying with this expectation creates consequences for women's everyday life, convincing them that they are not able to participate in competing activities. Second, the political world is equated with the public world and is considered to be different—often very different—from the private world. Thus, the political world is defined as adversarial and as involving mostly men. Third, since the public/private division of labor in the social order is seen as normal and natural by those in power, there is a lack of political commitment by governments and subjects alike to social and gender equity policies that would support women (Ashworth 1996). Gender is not merely a social invention but the crystallization of a political construction, because it is both the result of power differences as well as the producer of conditions that sustain historically established power differences.

In the academic world, disciplines central to the understanding of citizenship, such as political science and comparative politics, operate within narrow definitions. The dominant paradigm of citizenship examines political behaviors (especially voting frequencies and attitudes), women in political elites (or rather their absence), how politics affects women in a general "status-of-women" framework, and presents a few policy analyses concerning women's issues (Vickers 1989). These foci take current political situations for granted and, as Vickers notes, sustain a "normal integration model" (29) that seeks to understand barriers to women's integration, while failing to question whether something intrinsic to the nature of the contemporary and dominant liberal-democratic political system keeps women outside politics on a profound and permanent basis.

RECOGNIZING CITIZENSHIP AS GENDERED

Democracy's two main pillars are supposed to be freedom and equality, but women cannot be "free and equal" because of two prevailing conditions: (1) the physical and psychological limitations on women's participation in politics created by the sexual division of labor and (2) ideologies regarding masculinity, femininity, and motherhood norms that not only exclude women from politics, but that also define the political world in ways that ignore salient aspects of women's lives that need to be regulated to avoid further oppression or subordination.

Citizenship, as we know it in contemporary democracy, on deeper analysis depends on the citizen being supported by a functioning patriarchal household. The responsibilities toward others by women who are mothers usually are very absorbing, and therefore reduce other expressions of social, political, and economic life. In societies where domestic technologies are limited, the roles expected of women are all the more restricted and demanding. Developing countries, in consequence, create women's and motherhood roles that are difficult to question at both ideological and material levels. Social practices naturalize the world, leading many women themselves into definitions of self as nurturing and caring human beings. While these self-definitions have a strong ethical component, at the same time they operate to make women postpone their own needs and desires until other persons have been satisfied.

In Western political and economic theory, men are placed at the center of public and private life, while women occupy the household as social, political, and economic dependents. A clear manifestation of this is the taxation system, which in most countries, Western and non-Western alike, assumes a single breadwinner, usually the man, operating in the context of a nuclear family.

The contemporary women's movement has sought greater representation of women in all decision-making bodies, and more legal and educational programs for women's empowerment, but it has been very slow and reluctant in recognizing the need to hold power, to enter public office, and to engage in open conflict with oppressive public institutions.

So, what do we mean by citizenship when we aspire to have a nonsexist democratic society? Is it mere parity of formal political (i.e., voting) rights between men and women, or is something *else* needed to create this democratic society? Should attention be focused on the different duties men and women face on account of social representations of masculinity and femininity? Is having the right to vote and be elected enough to move social institutions, or must these institutions undergo some sort of change to make democracy gender-free? Do we want and can we have an entirely equal-rights democracy, or should we seek ways to live with some gender differences (e.g., pregnancy and child nursing) in a creative and nonoppressive way?

Connell (1989) observes that the treatment of the state in feminist literature has taken three main forms: accounts of the political history of feminism and its encounters with the state, generally to demand voting rights; survey studies focusing on the gender gap in voting patterns, primarily in the United States; and studies of state action in particular areas of sexual politics, such as family, labor, and education laws. I would argue that a fourth treatment of the state has also occurred, albeit in weaker and more incipient form. It is the study of the nature of democracy within the patriarchal state. I agree with Connell's assertion that a "very important image of our future should be a feminist state that is an arena for radical democratization of social interaction" (31).

The best known discussion of citizenship rights is that elaborated by Marshall (1964), who proposes a linear development that moves from civil to political rights and ultimately to social rights. For Marshall, civil rights are those having to do with individual freedoms, such as "liberty of the person, freedom of speech, thought and faith, the right to own property and to conclude valid contracts, and the right to justice" (72).

Political rights are those having to do with electing political representatives and being elected to public office; social rights are those addressing the social welfare of persons, and would include such rights as health, education, housing, and so on, in amounts that would greatly reduce inequalities among the members of the nation-state.

Using different terms, Patterson (1991) offers a typology that is also worth considering. He recognizes three types of freedom: personal freedom—freedom from coercion or restraint restrained by another person, or the conviction that one can do as one pleases; sovereign freedom—the power to act as one pleases, regardless of the wishes of others; and civic freedom—the capacity of adult members of a community to participate in its life and governance (this implies that a person belongs to a political community with clearly defined rights and duties, and, to some degree, is involved in the way it is governed). Patterson's personal and sovereign freedoms intersect with Marshall's civil freedoms; what Patterson calls civic freedoms are what Marshall calls political freedoms.

Concentrating on what Patterson terms personal and sovereign freedoms (and Marshall calls civil rights), it would appear that women encounter little freedom to do as they please and to go against the wishes of others in areas dealing with their autonomy as persons. This occurs primarily because of the social control over their sexuality, translated in the prohibition in many countries against self-determined abortions, and in the pressing social norm to marry. Regarding other freedoms, women do have freedom of speech, thought, and faith, but because they live within formal and informal marriage contracts that hold them as subordinates of husbands in many countries, they experience degrees of dependence that seriously curtail their rights, both publicly and privately. A major right for men has been that of *habeas corpus,* which protects men against arbitrary imprisonment. For women, who have not been allowed to be actively political and thus to play oppositional roles in the public sphere, *habeas corpus* is not the most salient right. For women, their most precious civil right is that of control over their own bodies.[3] Many feminists have called this a woman's "reproductive rights." I prefer to call it the right to have an autonomous life, because motherhood in many ways seals the fate of women by placing them in the service of others—their children's—for several years.

Other civil rights identified by Marshall, such as the right to property, the right to conclude valid contracts, and the right to physical movement, are also important for women. Though in principle these rights are being gradually gained, their implementation remains problematic due to marriage practices and to cultural norms that prevent women from claiming these rights. Citizenship, therefore, must be seen not merely as the collection of rights that individuals have, but also as the set of societal norms that facilitate the use and application of these rights.

The typologies proposed by Patterson and Marshall are quite helpful in the analysis of women's citizenship. The control of a woman's body through restrictions on abortion, and the control on women's ability to act as they please (by virtue of the prevailing norm of motherhood) clearly puts limits on their personal and sovereign freedoms, or civil freedoms in Marshall's words. It is clear that today in most countries women's political freedoms are much greater than their personal/sovereign or civic/social freedoms.[4] It is obvious that political freedoms are not enough for full citizenship. Without the foundation provided by civil rights, political rights may not be fully invoked by either men or women, and not having leverage to determine state policies, the third level of citizen rights—those concerning social rights—will emerge primarily under conditions of paternalism, thus keeping the "beneficiaries" under conditions of dependency on existing rulers.

The suffragist era, the first wave of the feminist movement, was concerned with citizenship in terms of duties: women argued that by giving women access to the vote, their virtuous traits for leadership and education would improve the democratic state (Vickers 1989). At that time suffragists gave little thought to the problems of combining motherhood and politics (Vickers). The understanding that "the personal is political," which occurred during the second wave of the feminist movement through the writings of persons such as Millett (1970) and Ware (1970), was a conceptual milestone. This principle functioned also as a major mobilizer of women who had never been active before and enabled others to develop a new relationship with the political world (Miles 1996).

Through increased feminist theoretical understanding, the specificity of women around sexuality and reproduction was identified as a major consideration in shaping women's citizenship. Millett's (1970) argument that power structured all relationships, including those of our so-called private world, and that these "sexual politics" transitioned from intimacy to wider social contexts, brought great analytical sensitivity to the functioning of the private sphere.

Today, most feminist thought acknowledges that the sexual division of labor in the household offers differential spaces for men and women in conducting productive and reproductive tasks. It is also well accepted that these tasks carry differential symbolic value but, by and large, end up placing women in subordinate positions. The domestic sphere is a busy site for economic and political transactions, characterized by different access to economic resources, types of decision making, and vested authority. To be sure, gender is not the only determinant of these transactions, as they are also affected by age, generational rank, and kinship ties. Ideological construction regarding motherhood and fatherhood, and the concomitant obligation of the various members to the maintenance of the domestic group, also enters the picture.

The astute observation by Foucault (1977) that individuals are socialized not just by amorphous processes but through specific "technologies of subjugation" (p. 27), which include all institutions of society, has further assisted feminist theory to consider the family and the school as particular sites of gender construction. Women, then, are not only rational individuals but also embodied entities. A corollary to this assertion is that citizenship, in the sense of equal participation by women and men in the political sphere, cannot be attained without changing first the division of labor, and ideological and material conditions. So, it is not only whether citizenship rights have been enacted but whether they can be exercised. Citizenship, in the sense of providing a reality suitable to women's liberation, cannot be attained without first redefining it.

In several regions of the world, particularly Latin America, feminist women have known from the earliest moments that part of the democratic struggle must include consideration of the private sphere. Domestic inequality, conceptions of femininity and masculinity linked to motherhood and derived from it, and control over women's sexuality deeply affect the democratizing efforts. Feminist awareness that democracy is gendered and that citizenship is consequently gendered is part of a modern project, in which the state is considered necessary to establish a just and fair society and is to be held accountable for its failure to provide.[5] To this effect, many feminists— especially in developing countries where social justice remains a distant dream—hold that feminism is a modern project, albeit a yet unrealized modern project.

In the new democratic project it will be essential to think about how to reconstitute the current political systems and institutions, to recognize how political transactions occur, and to invent new ways of doing politics. It will be crucial to recognize the private world and its intimacy and sexuality dimensions as areas of political engagement and therefore as terrains to be renegotiated. New political definitions will also have to acknowledge that local and community politics have often been the primary arenas of women's activism. Consequently, the expanded definition of "the political" will include new terrains and issues to which politics, and thus policies (i.e., governance) would apply. A full citizenship would give legitimacy to the design and implementation of policies not only at the levels of national and international government, but also at the levels of the household and the community (Ashworth 1996). For example, this will mean going beyond the sexual division of labor in society to understand how relationships between the genders occur in the intimacy of the home and to understand why domestic violence is so prevalent throughout the world, why unwanted pregnancies occur so often, and how micro relations of power within the household reproduce gendered versions of the human subject.[6] In the case of domestic violence, what becomes increasingly evident is that the large variety of family arrangements today (consensual unions, female-headed households, extended families, and so on) has not significantly altered the widespread nature of domestic violence.[7]

Not only would new levels of governance come into the picture, but the nature and processes of the key elements of established political power—the executive, the legislative, and the judicial—would come into closer scrutiny. For instance, the degree of sexism within the judicial profession would be probed to ascertain how it affects the equitable distribution of justice among the population. This position would go well beyond the conventional requirement that the judiciary should be free from executive or legislative interference as a criterion of good governance (Ashworth 1996). A feminist view of democracy would also consider profound reform of the social services so that they would provide both equal opportunity and affirmative action measures, and it would precede these measures with understanding gained through techniques of gender analysis and planning. These changes would in turn be reflected in budgetary planning and fiscal reforms and redirection of social services.

This expanded political agenda meets a harsh reality in many countries, particularly in the Third World countries. In several societies, including those with long-standing nation-states (formally independent for about 180 years) such as those in Latin America, "the granting of political rights in many new democracies has been accompanied by the increasingly precarious nature of civil rights and growing limits—if not actual reversals—of the social rights of citizenship" (Oxhorn 1998, 3).

Returning to the typology of citizenship rights proposed by Marshall, it can be said that women do not enjoy full civil rights, their political rights cannot always be asserted, and their social rights do not cover their most direct needs.

DEFINITIONS OF DEMOCRACY AMONG INTERNATIONAL DEVELOPMENT AGENCIES

With the general demise of socialism in Eastern Europe and the drastic changes socialism is undergoing in China, there is a firm belief among many countries in the power of capitalism and the promise it brings for democracy. To accelerate the process of democratization, international development agencies, both bilateral and multilateral, are working on a new area of development: political development. Their programs usually go under the names of good governance, democracy, and human rights.

Bilateral and multilateral agencies, no less than the states they represent, are still male-dominated and patriarchal in orientation (Jain 1996; Stromquist 1995; Walby 1990). Despite recent recognition of the importance of nongovernmental organizations in the development process, the development agencies privilege the state. "Country responsiveness" and "policy dialogue"—current principles of international cooperation—place the government of the developing country (or recipient state) in first position vis-à-vis other national entities. While these principles are commendable from the perspective of respecting the autonomy of the recipient government (which has been promoted these days to "partner" government), the reality is that since governments are male dominated, men end up speaking for women, even in programs designed to benefit women. In so doing, current agency policies—whether they want this or not—relegate women to subordinate positions, despite the agencies' constant discourse calling for the full participation of women.

It is essential to analyze how democracy is being treated by these agencies and what is present or absent in their definitions. It is important also to see how women and gender issues are framed in the "improved" conceptions of democracy. Below, we examine two institutions, one multilateral (the World Bank) and the other bilateral (the Canadian International Development Agency [CIDA]). They are selected because of the salience they give to gender issues and their position along different ends of the agency spectrum.

The World Bank, having become the largest think tank on questions of development, profoundly shapes this debate. In the early 1980s it called for a minimalist state that would enforce deregulation, liberalization, and the reduction of an overexpanded bureaucracy. Since 1992, however, the World Bank has advocated the concept of "good governance," a concept justified as "an essential complement to sound economic policies" (World Bank 1992, 1). The four dimensions of "good governance" on which the World Bank focuses are: capacity and efficiency issues in public sector management; accountability; predictability and the legal framework for development; and information (World Bank 12).

This definition of the state, while more explicit than in the past, positions it as a competent manager of civic transactions rather than a mediator of conflict and a promoter of equity. The World Bank's *1997 World Development Report* argues for an "effective state" to bring about socioeconomic development. In this document, the World Bank identifies five core missions of every government: establishing a foundation of law, maintaining effective macro-economic policies, investing in basic social services and infrastructure, providing a comprehensive safety net for vulnerable members of society, and protecting the environment. These are objectives that could promote a productive and efficient government; these are objectives that perhaps may even foster a democratic environment. But, being gender blind, they are not objectives that will ensure that women will enjoy full citizenship, especially in societies with deeply rooted patriarchal beliefs and norms.

In a brief but influential document titled *Toward Gender Equality: The Role of Public Policy,* the World Bank does recognize women and argues that targeting women specifically in development projects is appropriate:

> Targeting women directly is justifiable on two grounds: First, to the extent that gender inequalities prevent an economy from realizing its full potential, targeting to women can be an effective strategy for increasing productivity and output. Second, where gender differences are wide, targeting may be needed to capture social gains, and to increase internal efficiency. Targeting women is especially appropriate when doing so contributes directly to reducing poverty or when women have particular needs—for example, when maternal mortality is very high. The exceptionally high gender gap in educational enrollments in some countries can be reduced only by policies (including subsidies) that target girls. An obvious example would be policies that affect the private costs of schooling. (1995, 59–60)

On the positive side, it can be observed that the World Bank now agrees that public policies matter and that some should be in place specifically to help women. On the negative side, it can be seen that defined as women's issues are only those problems that block women's participation in the economy or that prevent them from being efficient household managers (reflected in the argument that they are the main providers of health, care, and hygiene to family members, mostly their own children) (25). This definition ignores the need to actively promote women's participation in civic life sufficiently to overcome the often strong traditional, paternalistic opposition to such participation.

Toward Gender Equality does call for policies in favor of women by calling for the abrogation of repressive laws dealing with such issues as land and property rights (e.g., laws that prevent women from having property titles, equal rights to inheritance), labor market and employment policies (e.g., laws that restrict women's access to employment or laws that in calling for "generous" maternity and childcare benefits make female workers more costly than male workers), and instead drafting positive family laws (such as those setting minimum age of marriage, providing women with rights following marital separation, penalizing domestic violence) and financial laws and regulations (such as those enabling women greater access to credit) (45–51). While this World Bank document acknowledges the need for a "gendered approach to public policy" (45), all the policies—in merely calling upon the state to behave in a different away—assume a friendly state that will respond to the need for new actions on the basis of rational thought. No policies are proposed on how to deal with conflict or with gender ideologies. Therefore, the roles of the mass media, cultural beliefs and norms, and the educational system are overlooked, as is the need to transform them so that women, through increased consciousness, may become advocates of their own advancement. CIDA provides a detailed example of how bilateral agencies are working on the question of democratization and women. CIDA's (1996) *Policy on Human Rights, Democratization and Good Governance* defines "good governance" as the exercise of power by various levels of government that is effective, honest, equitable, transparent, and accountable. This Canadian policy proposes to intervene to build the role of organizations in civil society, and to "build the participation in civil society and the political process more generally of women and other marginalized groups in society" (12). It also recognizes the need to support law reform, for example in relation to gender equality, land rights, family law, the media, and conditions of work.

In practice, however, CIDA's good governance emphasizes efficiency over equity, and the projects it has supported often result in efforts to improve the capacity of the legislature, the judiciary, and the executive for transparency, accountability, and public participation (CIDA 1997). Content analysis of eighty-one projects on human rights and democratization funded by CIDA in over twenty-six countries in Latin America and the Caribbean (amounting to $8.5 million for 1995–1996) indicate that most of the support has gone to strengthen established democratic features such as elections, legal systems, and human rights. The projects addressing women have focused on practical gender needs such as legal information about and assistance for domestic violence, the training of women leaders in decision making and participation, and the dissemination of information on women's rights. Support to strengthen women's organizations is also present and has amounted to 62 percent of the funds within this program (CIDA 1997). This analysis reveals that in the case of Latin America and the Caribbean, CIDA's assistance is promoting groundwork in support of women as citizens. It also suggests that as women become organized—evident in the large number of women-based nongovernmental organizations (NGOs) in the region—they can make inroads with the assistance of gender-responsive development agencies.

International development agencies are currently engaged in the production of indicators that reflect a gender-sensitive political development. An example of such efforts suggests a limited understanding of citizenship from a woman's perspective. Thus, Kapoor (1996) identifies as pertinent indicators those that measure project impact on women by collecting and reporting sex-disaggregated data. This measure, while correct, might be considered an initial indicator at best. Kapoor's treatment of gender-sensitive indicators also states that the data must be "culturally and historical sensitive" (13). The potential contradiction between indicators that might reflect new perceptions about the relative roles and situations of women and men in society and "cultural and historical sensitive" approaches that tend to reproduce women's subordination and marginality are left unexplained.

Another effort focusing on gender and democratization addresses election of more women to political office. Projects under this rubric involve providing women with training to run as candidates for political office and encouraging them to participate in official elections at community and national levels. Connell (1989) reminds us that

> For liberal feminism the state has provided leverage for reform mainly through the citizenship/legitimacy nexus. But an exclusive focus on those opportunities leads to a form of politics organized around "representation" rather than mass participation, and emphasis on reforms such as "equal opportunity" programs conceived in terms of career path. This prioritizes the interests of an educated minority of women; working-class women do not have "careers" and are unlikely to be picked out as "representatives."(29)

Getting women into the mainstream of public office and bureaucracies might foster gender-sensitive governance, yet the presence of women in public office will not ipso facto lead to a reframing of the nature of politics and of citizenship in particular because women, as men, are socialized into dominant norms of femininity and masculinity. Moreover, the interests of women in general may not necessarily be recognized by the women who will gain political office (Beall 1996). It is clear that to address gender issues, political representatives—both women and men—will have to be trained to gain a greater understanding not only of class and ethnicity issues, but should also receive training in gender analysis.

It can be asserted that current efforts by development agencies emphasize the creation of efficient government institutions but only to a very small degree do they aim at the modification of the basic features of capitalist gendered societies. The institutionalized masculinity of key public institutions, the forced separation of domestic life from the money economy and the political world, and the unquestioning posture toward institutions such as the family, the school, and the workplace, which reconstitute gender relations on a day-to-day basis, is an obvious indication of how the gender system is essentially left untouched by the numerous policies to democratize life and create better citizens.

Proposals for citizenship promoted by agencies tend to be theoretically groundless. They treat patriarchy as an undesirable situation without looking beyond to examine the structures and dynamics that create and maintain it. According to liberal feminism—the type of feminism accepted by the state and its national and international machineries—the women's situation is defined as a case of imperfect citizenship. Since full citizenship is seen as the answer, the solution is increased rights, until parity is achieved. Feminism as an oppositional culture trying to reshape the nature of the state and as a force seeking to change the state in order to implement policies that would indeed augment the rights women can have is lost in current democratization efforts by donor agencies.

TOWARD DEMOCRATIC EDUCATION
AND THE REDEFINITION OF CITIZENSHIP

While within feminist perspectives there is increasing clarity of the need to educate women and men in new conceptions of citizenship, concrete efforts to modify practices and social representations of gender, democracy, and politics are few. Moreover, important crosspressures supported by international donor agencies are at work. We explore some of them in this section.

International Agencies' Views of Democratic Schooling

As a consequence of the limited-problem definition that international agencies accept regarding the condition and situation of women, many educational efforts attempted by governments and the development agencies funding them have centered on educational access and attainment issues, not on challenging the school as a site for the production of gendered identities. Further, the initiatives to promote access to education have concentrated on the access of girls, not women, and on the access to primary education, not all levels of education. This is a common practice among all agencies and one that has prevailed despite international agreements to work on a larger number of educational issues and problems (Stromquist 1986a, 1994, 1998a, 1998b). Only in a handful of projects are there efforts to modify curricula or to provide nonsexist or antisexist knowledge to teachers in pre- and inservice training programs.

The lack of attention to gender issues in the formation of citizen values through schooling is reflected in recent research to assess achievements in the area of civic education. In 1993 the International Bureau of Education (IBE), part of the United Nations Educational, Scientific, and Cultural Organizations, launched a project called "What Education for What Citizenship?" The first step was a comparative survey in thirty-four countries asking students and teachers their opinions about various actors and events in contemporary social life, of which gender issues were a very small part. The preliminary findings of the study indicated that students give low importance to even the most basic rights of women. For instance, most of the students agreed with the statement that "In a family, it is enough if the man votes." Most students also agreed with the statement "It is normal that a woman gets lower wages than a man for she may get married and be supported by her husband" (Albala-Bertrand 1997). Unquestionably, these are opinions shaped by social and family influences, but it is surprising to observe how little schools seem to modify these traditional views.

Over time, the world has been experiencing an increase in the number of years of education among both men and women. The gender gap persists but it is decreasing in many countries. It is estimated that in 1990 the average six-year-old girl could expect to attend school for 8.4 years and the average boy of the same age could expect to do so for 9.7 years (World Bank 1995), a gender gap now of about 1.5 years. The decreasing gender gap is welcome for it is hoped that increased schooling will increase people's capacity to reflect upon their reality. Yet, without an explicit effort to combat gender stereotypes and limited representations of women in the curriculum and through school practices, the schooled woman will not question the patriarchal structures in her surrounding environment. And despite the fact that in several developing regions, women are increasing their participation as teachers (Latin America, for instance, has a strong majority of female teachers at primary and secondary school levels), they will not function as gender change agents in the absence of specific efforts to make them more gender-aware and capable of addressing gender inequalities through curriculum content and equity-sensitive teaching practices. Evidence in this regard is beyond contestation, as many countries with parity, or almost parity, in the enrollment of girls and boys at primary education levels, and even at secondary and tertiary education levels, have not been able to create social environments in which women and men have comparable social, political, and economic status.

Countering Political Stereotypes of Women through Action and Nonformal Education

To understand efforts to improve the political understanding of adult women it is also necessary to understand the work of social movements. Social movements offer an alternative rationality (Touraine 1979). In the case of women, it is the NGOs led by women that are formulating different ways to create citizenship values among women.

These women-led NGOs are doing so through a threefold agenda: addressing previously ignored women's issues, providing support for other groups, and training women for political activism. Their work is not always documented; we will give but a few examples of the ways in which political rights for women as citizens are being gained.

Increasing the presence of women in politics at the local level. A notable example is drawn from the constitutional amendment in India (73rd Amendment), which has reserved one third of seats at district, intermediate,

and village levels for women since 1992.[8] While this measure still emphasizes formal representation rather than efforts to change the nature of the
patriarchal state, it appears that local levels, especially municipalities, are
very well suited for development purposes—all the more so if there is an
institution to support it. Heralded as a process that is "transforming the state
from within," some 330,000 Indian women have entered the arena of formal
politics (Jain 1996, 8).

Through participation in the Panchayat Raj institutions, women are
engaged in formal politics at village and district levels, not only now representing 25–40 percent of the elected officials, but also bringing in a new political agenda focusing on issues such as water, alcohol abuse, education, health,
and domestic violence. Indian women in the Panchayat Raj are bringing an
agenda that is more sensitive to social and economic security, the protection of
livelihood and the environment, and the reduction of domestic violence and
other forms of oppression of and discrimination against women. Some
progress has obviously taken place: identified as obstacles to transformation
are inadequate education, the burden of productive and reproductive loads,
lack of self-confidence, and the opposition of entrenched cultural and religious views (Jain 1996, 16–17). Among the lessons learned from the electoral
quota system in India are that it is possible to organize community human
rights programs around productive activities, and that simultaneously supporting government organizations and NGOs can be quite effective (Brown 1996).

Amending the definition of human rights. The original Universal Declaration of Human Rights (signed in 1948 in the aftermath of World War II)
was a product of its times. It did not consider the specificity of women as citizens. In fact, it considered the home a special "private" site (Article 12) and
defined the family as "the natural and fundamental group unit of society
(Article 16). Moreover, it set principles in potential opposition to gender
equality (in the sense that protecting the status quo might be inimical to
women in some cases), as in holding that education should "promote tolerance . . . among all nations, racial, or religious groups" (Article 26) and that
parents "have a prior right to choose the kind of education that shall be given
to their children" (Article 26).

The Comité de América Latin y el Caribe para la Defensa de los Dere-
chos de la Mujer (CLADEM), a women-led NGO composed primarily of
women lawyers, has been working in recent years on a set of principles to
amend the original declaration so that it may be more explicitly inclusive of
women and other groups, such as indigenous peoples, homosexuals, children,
the elderly, and disabled people. Regarding women, the new human rights
declaration states that "all women and men are born free and equal in dignity
and rights" (Article 1), "all states shall eliminate obstacles to the full and
equal enjoyment of citizenship rights by women" (Article 3), and "all forms

of violence against women constitute a violation of their human rights" (Article 7). Section III of this new declaration, "Sexual and Reproductive Rights," is notable for its focus exclusively on women: Article 10 asserts "autonomy and self-determination in their exercise of sexuality, which includes the right to physical, sexual and emotional pleasure, the right to freedom in sexual orientation, the right to information and education on sexuality, and the right to sexual and reproductive health care of the maintenance of physical, mental, and social well-being." Article 11 states that "women and men have the right to decide on their reproductive life in a free and informed manner and to exercise the voluntary and safe control of their fertility, free from discrimination, coercion or violence, as well as the right to enjoy the highest levels of sexual and reproductive health" and that "women have the right to reproductive autonomy which includes access to safe and legal abortions" (Red de Educación Popular entre Mujeres 1998).

This new declaration has been under discussion in global feminist networks and there is widespread support for its approval. The document was brought to the UN General Assembly in 1998 for discussion and approval, but it was not able to obtain the official government endorsement that it needed for inclusion in the debate. The efforts by women in this arena will continue in the years ahead.

Empowering women through nonformal education approaches. Other changes to promote gender-sensitive citizenship involve working with adult women. Such initiatives have involved the creation of settings for adult women where they can discover and re-discover their identities and problems as women, and mobilize around issues that are of priority to them. This has been the process promoted by the successful case of Mahila Samakhya in India. The issues discussed in the frequent meetings of the women's committees made possible by the project have included wife beating, rape, mental torture, humiliating treatment of infertile women, inhuman treatment of widows, forced abortions and female infanticide, humiliation of wives who do not please their husbands, and sexual harassment (Jain and Krishnamurty 1996). Following these discussions and the subsequent empowerment they have fostered, women have asked to plan and monitor their own education, an education that has addressed building a positive self-image, developing critical thinking, building group solidarity, and engaging in collective decision making and action.

In Latin America several efforts have occurred to modify primary school textbooks by eliminating sexist language and removing sexual stereotypes. Yet, there is still very little in producing alternative, women-affirmative curriculum content to promote women's autonomy. While there are limited instances of change within the school system, a silent revolution is occurring among many women NGO networks, many of which are working for transformative adult education programs, including those stated in the full plan of action approved at the most recent world conference on adult education (in Hamburg in 1997). A key reflection from this Latin American experience is whether citizenship norms can be obtained in the formal school or perhaps be better attempted with adult women—after they encounter difficulties and obstacles in the actual world. The latter looms as the more effective so far.

The experiences cited are not the only ones, they simply reflect the best documented attempts to modify the concept of citizenship. What these limited experiences (except the CLADEM initiative) do suggest is the tremendous force of immediate problems over long-term ones in constructing a new citizenship for women. Several years ago, Maxine Molyneux (1986) highlighted the importance of distinguishing between practical gender interests (i.e., immediate problem solving, usually addressing survival issues) and strategic gender interests (i.e., working on structural and systemic changes to improve/transform gender relations in society). It would appear that while the two actions are not mutually incompatible (as strategic work might be built on the experience of solving practical needs), many efforts may not go perceptibly further than immediate problem solving.

SCHOOLING AND THE TEACHING OF DEMOCRACY

When the average person thinks of citizenship and schooling, there is an immediate reaction to consider that schools are, of course, cradles of citizenship. Since schools tend to be seen as neutral institutions imparting objective knowledge, it is assumed that schools automatically convey democratic norms and thus develop citizenship values.

Unfortunately, schooling so far has played a greater role as mediator of the nation-state than as a vehicle to alter it (Walkerdine and Lucey 1989). Through discourses in the formal and the informal curriculum, sexuality has been controlled to produce "normal femininity" and "normal masculinity" (Connell 1996; Walkerdine 1987). The evidence from the schools is that, by and large, they promote a process of assimilation into the status quo. Under these conditions, it can hardly be expected that schooling access, completion, and achievement will affect the existing social order. School serves to construct gendered citizens and to make gendered society accepted as normal. What can be done in schools to make them more democratic and how should schools/classrooms address democracy and citizenship? Citizenship must be translated into expanded civil and social rights, but to accomplish this, changes are needed in the political culture. This is an area in which education can help.

Teacher training and content of curriculum would be the two key axes of intervention in the schools. Teachers are the mediators between knowledge and students, and the curriculum offers the official discourses in education that greatly contribute to shaping gender identities. Schools seldom address the hidden curriculum in teacher-training practices. To expand the notion of citizenship and to develop citizenship norms much more sensitive to gender dimensions, we need not greater allegiance to existing institutions (the usual emphasis of civics courses in school) but critical education leading to greater gender awareness and legal understanding, and education programs for empowerment within women-led NGOs.

Feminist definitions of democratic schooling would contend that gender awareness within educational programs is essential to develop a new concept of citizenship among women. The task ahead for the schools is both complex and difficult. It will call not merely for the teaching of democratic values but also for empowerment of all students through the ability to analyze gender subordination, seeing how public and private discourse mesh with and are supported by structure and institutions to create and sustain gendered representations and practices. It will call, therefore, not for conflict resolution but for conflict perception and engagement, not only for understanding of sex roles but for renegotiating them. A gender-sensitive teaching and learning process will enable girls to become aware of how gender ideology and norms of femininity conspire to their subordination and will enable boys to perceive and reflect on how norms of masculinity situate them in positions of social privilege. Finally, it will not assume that teachers are ready to serve as change agents for gender equality and equity, but will prepare them to change both their own lives and their professional practices.

To accomplish these objectives, much more work needs to be done in the development of a graduated nonsexist and antisexist curriculum that takes students from kindergarten all the way to the end of high school through messages and discussions suitable for their age and their moment in the life cycle. It also needs incentives for new and practicing teachers to engage in gender analysis, including the understanding of the influences that emerge from the hidden curriculum. Nonformal education programs also will be important to create gender awareness and make women aware of the different roles and responsibilities women and men evince not only in urban settings (Beall 1996), but in rural areas as well. At this moment, what needs to be done is clearer than where to find the political will to get into the action.[9]

CONCLUSION

The concept of citizenship is crucial to feminism because it brings back the importance of the individual in the examination of both democracy and politics. Because women's experiences are greatly shaped by their private world, their individual roles and agency in that arena must be captured and reclaimed. We have amassed clear evidence that the right to vote has not resulted in more women politicians and that much more than participation by women in a one-time voting exercise is needed to transform the political culture. Impediments at microlevels in women's lives need to be considered in order for political rights to be accessible to women. The narrow, but still prevailing, conceptualization of politics as election to office and party involvement is no longer tenable.

The examination of the private world, especially of areas of intimacy, long considered beyond the concerns of democracy, await further reexamination. This is an area not without contradictions. Feminist demands on the state run into conflicting demands concerning the role of the state. For example, in the case of abortion, the demand is for the state to *keep out* of women's decisions on whether or not to carry a fetus to term. In the case of domestic violence, the call is for the state *to intervene.* And in instances of allowed abortion sometimes the question is, should we ask the state to pay for this service? The road is long and much remains ahead. I agree with Connell's (1989) assertion that a "very important image of our future should be a feminist state that is an area for radical democratization of social interaction" (31). The state has to be a target of feminism if feminism is indeed going to challenge patriarchy. Some feminist writers and activists in the women's movement do not hold much hope regarding the state's willingness to redress gendered structures and norms; thus, they argue for staying out of the state and seeking transformation through independent, albeit very incremental, means. Others disagree. Young (1985), for instance, argues that, "feminists cannot undermine masculinist values without entering some of the center of power that fosters them . . . [otherwise] it can only be a moral position of critique rather than a force for institutional change" (182).

In addition to challenges that the state must resolve, there are external pressures against the process of social change. First, international development agencies, while promoting attention to women and particularly women's education, foster a promotion of citizenship purely along formal dimensions, thus weakening feminist demands for considering the private and intimate as areas of power that affect the definition and exercise of citizenship. The work of international development agencies appears to be frozen in time and incongruent with current appreciations of political life that have been put forward by feminist thought. Especially relevant within the new dimensions of citizenship are the areas of intimacy, the still-private spheres of family life, the dominant societal versions of motherhood, and the lack of women's autonomy in areas that are crucial to their freedom as individuals.

Second, attempts to expand women's citizenship face the crosspressures of globalization. States now have a diminished capacity for expanding the basic rights of citizenship due to global processes of economic and technological change and the rise of ethnic nationalism (Oxhorn 1998). In many developing countries, democracy is still seen as little more than institutionalized democratic procedures, or rather a largely nominal commitment to human rights and dignity (Selbin 1998). The fragility of democracy is being put to test further by the increasing forces of globalization that call for a minimalist state, especially regarding social rights. For women, globalization trends, on the one hand, offer the potential for the rapid expansion of ideas about the importance of women as individuals in their own right, making the decision to become mothers and wives, for instance, an option among several alternatives. On the other hand, globalization gives priority to the market over social justice by focusing on ensuring fair rules for production and profit making and being much less interested in promoting social equality and equity; further, globalization is creating new forms of labor processes that for the most part are contributing to reinscribe gender inequalities in new occupational forms.

The challenges to women as full citizens are numerous. Understanding the nature and range of these challenges is a first step. Not losing hope, deploying creative responses, and developing endurance and resilience are the next steps.

NOTES

[1]There are powerful instances where motherhood has served to politicize private and social life. One example is the well-known case of the Madres de Plaza de Mayo (Argentina, mid-1980s to mid-1990s). Another example concerns the mobilization by women's organizations in Ecuador to protest Citibank's freeze on $80 million from the Ecuadorian Central Bank account. The women protested as mothers of families against the economic crisis, but in so doing asserted their social and economic rights—clearly a political act (Lind 1997).

[2]An example of the "public" definition of democracy is well represented in an influential book on democracy (Diamond, Linz, and Lipset 1995) that identifies three conditions for democracy to exist: competitive elections, broad participation, and civic and political liberties. The civic liberties, however, do not include those within the household.

[3]In the United States, the Supreme Court upheld women's rights to have abortions, justified on "privacy grounds." Such a principle, though linked to civil rights, needs revision because it is not simply an issue of individual privacy but rather a fundamental principle of human freedom, subject of course to the fetus becoming what has been called "viable for life."

[4]We should remind ourselves that political rights do not necessarily imply a complete democracy. In Greece the principle of participative politics through the extension of the franchise was made possible by the exclusion and domination of others—slaves and women.

[5]As an aside, I should state that postmodernism has influenced feminism by generating greater awareness of the importance of the multiplicity of women's identities, voices, and experiences. In this respect, postmodernism has brought in new ideas regarding the particular and the everyday; yet, to engage in a critique of general relations and the social positioning of men and women in society, we need to consider the collective, institutional, and macrosocial structures.

⁶The latest UN data indicate that each year 80,000 women die as a result of abortion attempts and 75 million women experience unwanted pregnancies.

⁷Domestic violence is not only perpetuated by husbands against wives but also by adult brothers against adult sisters, and by uncles against adult nieces. Transcriptions of a hot line violence telephone service in Lima, Peru, for instance, revealed this wider pattern of violence (Stromquist, personal observation 1998). Another important dimension of violence is not the physical or psychological suffering per se but the fact that women do not fight these conditions because of numerous forces against resistance—their economic dependence on men, the influence of social messages about women's commitments to their complete family, the stigma of being a lone woman, their reluctance to make public what should be kept a personal secret, among others.

⁸This amendment, which sets quotas specifying the number of positions to be filled by women as a result of elections, can also be observed in several other Third World countries. In Latin America today there are ten countries whose political parties have endorsed the principle of electoral quotas for women, or whose constitution considers it.

⁹A complete set of interventions through schools, mass media, and other social institutions is detailed in the Platform for Action, signed unanimously by all states at the end of the Fourth World Conference on Women in Beijing, 1995 ("Platform for Action" 1996).

REFERENCES

Albala-Bertrand, L. (1997). "What education for what citizenship?" In *Educational innovation and information*, 4–8. Geneva: International Bureau of Education.

Ashworth, Georgina. (1996). *Gendered governance: An agenda for change*. New York: United Nations Development Programme.

Beall, Jo. (1996). *Urban governance. Why gender matters*. New York: United Nations Development Programme.

Canadian International Development Agency. (1997). *Government of Canada policy for CIDA on human rights, democratization and good governance*. Hull, Quebec: Author.

Connell, Robert. (1989). "Cool guys, swots and wimps: The interplay of masculinity and education," *Oxford Review of Education* 15(3): 291–303.

Connell, Robert. (1989). *The state in sexual politics: Theory and appraisal*. Mimeo. Los Angeles: University of Southern California.

"Convention on the elimination of all forms of discrimination against women." (1979). UN Document A/34/830 (1979). New York: United Nations.

Diamond, Larry, Juan Linz, and Seymour Lipset. (1995). *Politics in developing countries: Comparing experiences with democracy*. Boulder, CO: Lynne Rienner.

Foucault, Michel. (1977). *Discipline and punish: The birth of the prison*. New York: Vintage Books.

Jain, Devaki. (1996). *Panchayat Raj. Women changing governance*. New York: United Nations Development Programme.

Jain, Sharda, and Lakshmi Krishnamurty. (1996). *Empowerment through Mahila Sanghas. The Mahila Samakhya experience*. Tilak Nagar: Sandhan Shodh Kendra.

Johnson, Isabelle. (1997). *Redefining the concept of governance.* Hull, Quebec: Canadian International Development Agency.

Kapoor, Ilan. (1996). *Indicators for programming in human rights and democratic development: A preliminary study.* Hull, Quebec: Canadian International Development Agency.

Lind, Amy. (1997 April). "Negotiating boundaries: Women's organizations and the politics of restructuring in Ecuador." Paper presented at the twentieth annual meeting of the Latin American Studies Association, Guadalajara, Mexico.

Marshall, T. H. (1964). *Class, citizenship, and social development.* New York: Doubleday.

Miles, Angela. (1996). *Integrative feminisms: Building global visions 1960s–1990s.* New York: Routledge.

Millett, Kate. (1970). *Sexual politics.* Garden City, NY: Doubleday.

Molyneux, Maxine. (1986). "Mobilization without emancipation? Women's interests, state, and revolution." In R. Fagen, C. D. Deere, and J. L. Coraggio (eds.), *Transition and development: Problems of Third World socialism.* New York: Monthly Review.

Oxhorn, Philip. (1998 September). "Social inequality, civil society, and the limits of citizenship in Latin America." Paper presented at the twenty-first annual meeting of the Latin American Studies Association, Chicago.

Patterson, Orlando. (1991). *Freedom in the making of Western culture.* New York: Basic Books.

Platform for action and the Beijing Declaration. (1996). New York: United Nations.

Red de Educación Popular entre Mujeres. (1998 May). *Voices rising.* Special issue. Repem@chasque.apc.org.

Selbin, Eric. (1998 September). "Social justice in Latin America: Dilemmas of democracy and revolution." Paper presented at the twenty-first annual Latin American Studies Association, Chicago.

Stromquist, Nelly P. (1986). "Empowering women through knowledge: Policies and practices in international cooperation in basic education." Report prepared for UNICEF. Stanford, CA: Stanford University.

Stromquist, Nelly P. (1994). *Gender and basic education in international development cooperation.* New York: UNICEF.

Stromquist, Nelly. (1995). "Romancing the state: Gender and power in education." *Comparative Education Review* 39(4): 423–454.

Stromquist, Nelly P. (1998a). "Inventory of efforts to mainstream gender in education—UNICEF." Mimeo. Los Angeles: University of Southern California.

Stromquist, Nelly P. (1998b). "Inventory of efforts to mainstream gender in education—CIDA." Mimeo. Los Angeles: University of Southern California.

Stromquist, Nelly P. (1998c). Personal observation, Lima, Peru.

Vickers, Jill. (1989). "Feminist approaches to women in politics." In Linda Kealey and Joan Sangster (eds.), *Beyond the vote: Canadian women and politics.* Toronto: University of Toronto Press.

Walby, Sylvia. (1990). *Theorizing patriarchy.* Oxford: Basil Blackwell.

Walkerdine, Valerie. (1987). "Femininity as performance." *Oxford Education Review* 15(3): 267–279.

Walkerdine, Valerie, and Helen Lucey. (1989). *Democracy in the kitchen.* London: Virago.

World Bank. (1992). *Governance and development.* Washington, DC: World Bank.

World Bank. (1995). *Toward gender equality: The role of public policy.* Washington, DC: World Bank.

World Bank. (1997). *World development report.* Washington, DC: World Bank.

Young, Iris. (1985). "Humanism, gynocentricism, and feminist politics." *Women's Studies International Forum* 8(3): 173–183.

DISCUSSION QUESTIONS

1. What would constitute full citizenship from a feminist perspective? In what ways would this concept mean an expansion of current notions of citizenship?

2. Who speaks on behalf of women in the school system? When and how are the concerns of women regarding schooling and education heard? How can these voices be heard in a more systematic and sustained way?

3. How do donor agencies tend to define citizenship? Why is it important to know and contest their views? Since external financial resources are needed, what are the best ways to use these funds if the objective is to create a full citizenship for women?

4. What measures have women-led NGOs taken to expand the notions of citizenship? In what ways have they succeeded? In what ways have they been unable to surmount both conceptual and practical obstacles?

5. What kinds of issues should an education for full citizenship cover? What kinds of activities could be conducted at the school and classroom level to create conditions that promote the development of gender-sensitive citizenship norms? What initiatives could you and your peers, as students in a particular school, take to develop a more gender-sensitive society?

CHAPTER 2

The Democratic Politics of Theory in Comparative Education

VAL D. RUST AND LISA LAUMANN

> *Reunification of Germany has meant former East German*
> *teachers and students must learn about democracy and*
> *citizens' participation to make it function for the benefit of*
> *the people.*
> — SUSANNE SHAFER (N.D.)

This book honors Susanne Shafer, a comparative educator, who dedicated her professional life to extending democracy and the rule of the people. In this chapter we deconstruct the historical landscape of comparative education theory, and assess the political and ideological overtones of this landscape. The focus of our inquiry shall be on the commitments comparative educators have expressed toward democracy. The word derives from the Greek *demos,* meaning "the people," and *kratein,* "to rule," as opposed to the rule of the few or the one. Beyond this, though, we enter into troubled waters, because democracy has been variously defined. We suggest that most of the theoretical work that drives comparative education is based on assumptions not unlike the commitment of Shafer, though the ways in which these assumptions were expressed vary considerably.

We maintain that comparative education theory, like other disciplines and fields, has never been free of politics and ideology but has always been grounded in convictions, preferences, and interests framed in paradigmatic forms and biographical experiences. Theorists' ways of knowing come in large measure from their own history and geography, from their cultural and social context, from their physical and emotional perspective. As Brian Holmes and Joseph Lauwreys (1957) observed in a *Year Book of Education* article, educational treatises contain "a doctrine of man in society and a doctrine of the nature of knowledge; both being themselves coloured by assumptions in part explicit, in part implicit, drawn from the cultural ground" (48). Part of the cultural ground is the ground of comparative education discourse itself. Jürgen Schriewer (1988) notes that the "contradictory traditions" of the field of comparative education shape the field in a process largely self-referential (27–28). While the content of paradigmatic forms/frames varies by era, by individual, and even by specific work, and may be strongly contested, we suggest that the ways comparative educators juxtapose this content shape their approaches to policy, their relationships with theory, and their views on democracy.

COMPARATIVE STUDIES BEFORE WORLD WAR I

Nineteenth- and early-twentieth-century inquiries about state educational systems from an international perspective were decidedly practical and politically motivated. MarcAntoine Jullien's 1817 plan for the establishment of an international commission on education, a multilingual journal to disseminate the findings of comparative research, and a network of teacher training institutions throughout Europe, illustrates our contemporary failure to recognize such motivations. Today we refer to Jullien, the so-called father of comparative education, as one of the earliest advocates of the science of education and a proponent of systematic data collection for comparative purposes (Fraser 1964, 1–2). Less well known, however, is Jullien's intense commitment to education as an instrument of social change. He believed education was the best means of overcoming the corruption of morals and character that he believed had infected European society. The purpose of comparative education was to collect information on all educational systems, whether democratic or autocratic, so that nation-states could make informed judgments as to what practices were the most suitable for improving and regenerating morality.

Nineteenth-century scholars engaging in international education activities acted on clear assumptions and categories of education within the nation-state being investigated. They generally took for granted that their own educational system fell somewhere along a continuum in terms of its state of development, better than some and worse than others. Foreign educational studies were of three major types: rejecting, giving, and borrowing.

The rejecting mode of relationship is illustrated by certain Russian scholars, who rejected foreign influences in favor of internal developments. Leo Tolstoy ([1861], 1967), for example, devoted himself extensively to Western European education in hopes of finding appropriate models for Russia, but he returned home convinced that the foreign models he observed were totally unsuited to the democratic schools he had in mind in Russia, which would set men free and allow them to flourish in terms of individual personality.

The giving and borrowing modes were prevalent during that time. In 1831, for example, Victor Cousin, a French scholar, was sent to Prussia by the French Ministry of Education and published a report of education in Prussia that inspired the French Guizot Educational Law of 1833 (Knight 1930). In England Matthew Arnold was active in studying German and French education in an attempt to provide illustrations to his countrymen of national systems of education that might serve as models for an English national system of education (Arnold 1861, 1864, 1868).

The giving and borrowing modes are well illustrated in Prussian educational relations. The Prussian schools of that period typify a giving type of orientation. Prussian aims were then directed toward monarchical nationalism rather than democracy and Prussians assumed their schools were superior to schools in other countries. Foreign educational studies consisted of three notions. First, Prussian educators wished to publicize how much other countries had copied their education. Second, they wished to publicize German educational superiority. Third, they wished to expose faulty foreign educational reforms because they had not followed the German model.

This giving orientation was especially evident regarding the interests Prussians showed in America education. Prussia saw itself as one of the dominant cultural centers of the world and viewed America as a cultural infant. Rudolph Dulon (1866), a German-American educator living in Illinois, wrote that the "German school is a product of the work, power, creation and studies of a thousand years," and stands on the foundation of a strong culture, while the "American school came forth as if a product of a magic wand from nothing" (289), springing from a barely cultivated foundation, and growing in the wilderness, without the protection required by something noble.

In the last half of the nineteenth century, a decidedly practical and helping side emerged regarding German interests in American education. Large numbers of democratically oriented German educators were among those participants of the 1848 revolution, who ultimately fled repression in Germany and settled in the United States. Even though they were committed to democracy as practiced in the United States, the German educators retained a conviction of German educational superiority. One of the conscious purposes of the German/American Teachers' Association was to help remake the American schools, which Germans believed to be of English origin. Even Dulon (1866) felt compelled to conclude his study of American schools and German schools in America with the observation: "My American colleagues . . . in your schools you must indeed bow to the German genius! We wish to help."

The nineteenth-century American orientation toward Germany reflected a borrowing type of relationship. Americans generally recognized that the German system was worthy of emulation. Following a trip to Europe, Calvin E. Stowe (1910) declared before the Ohio legislature that the Prussian system was no "visionary scheme," but a course of instruction "in the best school districts that have ever been organized." It was a system worthy of emulation. Alexander Dallas Bache (1839) returned from a two-year study of European schools to report that Prussian primary education was the "most perfect of the centralized systems" (179). In his *Seventh Annual Report of the Secretary of the Board,* Horace Mann (1844) stated, "Among the nations of Europe, Prussia has long enjoyed the most distinguished reputation for excellence of its schools," and Americans must adopt a system similar to that in Prussia. The same praise was expressed by the superintendent of Common Schools in Connecticut, Henry Barnard (1854), who claimed that the Prussian schools had "attained a degree of excellence, which has attracted attention of statesmen and commanded the admiration of intelligent educators in every part of Christendom" (27).

The appeals of American educators that America adopt the Prussian model was challenged by certain Americans who claimed the Prussian education system intended to perpetuate and strengthen monarchical aims and to check the revolutionary aims of those wishing to create a more democratic form in Germany. However, the American reformers countered these arguments by pointing out that the best means of cultivating democracy was through the schools. Horace Mann (1844) stressed that America could copy the modes of instruction and the school structure of the Prussian educator without "adopting his notions of passive obedience to government" (73). And he argued that a system of education used to support arbitrary power should surely be able to support and perpetuate democratic institutions.

We have stressed that German interests in American education were proscribed by the fact that American education was in its infancy. However, by 1911 the uniqueness of American democratic principles and schools had been recognized to the degree that people such as Georg Kerschensteiner (1945) claimed that a number of American schools existed "from which we Germans can learn as much as the Americans could at one time learn from us" (243). Johannes Tews, the great exponent of the *Einheitsschule*, enjoyed quoting Goethe's famous statement, "America, you have it better than our continent, the old thing" (15). During the great general interest shown toward America in the middle of the Weimar period, Erich Hylla (1928) returned to his Prussian Ministry of Education post after a year in America. He openly admitted that he had developed a great admiration for American schools and advocated that the Germans adopt many things related to them. The title of his book reflects the attraction America held: *Die Schule der Demokratie (The School of Democracy)*. In addition, Hylla published a companion volume, a translation of Dewey's *Democracy and Education.*

COMPARATIVE STUDIES IN THE FORCES-AND-FACTORS PERIOD

The era of comparative education as an academic enterprise began to emerge in the second quarter of the twentieth century. As the field developed, scholars who identified themselves as comparative educators expressed a commitment to theory, but their theoretical orientation was quite different from the orientation seen in the field as it became aligned with the social sciences. The theorists of this period held explicitly to normative views of people in society, projecting individuals as citizens with rights and responsibilities. Scholarly knowledge focused on description, discovery, and policy prescription for building a better society. The norm they held was democracy.

Michael Sadler and P. E. Levasseur exemplify the work of early comparative education theorists. Their focus was on national education systems in Europe but was guided strongly by historical, empirical, and comparative analysis. Sadler's aim was not simply to catalogue educational changes taking place but to develop theories that would enable him to anticipate events. However, such predictions were not intended to be of a neutral kind, but to inform national leaders and to promote the wisest, most democratic and fruitful line of development (Sadler, quoted in Higginson 1961). Levasseur (1892) was a French statistician who attempted to rank European countries according to educational criteria. He then related these criteria to cross-national forces and factors, including politics, race, religion, and climate. He found, for example, that by holding race and religion constant, democratic governments exhibited a stronger tendency to make provision for public education than did autocratic governments.

Isaac Kandel (1937) considered comparative education to be the study of educational theories and practices as influenced by different backgrounds. In other words, early comparative education specialists saw theory as an object of national study rather than something that drives inquiry. They assumed various nations adopted different theoretical orientations and the work of the comparativist was to understand these as foundational norms of a given educational system.

Comparativists such as the German educators Franz Hilker (1964) and Friedrich Schneider, as well as scholars such as Kandel and Nicholas Hans, were not content to identify the theoretical orientations of various nations, but they were intent on making judgments concerning their relative merits. Kandel typifies the orientation of these educators. He was deeply committed to democratic citizenship and judged educational systems on the basis of their capacity to instill in the youth of the system a commitment to democracy. He defined democracy as much more than "the rule of the people." He believed democracy to be a way of life, "a body of principles, ideals, and values which is constantly expanding in scope and depth of meaning . . ."(Kandel 1955, 27). He claimed education does not satisfy its potential if it merely engages the students in an "uncritical and unquestioned transmission of the cultural experience" of a nation. It must be judged on its capacity to "equip the individual with knowledge and skills necessary to understand the society in which he lives," and to help develop "a critical attitude which will enable him with freedom and discrimination to modify and adapt the social conditions around him to his own needs." In other words, for Kandel a comparative educator must not be content to learn of educational theories in a society, but he must act as a voice for the "development and progress of humanity" (Kandel 1933, 866–867). His was a voice for democratic political action and inspiration.

The other comparativists mentioned above were not as forthright as Kandel in their commitment to a singular road called democratic progress. In Nazi Germany, Friedrich Schneider (1961) found himself in the middle of radical political currents and, though his writings were understandably framed in rather abstract terms because he could not directly address the totalitarian conditions of his country, the underlying political message was clearly in favor of a more liberal, democratic educational form.

And Nicholas Hans (1949) recognized that the concept of democracy was multifaceted. Kandel's (1933) notion of democracy focused heavily on its expression in America and England with their representative governments and emphasis on individualism and capitalism. However, Hans also recognized the importance of what he called "social democracy" as practiced in the Soviet Union and other socialist countries, based on a socialist economy and state monopoly. Hans's basic thesis was that a national system of education constitutes the "outward expression of national character" and it therefore represents a distinct institution in each national setting (236–238). Because each system of education is unique, Hans is reluctant to advocate a system that is universal; rather, he takes a normative stand on certain basic principles of society, such as equality of opportunity. However, he maintained that these normative principles can be fully expressed in different ways, and different national systems should be free to follow their respective national traditions and adapt themselves to local traditions.

COMPARATIVE EDUCATORS ADOPT THE SOCIAL SCIENCES

In the late 1950s and 1960s the field shifted its focus toward becoming a social science. In the process, the concept of theory underwent a dramatic shift. In the social sciences, theory referred to the lens through which the social scientists viewed the subject of study, rather than the object of research itself. Three major volumes by George Z. F. Bereday (1964), Brian Holmes (1965), and Harold Noah and Max Eckstein (1969) formed the basis of the discussion, though subsequent scholars contributed to the debate. Lê Thành Khôi, a professor at the Sorbonne, not only wrote about comparative education as a scientific enterprise but argued that a general theory of education must necessarily be based on comparative education (Lê Thành Khôi 1981, 1986). Specialists pointing toward making comparative education a more "scientific" enterprise complained that comparative education had been linked too closely with "comparative philosophy of foreign education," and they wished to shift it toward an "empirical approach of the social sciences" (Noah and Eckstein, viii).

We understand social science to be the systematic study of social phenomena, and it involves observation and experimentation for the search of laws, predictions, and explanations related to those phenomena. The value orientation of the social sciences is also quite different from that of social philosophy. Even while social scientists attempt to be neutral, objective, and distant from their work, the comparative educators attempting to bring the field into the sphere of the social sciences identified their work with democratic processes. Holmes (1965, 32), for example, identified his "problems approach" to comparative education with John Dewey's *How We Think*. It was Dewey who connected social scientific inquiry with democratic processes, and Holmes propagated the notion that both scientific inquiry and democratic action liberate human intelligence and human sympathy. For Holmes, if inquiry is truly scientific it must occur in the context of democratic thought.

Though Holmes (1965) attempted to create a field of comparative education that is scientific, he recognized that science does not necessarily disregard normative laws in favor of social science laws (51–53). Drawing from Karl Popper (1962), who openly advocated an "open society" that is consciously pluralistic in nature, Holmes asserts that every society has normative laws and "sociological" laws. For the comparative educator science is to be put in the service of such an open society and humankind, in that it would be "used as an instrument of educational reform" (3). Holmes makes clear paradigmatic assumptions about the direction educational reform ought to take. He does not believe that his scientific enterprise can define what educational policies and practices are to be adopted in a particular country. Rather, his science ought to tell policy makers what consequences their policies might have on an educational system and on other aspects of society (308).

In spite of proclamations about dispassionate inquiry, objective research, and value neutrality on the part of scholars, certain comparative educators were highly motivated by moralistic and progressive intentions. Bereday (1964), for example, forthrightly admitted that a primary purpose of comparative education is its "practical application" (5), just as the purpose of mathematics is occasionally to be applied.

Certain comparative educators of this period were more narrowly committed to the social sciences, including C. Arnold Anderson and Noah and Eckstein. Anderson is singularly devoted to structural functionalism and its evolutionary trends. And Noah and Eckstein (1969), advocates of a science of comparative education, were nevertheless fully aware that the findings of their science ought to have utilitarian consequences. They explained that the potential of the field lies in four spheres. First, it promises to extend the generality of social and educational propositions beyond the confines of a single society. Second, it has the potential to test propositions that can only be tested in the cross-national context. Third, it has the capacity to further cross-disciplinary activities. Fourth, and most important for our discussion, it has the potential to serve "as an instrument for planners and policy makers" (190).

In other words, while comparative education has significant theoretical potential, it also has important instrumental potential.

Other science-oriented comparative educators were even more direct in terms of the utilitarian nature of their work. Edmund King (1958) maintained that even though comparative education is a reliable and accurate study presented as scientifically as possible, it is "practical and reformative" in nature (349). The young beginner of comparative education studies must become aware that the ultimate implication of comparative study is a "reformative intention." King believed that comparative education, like democracy, teaches us that the work of our educational neighbors does not necessarily go in the same direction as our own reforms; however, they ought to teach us that each endeavor contributes to the general pool of "truth" (1958, 12).

Most of these science-oriented comparative educators were not explicit regarding their commitments to democracy and liberty. They recognized that such concepts become difficult to manage if subjected to scientific scrutiny, though certain students of these early scholars remained explicitly committed to democratic ideals. Susanne Shafer exemplifies one such student. She had spent her early life in Germany and later immigrated to America, where she became a student of Claude A. Eggertsen. She was joined by a number of scholars, including Robert Lawson (1965) and Val D. Rust (1967), who concentrated their dissertation research on the democratization processes taking place in postwar Germany. Her dissertation (Shafer 1964) highlighted the democratization efforts in the German *Volksschule* (vocational secondary school), and she then devoted her professional life to democratic facets of social studies programs.

During the period of theoretical hegemony of the 1950s and 1960s, comparative education scholars joined with social scientists to advocate a distinct form of political development, which is best outlined as modernization theory. The paradigm was attractive because it inevitably took on the character of certain nations and implied the emptiness or lack of development in other nations. The United States was usually the "model modern nation" because of its enormous gross national product, its pluralistic life style and its optimistic attitude.

Implicit in the modernization paradigm is the notion of a linear movement between the two extremes. A nation is believed to modernize when it emulates model nations such as the United States, Germany, England, or Sweden. A number of studies appeared that began to provide empirical evidence that relationships between modernization variables exist (Almond and Coleman 1960; Cutright 1963; Lerner 1958; Lipset 1959, 1963). A number of studies found positive correlations between the spread of education and other indicators (e.g., Bowman and Anderson 1967; Harbison and Myers 1964). In fact, the education community was quickly caught up in efforts to apply education as an intervention strategy for national development. The correlation work being done might be regarded as scientific, but the primary intention of the efforts of comparative education scholars was openly and consciously political in favor of justifying education for the purpose of economic and political development. Included in the catalogue of descriptors of modernization was the notion of political democratization. That is, modern nations are characterized by mass popular participation in the political system and by the impersonal rule of law (Rust 1977).

The modernization orientation contributed in large measure to two major practical movements within comparative education: planning and development. Even though these movements grew out of theoretical orientations, they were directly and deliberately interventionist in nature.

Planning. Educational planning emerged as a strategic subfield focused on identifying optimal national investments in education, particularly with respect to projected labor force needs and to education's proposed role as a stimulant to aspirations and demands for goods and services. Planning, therefore, should facilitate the direction of scarce educational resources such that they optimize economic expansion. The challenge, of course, lay in how to figure this out, and planners developed a number of models and strategies to use. The manpower planning model started from personnel needs projected into the future, with education planned back from that point, while cost benefit analyses and rates of return calculations drew on neoclassical economic theory to portray education as investment. Social demand approaches viewed policy formation as a response to political claims, and political economy approaches started from the idea that education systems reproduce structural inequalities. Though early planners focused on preparing students for a world of work, they acknowledged other purposes for education, including the cultivation of a responsible and participatory citizenry and the promotion of social stability and harmony (Adams 1965; Anderson and Bowman 1964; Easton and Klees 1990; Farrell 1997; Parnes 1964). Embedded in the concept of planning was the notion that citizens become better equiped to participate in individual and social choices, which are requisites of democratic participation.

According to Farrell (1997), formal education planning was first associated with state socialist economies, but was also used in post–World War II Western Europe to facilitate reconstruction and to cope with the postwar population increase. In the United States, educational planning took off in the post-Sputnik era. He notes that educational planning in capitalist nations has tended to be more indicative than directive, and that skepticism about it encouraged an emphasis on qualitative aspects and participation. Farrell reports that planning grew tremendously as a field as a result of its use in developing nations, and largely with the support of international and national agencies such as the United Nations Educational, Scientific and Cultural

Organization (UNESCO), the World Bank, and the Institute for International Education. In the case of the World Bank, planning was a prerequisite for the receipt of assistance (Farrell).

Unfortunately, planning has focused almost exclusively on economic development and has failed to consider broader issues related to democratic processes and individual moral and cultural interests. In fact, issues related to democracy and democratic processes are rarely even raised by those advocates of planning. They focus almost exclusively on economic development.

Development education. The term "development" has been in the comparative education literature since the late 1950s (Hylla 1958). It received a notable degree of publicity with the 1961 publication of *Education, Economy, and Society,* edited by A. H. Halsey, Jean Floud, and C. Arnold Anderson. In that book various specialists in comparative education argue that there is a close link between education and economic/social growth. Various authors point out that the link is not necessarily one of cause and effect. In certain respects each acts as both a stimulus and an effect. That is, education certainly stimulates economic and social growth, but they also stimulate educational provision.

Andreas Kazamias and Karl Schwartz (1977) mark the major inception of development education in the field in the year of 1963 with two major events. The first was a conference held at Syracuse University, organized by Don Adams, entitled Education and the Development of Nations. The second was the announcement by Stanford University that it was establishing the Stanford International Development Education Center, or SIDEC. As noted, the University of Chicago had already begun efforts toward development activities, through the work of scholars such as C. Arnold Anderson, Philip Foster, and Mary Jean Bowman.

The work of these comparative educators was clearly within the so-called liberal democratic tradition, which promotes "market forces and an aggressive individualism" (Giddens 1994, 9). While liberalism has a long tradition of communitarian attachments, it has dislodged itself from the tradition of John Locke, John Stuart Mill, and Condorcet and has become identified with Adam Smith and Milton Friedman. In other words, its identity is now with capitalism and individualism (Spragens 1995). Kazamias and Schwartz (1977) note that the movement for development education quickly attained considerable prominence, and they also note that its development marked a distinct increase in activities that were intentionally "instrumental" in nature, in that it fostered market forces in the economy. That meant that comparative education studies would no longer be content with understanding education, explaining educational conditions, or analyzing interconnections between education and the broader social situation. Rather, these studies would extend themselves to applying comparative education knowledge, to defining educational policy implications of research. They maintained that education was a key to improving the conditions of people's lives or to unlocking the door to modernization. Education would produce people who would be activists in society, who would help transform society (Adams 1977; Anderson and Bowman 1964).

Accompanying the theoretical commitments to development was the growing influence of international agencies, including the World Bank, the Organization for Economic Cooperation and Development (OECD), as well as UNESCO and its subsidiaries such as the International Bureau of Education (IBE), and the International Institute for Educational Planning (IIEP). Not only have the organizations dedicated themselves to global planning and development activities, but certain scholars in them have had a direct impact on the field of comparative education itself. For example, Pedro Rosello, who was associated with the IBE in the 1960s, was the first to develop the so-called steps of comparative analysis: description, interpretation, juxtaposition, and comparison, which were popularized by scholars such as Hilker and Bereday (Hilker 1962). But other comparative educators had a direct impact on work that we would associate with democracy. Comparativist Leslie Limage brought her concerns for democratizing access to literacy through analysis of the politics of literacy in both developing and industrialized countries to her work at UNESCO. That organization has had a long-standing, albeit uneven, commitment to literacy as a basic human right. Her work focuses on demystifying literacy issues and promoting participatory autonomous basic skill acquisition in international fora as more than rhetoric (Limage 1986, 1993, 1999). And World Bank scholars such as Stephen Heyneman, Dean Jamison, and George Psacharopoulos contributed to a growing body of comparative education literature linking educational investments to economic development (Farrell and Heyneman 1989; Heyneman and White 1986; Jamison and McAnany 1978; Psacharopoulos and Woodhall 1985).

Even though development advocates have maintained a strong voice in comparative education, by the end of the 1960s the modernization paradigm had begun to fragment, in part, because it had been naïve to believe that all nations are moving toward a colossal homogeneity of social processes and structures. It had also been naïve to believe that all nations had come out of a single social, political, and economic form called traditionalism. Further, the United States, where comparative education was centered, was moving quickly toward becoming a pluralist society, which began to decenter the field away from a single orientation and toward multiple orientations. In addition, the scientific paradigm itself was coming under increasing attack. However, the primary challenge to the pervasive social science paradigm came from within, as the conflict theorists launched a broad attack against the prevailing ideology of the academic world.

CONFLICT ADVOCATES

Philip Altbach (1991) writes that in the 1970s the field of comparative education fell into decline. In the United States, higher education budgets fell, population stabilized, and the US/Vietnam war experience led to a decrease in foreign involvement. The purpose of comparative education also came into question: "Finally, the bright promise of education as the engine of national development and renewal, both at home and abroad, proved false, as many Third World economies failed to reach the takeoff point despite significant educational inputs" (500). Indeed, some scholars began to argue that education systems and institutions served to oppress rather than liberate people.

The label these new scholars were identified with was conflict. Though conflict theorists differed in many ways, one underlying current in the movement was the importance of Karl Marx and Marxism. People such as Alvin Gouldner (1971) were mainline Marxists, while others combined Marxist thinking with that of other scholars. Rolf Dahrendorf (1957), for example, relied heavily on both Max Weber and Marx.

The connection of Marx with democracy has long been one of differing interpretations. He most certainly was a critic of liberal democracy for two reasons. First, he maintained it fell far short of its claims to provide universal rights. Rather, it provided these rights mainly to the privileged few. Second, the resources and rewards of society are unequally distributed. It is around these criticisms that Western Marxism has focused its attention. The underlying idea is that the aims of democracy are not wrong. Capitalism simply prevents them from being fulfilled and they could better be fulfilled in a socialistic state (Giddens 1994).

Marx had been popular in certain European circles since the early 1920s, when the Frankfurt Institute of Social Research Science was founded. Since that time a flourishing body of literature had been generated in Germany, France, and Great Britain. Marxism had never gained a foothold in American politics, and it had usually either been rejected outright or simply ignored. And so the advent of Marxist ideas in the American academy represented a novel and troubling perspective to those who had taken for granted that their perspective would prevail.

The work of Marxists was decidedly political in nature. It emphasized power relationships, the exploitation of one class over the other, and contradictions in the economy, political structure, and society in general. In addition, conflict-oriented academics in America were not content to sit in their chambers and write about the situation, but they joined the activists in their protests, marches, and political rallies.

Here we find the first frontal assault in comparative education circles against an ideal that had almost been held sacred: liberal democracy. Political liberals had defined democracy as the form of government where all citizens shared in political power, a form of government that grants its people, through suffrage, the right to choose its elected officials and even its form of government. This was the notion that guided scholars such as Kandel and Bereday to proclaim it as the highest political virtue. Neo-Marxists held quite a different view of democracy. As practiced in Western Europe and America democracy was seen as little more than a sham on the part of the owners of the capitalist economy that veiled the dictatorship of the bourgeoisie. Democracy was little more than a shameless and cruel process of exploitation. At home the exploited were the working class masses, while abroad the exploited were the poor countries on the periphery.

The primary theoretical challenge of the early 1970s came from the French philosopher Louis Althusser, who, as much as any other individual, inspired the current renaissance of Marxist philosophy. He developed what has since become known as the correspondence theory. That theory establishes theoretical beliefs about the relationship of school to society, and it solidified the assumption that schools could not be used as instruments of social change.

In the United States, Martin Carnoy and Henry Levin (1976) argued that, according to the "correspondence principle," schools exist as an agent of the larger social, economic, and political context that fosters them. This principle suggests that schools serve only to reinforce the existing social order and that stable and enduring educational systems are those that closely mirror the social, economic, and political conditions of the society of which they are a part. If change occurs in these broader spheres, we can expect change to occur in education; the latter with the intent to bring schools in line with social conditions and economic demands. It would be unlikely that school reforms would extend beyond the limits of the social order. This does not mean that attempts at school reforms do not take place, but they are only accepted if they "correspond to modifications in the larger social order" (43).

We find that a new focus has emerged on social conflict as enacted through education systems, and on school processes rather than policy. In *Education As Cultural Imperialism,* Martin Carnoy (1974) asserted that the spread of schooling has been an important force in the spread of capitalism, and that rather than fostering individual participation in social change, schools reinforce the economic and social hierarchy. He argued that a new education should be created to reinforce a nonhierarchical society. Samuel Bowles and Herbert Gintis's *Schooling in Capitalist America* (1976) proved an influential text for comparative educators as well as for scholars focusing on the United States. Bowles and Gintis developed a new functionalist argument, claiming that education operates to perpetuate the inequities inherent in the capitalist mode of production and links democracy with economic equality: "An educational system can be egalitarian and liberating only when it prepares youth for fully democratic participation in social life and an equal claim to the fruits of economic opportunity" (14). An important element in conflict approaches was the linking of education, political and economic equality, and democracy via participation. This relationship is poignantly articulated by Paulo Freire (1983):

> Nothing threatened the correct development of popular emergence more than an educational practice which failed to offer opportunities for the analysis and debate of problems, or for genuine participation; one which not only did not identify with the trend toward democratization but reinforced our lack of democratic experience. (36)

As time went on, comparative educators moved beyond reductive and functional descriptions of the role of education to inquire more specifically into how education could indeed more adequately support the goals of freedom and democracy.

While this information was probably unsurprising to those on the left, intellectual developments, in particular rereadings of the work of Antonio Gramsci and elaborations of theories of the state, encouraged radicals to consider how schools might operate to promote social and political change. Thus, Martin Carnoy (1982) saw in schools the potential to exacerbate contradictions in the superstructure by increasing access to knowledge through mass primary education, increasing parental control of decision making, and linking education to self-reliant development. Following their interest along these lines, Carnoy and Samoff (1990) came to conclude that in transition societies, and perhaps in others as well, the state and politics, more than the system and relations of production, led social development. This logic is echoed by David Plank (1990), who reported it was not a "disembodied political will" that hampered Brazilian basic education but competing social and educational interests (551).

In many respects, the proponents of conflict were proposing a new version of democracy that would contrast with that of liberal democracy. Rolf Dahrendorf (1957) most explicitly spells out a distinction between democratic and totalitarian societies. Totalitarian societies demand conformity and uniformity, while functioning democracies encourage and promote divergence. They are not intimidated by divergence and believe in the justice of creativity, diversity, difference, and conflict.

RECENT DEVELOPMENTS

The disputations between equilibrium and conflict points of view have been superseded in the 1990s by a wide array of knowledge communities that have come to recognize, tolerate, and even appreciate the existence of multiple theoretical realities and perspectives. According to Anthony Giddens (1994), essentially all of these orientations express a firm commitment to democracy.

Why have all theoretical positions made claim to being democratic? With the disintegration of communism, the decline in popularity of the welfare state, and the terrible reputation of fascism and other authoritarian forms of leadership, the only orientation left is democracy. It would be a mistake, however, to assume that the situation has changed in a fundamental way. Of course, people such as Francis Fukayama (1992) announce the death of everything except liberal democracy as a clear sign that liberalism has finally become victorious and that democracy stands today as the only viable form of governance. However, a multitude of theoretical positions continue to be proposed, including those backers of equilibrium and conflict.

Many theorists also challenge the assumptions on which both equilibrium and conflict points of view are based. Certain points of view emphasize emphatically the desire to be noninvasive in certain dimensions of their sphere of study while also arguing for a more practical orientation regarding studies of schools and teaching. This is particularly the case with a recently popular type of inquiry, which we identify as qualitative, ethnographic, and even phenomenological. These orientations are based on quite a different paradigm than existed with regard to both equilibrium and conflict. They are particularly critical of conventional social science methods, claiming that the forms of knowledge the sciences have provided about nations, people, and social and educational processes are partial, deterministic, and not very useful. Vandra Masemann (1990) argues, for example, that "our conceptions of ways of knowing have limited and restricted the very definition of comparative education that we have taught students and used in our research and, indeed, have promulgated to practitioners. Additionally, our conceptions have created a false dichotomy between academics and practitioners. Moreover, they have led to willful ignoring or bypassing of large areas of teaching and learning that are not considered in the vein of valid knowledge." Thus, she claims, there is a "world of education where 'sacred knowledge' is generated by academics and researchers." Masemann argues that while "comparative education, as we now know it, is a creature of the Industrial Age," we are moving into a postmodern era in which paradigms of knowledge are changing and we will move toward using paradigms that are "holistic, context dependent, and integrative" (465–471).

The most striking challenges come from scholars who are directly interventionist in terms of their work. These scholars champion theories related to feminism, ethnicity, and race, complaining that the theoretical structures of mainstream social sciences have systematically excluded these voices and have put forward theoretical constructs that were totalizing and exclusive in nature.

Postmodernism. A main feature of this protest comes from postmodernism, which avoids what Lyotard calls "grand narratives" or "metanarratives," which are defined by Cherryholmes (1988) as something "similar to paradigms that guide thought and practice in a discipline or profession" (11). Lyotard (1984) claims postmodernists are those who are "incredulous toward metanarratives" (17–18) because metanarratives lock civilization into totalitarian and logocentric thought systems. They provide a restrictive, totalizing theory of society and history and are based on abstract principles and theoretical constructs rather than on direct, subjective human experience.

According to Rolland Paulston (1993), comparative education and the social sciences have finally transcended both orthodoxy and heterodoxy and have arrived at a period of theoretical pluralism and heterogeneity. This third period is consistent with postmodern sentiments. According to Val D. Rust (1991):

> Postmodernists would reject any claim that one way of knowing is the only legitimate way. Rather they would say our task is to determine which approach to knowing is appropriate to specific interests and needs rather than argue some universal application and validity, which ends up totalizing and confining in its ultimate effect. (616)

Of course, defenders of metanarratives continue to exist, but those in the field have generally tempered their claims and have reconciled themselves to a world that is largely eclectic, ambivalent, open-ended, and indeterminate, open to new voices in comparative education, which are factors that scholars such as Cleo Cherryholmes (1999) would identify with pragmatism and democracy.

Feminism. Some of the most visible voices come from those advocates of feminist theory. Concerns for gender issues began to emerge in comparative education in the late 1970s and early 1980s, as scholars sought to understand how increased participation of girls and women in schooling might improve their lives and society. Feminist theory is often roughly categorized into four broad categories ordered in terms of their sequential evolution: (1) liberal feminism aimed at asserting women's equality with men and the right to full inclusion in public life, (2) radical feminism emphasizing the value of women's experience and modes of being, (3) socialist feminism linking the personal to social structures of capitalism and patriarchy, and (4) poststructuralist feminism focused on understandlng how discourses shape both consciousness and social structures. In the field of comparative education, most feminist research has reflected the liberal, socialist, and—in the 1990s—poststructuralist approaches. Common to this work has been an emphasis on action and positive change in the lives of women.

Each of these positions also lays claim to some form of democratic practice. Each emphasizes aims for equity, greater freedom, and even progress, which replaces relationship descriptors such as fealty, order, and obedience

(Eisler 1987). Early feminist work in comparative education stressed both the liberating potential of education as a "force capable of generating new life opportunities for women" (Smock 1981) and the need to look under the surface at the nature and effects of educational processes and relationships (Biraimah 1982; Kelly and Elliott 1982; Kelly and Nihlen 1982). Authors noted the paucity of data available on women and girls and the difficulty of conducting comparative studies in the absence of good data (Smock) and relevant questions (Kelly and Elliot). And, they emphasized the need to understand how schooling relates to women's family relationships, stressing that the domestic sexual division of labor might be more persistent than inequality in public life (Kelly and Nihlen).

Much of the feminist research, or research on women, in comparative education has focused on the access for girls to schooling and educational attainment, and, to a lesser extent, the schooling experience, career choices, adult education, and benefits from education (Fuller, Hua, and Snyder 1994; Rose and Tembon 1999; Stromquist 1995a). Indeed, it appears that about half of the articles focusing on girls or women in the *Comparative Education Review* between 1957 and 1998 examined participation, attainment, achievement, gender orientations/expectations, and the relationship of education to work (see sections on gender, women and education, and social stratification in the *Cumulative Index of the Comparative Education Review, 1957–1998).* This research has tended, to the extent that it draws on feminist theory, to focus on the concerns emphasized in liberal feminism; it has also sometimes made use of the methodological features of feminist research, most particularly in studying women from their own perspectives.

Nelly Stromquist (1995a) observes that while a large number of publications (emanating from international organizations as well as from university-based scholars) extol the link between female education and the greater good—reflected in lower family size, better educated families, improved child health, and reduced infant mortality—educational benefits to women themselves appear to be indirect. Education does not seem to liberate women, but it can facilitate their ability to reflect and possibly initiate change. The failure of education to directly benefit women, she argues, is due to the patriarchal nature of the state, "the confluence of power, authority, and intention of dominant institutions in society" (Stromquist 1991, 112). Stromquist claims that "while feminist theory has shown increasing awareness of the role of patriarchy in creating and managing sexual relations and gender representations, it has failed to acknowledge the true importance of schools as instruments of the state—not part of civil society—and as major managers of social values and representations" (1995b, 445). The feminist focus on material needs rather than on ideological forces inhibits discussion of and confrontation over the role of education in the reproduction of gender identities. In the context of a hegemonic market economy, structural adjustment programs, and pressure for decentralization, feminists "romance" the state, constructing it as an "other" capable of developing responsive policies, but not holding it accountable for the reproduction of gender ideology or trying to amass sufficient formal political power to change it. State policies, in their turn, focus on female access to education, with less attention devoted to the content of the educational experience or strategies to construct alternative futures for women. States also fragment females as a group into specific categories targeted for intervention, shifting attention from "the relations and contexts in which problems present themselves" (442).

Critical theory. Probably the most audible voices of the past decade have come from a variety of theoretically orientated people calling themselves critical theorists. The influence of various critical theoretical perspectives in comparative education is undeniable. Critical theory represents an effort to bridge the epistemological gap between positivism and interpretivism; it is "a theory of knowledge that takes the emancipatory interest as fundamental. It recognizes the other types of knowledge but attempts to show that they, too, have their basis in human interests" (Bredo and Feinberg 1982, 275). In the field of comparative education, scholars have drawn on the work of Habermas, Luhman, Mouffe, and Freire to inquire into the relationship between the state, human agency, democracy, and liberation. Ray Morrow and Carlos Torres (1999) note that the critical theory of the state links neo-Marxian and Weberian insights, relating social class structure, "forces and instruments of political coercion," and understanding of "institutional mechanisms of the state, and especially the exercise of the authority of the state and the relationships among nation-states" (93). They contend that public policies reflect both domination and struggle, and suggest that the relationship between critical pedagogies and social movements imply a "radical democratic populism" intent on creating a democratic transformation. This transformation is no longer content with focusing on a socialist economy but on democratic populism along a broad front.

Martin Carnoy and Joel Samoff (1990) remain in the more conventional Marxist mode in that they report that consumption and productivity demands in states making a transition to a socialist model impel a move toward traditional, hierarchical, bureaucratized schooling and away from popular participative education.

Among critical theorists, Habermas (1987) and Giddens (1994) likely speak most directly in favor of a new type of democracy. Both call for a broader communicative democracy not unlike the recommendation of Riane Eisler (1987), that gives up the dominator model of human relations in favor of broader partnership relationships. The major difference in Habermas and Giddens is that Habermas believes consensus is possible through communicative action, whereas Giddens is satisfied with a "dialogic democracy," which presumes only that an ongoing dialogue is possible that provides for relationships based on mutual tolerance.

REFERENCES

Adams, D. (1965). "The study of education and social development." *Comparative Education Review* 9 (October): 258–269.

Adams, D. (1977). "Development education." *Comparative Education Review* 21 (June/October): 296–310.

Almond, G., and J. Coleman. (1960). *The politics of developing areas.* Princeton, NJ: Princeton University Press.

Altbach, P. G. (1991). "Trends in Comparative Education." *Comparative Education Review,* 35 (February): 491–507.

Anderson, C. A., and M. J. Bowman. (1964). "Theoretical considerations in educational planning." In D. Adams (ed.), *Educational planning,* 4–46. Syracuse, NY: Center for Development Education, All-University School of Education, Syracuse University.

Arnold, M. (1861). *A French Eton.* London: Macmillan.

Arnold, M. (1864). *The popular education of France with notices of that of Holland and Switzerland.* London: Longman.

Arnold, M. (1868). *Schools and universities on the continent.* London: Macmillan.

Bache, A. D. (1839). *Education in Europe.* Philadelphia: Lydia Bailey.

Barnard, H. (1854). *National education in Europe.* Hartford: Case Tiffany and Co.

Bereday, G. Z. F. (1964). *Comparative method in education.* New York: Holt, Rinehart and Winston.

Biraimah, K. C. (1982). "The impact of Western schools on girls' expectations: A Togolese case." In G. P. Kelly and C. M. Elliott (eds.), *Women's education in the Third World,* 188–200. Albany, NY: SUNY Press.

Bowles, S., and H. Gintis. (1976). *Schooling in capitalist America.* New York: Basic Books.

Bowman, M. J., and C. A. Anderson. (1967). "Concerning the role of education in development." In *Readings in the economics of education,* 113–131. Paris: UNESCO.

Bredo, E., and W. Feinberg. (1982). "The critical approach to social and educational research." In E. Bredo and W. Feinberg (eds.), *Knowledge and values in social and eductional research,* 271–291. Philadelphia: Temple University Press.

Carnoy, M. (1974). *Education as cultural imperialism.* New York: Longman.

Carnoy, M. (1982). "Education for alternative development." *Comparative Education Review* 26(2): 160–177.

Carnoy, M., and H. Levin (eds.). (1976). *The limits of educational reform.* New York: McKay.

Carnoy, M., and J. Samoff. (1990). *Education and social transition in the Third World.* Princeton, NJ: Princeton University Press.

Cherryholmes, C. H. (1988). *Power and criticism: Poststructural investigations in education.* New York: Teachers College Press.

Cherryholmes, C. H. (1999). *Reading pragmatism.* New York: Teachers College Press.

Cutright, P. 1963. "National political development: Measurement and analysis." *American Sociological Review* 28:25–35.

Dahrendorf, R. (1957). *Class and class conflict in industrial society.* London: Routledge and Kegan Paul.

Dulon, R. (1866). *Aus Amerika über Schule, deutsche Schule, amerikanische Schule, und deutsch-amerikanische Schule.* Leipzig: E. F. Winter'sche Verlagshandlung.

Easton, P., and S. Klees. (1990). "Education and the economy: Considering alternative perspectives." *Prospects* 20(4): 414–428.

Eisler, R. (1987). *The chalice and the blade.* San Francisco: HarperCollins.

Epstein, E. H. (1983). "Currents left and right: Ideology in comparative education." *Comparative Education Review* 27 (February): 3–29.

Farrell, J. P. (1997). "A retrospective on educational planning in comparative education." *Comparative Education Review* 41 (3): 277–313.

Farrell, J. P., and S. P. Heyneman. (1989). *Textbooks in the developing world: Economic and educational choices.* Washington: World Bank.

Fraser, S. (1964). *Jullien's plan for comparative education: 1816–1817.* New York: Teachers College, Columbia University.

Freire, P. (1983). "Education as the practice of freedom." In P. Freire (ed.), *Education for critical consciousness,* 1–84. New York: Continuum.

Fukuyama, F. (1992). *The end of history and the last man.* New York: Free Press.

Fuller, B., H. Hua, and C. W. Snyder, Jr. (1994). "When girls learn more than boys: The influence of time in school and pedagogy in Botswana." *Comparative Education Review* 38(3): 347–376.

Giddens, A. (1994.) *Beyond left and right: The future of radical politics.* Stanford, CA: Stanford University Press.

Gouldner, A. (1971). *The coming crisis of western sociology.* New York: Basic Books.

Habermas, J. (1987). *The theory of communicative action,* trans. Thomas McCarthy. Boston: Beacon Press.

Halsey, A. H., J. Floud, and C. A. Anderson. (1961). *Education, economy, and society.* New York: Free Press.

Hans, N. (1949). *Comparative education: A study of educational factors and traditions.* London: Routledge and Kegan Paul.

Harbison, F., and C. Myers. (1964). *Education, manpower, and economic growth.* New York: McGraw Hill.

Heyneman, S. P., and D. S. White. (1986). *The quality of education and economic development.* Washington, DC: World Bank.

Higginson, J. H. (1955). *Sadler's studies on American education.* Monograph no. 1. Leeds: University of Leeds, Institute of Education.

Hilker, F. (1962). *Vergleichende Pädagogik: Eine Einführung in ihre Geschichte, Theorie und Praxis.* Munich: Hueber.

Holmes, B. (1965). *Problems in education: A comparative approach.* London: Routledge and Kegan Paul.

Holmes, B., and J. Lauwerys. (1957). *Year Book of Education.* London: Evans Brothers.

Hylla, E. (1928). *Die Schule der Demokratie.* Berlin: Julius Beltz.

Hylla, E. (1958). "Recent developments in education in the Federal Republic of Germany." *Comparative Education Review* 2 (June): 12–16.

Jamison, D. T., and E. McAnany. (1978). *Radio for education and development.* Beverly Hills, CA: Sage.

Jullien, M.A. (1817). "Esquisse d'un ouvrage sur l'educaiton comparee et series de questions sur l'education." *Journal d'Education;* an abstract was published in 1826 in *American Journal of Education* 1:403–408.

Kandel, I. L. (1933). *Comparative education.* Boston: Houghton Mifflin.

Kandel, I. L. (1937). "National Backgrounds of Education." *Twenty-Fifth Yearbook.* Chicago: National Society of College Teachers of Education, University of Chicago.

Kandel. I. L. (1955). *The new era in education: A comparative study.* Boston: Houghton Mifflin.

Kazamias, A., and K. Schwartz. (1977). "Perspectives in comparative education." *Comparative Education Review* 21(2/3):153–174.

Kelly, G. P., and C. M. Elliott. (1982). "Orientations toward the study of women's education in the Third World." In G. P. Kelly and C. M. Elliott (eds.), *Women's education in the Third World,* 1–7. Albany: SUNY Press.

Kelly, G. P., and A. S. Nihlen. (1982). "Schooling and the reproduction of patriarchy: Unequal workloads, unequal rewards." In M.W. Apple (ed.), *Cultural and economic reproduction in education.* London: Routledge and Kegan Paul.

Kerschensteiner, G. (1965). "Die Volksschule der Vereinigten Staaten von Amerika." In Hermann Röhrs (ed.), *Die Reformpädagogik des Auslandes.* Düsseldorf: Helmut Küpper.

King, E. J. (1958). *Other schools and ours: A comparative study for today.* New York: Holt, Rinehart and Winston.

Knight, E. W. (1930). *Reports of European education.* New York: McGraw-Hill.

Lawson, R. F. (1965). "Reform in the West German school system: 1945–1962." Ph.D. diss., Comparative Education Dissertation Series 4, University of Michigan, Ann Arbor.

Lê Thành Khôi. (1981). *L'éducation comparé.* Paris: Armand Colin.

Lê Thành Khôi. (1986). "Toward a general theory of education." *Comparative Education Review* 30 (February): 12–29.

Lerner, D. (1958). *The passing of traditional society.* New York: Free Press.

Levasseur, P. E. (1892). *La statistique de l'enseignement primaire.* Rome: Imprimerie Nationale de J. Bertero.

Limage, L. (1986). "Illiteracy in industrialized societies." *Comparative Education Review* 30 (February): 50–72.

Limage, L. (1993). "Literacy strategies: A view from the international literacy year Secretariat of UNESCO." In A. Welch, Anthony, and P. Freebody (eds.), *Knowledge, culture and power: International perspectives on literacy as policy and practice,* 23–34. London: Falmer Press.

Limage, L. (1999). "Literacy practices and literacy policies: Where has UNESCO been and where might it be going?" *International Journal of Educational Development* [Special Issue: UNESCO's Multilateral Role for the Twenty-First Century] 19(1):75–91.

Lipset, S. (1959). "Some social requisites of democracy: Economic development and political legitimacy." *American Political Science Review* 53:69–105.

Lyotard, J.-F. (1984). *The postmodern condition: A report on knowledge,* trans. G. Macpherson and B. Massumi. Minneapolis: University of Minnesota Press.

Mann, H. (1844). *Seventh annual report of the secretary of the board.* Boston: Dutton and Wentworth.

Masemann, V. (1990). "Ways of knowing." *Comparative Education Review* 34(4): 465–73.

Morrow, R. A., and C. A. Torres. (1995). *Social theory and education: A critique of theories of social and cultural reproduction.* Albany: State University of New York.

Morrow, R. A., and C. A. Torres. (1999). "The state, social movements, and educational reform." In R. F. Arnove and C. A. Torres (eds.), *Comparative education: The dialectic of the global and the local.* New York: Rowman and Littlefield.

Noah, H., and M. Eckstein. (1969). *Toward a science of comparative education.* London: Collier Macmillan.

Parnes, H. S. (1964). "Assessing the educational needs of a nation." In D. Adams (ed.), *Educational planning,* 47–66. Syracuse, NY: Center for Development Education, All-University School of Education, Syracuse University.

Paulston, R. (1993). "Comparative education as an intellectual field." *Comparative Education* 23(2):101–114.

Plank, David N. (1990). "The politics of basic education reform in Brazil." *Comparative Education Review* 34(4):538–559.

Popper, K. (1962). *Conjectures and refutations: The growth of scientific knowledge.* New York: Basic Books.

Psacharopoulos, G., and M. Woodhall. (1985). *Education for development: An analysis of investment choices.* New York: Oxford University Press for the World Bank.

Rose, P., and M. Tembon. (1999). "Girls and schooling in Ethiopia." In C. Heward and S. Bunwaree (eds.), *Gender, education and development: Beyond access to empowerment,* 85–99. London: Zed Books.

Rust, V. D. (1967). "German interest in foreign education since World War I." Ph.D. diss., Comparative Education Dissertation Series 13, University of Michigan, Ann Arbor.

Rust, V. D. (1977). *Alternatives in education: Theoretical and historical perspectives.* London: Sage.

Rust, V. D. (1991). "Postmodernism and its comparative education implications." *Comparative Education Review* 35:610–626.

Schneider, F. (1961). *Vergleichende Erziehungswissenschaft.* Heidelberg: Quelle und Meyer.

Schriewer, J. (1988). *Theories and methods in comparative education.* Frankfurt: Peter Lang.

Shafer, S. (1964). "Postwar American influence on the West German Volksschule." Ph.D. diss., Comparative Education Dissertation Series 3, University of Michigan, Ann Arbor.

Shafer, S. (Undated). *New social studies teachers for Eastern Germany.* Unpublished manuscript.

Smock, A. C. (1981). *Women's education in developing countries.* New York: Praeger.

Spragens, T. A. (1994). "Communitarian liberalism." In A. Etzioni (ed.), *New communitarian thinking; persons, virtues, institutions and communities,* 37–51. Charlottesville: University Press of Virginia.

Stowe, C. E. (1930). "Report on elementary public instruction in Europe." In Edgar Knight (ed.), *Reports on European education.* New York: McGraw Hill.

Stromquist, N. P. (1991). "Educating women: The political economy of patriarchal states." *International Studies in the Sociology of Education* 1:111–128.

Stromquist, N. P. (1995a). "Gender and education." In T. Husén and N. Postlethwaite (eds.), *International encyclopedia of education,* 2d ed., 2407–2412. London: Pergamon.

Stromquist, N P. (1995b). "Romancing the state: Gender and power in education." *Comparative Education Review* 39(4):423–454.

Tews, Johannes. (1916). *Die deutsch Einheitsschule.* Leipzig: Julius Klinkhardt, 15.

Tolstoy, L. ([1861] 1967). *Tolstoy on education,* trans. Leo Wiener. Chicago: University of Chicago Press.

DISCUSSION QUESTIONS

1. What kinds of contexts have influenced the thinking of comparative educators about the nature and role of democracy and the ways in which education contributes to it?

2. How did the concerns of comparative educators differ in the pre–World War I era and "Forces and Factors" periods? In later periods?

3. What did comparative educators such as Noah and Eckstein, Bereday, and Holms feel that the field would gain by becoming more scientific? How realistic and appropriate were their ideas? What was their impact? Describe the potential and limits of scientific approaches to comparative education.

4. How have emphases on modernization, development, and planning affected how comparative educators have viewed the role and purpose of comparative education?

5. How have conflict approaches influenced the development of the field? How legitimate were the concerns of scholars working in the conflict paradigm?

6. How would you characterize the current state of comparative education? How has the field's past influenced the direction in which it is heading now? Have issues of concern to comparative educators changed? What new contributions to thinking about education and democracy is the field likely to make?

PART II

Democratizing Education
Reform Efforts in Societies in Transition

CHAPTER 3

Reconstructing Education in Germany

Some Similarities and Contrasts in the Postwar and Post-Unification Rethinking of Educational Provision

DAVID PHILLIPS

There have been two periods in recent German history when, as a result of enormous political and social upheaval, there has been an opportunity to rethink educational provision in all or part of the country. The first period is that immediately following the cessation of hostilities in 1945, when the victorious Allies were able to embark on a program of reconstruction of the education systems in the four Zones of Occupation. The second encompasses the time that has elapsed since the collapse of the German Democratic Republic (GDR) and the Unification of the two Germanies.

Elsewhere I have drawn attention to certain parallels that might be identified between the two periods, as far as efforts at rethinking educational provision in all its aspects is concerned (Phillips 1992, 1995a, 1999). The purpose of this chapter is to look more closely at these parallels in order to explore the extent to which they constitute either similarity or contrast, and to determine how instructive the comparison of developments in the two periods can be.

EDUCATION IN GERMANY, 1945–1949

For much of World War II it was not anticipated that the Allies would need in any significant sense to "govern" Germany once victory was secured. The assumption was that there would be some kind of government in place and that with proper peace negotiation, followed by control and supervision from the victors, a degree of normalcy in government and administration might be restored. With the demand for unconditional surrender, the widespread destruction of cities and major towns, and the huge displacement of populations, it became clear that the Allies would have to assume complete responsibility immediately following the surrender, and that such assumption of power and authority would probably last a considerable time—some estimates put the time needed at several decades.

The Allies were generally ill prepared to assume responsibility for education, though much planning was swiftly undertaken once the potential enormity of the task ahead was realized. Some special training took place, for example, though for the British at least it was rather desultory (Phillips, 1984). Policy was largely developed "on the hoof," with the starting point being Section II A 7 of the Potsdam Agreement of August 1945:

> German education shall be so controlled as completely to eliminate Nazi and militarist doctrines and to make possible the successful development of democratic ideas.

The basic principles enshrined in this brief text agreed on by the Four Powers were meant to inform subsequent directives that provided frameworks for the development of educational provision at various levels.

We might divide the tasks in education in Germany faced by the occupiers into two groups. The first overarching group would involve the following first-order priorities: physical reconstruction, denazification, and reeducation. On these immediate priorities would depend a series of other activities to facilitate progress at a practical level, among them:

- reform of curricula
- production of new textbooks and other teaching materials
- reframing of admissions procedures
- recruitment and retraining of teaching staff
- renewal of contacts with the outside world
- provision of ancillary services (health, welfare)
- creation of new library holdings

It has sometimes been assumed that the Allies were able to regard education as a tabula rasa, so that they might design education systems from scratch in their respective zones. The reality was quite different, at least for the three Western Allies. The first preoccupation—far removed from any wish to introduce fundamental systemic reform—was to tackle the immediate and pressing problems of physical reconstruction. Alternative buildings had to be provided in the worst-hit areas, damaged buildings had to be made safe, glazing and roofing materials had to be found, furniture and writing paper had to be provided. Many of those charged with "controlling" education on the ground found that most of their time was taken up with such tasks. The German administrators had a hard time of organizing even sufficient office space to allow them to function properly. *Ministerpräsident* (Prime Minister) Schäffer said of working conditions in Munich: *"a Sauerei is"* ("it's an utter disgrace") (Müller 1995, 16).

Denazification was a major problem. "White," "grey," and "black" lists had been drawn up on the basis of such evidence as the Allies had been able to gather about individuals and their past involvement with the Nazi party and its organizations. Following the initial dismissal of those considered unsuitable to remain in post, there was a long-drawn-out process of evaluation by means of questionnaire (the notorious *Fragebogen*). There was inevitably much injustice, and there were many denunciations. Very difficult problems were encountered. If, say, the only specialist pediatrician available to work in a university clinic were found to have had an unacceptable Nazi past, should that person be dismissed? Or should there be exceptions to the normal rules, however unfair in comparison to the cases of others? The denazification process inevitably remained incomplete and controversial, and it still haunts Germany today (Bower 1981).

Figures for dismissals are slippery. A few sample figures will illustrate the scale of the problem. Among the information we have, it appears, for example, that in the Soviet Zone some 28,000 teachers (out of a total of 39,000) were replaced; in the British Zone 16,000 teachers "were forbidden to carry on their profession" (Birley 1978, 52). The University of Leipzig had 170 of its 222 academic staff dismissed (Webb 1998) and Pingel (1983) estimates for the British Zone that about one-third of the teaching body of each university was affected by the early stages of denazification (about 150 professors per institution). By mid-autumn of 1945 about 30 percent of the university teachers in Hamburg had been removed. By early 1946 a total of 125 members of the teaching staff in Göttingen University had been dismissed, some of whom were later reinstated. Robert Birley, the distinguished educational adviser to the military governor of the British Zone, felt that it was "an extraordinarily difficult, perhaps an impossible task to decide which teachers should be forbidden to teach on account of their previous connection with the Nazi movement" (Birley 1978, 52).

To replace those dismissed—as well as the many who had been killed on active service, or were displaced, or were still in prisoner-of-war camps—retired teachers were drafted into service and emergency training programs were introduced. At the same time it was essential, in the terms of the Potsdam Agreement, to encourage "the successful development of democratic ideas."

Here the Allies faced a plethora of problems. First, there was the question of what might constitute "democracy." With the founding of the German Democratic Republic in 1949, it would become clear that the word "democratic" might even be used to describe a regime that was in essence undemocratic, at least as far as the term is understood in Western nations:

To the Western nations democracy meant free elections, freedom of speech and religion, preservation of the traditional rights of man. To the Russians these were merely the forms of democracy, and to the idea of a "formal" democracy they opposed their conception of a "true" democracy, wherein the workers or their representatives (who might be self-appointed) controlled the State. (Hill 1947, 12)

But even the Western Allies incorporated three distinctive approaches to democracy into their political systems, which made the differences in interpretation possible. It was said that at one Four Power meeting it was concluded that the only definition of "democracy" that could be agreed upon was that it was what "four Powers could agree to inflict upon a fifth" (12).

The problem of "inflicting" or "imposing" anything within a policy of encouraging democratic behavior is of course itself highly problematic: if you wish to teach people to be democratic, it was concluded, you must proceed principally by example. And so in the Western zones of occupation a policy of encouragement and persuasion was quickly adopted. In this spirit, responsibility for most areas of public administration, including education, was to be handed over to the German authorities as early as January 1947, with the occupying forces thenceforth exercising a largely supervisory function.

The means by which democratic ideas were to be encouraged and developed was the process normally called "reeducation." This too was an aspect of the control of Germany fraught with difficulties (Jürgensen 1985). The term itself is ambiguous, since the prefix *re-* in English has the force of doing something again and that of doing something anew: that is to say, as far as education is concerned, it can either imply a complete starting from scratch or a process of amendment. One of the German terms used, *Umerziehung,* embraces, through the prefix *um-,* the sense of turning around; here there is a clearer immediate sense of a change of direction. The terms and the interpretations put on them are perilously close, however, to indoctrination. Robert Birley disliked the term "reeducation" (Birley 1978), and the deputy director of the education branch in the British Zone insisted that it was an education branch he was running and not a reeducation branch (Jürgensen 1983). Most of its members would have been strongly opposed to any attempts at the imposition of ideas.

The most successful form of reeducation was contrived through the example of democratic decision making, through discussion and debate, through access to visitors from outside Germany representing the widest possible range of ideas, and through contact with the outside world generally. There were now opportunities to travel, books previously banned or unavailable could be obtained, information of all kinds (through official information centers like *Die Brücke*) was now easily accessible, the press and radio services were reestablished, and cultural activities resumed. There was a constant flow of visitors to the Western zones, many of them liberal spirits who had a wish to "do something from Germany." A report on British summer vacation courses for university students in 1948 encapsulates the strengths of learning by example:

> [O]ne of the deepest impressions made on the Germans in these courses was the contact they were able to make with British methods of lecturing, discussing and debating. They admired the frank and easy manners of the British participants, their tolerance, their humour, their appreciation of the other man's point of view, their refusal to talk down to the Germans or to suggest anything that implied "reeducation." What the British participants put across was done more by example than by instruction. (Murray 1948, 100)

It was important, too, to be positive in order to create confidence in those who would be creating the new democratic Germany. Jürgensen quotes a one-time head of the German education department of the British Foreign Office as offering the following advice to the warden of Wilton Park, the British conference center that ran courses for visiting Germans:

> We must avoid doing anything which suggests that we think the Germans unready to set up an independent democratic government and we must make it clear that our aim is to help them to do so. Therefore, in all discussions and lectures [in Wilton Park] we should not probe for the weak points in German history or in the German character, but for the strong points. The aim should be to encourage the Germans to build on the good elements in themselves and in the country as a whole and to develop a well founded self-confidence in their ability to conduct a democratic state. (Jürgensen 1985, 91)

Susanne Shafer was among the first to document the development of American-style social studies classes *(Sozialkunde)* in West German elementary schools after the war (Shafer 1964, 1979). This curricular innovation included civic education—what would now be called education for citizenship—a subject in which there was a lot of renewed interest in the late 1990s. After the war the American example in this area of the curriculum proved helpful in attempts to introduce to school children brought up under Nazism some of the principles of a democratic way of life:

> No longer was history to be taught to German youth so as to glorify war as well as to avoid its controversial aspects. Pupils should learn about German history since the founding of the German empire in 1871, they should learn much more about the history of the other nations of the world, and they should understand the background of the political, economic, and social developments which they were witnessing in the world around them. (Shafer 1964, 1)

There was an enormous effort after the war to produce new teaching materials, especially textbooks, that would facilitate the new styles of teaching and learning. Work began in 1944 on the selection of suitable material, and it was originally hoped that many books dating from before Hitler's rise to power in

1933 might be used. In the event this proved unrealistic, as only eight such books were considered suitable for use with children of primary school age (Davis 1978). Thereafter, despite all the problems with the supply of paper and printing and binding materials, a whole new generation of textbooks was slowly produced. Much reading material was donated to assist the building up of library stocks. The international scholarly community did much to assist the universities (Lagler 1993), but other needs were not neglected, including those of younger children, for whom special libraries were created (Lepman 1969).

We have seen, then, that Germany after the war did not present the tabula rasa in education that might have been imagined. There were many who thought that widespread structural and conceptual reform of the education system could and should have been effected while the situation appeared ripe. Indeed, such radical change was to happen in the Soviet Zone, and to continue under the governments of the German Democratic Republic. But in the Western zones, despite some enthusiasm for radical change, the basic principles of encouragement and persuasion in place of *Diktat,* of proceeding by example instead of by prescript, and of allowing the Germans themselves to seek to solve the problems they perceived in their education system rather than attempting to solve those problems for them, resulted in a lack of willingness to depart from the tried and tested system that prevailed before Hitler came to power. This is often characterized as a policy of "On from Weimar," an approach that was to be reinforced by Chancellor Adenauer's catchphrase *keine Experimente!* (no experiments). Stabilization became a prime political imperative in the newly created Federal Republic, and risks could not be taken.

There are five reasons, I believe, for the failure of the Germans after the war to make a completely fresh start with a redesigned education system (Phillips 1987):

- The force of tradition was, despite the intervening years of Nazi hegemony, too strong to allow any drastic departure from a system that had once been the envy of the world.
- There was an understandable fear of any centralized control—Allied or German. The only time there had been a Federal [national] Minister of Education had been under the Nazis.
- The teaching body—at all levels—was not the most progressive: in Nordrhein-Westfalen only 6.2 percent of secondary school teachers were under age thirty, and 55 percent were fifty and over; in Berlin the average age of fully trained teachers was fifty-seven in 1948.
- There was a feeling that the Allies did not necessarily have the answers to many of the important educational issues of the time, despite, for example, the British enthusiasm for the 1944 Education Act.

- Counteracting the enormous physical and material hardships of the time naturally took precedence over projected reform plans.

Examination of the condition of education in Germany after the war and its consequences for later development inevitably invites comparison with post–Unification Germany, to which we now turn.

EDUCATION IN EAST GERMANY SINCE 1990

After the collapse of the government of the GDR and the subsequent Unification of the two Germanies in October 1990, the practical problems facing those charged with reorganizing the education system in what became known as *die fünf neuen Länder* ("the five new states") were not as great as those the Allies had to cope with after the war, but they were huge problems nonetheless (Pritchard 1999; Rust and Rust, 1995; Weiler, Mintrop, and Fuhrman 1996). The rapidity of change caught almost everyone by surprise. After a visit to the GDR as late as spring of 1989, I noted the following in my journal:

> The overwhelming impression is of a society which has gone its own way and which will probably survive much as it is, while becoming outwardly more and more "Western" (i.e., West German, principally) in its [outward] look. . . . Few changes look possible on the ideological front, since it is so firmly established in the people's consciousness.

And even so acute an observer of the German scene as Timothy Garton Ash could write in January 1989 "an article pooh-poohing suggestions that the Berlin Wall might soon be breached" (Garton Ash 1999, xiii). Remarkably—since a unified Germany had been spoken for by Western politicians with a rhetoric of high commitment—a future unification had not been planned for. No proper contingency arrangements existed for the pressing eventualities that would follow from the bringing together of the two countries.

An education system (see Appendix II) was, of course, in place, and functioning normally, but its controlling central ministries were quickly disbanded and new *Land* (state) ministries assumed powers of the kind enjoyed by their "old" Western counterparts. Makeshift premises were soon in operation, and ministers were appointed following the elections of December 1990. Much advice was sought from the West, and civil servants were borrowes from Western ministries. Pairings with Western *Länder* were organized, some of them resulting in fruitful support and collaboration in a variety of fields. I visited the Brandenburg Ministry of Education in January 1991 and made these notes in my journal:[1]

> We visit the *Landesregierung* [state ministry] of Brandenburg, where we meet the Minister . . . (who was not expecting us) and three of his staff (one

of whom is on loan or has moved from Nordrhein-Westfalen). It is clear from our discussions that everything is in a most almighty muddle, despite the frenzied activity to get a new *Schulgesetz* [school law] formulated and to arrange *Sofortprogramme* [emergency programs] to cope with immediate needs. . . .

The ministry is accommodated in a building with makeshift signs everywhere, and its administration seems very precarious. I begin, in these rundown surroundings so typical of East Berlin, to be reminded of the postwar years, and the improvisation that informed everything then.

Academics from West Germany began to become involved in East German institutions and here a curious mix of motives could be discerned. While there were those of high standing and established credibility who gave freely of their time and energy to support colleagues in the East, there were many others who saw a role for themselves that might further their careers in the West. In February 1991, I recorded the views of an academic in Magdeburg who spoke with strong feeling about the behavior of West German members of a newly established *Strukturkommission* (structural committee charged with reorganization) for the university:

[The West Germans] asked about the openings in Magdeburg—would they be offered C3 or C4 professorships? Would financial support be available so that their existing living standards could be maintained? When we react with incredulity, they say that this has happened elsewhere too. Our interlocutor says it is for them not a question of C3 or C4 professorships but one of whether they will have a job at all.

Such people with an eye to the main chance caused much confusion and considerable resentment, just as some visitors did who breezed into the British Zone from time to time after the war, "full of wise saws and modern instances." In February in Berlin, I noted:

We keep hearing people say to us: "I've made contact with Prof. X in Frankfurt, or Prof. Y in Bremen or Hamburg," etc.—there seems to be enormous faith in the simple process of contact, but I wonder about the quality of much of the advice they might be getting.

But of course, as was the case after the war, urgent contact with the West was necessary if quick advances were to be made, and academics who had been cut off from normal association with colleagues in universities in Western countries quite naturally sought such contact wherever it could be quickly established. After the war, attempts were made to "pair" British and German universities; exchange programs were established and German teachers at all levels were allowed to travel to England for conferences at Wilton Park and elsewhere.

Visiting higher education institutions in East Germany in the early 1990s was in some regards like stepping back to the 1950s. The material conditions were very underdeveloped, with many buildings still bearing the scars of war; library holdings were minimal; laboratory equipment was severely outdated by Western standards; and the administrative infrastructure was primitive. The prospective task of rebuilding and developing sites was huge. A rationalization process was necessary too, since higher education institutions were very generously staffed in comparison to those in the Western *Länder*. The *Wissenschaftsrat* (German Science Council), responsible for advising the federal government and the parliaments of the *Länder* on higher education matters, was charged with the task of establishing a lengthy and complex process of evaluation of East German institutions.

At the start of the 1990–1991 school year head teachers in the still existing GDR were elected by *Schulkonferenzen* (committees of teachers and parents); many were simply confirmed in their old posts at this early stage. It had been a prerequisite for head teachers in the GDR to be Party members, and so such membership in itself could not be grounds for dismissal—and certainly not grounds that could be comfortably used by people who had most likely themselves been members of the Party. In the same period it is estimated that about half the entire workforce in the Eastern *Länder* lost or changed their employment. By 1991–1992 some 10 percent of the teaching force had lost their jobs (Weiler et al., 2). It is an uncomfortable thought, but clearly some teachers must have survived whose behavior under the GDR regime would not bear scrutiny by any Western standards. Hämäläinen (1994) reminds us that "teachers were forced to lie to their pupils in schools and were pressured by the *Stasi* to extend punishment of parents to their children in classrooms and playgrounds. One way was the freezing out or isolation of these children from their classmates. The Nazis had practised the same chilling methods" (60). The *Stasi* (security police) were more prominent in the GDR than their counterparts under the Nazis—Hämäläinen estimates they had double the personnel for a population only one-quarter the size. Now that the *Stasi* records have been made available, the pervasive extent of the organization's activities is very clear. A large proportion of the GDR population was caught up in the process of checking and reporting, often in the most trivial detail. Garton Ash (1997) provides some chilling examples from his own *Stasi* file.

There was a greater proportion of dismissals in the university sector, where the processes of evaluation were much fiercer. There were many tragic cases, where otherwise quite worthy academics could not compete—for their own jobs—with Western applicants who had had all the benefits denied to their colleagues in the east.

As mentioned, I had postulated in a piece written in 1992 that there were several parallels between the postwar and post-Unification situations in education in Germany. At the same time, I had intimated that such parallels are deceptively alluring. With the benefit of rather more hindsight, it is possible to reconsider the obvious similarities and to consider how informative they might be. The following is a basic checklist:

- the collapse of the old system and its accompanying trauma and consequent nostalgia
- the need to reestablish contact with the outside world
- the purging, retraining, and reorientation of the teaching force
- the revision of courses, curricula, and teaching materials
- the democratization of education generally

The collapse of the old system was rapturously received, and there was excitement at the prospect of a coming-together with the prosperous Federal Republic. People were willing to seize opportunities. But it was not long before a certain nostalgia—*Ostalgie* (Eastalgia) was the German term coined for this—crept in, just as there had been times in the long period of hardship for German citizens after the war, when even the Nazi period had begun to look attractive in retrospect.

The nostalgia for a securer past is understandable. Change had been slow, and East Germans are still on pay scales pegged at lower levels than their Western counterparts. Unemployment and less secure social support have been new phenomena for those in the eastern parts of Germany. Crime and violence have increased alarmingly. Neofascist groups have found an uninhibited voice. Psychological problems abound as people contemplate the "loss" of their country, however attracted they might be to the Federal Republic and its traditions and institutions. There is still talk of *Ossies und Wessies* ("Easties and Westies") and the divided nation is characterized by the term, alluding to the Berlin Wall, *die Mauer im Kopf* (the Wall in people's heads).

Specifically in the field of education there is a widespread feeling of being let down, or unnecessary restructuring of the education system for the sake of conformity with Western models, without sufficient thought having been given to what had been worth preserving in the GDR system—not only in structural terms but also with regard to its approaches to teaching and learning (Phillips 1999; Streitwieser 2000). Kindergarten provision in the GDR, to take one example, was highly regarded, and the ten-year polytechnical school—which was the basis of the GDR system—provided an undifferentiated education for all children throughout the period of compulsory schooling. In effect, it constituted the purest type of comprehensive education (never achieved in the West), since there were no competing school types (such as independent schools).

As was the case after the war, when pre-1933 models for the structure of schooling were reintroduced, so in the post-Unification period trust has been placed in the traditional structures of schooling in the West, with the comprehensive school (the *Gesamtschule,* the closest Western school type to the former GDR model) figuring only partially (in Brandenburg and Mecklenburg-Vorpommern) in the new systems for the five Eastern *Länder* (Führ 1992). Great faith was placed in the academic secondary school, the *Gymnasium,* which all the new *Länder* introduced (for details of the structure of education in the "old" Federal Republic, see Appendix I).

Contact with the West has been easier than was the case after the war. A great deal of practical assistance has been provided, but there has been a much resented "colonization" of some Eastern German institutions (not schools, where the teaching force is predominantly East German in origin). Pritchard gives the following figures for the origins of staff in higher education in East Germany in 1991: At universities, colleges of art, and polytechnic schools, respectively, there were 52 staff rom new *Länder* and 45 staff from old *Länder,* 71 staff from new *Länder* and 22 from old, and 58 staff from new *Länder* and 41 from old (171).

Rapid expansion of library holdings and the provision of information technology support of all kinds have given East German teachers at all levels the chance to catch up with their Western colleagues. Nonsense such as the banning of books—one East German professor told me in 1991 that he had even been unable to get permission to read Henry Ford's autobiography—quickly became a thing of the past.

Denazification after the war and the evaluation of the East German teaching force following Unification are deceptively similar. But the processes involved, and their consequences for individuals, are somewhat comparable. In both situations reliance was placed in a questionnaire (see Pritchard 1999, 217–218, for an example; FitzGibbon 1969, 185–194, gives the text of the postwar *Fragebogen*), with all the problems that questionnaire returns and their interpretations create. In both situations much injustice was evident, and there was little consolation in the fact that many who deserved to be punished for an unacceptable past lost their posts. In February 1991 I found myself recording sympathy for the academics involved in teacher education in Halle of a kind that would have been inconceivable in the context of the postwar situation:

Frau H. says that . . . she was worrying . . . about the fate of the good people we have been meeting with. It is *tragic* to see the position they are in and not to be able to do much—if anything—to help them. Most of them—I would have to exempt most of the professors—are forward-looking, positive people, who feel very strongly about their professional skills and the good experience they have of training teachers *to teach.* They are now in a state of shock and clearly feel very bitter and, in many cases, angry, about their situation. They are not happy with the *Abwicklung* [unwinding] processes, and they are worried, while not being at all anxious about *Evaluierung* [evaluation of their professional abilities] or about their jobs.

Retraining was a priority in both periods. In the Eastern *Länder*, teachers of Marxism-Leninism have not been needed. Some have turned themselves into *Gesellschaftskunde* (teachers of social studies) after the collapse of the GDR regime and before Unification (Neather 1998). Nor have so many teachers of Russian (the compulsory first foreign language in the GDR) been required. Many retrained, from a very early stage, as teachers of other languages, principally English (Klapper 1992), in special courses such as those run in Güstrow at the *Landesinstitut für Schule und Ausbildung* (*Land* Institute for Schools and Teacher Training).

Courses and curricula have been revised and restructured, so that there is comparability between the Eastern and Western *Länder*. Teaching materials were a problem in the early post-Unification period, when much ad hoc adaptation had perforce to take place, but at least appropriate materials were potentially available, unlike in the postwar years, when most textbooks had to be entirely rewritten.

Democratization of institutions began to happen quickly following the events of 1989. With Unification in October 1990 came the framework of the democratic government and its expectations of the Federal Republic, and so Eastern Germany had the advantage—not available to other ex-communist countries—of immediate models in existence in the nation-state into which it was now absorbed.

How informative, then, is the comparison between the postwar and post-Unification rethinking of education in Germany? As I have attempted to show, there are superficial similarities that can be seen to contain clear contrasts when the detail is examined. In terms of any theoretical consideration of what tends to be necessary in post-crisis situations in education (Arnhold et al. 1998), it can be seen that both periods under consideration here involved the solution of problems to do with the following:

- physical reconstruction
- ideological reconstruction
- psychological reconstruction
- provision of materials and curricular reconstruction
- human resources
- population and demography

The education systems of the German *Länder* have passed through both periods with a faith in their long historical tradition, a tradition that at various times has attracted the attention and admiration of observers from Britain, the United States, Japan, and elsewhere. Despite the many problems in education still evident in the eastern *Länder*, and the unease felt particularly by teachers who believe that there was much that was good in the hastily abandoned educational provision of the German Democratic Republic, education in Germany seems for a second time to have survived a period of quite extraordinary change with its fundamental strengths intact.

APPENDIX I: ASPECTS OF EDUCATION AND TRAINING IN GERMANY

Germany, as a federal republic, devolves responsibility for educational and cultural matters to the *Land* (state) parliaments. Each *Land* (in the old Federal Republic there were ten *Länder* plus West Berlin; with the accession of the former German Democratic Republic (GDR) there are an additional five) therefore has a degree of autonomy that does not exist in countries with centralized education systems.

The autonomy the *Länder* enjoy, however, cannot allow them to deviate too far from "natural" expectations of what the education system should deliver, and so there are also federal planning and policy bodies, the KMK (the standing conference of ministers of education) being the most obvious for the coordination of policy for the period of compulsory schooling.

A process of *Verrechtlichung* (juridification) results in educational provision being enshrined in law, and so it is clear to all involved with the system within an individual *Land* what types of schools are provided, what the syllabus content is for particular years in particular types of schools for the various subjects taught, how and at what stages children will be assessed, and so on. This unequivocal clarity regarding provision must be seen as one of the strengths of the system, despite criticisms of bureaucratization.

Since education is a matter for *Land* parliaments, it is also a subject for political decision making. Whether or not to introduce the *Gesamtschule* (comprehensive school), for example, has been a political matter that has resulted in some *Länder* experimenting widely with such schools, while others have resisted them. Decisions reached in the five new *Länder* of the former GDR have been determined by Christian Democratic Union (CDU) thinking on education, and so all of them quickly envisaged the rapid introduction of the *Gymnasium* (grammar school) and other "selective" schools, to replace the ten-year common school, which had provided a wholly undifferentiated education for all children between the ages of six and sixteen.

The eleven *Länder* of the old Federal Republic have retained a school system that is arguably the most conservative in Europe. With various exceptions it consists of the *Gymnasium,* the academic secondary school preparing pupils for university entrance; the *Realschule,* an intermediate school with a long and distinguished history of preparing pupils for a range of technical and middle-management careers; and the *Hauptschule,* the main type of secondary school, actually for a minority of pupils in Germany's tripartite system and now having the unenviable label of "sink school," since it is no longer clear for what professions its products are qualified. Alongside these schools there exist in some *Länder Gesamtschulen* (comprehensive schools) that cannot be considered truly comprehensive owing to the competitive presence of other types of school.

The five *Länder* of East Germany all proposed, following Unification, to introduce the grammar school and a *Realschule* of some kind; only one envisaged the *Hauptschule;* three did not foresee the introduction of comprehensive schools in any form. The conservative nature of German school provision has thus been confirmed and strengthened by the new *Länder.*

Defenders of the differentiated German system point to several features that mitigate its apparent rigidity:

- parents may choose which type of school their children attend;
- there is the possibility of lateral transfer from one type of school to another, syllabuses being devised with this in mind;
- the leaving certificate from each type of school is not restrictive, but provides vertical access to other stages of education; and
- some *Länder* in any case have an orientation stage before a final decision is reached as to which type of school a child is best suited to attend.

But the greatest strength of the school system up to age sixteen is probably the strong *Realschule* (intermediate school), which provides essential education and training for pupils not aiming specifically at a university education. The new German *Länder,* while mostly rejecting the *Hauptschule* on the grounds that it has failed in the West, are putting their faith in the expanded *Realschule* for non-grammar-school pupils.

Assessment in German schools is continuous and regularized. A six-point scale is used, with grades 1 to 4 representing satisfactory attainment or above. Pupils may score only one average of 5 in their end-of-year report; a 6 or more than two 5s will in most cases result in their not being able to proceed to the next class. A class can only be repeated once; thereafter a pupil who has failed to reach the goal of the class will have to transfer down to another type of school.

Vocational training, based on a Dual System of cooperation between employers and the state, has long been regarded as exemplary in the Federal Republic. It is compulsory—on a part-time basis—for all pupils up to age eighteen who are not in full-time education. At age sixteen some 70 percent of school-leavers enter vocational training of some kind. There is a noticeable trend for eighteen-year-olds to enter the Dual System, even though they have gained the right to a university place by passing the final *Abitur* (school-leaving examination).

In higher education the *Fachhochschulen* (roughly equivalent to our former polytechnics) are enjoying great favor, and they have grown in numbers.

They provide a shorter (three-year) course than the universities, with a strong bias toward practical subjects and their application. These institutions, building on the traditions of the *Realschule* concept and the highly developed vocational training system, provide a further indication of the seriousness of purpose of education in Germany when it comes to assessing and meeting the needs of a modern industrial society.

Source: Adapted from Phillips.

APPENDIX II: A NOTE ON EDUCATION IN THE FORMER GERMAN DEMOCRATIC REPUBLIC

The basic structure of general educational provision in the former German Democratic Republic is characterized by uniformity and so is relatively straightforward to describe. In 1989, the year in which so many countries of Eastern Europe, including the GDR, underwent sudden and dramatic political change, the education system of the GDR looked as follows:

Preschool education: crèches for children up to age three (places available for something over 60 percent of children)

Kindergarten: provided for in excess of 90 percent of children aged three to six

Ten-year general polytechnical school: for children aged six to sixteen, general comprehensive school with curricular emphasis on science and technology; no general differentiation according to ability; from grade 7 pupils gained work experience through attachment to an industrial enterprise of some kind, as part of the curriculum for what was called "introduction to socialist production"

Extended upper secondary school: providing a two-year course leading to university entrance

Sources: Moore-Rinvolucri (1973) and Hearndon (1974).

NOTE

[1]During 1990–1991, I served as a member of a commission set up by the *Wissenschaftsrat* (Science Council) to report on the future of teacher education in the new *Länder.* I kept a detailed account of my experiences as a member of the commission, and extracts are presented herein.

REFERENCES

Arnhold, Nina, Julia Bekker, Natasha Kersh, Elizabeth McLeish, and David Phillips. (1998). *Education for reconstruction: The regeneration of educational capacity following national upheaval.* Wallingford, CT: Symposium Books.

Birley, Robert. (1978). "British Policy in Retrospect." In A. Hearnden (ed.), *The British in Germany: Educational reconstruction after 1945,* 46–63. London: Hamish Hamilton.

66   *Democratizing Education and Educating Democratic Citizens*

Bower, Tom. (1981). *Blind eye to murder. Britain, America and the purging of Nazi Germany—A pledge betrayed.* London: André Deutsch.

Davis, Kathleen Southwell. (1978). "The problem of textbooks." In A. Hearnden (ed.), *The British in Germany: Educational reconstruction after 1945,* 108–130. London: Hamish Hamilton.

FitzGibbon, Constantine. (1969). *Denazification.* London: Michael Joseph.

Führ, Christoph. (1992). *On the education system in the five new laender of the Federal Republic of Germany.* Bonn: Inter Nationes.

Garton Ash, Timothy. (1997): *The file. A personal history.* London: HarperCollins.

Garton Ash, Timothy. (1999): *History of the present. Essays, sketches and despatches from Europe in the 1990s.* London: Allen Lane/Penguin Press.

Hill, Russell. (1947). *Struggle for Germany.* London: Gollancz.

Hearnden, Arthur. (1974). *Education in the two Germanies.* Oxford: Basil Blackwell.

Hearnden, Arthur (ed.). (1978). *The British in Germany. Educational reconstruction after 1945.* London: Hamish Hamilton.

Jürgensen, Kurt. (1983). "British occupation policy after 1945 and the problem of 're-educating Germany.'" *History* 68(223): 226–244.

Jürgensen, Kurt. (1985). "The concept and practice of 're-education' in Germany, 1945–50." In Nicholas Pronay and Keith Wilson (eds.), *The political re-education of Germany and her allies after World War II,* 83–96. London: Croom Helm.

Klapper, John. (1992). "German unification and the teaching of modern languages: The methodological legacy of the GDR." *Comparative Education* 28(3):235–247.

Lagler, Wilfried. (1993). "Die Rezeption ausländischer Einflüsse." In Peter Vodosek and Joachim-Felix Leonhard (eds.), *Die Entwicklung des Bibliothekswesens in Deutschland 1945–1965,* 379–392. Wiesbaden: Harrassowitz Verlag.

Lepman, Jella. (1969). *A bridge of children's books.* Leicester, UK: Brockhampton Press.

Moore-Rinvolucri, Mina J. (1973). *Education in East Germany.* Newton Abbot, UK: David & Charles.

Müller, Winfried. (1995). *Schulpolitik in Bayern im Spannungsfeld von Kultusbürokratie und Besatzungsmacht 1945–1949.* Munich: R. Oldenbourg.

Murray, George. (1948). "University summer vacation courses in the British Zone of Germany, 1948." Public Record Office Report no. F0371-70715. London: Public Record Office.

Phillips, David (ed.). (1983). *German universities after the surrender: British occupation policy and the control of higher education.* Oxford: Oxford University Department of Educational Studies.

Phillips, David. (1984). "British university officers in Germany after the war." *IJED* 4(1):65–76.

Phillips, David. (1987). "Lessons from Germany? The case of German secondary schools." *BJES* 35(3):211–232.

Phillips, David. (1992). 'Transitions and traditions: Educational developments in the new Germany in their historical context." In David Phillips and Michael Kaser (eds.), *Education and economic change in Eastern Europe and the former Soviet Union,* 121–136. Wallingford: Triangle Books.

Phillips, David. (1995a). "Rééducation et réforme de l'enseignement supérieur dans la zone d'occupation britannique." In François Genton (ed.), *France-Allemagne.*

De Faust à l'Université de masse, Chroniques allemandes, 4, 223–240. Grenoble: Département d'études germanîques, Université Stendhal-Grenoble III.

Phillips, David (ed.). (1995b). *Education in Germany. Tradition and reform in historical context.* London: Routledge.

Phillips, David. (1999). "Das 'Zusammenwachsen' Deutschlands in Bereich des Bildungswesens. Perspektiven und Probleme aus britischer Sicht." In Wolfgang Hörner, Friedrich Kuebart, and Dieter Schulz (eds.), *'Bildungseinheit' und 'Systemtransformation'. Beiträge zur bildungspolitischen Entwicklung in den neuen Bundesländern und im östlichen Europa,* 51–59. Berlin: Berlin Verlag Arno Spitz.

Pingel, Falk. (1983). "Attempts at university reform in the British Zone." In David Phillips (ed.), *German universities after the surrender: British occupation policy and the control of higher education,* 20–27. Oxford: Oxford University Department of Educational Studies.

Potsdam Agreement. (1945). *Protocol of the Proceedings of the Berlin Conference, Berlin, 2nd August, 1945.* Cmd 7087. London: HMSO.

Pritchard, Rosalind M. O. (1999). *Reconstructing education. East German schools and universities after unification.* New York: Berghahn.

Rust, Val D., and Diane Rust. (1995). *The unification of German education.* New York: Garland.

Shafer, Susanne. (1964). *Postwar American influence on the West German Volksschule.* Michigan: University of Michigan School of Education.

Shafer, Susanne. (1969). "American origins of civic reeducation in the American Zone of Occupation in postwar Germany." Paper prepared for a symposium on the educational policies of the Occupation Powers, Bielefeld, Germany.

Streitwieser, Bernhard Thomas. (in press). "Memory and judgment: How East Berlin teachers have been regarded in the post-Unification decade." In David Phillips (ed.), *Education in Germany since Unification.* Wallingford: Symposium Books.

Webb, Adrian. (1998). *Germany since 1945.* London: Longman.

Weiler, Hans N., Mintrop, Heinrich A., and Fuhrmann, Elisabeth. (1996). *Educational change and social transformation. Teachers, schools and universities in Eastern Germany.* London: Falmer Press.

DISCUSSION QUESTIONS

1. Following periods of great political crisis and upheaval, what measures can be taken to ensure and preserve the democratic development of education systems?
2. What would constitute an undesirable background in a teaching context?
3. Is it possible to "purge" a teaching force of people with undesirable backgrounds?
4. Is reeducation a viable concept?
5. Might it have been feasible, in the context of the immediate post-Unification period in Germany, to have retained something of the structure of the school system of the former German Democratic Republic?

CHAPTER 4

Democracy and the Study of Germany
ROBERT F. LAWSON

After studying archival sources, observing schools, and interviewing educationists, Susanne Shafer, in *Postwar American Influence on the West German Volksschule* (1964), presented evidence to conclude positively on both the American Occupation effort to liberalize the social studies in elementary schools and the response of German teachers, administrators, and curriculum institutes.

> It is noteworthy that [the] examples agree with postwar American proposals for German school reform. In general, these and other proposals which were adopted came to be recognized as consistent with the new German national goals. This study seems to indicate that the evolving national goals of a new nation, as well as the current social, political and economic milieu, may have at least as much influence as its traditions upon the adoption of new educational practices. (249)

> The postwar years have been years of widespread reevaluation by Germans. Adenauer, Heuss and other leaders within Germany have turned to Western Christian values to guide them in the rebuilding of Germany. This orientation has allowed them, as well as teachers and other West Germans, to accept the fifteen years of national Socialism as totally lost. The same orientation enabled West Germans to be receptive to the Western Big Three's proposal that representative government be established in their zones of occupation. The accompanying postwar American proposals for social studies education were gradually received in the same spirit. Along with the study of contemporary affairs, teachers presently stress such democratic ideas as equal justice for all, the inviolability of the individual, and the responsibilities of citizens. (247)

She noted, however, some questions for democratic education:

- About carrying knowledge into practice—"... whether in the present educational setting German youths are truly learning to accept and *fulfill their part* in their country's democracy" (247).
- About understanding the practical as well as the form of democratic education—"... in the West German *Volksschule* [vocational secondary school] the requisite critical faculties today receive little more than token recognition. When a teacher talks about the Third Reich, he may be so highly critical and condemnatory that a form of reverse indoctrination of pupils occurs. Critical discussions of communism have the same condemnatory character. They shortcut a more scientific analysis of the appeal of communism and its successes" (248).
- About independence in searching widely through political information and views—"... unlike many American teachers, he does not encourage the pupil to read widely exploring his interests through the large variety of books and magazines in existence. No doubt, present educational practices in the Volksschule limit the pupil's freedom to explore, to question, and to criticize. If social studies education were to reverse this pattern, Germany might produce not only an informed electorate but one less indifferent to party politics, an indifference which weakens representative government" (248).
- About social class—"... German democracy might also be strengthened if social fluidity were further increased. Rigidity of social class runs counter to democracy with its respect for individuality" (248).

She was ambivalent about the forcefulness of the American role, mainly in regard to timing, since both American initiative and German participation seemed to be equally necessary.

> Might American proposals for educational reform have been more completely adopted if the United States occupation authorities had forcefully instituted the changes recommended? Some German teachers wish such measures had been taken. In actual fact, by 1949 reform was made the responsibility of German educators. When initially they failed to go far enough, teachers and the lay public have had to rely on themselves to seek additional improvements." (248)

I will return to the question of American influence as a macro concern in the discussion on democracy.

Professor Shafer's work and mine from about the same period of time *(Reform of the West German School System, 1945–1964)*, were complementary (Lawson 1965). We agreed on the events, the roles, the questions—perhaps not surprisingly since we had both been social studies teachers and students in Ann Arbor, and were subject to the academic environment of the University of Michigan and the Ann Arbor community. We agreed on what democracy means, and what it means to teach democracy in form and practice. We agreed on the value in the postwar situation of American imposition, but also about a necessary limitation on and reciprocity in that imposition. We accepted the cultural sources of the "reluctance displayed [by Bavarian officials] to accept American proposals for change" (57) as a research fact, but as a hindrance to developing a context for liberal change, which we understood primarily in institutional terms. We believed that tolerance of difference means intolerance of cultural-political ideologies that lay claim to truth but deny dissent. We believed in the efficacy of the American path to social unity, though that would change in our respective concerns—not in principle—over the years. We shared the value that Shafer attributed to George Eckert's writing, ". . . in the course of a calm analysis of the lives of people through history, basic common humanity was put above cultural differences" (222).

It is also appropriate to say that we lacked sophistication about a number of comparative, methodological, and research issues. Obviously, American assumptions in 1945 about democracy were not universal. The United States led Germans to believe our emphasis on equalization was not only transferable but also the central issue of democratization. We were, like our politicians and our respondents, guilty of subordinating the context to an American analytical model—an error now more obvious in North-South interactions (*African Renewal* 1997).

Of lasting moral consequence was the political conclusion that reeducation of the vanquished was more civilized than rape and pillage. That is one of those simplistic moral truisms, but the issue, of course, is the concept of total peace following total war. For some decades the unholy wartime alliance between the United States and the Soviet Union, followed by their agreement on spheres of influence, kept this from emerging in an uncontested hegemonic form, but the contemporary version of moral (not religious) absolutism—cultural cum political subordination of dissent employing education as a primary vehicle—may have been launched, or at least programmed through this substitution of conversion for force. Similarly, the model of reeducation (Shafer 1964) proved so successful, in the enthusiastic response of the captive public, in the initial visibility of structural change, and in the political colonization of the losers, that it became a cornerstone of international education policy in the United States.

In retrospect, formal education was believed to have the independent potential through the curriculum and method of teaching to effect significant changes in individual attitudes, values, and eventually social structure. Following the intensive effort from about 1870 to 1940 on teaching children and on socializing them in national systems, the view was that education could be a potent vehicle for social melioration. It was framed however by a benign policy emphasizing general outcomes (equality, mobility, unity, respect, success) and through particular *educational* means (access, cooperation *and* competition, achievement, work, inclusiveness) articulated in classroom practice and system structure. This differs in principle from what has come to be an acceptance of the legitimacy of education not only to reflect societal directions but to act as a political agent of a professional class. This shift was foreshadowed in zonal policies of the Allied Occupation in Germany. Only in the Soviet Zone, later in the German Democratic Republic, was education directly enslaved to the remaking of personalities and collectivities in the Party image and according to Party specifications. In this the Communists were much more thoroughly prepared, organized, dedicated, and overseen than were the Nazis, who were never able to completely subordinate other groups and who settled for minor intrusions in formal education, believing the child-oriented lower school and the humanistic upper school would naturally yield either political indifference or values amenable to patriotism and authority. Using education in the social engineering of Soviet-dominated countries proved to be contagious, but even more pervasive is the principle agreement on the central social role of education between the United States and the Soviet Union, whose ideologies became uncontested in international development. Brief attention to the zonal histories is instructive.

The Soviet zonal authority was thoroughly prepared in procedures and aims, both general and specific, for German educational reconstruction. By 1946, a school law for this zone was in effect, the main guidelines of which specified an elimination of the private sector in education, the extension of common schooling in the form of the unified eight-year school, a reorientation of content and organizational emphasis toward occupational and technical training, and a permeation of communist doctrine in the school.

In the French Zone, the reestablishment of a traditional European school organization required little active educational effort beyond that agreed upon by the Occupation Powers in consort. Only the restatement of classical educational values and an insistence on at least minimal concessions to French cultural universality were particular characteristics of French Occupation policy on education.

Although important differences existed between the United States and British zones, both in policy formulation and in procedures employed (Lawson, 1965), these differences become matters of detail here. Both can be characterized by an effort to cooperate with German authorities in the reconstruction of education and to allow, at least gradually over the course of the occupation period, increasing independence of decision making to German officials and educators. This policy resulted in wide variations among the school programs finally adopted in the *Länder* (provinces) of the American and British zones.

There were no more serious differences among the occupying powers than among the German regions themselves in the Western zones by 1947, and what differences there were did not constitute any critical hindrance to the general political integration of these zones taking place from 1947. The basic East-West difference remained the crucial one, and in that it did, this difference constitutes a major piece of evidence in support of the contentions that (1) foreign intervention in anything less than total social reconstruction is not decisive for specific institutional change and (2) specific institutional form is determined largely by the political and economic means and objectives pervading all institutions of the society. Furthermore, in the one instance in which circumstances dictated a laboratory-like situation, relatively free of the direct foreign or indigenous cultural baggage of Berlin, the educational outcome was precisely as determined by that sociopolitical environment (Lawson 1972).

EDUCATIONAL DEVELOPMENTS IN EAST GERMANY

The goals of education and the structures established to achieve them in East Germany were initially determined by the Soviet Union, and the Soviet influence continued to be decisive for policy. Basic educational decisions were thus made externally, but this is not to deny the existence of tension between the German tradition in education and the philosophy of communist education as interpreted in the Soviet Union or defined by the German communist party. Nor is it to deny any connection between these two schools of thought. European communism carries a particular theme of social organization with European cultural content. Moreover, the development of socialist thought, organizational strength, and political voice in Germany had prepared a social alternative to prevailing forms long before the middle of this century. While a basis for the social change did exist in Germany, however, it had never been dominant or instrumental in the ordering of institutions. As a result of the political solution after 1945, institutions were abruptly restructured. From that time, education was organized so as to reflect a current interpretation of socialist institutional form, and accepted the task of operationalizing the social philosophy through behavioral change and direct contribution to economic growth.

In the Western zones, military governments, while exerting relative degrees of pressure on Germans to conform to British, French, or American institutional patterns, moved rather early toward restoring local autonomy. As the military governments relinquished their control, Germans in the West became free to resist Occupation pressures, and did so—vehemently in some cases. The prepackaging in Moscow of the Soviet Zone, however, meant that the aims of the Soviet military government and those of the local German authorities were in full accord. The National Committee, *Freies Deutschland,* had been working in the Soviet Union since 1942, and specific proposals for Communist reconstruction of German society had been prepared by 1944 (Gunther and Uhlig 1969). Furthermore, the Soviet advisors were prepared for political tasks pertaining to their respective areas of responsibility in a way that was not generally true in the Western zones. In education, the military advisors were intimately acquainted with the history of German education, and were able to select the periods and actions from that history that would support a cultural interpretation favorable to a socialist reconstruction of school and society. Thus, whatever reaction the general population may have had to the Soviet military occupation, the governance of the Soviet Zone was tidy and total, with apparently smooth working relations between the German leaders and military authorities.

The educational literature of the Soviet Zone in the early postwar period and thereafter reflects only this smoothness and agreement. In contrast to West German reaction to some points in the basic military government educational directives, Soviet Order No. 40 was credited unequivocally for its value in establishing the goal and content of a democratic school reform. Allegedly, only the Soviet Union among the Occupation powers fulfilled the obligation undertaken in the Potsdam Agreement to effect a democratic reconstruction of German society, and only the Soviet Union followed through on the joint educational agreement requiring the cleansing from German education of Nazi, militarist, and racist contaminants (Schneller 1955); only the Soviet Occupation Authority assisted Germans in the restoration of economic stability, using "the long experience of the Soviet Union in the development of the best tradesmen, technicians, and engineers in the world" to advise on plans, quotas, and training mechanisms, which, without exploiting workers, would increase the industrial potential of the society and the well-being of its members (Beilken and Weber 1959, 473). It is impossible to be more unreserved in praise of a military occupation than East German writers were. For example, "there has scarcely been a government in the history of Germany which has had so much understanding for the cultural concerns of our people, which has so applied itself to the extension and expansion of the school, as the responsible organs of the Soviet Military Government" (Schneller, 18). Such phrases were stated, and repeated, as truth until for all practical purposes, they became so for East German society.

Justification of the strong hand of the Soviet Union in the reconstruction of East Germany, and corollary justification of the strong hand of the SED in the internal operations of the society, allowed for an unquestioned channeling of Soviet principles and practices into each institutional area. The Soviet example continued to be followed in education throughout the 1950s and 1960s, not only in terms of the fundamental assumptions and of administrative practices but also in terms of specific structural and curricular developments. The ten-year school, the polytechnical curriculum, the primacy of Russian in foreign-language instruction, the inclusion of vocational training in schools of general education, the emphasis on vocational paths to higher education, the development of special schools for the highly talented, revisions in the university curriculum and stipulation of degrees, the inclusion of youth groups and other social agencies in educational policy making, the organization of teacher training according to school levels, and the ambitious development of means of part-time correspondence education—all followed examples set in the Soviet Union (Baske and Engelbert 1966).

Such an educational process is defined by (1) the ideological foundation of school instruction, which determines the active role incumbent on education in the society; (2) the structural developments, which show education to be the object of institutional decisions made in general social terms; and (3) the planning procedure, which powers the cycle of socioeconomic input and output through schools.

Education in such an ideologic system must be defined in terms of three basic, perhaps concentric areas of effort: (1) the systematic instruction given in schools (Kohlsdorf 1965), (2) the extracurricular involvement of youth in collective activities that supplement both social and academic learning, and (3) the continual reeducation of the total population through the communication of Party decisions and propaganda. While qualifications and responsibilities are discrete, the various educational agents are not permitted to become independent of one another or isolated from the collective social effort. Correspondingly, youth are not allowed to withdraw from their obligations to the society, and these obligations were spelled out in both procedural and normative terms in communist pedagogics, for example by Gerhart Neuner, director of the Central Research Institute (abbreviated in German as DPZI), referring to the research of the Soviet psychologist, L. J. Boshowitz (Baske and Engelbert 1966).

For education to develop the human product desired in the new East German society, the institution had first to be structured and equipped to perform its active role. In this structuring, education was defined much more broadly than was common in European history and practice. Although the emphasis here is on formal schooling, the definition of education was extended in a real and systematic way to include youth movements, mass communication media, social-induction rituals, farm and factory training programs, artistic and sport activities, paramilitary and social tasks, and a variety of youth and adult pursuits outside the formal curriculum.

The use of an institutional model implemented in another society inevitably produces certain conflicts. In the East German situation, these conflicts were muted through the use of two basic strategies. The first was use of Party interpretation to strike a subtle, shifting balance between national independence and the interdependence of socialist countries.

Shifts in the balance were motivated by Party assessments of the appropriate relationship between the Soviet Union and the GDR in a given development period. Hence, the postwar fusion of Soviet-German interests gave way, after independence, to a general linkage of the two systems with increasingly discriminatory action on educational particulars. Neither the ultimate control of the Soviet Union nor the application of Soviet experience to the East German system were ever questioned, but these realities came to be more assumed than advertised, and the relationship was overt only in reference to particular institutional questions.

The second strategy required the reestablishment of a national identity compatible with international communism. The historical dimension was accommodated by a logic that diverted the progressive ideas from German educational history through the Soviet Union and back into the German flow in the GDR. These ideas returned verified by Marxist universals, so the national question was made irrelevant. To the extent that they were interpreted under Soviet conditions, however, they had to be reinterpreted to accord with social conditions and requirements in the GDR, and this became a continuous process. Theoretically then, educational forms were national in their reference to German history and the present society of the GDR, but, being based on common communist socioeconomic assumptions, were coincident with developments in other communist countries and divergent from developments in Western Europe, including West Germany.

The educational structure established in East Germany immediately after World War II was a rather simple, makeshift conglomerate, but one that embodied the educational demands of German socialists over more than one hundred years and laid the foundation for subsequent development. The basic system principles were equality, unity, and secularity, and these were structurally implemented by building around an extended eight-year common school—before it, a program of preschool education, and after it, alternative vocational and academic high schools, both leading to forms of higher education.

The initial reform effort was characterized largely by negative thinking; the elimination of old structures and norms had to be accomplished before real, positive reforms could take place. After 1959, the development of the unified socialist school system was dealt with positively. The central link in the system became the ten-year general polytechnical school, common for all children, and interlocking with differentiated types of intermediate schools offering alternative avenues to work and further education. Without going into the details, the reforms after 1959 must be seen as a progressive development, implementation, and consolidation of principles firmly established by then for education. The preschool program was steadily expanded to provide more equality of opportunity and to free women for the work force. The ten-year school was structurally refined to include three levels; continuous research was directed toward scientific significance and productive application in the curriculum, and toward more effective, systematic teaching. Upper-level programs were further elaborated and differentiated, and their links to the common school strengthened—thus securing the integration of vocational and general education, and providing horizontal mobility while promoting individual talents in the interest of economic development (Anweiler 1970). These ideological directions were determined by certain fundamental principles, the two most crucial being *unification* and *polytechnical education.*

Unification in communist education is a significant and extensive concept. It includes not only the combined parts of the system but the "essential couplings" among them. It includes all the schools, all levels and types of schools, the links between schools, between schools and other educational agencies, and between education and other institutions of society. It implies *totality,* and it requires singular central planning and authority. Education, through this concept, was treated in terms of the total social policy of the GDR, and its treatment was determined by the state authority for that policy. Also, since unification refers to a standardization of goals and a collectivization of the school population, the same concept was used to promote conscious, active popular participation in the implementation of social policy.

Polytechnical education as a Marxist educational concept centralizes the industrial society in the curriculum of the school. It is, like social studies in the United States, both a subject and a principle permeating the entire school program. The curriculum is organized around major areas of production, and pupils learn to use tools, service machines, and otherwise to acquire skills of the factory or farm. Its nearest specific reference to vocational education, however, is its function of preparing the young to make appropriate vocational choices. More important in general education is the utilization of polytechnical studies to induce "technical thinking," the positive orientation toward work, and the acceptance of collective relationships that are characteristic of life in a modern industrialized socialist society. The reforms progressively emphasized more strongly the intention to develop a general science of technology and the centrality of this study in *general education.* While there is some recognition in Western countries of the appropriateness of this effort, nowhere outside the socialist bloc did it so redefine the content of education (Klein 1962; Baske and Engelbert 1966; Anweiler 1969).

EDUCATION DEVELOPMENTS IN WEST GERMANY

For West Germany, the change pattern tends to be concentrated in those institutional rearrangements that will underscore and develop selective social characteristics and facilitate the society's capacity to accommodate modern conditions and change pressures.

Analysis of this change pattern has essentially two parts: identification of the social and political factors bearing on educational policy decisions, and projection of these determinants through policy to the actual institutional changes. While cultural continuity has been assumed in West Germany, thus dismissing one of the largest interpretive problems in East German education, there can be no simple assumption about social organization, no singular direction of institutional development, no central authority to reconcile differences or overrule dissent. The cloth of development has to be made up from the patches of special interest and philosophy present in a pluralistic society, and woven together by the many seamstresses of a decentralized system.

The extranational control that West Germany was subjected to during the Occupation period was weakened by its distribution through three governments having themselves differing of views of society and education. Furthermore, it was perceived as extracultural, without general, integrative, or permanent application. Thus, with some new international content of educational ideas and with vague liberal democratic goals for education, West Germany reestablished the form and structure of schooling that had evolved in that society.

The need for social reform, initially referred to as the National-Socialist disaster, necessarily impinged on education. The debate on school reform has been active ever since. This debate has been complicated by the difference of opinion within and between various group sets, which had traditionally resulted in a nonsystem made up of a compromise of separate schools representing the variety of interests. In a very real sense, the question of reform in West German education can be seen as an effort to unify these diverse interests in a modern educational progression.

The main public issues in the postwar debate were: the length and function of the common school; the time and procedures for separation of pupils into ability groups for secondary education; the place of religious education, and, closely associated, the community school in the public school system; and the appropriate basis for curriculum, in general or according to school type. All of these issues could be referred to the question of the school's role in social change, and positions were dichotomized on this question. Basically, those parties viewing the school as a social instrument wanted to change education itself most radically; those attempting to preserve established traditions could countenance educational change according with modern conditions, but not to the degree that the essential character of schools would change or that they would act to accelerate social change. Specific decisions were made regionally, according to the principle of *Land* autonomy in cultural affairs, and were determined by the regional strength of the respective disputants and by the compromises acceptable to the professionals involved. It has been politically impossible to overcome "states' rights" in West German education. Although the resulting unevenness in educational reform has been criticized by liberal interests, provincial autonomy has protected local cultures to some extent. Furthermore, that principle made feasible the accommodation of educational systems of the Eastern *Länder* after Unification. In spite of their immediate structural shift to West German forms, it allowed room for difference and time for self-determination.

Certain impulses to reform have cut through this diversity. These impulses have not come from the schools, but they do course through education to affect certain social expectations. They are primarily the impulses of economic development, social democracy, and political participation—all of which are seen to be sustainable only with educational support. Moreover, the reference of these terms becomes clear only in the framework of a particular political community, and that community is increasingly defined by West European agreement—which overrides particularistic differences. The standards and common expectations deriving from the European interpretation of these impulses have in fact dictated certain educational actions and thus forced a degree of conformity in normative and structural decisions. There is no longer any real argument against the extension of schooling for all, the restructuring of higher levels to accommodate various interests and talents, or the modernization of curriculum through core studies and differentiated courses, both having reference to the society outside the school. There is no tenable argument against the proposition that social welfare and economic advancement require the encouragement of generally higher levels of educational attainment across the school population. There is no objection to the central importance of political education, to the school's responsibility to communicate directly the principles and behaviors of democracy to the youth of the nation.

What emerges from these changes is a conception of the school system that still retains the principles of differentiation on a common base, but that extends both the horizontal and vertical dimensions to encompass a greater school population and a wide variety of curricular programs. To make this concept workable, the structure of the school system has to be seen to have some openness; the teaching body has to be better equipped to handle the new tasks expected with continuous educational change; the strategy of "inner reform," criticized as protective of areas and school types, needs to relate directly to a reform dynamic that at any given historical moment meets democratic as well as achievement criteria.

CONCEPTUALIZING EDUCATION FOR DEMOCRACY IN GERMANY TODAY

Institutionally, because of *Land* autonomy and because the structural principles were not essentially different in the two Germanies, the difficulty of including a decommunized East German education was not insurmountable. The tensions that still persist are more than economic however. They are the residual tensions of clashing beliefs about democracy in education.

Ideas are the toys of intellectuals until they are given life in social response; by their results they are proved right or at least right-headed, even though momentum and power can delay consciousness of misguided ideas, and human error, mental or moral, can derail an idea going in the right direction.

In dealing with the reactions to an extreme, like the Communist socialization of Eastern Europe, it is easy to yield to an opposite extreme. Democracy is by its nature not an extreme, however, and it is never subsumed within another sociopolitical concept, nor compromised by excesses of *a* community or of *an* idea other than of itself.

We have learned in the contemporary period to question both philosophically and empirically some of our assumptions about democracy, questions that should now inform our impositions abroad. Given the historical results of grand abstractions about political ideas and about societies, *it* appears that universals are treated with considerable suspicion in the most viable democracies, and that pragmatic, relative decisions about social development are most likely to represent the will of the people, *provided* that the process is guided by a simple, powerful, and unyielding principle of justice.

For the transfer task, educators have to consider seriously the question of how democratic practice takes place. What are the practical community dimensions of making an individual socially conscious in a way that preserves individual autonomy and also builds social commitment? The experience of all societies is relevant to answering those questions. In the transfer situation, however, American educators can only bring American democratic practice—that is, principles, strategies, and mechanisms to use as points of consideration and possibly of departure. Have we learned not to replicate mistakes of an earlier, perhaps imperialistic America? Have we learned that to democratize is not necessarily to Americanize?

I would have answered that we have learned those things intellectually, and that the changes in American society, however painful, show the continued working of the best of American democratic principles. After observing policies and projects for assistance to Eastern Europe (among others) under the rubric of education for democracy, I must conclude that the actions of American educators do not appear to have been substantially altered by changes in American society or by the transfer and development of literature.

There is not a great deal of agreement in American society about the vehicles of implementation of democratic principles, let alone the contents. For some, the implementation of democratic principles does not seem to require substantial change. They do not expect normative changes affecting cultural monopolies or political assumptions to result from the societal operation of such principles. Structures are sufficient, and eventually come to be used against change. Others see the task as "instructing a pedagogical and political vision that recognizes that the problems [with American schools] lie in the realm of values, ethics, and vision" (Giroux 1992). The gulf between those who see democracy as essentially political, within a predetermined moral frame, and those who emphasize the economic conditions of democracy, the primacy of market forces for politics and human relations is at this moment in American history as unbridgeable as it was in nineteenth-century

Europe. It seems pretty clear, however, that the transfer effort in Eastern Europe is now governed by structure and market assumptions. Privatization is so pervasive in the general American literature on development that it is inevitable that the values associated with competition and ownership be made the basis of economic reference in the curriculum.

> The shift to a Western European ownership structure will require that enterprise governance be removed from the workers' councils and managers and placed squarely on the supervisory board controlled by the owners of the enterprise. In essence privatization requires first that certain ownership rights now vested in the enterprises, and particularly in the workers' councils, be eliminated so that the property rights can be transferred to the real owners. (Lipton and Sachs 1991)

Do transfer projects (in Eastern Europe) now show consciousness of an altered American approach to international exchange of democratic ideas? Perhaps, but they still show a continuity of American-centered policy—in fact mirroring expressions from the American Occupation in postwar Germany. The assumption is generally that the task of American educators is to teach American practices directly. Curriculum guides, organized around "basic concepts about democracy" use instructional strategies developed out of American content and using educational "methods" familiar to U.S. teacher training and for the level and teaching style of American schools.

REFERENCES

African Renewal: Report of a conference on state, conflict and democracy in Africa. (1977). Cambridge, MA: Massachusetts Institute of Technology.

Anweiler, Oskar. (1970). "Strukturprobleme des allgemeinbildenden Schulwesens der DDR." In W. Hilligen and R. Raasch (eds.), *Pädagogische Forschung und padagogischer Fortschritt.* Bielefeld: Bertelsmann.

Baske, S., and M. Engelbert. (1966). *Zwei Jahrzehnte Bildungspolitik in der Sowjetzone Deutschlands.* Berlin: Quelle and Meyer.

Beilken, Gustav, and Walter Weber. (1959). "Zehn Jahre Deutsche Demokratische Republik—Vierzehn Jahre Sorge um die Jugend," *Berufsbildung.*

Giroux, Henry A. (1992). "Educational leadership and the crisis of democratic culture." Pennsylvania State University: University Council for Educational Administration.

Gunther, Karl H., and Gottfried Uhlig. (1969). Aktionsprogramm des Blocks der hämpferischen Demokratie." In *Geschichte der Schule in der Deutschen Demokratischen Republik 1954 bis 1968.* Berlin: Volk und Wissen.

Klein, Helmut. (1962). *Polytechnische Bildung und Erziehung in der DDR.* Reinbeck: Rowohlt.

Kohlsdorf, F. (1965). " Marzistische Philosophie und sozialistische Bildungskonzeption," *Pädagogik.*

Lawson, Robert F. (1965). *Reform of the West German school system, 1945–1962.* Ann Arbor: University of Michigan Comparative Education Series.

Lawson, Robert F. (1972). "The ring and the book: Educational change in Berlin." In R. D. Heyman, R. F. Lawson, and R. M. Stamp (eds.), *Studies in educational change.* Toronto: Holt, Rinehart and Winston.

Lipton, D., and J. Sachs (1991). "Privatization in Eastern Europe: The case of Poland." In V. Corbo, F. Coricelli, and J. Bossak (eds.), *Reforming Central and East European economies: Initial results and challenges.* Washington, DC: World Bank.

Schneller, Wilhelm. (1955). *Die Deutsche Demokratische Schule.* Berlin: Volk und Wissen.

Shafer, Susanne M. (1964). *Postwar American influence on the West German Volksschul.* Ann Arbor: University of Michigan Comparative Education Series.

SUGGESTED READINGS

Budge, I., and D. McKay. (eds.). (1994). *Developing democracy.* London: Sage.

Edwards, L., P. Munn, and K. Fogelmann. (eds.). (1992). *Education for democratic citizenship in Europe: New challenges for secondary education.* Lisse: Swets and Zeitlinger.

Führ, C. (1979). *Education and teaching in the Federal Republic of Germany.* Munich: Hansa.

Halls, W. D. (1990). *Comparative education: Contemporary issues and trends.* London: Jessica Kingsley/UNESCO.

Hearnden, A. (1974). *Education in the two Germanies.* Oxford: Blackwell.

Inkeles, A., and M. Sasaki. (eds.). (1996). *Comparing nations and cultures.* Englewood Cliffs, NJ: Prentice Hall.

Kodron, C., B. von Kopp, U. Lauterbach, U. Schäfer, and G. Schmidt. (1997). *Vergleichende Erziehungswissenschaft: Herausforderung, Vermittlung, Praxis.* Frankfurt am Main: Deutsches Institut für luternationale Pädagogische Forschung.

Lawson, R. F., V. D. Rust, and S. M. Shafer. (1987). *Education and social concerns: An approach to social foundations.* Ann Arbor, MI: Prakken.

Lowenthal, A. F. (ed.). (1991). *Exporting democracy.* Baltimore, MD: John Hopkins University Press.

McGinn, Noel, and Erwin Epstein. (eds.). (1999). *Comparative perspectives on the role of education in democratization.* 2 vols. Frankfurt am Main: Peter Lang.

Mitter, W. (1988). "Secondary Education in the Federal Republic of Germany." In R. Lawson (ed.), *Changing patterns of secondary education: An international comparison.* Calgary: University of Calgary.

Pritchard, R. M. O. (1999). *Reconstructing education: East German schools and universities in transition.* New York: Berghahn.

Treverton, G. F. (ed.). (1992). *The shape of the new Europe.* New York: Council on Foreign Relations.

Weiter, H., H. Mintrop, and E. Fuhrmann. (1996). *Educational change and social transformation: Teachers, schools, and universities in Eastern Germany.* London: Falmer.

DISCUSSION QUESTIONS

1. What do you consider to be the limits on transfer of American educational ideas and practices to other countries? Do you distinguish between transfer to and from European countries and countries of the southern hemisphere?

2. How context-bound is the American conception of democracy and American practices stemming from that conception? Have contemporary changes in education and society made our idea of democracy more or less certain, consensual, and transferable?

3. Do you see ideas and practices in communist education that might be studied for applicability elsewhere (or continuation in Eastern Europe)? Can they be separated from their political-ideological context?

4. What does the study of authority and ideology in fascist/communist political and educational systems employ for international relations, for institution building, and for "political correctness"?

5. Both Germany and the United States are structurally decentralized systems. In what sense can we talk about "German education," and "American education"? To what extent is the decentralization integral to democratic politics?

6. How effective is education in changing individual attitudes and values? (Does this question itself imply a value stance?) Does the effectiveness of education in shaping individual behavior and social behavior depend on other institutions?

7. Do you think the bases of educational policy in European countries have converged with European union? Would you expect them to be more alike than they were in 1945?

CHAPTER 5

Decentralization, Choice, and Charter Schools in the United States
Equity or Radical Transformation?

ELIZABETH SHERMAN SWING

Public schools in the United States are in flux. Buffeted by large, bureaucratic school districts, parents look for schools that will hear their voices. Buffeted by escalating real estate taxes, parents look for new sources of funding. Buffeted by the legacy of the "excellence movement," parents look for solid curricula and better instruction. Magnet schools, originally a tool of desegregation, offer racially mixed populations programs in specialty areas: music and art, agriculture, diplomacy, engineering, science, or even old-fashioned academics. Schools-within-schools, administrative units of as few as one hundred students who stay together for their entire secondary school career, coexist within the walls of dinasaur-like urban high schools built for 4,000. Home schooling, for years embraced by intellectuals, has become a tool of their unlikely allies—Christian fundamentalists seeking escape from public school "secularism." The spectrum of transformations is immense (Finn and Gau 1998).

This chapter examines three of these transformations: *decentralization,* control of schools by local administrative units or, in some cases, by private groups instead of a centralized bureaucracy; *choice,* acceptance of a market economy in education through redistribution of public money in the form of *vouchers* or *tuition tax credits;* and *charter schools,* schools that receive public funds but are run semi-autonomously, free from state and local regulation, often by parents and teachers. Each of these transformations is based on the premise that the expectation that reform will provide parents with greater control over their children's lives than public schools have heretofore provided, that it will bring academic benefits to their children, and that it will guarantee greater social equity. Each could signify a radical change in public education as we have come to know it.

THE PROMISES AND PITFALLS OF DECENTRALIZATION

Decentralization is a concept that has particular resonance in the United States. There is no centralized oversight of education in the United States, no real analogue to the national Ministries of Education that set education policy in some, but not all, European countries. Instead, each of the fifty states is in charge of education within its own borders. The federal Department of Education, which only gained cabinet status in 1979, has relatively limited power. It gathers statistics and oversees distribution of federal aid in the form of block grants to states. It, or in some cases the federal courts, may also monitor compliance with relevant judicial decisions, with regulations guiding application for federal grants, and with certain federal laws—civil rights legislation, for example, the area where federal presence is particularly noticed by state and local officials. But the United States has no national curriculum, no national standards, and no national tests administered by the national government—despite repeated attempts of public officials to institute such reforms.

Each of the fifty states writes its own school code. Each sets its own standards for certification and testing of teachers. Each determines minimum levels of taxation for schools within local school districts. Each prescribes the length of the school year. Each specifies safety standards for school buildings, mandates minimum curriculum requirements, sets the boundaries of school districts. That there is remarkable similarity among these fifty school codes does not change the fact of individual state responsibility. Local school districts, on the other hand, are responsible for the day-to-day functioning of schools within their geographical boundaries. Some have adopted school-based management, whereby much decision making is put in the hands of teachers and principals. But such schools must nevertheless follow state standards in prescribing curriculum, in setting a school calendar, in hiring personnel, in designing school buildings. Local districts, the state, and (minimally) the federal government provide for the funding of public schools. Federal funds, however, although frequently an important part of *urban* school budgets, account for only approximately 8 percent of school financing throughout the country. More important are funds from local taxes, usually a real estate tax, and from state subsidies, frequently 50 percent or more of a school budget, although the proportion differs from state to state and even from district to district within a state.

There might have been Constitutional provision for *national* oversight of schools. A lively debate about what should constitute the civic education of political leaders in a republic took place in the late eighteenth century (Rush [1786] 1965). But no consensus was reached at the Constitutional Convention in Philadelphia in 1787, and there is no reference to *education* in the United States Constitution. Instead, the Tenth Amendment,[1] which reserves for the states or individuals the powers not delegated to the federal government, has become the constitutional basis for oversight and organization of public schools by each of the individual states. In the half century that followed adoption of the Constitution, the challenge for educational reformers such as Horace Mann in Massachusetts, Henry Barnard in Connecticut and Rhode Island, Calvin Stowe in Ohio—each of whom was Secretary of Education in his respective state—was not related to federal oversight of schools. The challenge was to garner sufficient power and resources to inaugurate a statewide system of free, tax-supported "common schools." The mission of these common schools was radical even by today's standards. Common schools (at first only elementary schools) would offer the same classroom experience to children from all walks of life, rich and poor alike. Education would become "the great equalizer of the conditions of men—the balance wheel of the social machinery" (Mann [1848] 1957, 87). As a consequence, the poor would develop intellectual self-assurance. They would, therefore, no longer defer to the rich. Common schools under the benevolent leadership of the state would produce a classless society.

Another nineteenth-century reform paralleled the emergence of statewide public education: the introduction of centralized urban school boards to replace the district boards that dispensed jobs to immigrants as part of a spoils system. In Philadelphia, for example, formation of a central school board provided opportunity for reformers, frequently represented by well-to-do individuals from old families, to crusade for the moral principle that only the best qualified teachers be hired (Hallowell 1900). In her memoirs, Anna Hallowell, a well-born Quaker and the first woman elected to the newly centralized school board in Philadelphia, provides an example of this process. Her attempts to get rid of "superannuated teachers" caused "a burly Irishman" in the 7th Section Local Board, on which she also served, to double his fist in her face (18). Miss Hallowell, in turn, viewed members of this 7th Section Local as "uneducated men," often drunk, "one habitually so"; and she notes that their expertness in using a row of spittoons down the middle of the floor "was astonishing!" Doing away with such local boards was a colorful chapter in the history of ethnic contact! The cyclical pattern of such reform is, however, illustrated by the appearance in 1998 of a proposal to reconfigure Philadelphia schools into twenty-two school districts, each with its own elected board—a proposal described in the *Philadelphia Inquirer* as nostalgia for a dimly remembered past when schools were not administrated by a distant and unresponsive bureaucracy, and as a bad idea that would lead to corruption and much rivalry between school districts ("Divide").

The first target in the *decentralization* battles of the 1960s were centralized urban school bureaucracies, some of which had become fiefdoms rivaling the state Department of Education as a site of power. The prototype for such conflict, also a chapter in the politics of race, was waged in New York City. A preamble to this power struggle, however, was the landmark Supreme

Court decision, *Brown v. Board of Education,* 347 U.S. 483 (1954), in which the Court declared: "Separate educational facilities are inherently unequal." In the wake of this major decision outlawing de jure segregation,[2] prominent New York African American intellectuals such as Kenneth Clark pointed to a disturbing pattern of segregation in the New York City schools caused, not by de jure segregation, but by much more subtle practices. African American and Hispanic students were clustered throughout the city in neighborhood schools that reflected what amounted to de facto segregation, schools that reflected housing patterns. Thereafter, the New York City school board initiated a system of citywide free enrollment, but in the eyes of social activists such a reform was inadequate. After the Brown decision, the social inequities implied by de facto segregation in New York City were no longer tolerable. The stage was now set for the civil rights confrontations that would mark this troubled decade (Ravitch 1974).

Decentralization as a cure for racial ills was actually the brainchild of McGeorge Bundy of the Ford Foundation (1969). The first stage in 1966 was Ford Foundation subsidy of three demonstration school districts: the Ocean Brownsville District in Brooklyn, IS 201 District in East Harlem, the Two Bridges District in the Lower East Side of Manhattan—districts that were to become models for subsequent decentralization. In 1967 the Ocean Brownsville governing board sought total community control. Thereafter, all three governing boards in the model districts refused to accept guidelines from the New York City Board of Education, which in turn refused to grant formal recognition of what was presented as total community control. Meanwhile, attempts to enlarge the number of prodecentralization members of the central school board were followed by confrontations between local leaders and the United Federation of Teachers—and by a crippling, lengthy teachers' strike. It is not the purpose of this chapter to rehearse in detail a history of these events. Suffice it to note that a major escalation of the aspirations for Black power took place over control of decentralized structures (Ravitch 1974, 1983).

The structure that emerged is based on transfer of decision-making authority from a centralized bureaucracy to locally elected lay boards, a structure similar to that found in federal antipoverty programs (Segal 1997). High schools remain under a central bureaucracy, but there are now thirty-two nine-member school boards, elected locally every three years to oversee 750,000 elementary and middle schools. These boards have control over promotions and, except for teachers who are safeguarded by the union, hire virtually all personnel. For advocates of reform in the 1960s, creation of smaller administrative units responsive to local needs emerged as a possible cure for the ills of overcrowded, low-achieving urban schools.

The jury is still out on whether such a cure might have been effected. We *do* know that the outcome is ambiguous and that school jobs have become a source of power and status for the previously powerless in New York City. Local control over money and jobs has meant maximum local discretion and minimum oversight and has led to widespread abuses: conferences in exotic places for recipients of patronage, the hiring of relatives, the temptation to engage in illicit profiteering. Decentralization has meant transfer of power in New York City schools, but it has not yet meant better education (Segal 1997). In the view of some critics, in particular conservatives like Diane Ravitch, the decentralization movement, often led by ethnic and religious groups, used schools for the transmission of *their own* identity and values and has, according to Ravitch (1974), given short shrift to the values and identity of others, and is, therefore, a direct attack on the concept of a common school and a serious threat to the future of public education (402). That reforms aimed at greater social justice should appear to pose such a threat is a special irony.

That big city schools throughout the United States are no longer governed by a white, middle-class central bureaucracy symbolizes many of the changes that are underway (Wong 1995). Suburbs provide increased competition. Teachers unions continue to act as autonomous powers; but there is a nationwide trend toward shared decision making, toward site-based autonomy, toward an increase in the number of administrators, toward rapid turnover of personnel and less stability in school governance, toward hiring superintendents from outside the city and even from outside the state. At the same time, New York City decentralization has become a partial model for other urban school boards seeking to share power with formerly disenfranchised groups. That decentralization has not become *the* primary model is a partial reflection of growth in the number of voucher programs and charter schools, structures that also challenge a central bureaucracy.

It is important to put decentralization in education into a larger context. Decentralization is a chapter in an ongoing process of devolution, a parallel to attempts to shrink government, to deregulate airlines, to break up telephone and software monopolies. From this vantage point decentralization also parallels widespread rejection of the regulations and standards set by a bureaucracy, whether that bureaucracy be federal, state, city, or local (House 1998). It is a movement fed by an ongoing attack on bigness in education, whether the bigness be large classes, big city bureaucracies, large consolidated school districts that have swallowed up smaller units, or schools designed for thousands of students. It is, however, a paradox that gargantuan urban school buildings and large consolidated suburban school districts are in large measure the reforms of a generation ago. For James Bryant Conant (1959), the former president of Harvard University who took on the task of examining public education in the United States after leaving Harvard in 1953, the problem was not bigness in education. The problem was fragmentation into small schools in small school districts unable to offer a challenging and varied curriculum, and thus limiting the life chances of students enrolled there. Conant called for larger districts and larger schools that could offer programs that would stretch a student's potential. Reform in education is littered with the unintended consequences of the innovations of the past.

CHOICE AND THE MARKET METAPHOR

Choice, a concept pioneered by Milton Friedman, a free market economist ([1962] 1982), is a direct challenge to what is sometimes referred to as the monopoly held by public education in the United States. Parents are, of course, free to select a private education for their children. This freedom, however, is constrained by their ability to pay the fees of most private schools. They are constrained, furthermore, by the geographical area in which they live, the area in which they pay school taxes, the area in which they are entitled to use of public schools for their children. Advocates of choice challenge this arrangement by advocating that local school taxes, usually and controversially real estate taxes, plus state subsidies, be returned to parents in the form of vouchers or tuition tax credits. These vouchers or tuition tax credits would, in turn, offset the cost of a school of choice, either public or private. In the utopian world of choice, a market economy would prevail. The schools selected would flourish. The schools not selected would wither and die. Choice, therefore, represents a direct attack on the hegemony of local school districts, which would lose funding as students look elsewhere to enroll. It is, not surprisingly, a concept favored by many conservatives but not by teacher unions (Brouillette and Williams 1999).

An important component of prochoice arguments is based on the premise that private schools—those responsive to a market economy—do a better job than do public schools. In a "voucher system—the public and private sectors compete to sell the unique strengths of their programs" (Fox 1999, 29). Critics such as John E. Chubb and Terry M. Moe (1990) argue that traditional reforms will not improve public education and that democratic politics make educational improvements in the public sector impossible, whereas schools in the private sector do not have to be all things to all people. According to Chubb and Moe, public schools are run by a rule-bound and formalistic bureaucracy. In their view, government on the local, state, or federal level cannot reform schools because government in education *is* the problem. Their attack is not just an attack on public education. It is by extension an attack on democracy itself. Democracy, according to Chubb and Moe, is coercive. The greatest impediment to public school improvement is democratic control. Private schools, on the other hand, are not infected by the democratic base of public education. Private schools, in their eyes, work because the strongest influence on overall improvement of the organization and academic performance of schools is autonomy for a school. The inventor of vouchers, Milton Friedman, even promotes the idea that vouchers should encourage the privatization of public schools (Friedman 1997).

Critics of the seductive appeal of the market metaphor counter such attacks with criticisms of their own. Advocates of market-based choice have played on public impatience (Henig 1994). Some question whether free market policies will improve schools, and note that schools and the economy are tied together only when education policies are formulated in the economic terminology of productivity and cost analysis rather than more worthy goals (House 1998). According to Peter W. Cookson (1994), the market metaphor is the cornerstone of a "struggle for the soul of American education." In Cookson's view the consensus that schools are mediators of merit where students learn democratic practices has come close to disappearing. In its place a market-based ideology will lead to erosion of public forums in which decisions are democratically resolved. There is also, according to Cookson, a curious faith in the market that comes close to religious conviction, a belief in market morality, a faith in educational competition as a "mission." The unquestioning acceptance of a market economy by those who want to change the structure of American education may, in Cookson's view, echo the intertwining of Protestantism and the rise of capitalism. A belief in a market economy reflects a loss of faith in public institutions and in democracy itself.

The apparently antidemocratic agenda of choice advocates is also a theme in a *Harvard Law Review* article, "The Hazards of Making Public Schooling a Private Business" (1999). The authors of this article are critical of the market metaphor because in their view the private groups found in *choice* projects do not necessarily have democratic goals. Counselors in the Edison Project, according to this report, have used an underhanded strategy to improve the profile of the children enrolled in their project by counseling parents of problem students to transfer their children to Boston public schools, a practice referred to as "counseling out." This project has had problems with the private deliverers of the education "product," a group who may have difficulty balancing a profit motive with the social and individual interests of students. There is, in the judgment of the authors of the article, a built-in conflict of interests between shareholders and customers in a private educational project. For-profit contracting amplifies these risks. Individual choice may *not* improve academic quality. Education becomes a business like any other. "The marketplace idea celebrates the notions of self-reliance and individual independence without recognizing that education is a precursor to those attributes" (709).

According to Henry Giroux (1999) the tradition of public education in a democracy is in jeopardy. Schools no longer take responsibility for creating a democracy of citizens. Instead, educators are viewed as consumers and advised to act like a corporation seeking a market niche to sell a product. Struggles to reclaim public schools are, therefore, part of a broader battle over the defense of the public good. In Giroux's view, the market metaphor is an example of social Darwinism in which schools mimic the free market. It is an attempt to transform a public good that is of benefit to all students to a private good that expands the profits of investors. Marketplace education, therefore, has ceased to be social investment. Privatization undermines the power of teachers to provide skills needed for responsible citizenship.

VOUCHERS AND CONSTITUTIONAL ISSUES

Unlike many European countries—the Netherlands and England come immediately to mind—denominational schools in the United States do *not* receive overt subsidy from the federal, state, or local governments. For many choice advocates, however, vouchers or tuition tax credits may be applied to public, private, or denominational schools. School choice is, therefore, a direct challenge to the concept of a wall of separation between church and state, a principle enunciated by Thomas Jefferson in a letter to a convention of Baptist ministers but not directly part of the United States Constitution. The issue is whether providing public money for tuition to a religious school breaches this wall of separation. According to Freeman Butts (1987), it does, and in so doing poses a direct constitutional challenge. According to Jonathan Fox (1999) and other choice advocates, it does not.

The Constitutional issue derives from the so-called establishment clause in the First Amendment: "Congress shall make no law respecting an establishment of religion, or prohibiting the free exercise thereof." These, the *only* words in the Constitution about separation of church and state, are open to a range of interpretations (Kneller 1971). For some, these words simply mean that the Constitution forbids promotion of a state religion but does not forbid subsidy of denominational schools—provided all such schools are treated equally, the situation that, to a large extent, exists in the Netherlands. For some, "establishment of religion" means no use at all of public money to fund religious schools. For others, however, even the tax exempt status of churches and church schools as nonprofit institutions is suspect. First Amendment Supreme Court decisions in the United States have avoided the extremes of this range of options, but the fact remains that use of vouchers to pay tuition to religious schools invokes scrutiny of the First Amendment.

The Supreme Court has produced a roster of court decisions limiting and occasionally extending the range of church-state relations in schools.[3] Parents, for example, have the right to select (and pay for) a denominational school for their children. The state cannot demand that parents use public schools. "The child is not the mere creature of the State" (*Pierce v. Society of Sisters* 268 U.S. 510 [1925]). Under the so-called child benefit theory, it is not unconstitutional for states or school districts to provide textbooks for students enrolled in private and parochial schools (*Cochran v. Louisiana State Board of Education,* 281 U.S. 370 [1930]) because it is the child who benefits, not the religion. Nor is it unconstitutional to provide transportation to denominational or private schools (*Everson v. Board of Education,* 330 U.S. 1 [1947]), provided the same benefit is also offered to public school students. The Supreme Court *did* rule against funding buildings and tuition in denominational schools (*Committee for Public Education and Religious Liberty v. Nyquist* 413 U.S. 472 [1973]), but allows parents in Minnesota to take a state income tax deduction for tuition, textbooks, and transportation for dependents in elementary and secondary schools, both public and private (*Mueller v. Allen* 463 U.S. 388 [1983]). The crucial detail is that deductions are allowed for public, as well as private and parochial, school expenses.

The Supreme Court has been cautious on the issue of religious observances in public schools. It is unconstitutional for the New York Board of Regents to call for a nondenominational prayer in public schools (*Engel v. Vitale,* 370 U.S. 421 [1962]), or for schools to begin the day with readings from the Bible and recitation of the Lord's Prayer (*School District of Abington Township v. Schempp,* 374 U.S. 203 [1963]), a widespread practice prior to the 1963 decision that Horace Mann in the nineteenth century viewed as a nondenominational opening exercise. It is unconstitutional for members of the clergy to provide religious instruction within the premises of public schools (*McCollum v. Board of Education* 333 U.S. 203 [1948]). Public schools, however, *may* send students to churches or synagogues for religious instruction during the school day (*Zorach v. Clausen* 343 U.S. 306 [1952]), a practice known as released time. Three tests are applied to legislation that might breach the wall of separation between church and state (*Lemon v. Kurtzman* 403 U.S. 602 [1971]): (1) Does the statute have a secular purpose? (2) Does it neither advance nor inhibit religion? (3) Does it avoid "excessive entanglement with religion"? The so-called Lemon test is still part of Supreme Court deliberations. The Court has ruled against displaying the Ten Commandments on the walls of a public school classroom (*Stone v. Graham* 449 U.S. 39 [1980]), a perennial favorite of conservatives, and against starting the school day with a moment of silence for the purpose of meditation or voluntary prayer (*Wallace v. Jaffree* 472 U.S. 38 [1985]). Neither practice has so far survived the Lemon test.

Given this constitutional frame of reference, it is not difficult to understand why the earliest choice plans were limited to choice between and among public schools. Such choice exists in Arkansas, Idaho, Iowa, Minnesota, Nebraska, Ohio, Utah, and Washington, among other states. In addition, cities such as Philadelphia and New York City allow parents to choose from among every public school in the district. Choice advocates, however, have pushed the issue of funding for denominational schools further than it has been in the past. *Mueller v. Allen,* 463 U.S. 388 (1983), the Supreme Court decision that allowed state income tax deductions for the cost of public, private, or denominational schools, implies that parochial schools may be "an educational alternative" (Bauknight 1998). The State Supreme Court in Wisconsin, moreover, has recently ruled that statewide vouchers may be used for religious school tuition. Privately funded voucher schemes, moreover, have built a powerful constituency for school choice among blacks and Hispanics, who see vouchers as a way to bypass inadequate inner city schools (Meyerson 1999), particularly in view of test scores that seem to indicate a superior performance by students in private schools (Peterson 1999). The accusation is sometimes made that vouchers will not serve children with disabilities. Voucher advocates, however, point to an increasing reliance by public school districts on special private schools for the disabled, an indication that vouchers can and do serve this population (Fox 1999).

There is, however, another issue, not always directly addressed by voucher advocates. Will religious schools dependent on vouchers become part of the government that funds them? Will their religious mission be compromised (Loconte 1999)? The critical question appears to pivot on *how* public funding programs reach private denominational schools (Lewin 1999). Direct designation of public funds for religious schools has met constitutional scrutiny, but funding of religious schools when vouchers go directly to parents as scholarships or when government funds are used for pupil benefit services has been increasingly successful.

These arguments notwithstanding, many remain skeptical of vouchers as a remedy for educational ills. Skeptics point, for example, to the fact that vouchers do not survive constitutional scrutiny in every state; challenges are underway in Massachusetts, New Hampshire, and Vermont. A federal court judge has recently blocked use of vouchers for parochial and private schools in Cleveland, Ohio, until a trial determines the constitutionality of the program. Skeptics also point to what they interpret as ambiguous results of school voucher plans in Britain, France, and the Netherlands, where the gap between privileged and underprivileged appears to have widened (Sianjina 1999). Another group of critics cite studies showing that private schools do not use educational resources any more efficiently than do public schools. Upper income families are more likely to benefit from voucher programs than are poor families (Goldhaber 1997). Another group of critics trace the genesis of the school choice movement to Adam Smith, John Stuart Mills, and Milton Friedman, but see its present-day incarnation as part of massive resistance to the Brown desegregation Supreme Court decision (Ryan 1999). According to them, Brown was followed by efforts to integrate urban and suburban schools. These efforts, however, failed when the Supreme Court ruled in *Milliken v. Bradley,* 418 U.S. 717 (1974) that suburban districts could not be forced to participate in a desegregation plan. Choice plans for affluent white families have become the remedy instead.

CHARTER SCHOOLS

Charter schools are in many ways the most significant example of transformation of public education in the United States. First created through Minnesota legislation in 1991 (Nathan 1996; Ridley 1999), they have grown exponentially, aided by state, local, and federal grants. The United States Department of Education (1999) reports that 110,00 students attended charter schools in 1996–1996. The 1998–1999 Charter School Directory lists 1,390 charter schools. To those who see public education as a monopoly dependent on a predictable and mandatory source of funding and an equally predictable and mandatory enrollment of children from a local attendance area rather than as an independent institution subject to market forces, charter schools are a harbinger of a better future, a marketplace innovation (Manno et al. 1998). Defenders of public education fear that charter schools will indeed do as much damage as these advocates predict.

These charter schools are quasi-autonomous institutions, organized and operated by a group of citizens, teachers perhaps, or parents, usually not professional educators (Finn, Manno, and Berlein, 1996). The chartering agency may be the local school district, the state, or even the national government. The schools are financed, however, with public money, usually with operational funding comparable to that used in public schools. In the process, a local school board suffers loss of the state and local funds used for students from its district who enroll in the charter school, a situation that makes this innovation less than popular with some local school boards. Once chartered, these schools operate for a limited, renewable term, frequently five years, on a performance-based contract that specifies student achievement goals, standards, or outcomes.

Unlike schools in privatization ventures in which district and state education requirements, as well as health, safety, and nondiscrimination (civil rights) statutes, still pertain, charter schools are free from state and local regulations, including teacher certification requirements. In addition, most charters set their own teacher salaries, which are likely to be lower than comparable salaries in the public domain. They may even bargain with and employ staff independently, a condition that puts them on a collision course with teacher unions (Brouillette and Williams 1999), which are fully aware that the rate of union membership is significantly lower in private and charter schools than it is in public schools. Unions are likely to seek certification requirements and collective bargaining agreements in exchange for endorsement of individual charters—or not to endorse the charters at all.

The charter for each school reflects the laws of the particular state in which it is located. But unlike magnet schools, which were originally a tool for integration but that are under the control of local authorities, charter schools provide for the constituent community that organizes it to retain control (Barnes 1997). They are, therefore, likely to be consumer-oriented institutions that reflect the values and orientation of the sponsoring groups. Some are former public schools. Less common are former private schools. A minority are "startups." All charter schools, however, are voluntary institutions that reflect the will and expectations of their founders. They are likely to be results oriented. They are also likely to be run by those who are sympathetic to the benefits of deregulation. They are, moreover, institutions that are demanding in terms of results but relaxed in terms of means (Turekian 1997). Charter schools are not necessarily elite institutions, although some are. They have considerable popularity among inner city residents, especially African Americans willing to try something new in response to a growing perception that neither enforced busing nor increased monetary spending have alleviated inadequate educational opportunities (Barnes 1997; Corwin and Dentler 1995).

Partially unresolved is the legal status of charter schools (Bauknight 1998). Each of the fifty states has a constitutional mandate to provide free and public education to the young within its borders. The state constitutions, however, delegate oversight of free public primary and secondary education to local and regional boards of education and to the State Board of Education. Local school board members are, therefore, agents of the state—monitoring state-mandated requirements—and they are municipal officials accountable to their geographical districts (Turekian 1997). Charter schools, however, although funded by the state and local district in an amount calculated as the average expenditure per child in the district, are usually free *not* to follow state or local education regulations. That charter schools drain money from existing districts but are nevertheless independent of them is a major concern.

Can charter schools maintain their educational, legal, and fiscal autonomy and still remain accountable to the public that finances their operation (Turekian 1997)? Are binding performance contracts better than regulation and oversight by state boards of education? Does the private entity that establishes a charter school become a state actor? This issue takes on special significance in defining the rights of teachers in their roles as employees of charter schools. Another issue concerns admission criteria. To what extent is a charter school public when admission criteria is based on something different from residency? Most charter school laws explicitly prohibit admissions on the basis of race; but even when the justification is enhancement of the quality of education, the legality of a charter school that admits a single sex is still unresolved. Also unresolved is whether a charter school may limit its population to only the talented and gifted as some magnet schools have done.

Proponents point out that charter schools provide choice, improve pupil learning through more rigorous standards, encourage diverse approaches to learning, foster innovative teaching, and lead to parental community involvement—all this without the financial barrier that alternatives such as private schools have always had. They also point out that charter schools include a cross section of the school universe, that as many as half of charter schools were founded to serve at-risk youngsters (Finn et al. 1996). Opponents, on the other hand, are likely to view charter schools as a direct threat to public education. Laws passed by state legislatures limiting the number of charter schools within a state and confining eligibility for organizing a charter to specific groups like teachers, may partially reflect this concern. Legislation may also forbid for-profit groups to organize charter schools, require mandated accounting procedures, even require education code restrictions.

Critics of charter schools note that charters do not have an unblemished record ("Charter School Closes" 1999; DeSpain and Livingston 1996; Mahtesian 1998). One set of problems involves attempts to use charters as revenue producers. Charter schools run by for-profit companies such as the Edison and Advantage Schools have produced financial results that are less than hoped for. Critics argue that flexibility and innovation can be achieved with fewer risks within public school systems. When a charter school is first established, there is likely to be a burst of enthusiasm, but then come problems that sap formative energy. Schools may be understaffed. Teachers may transfer back to public schools when a leave of absence expires. Charters, furthermore, may skim the cream, although a counterargument is that charters attract students doing poorly in public schools (Ridley 1999). They may be underfunded. It is difficult to know to whom they are accountable. Amy Stuart Wells (1999) points out that in California "accountability, in the sense of agreed-on and narrowly defined student outcomes . . . was not consistent with the way most charter school founders thought about their goals" (20). She goes on to note that charter schools may have no more autonomy than nearby site-management schools, that charter school administrators are likely to turn to the district bureaucracy when trouble breaks out, that most charter school teachers have not changed the way they teach. Each charter school, furthermore, has considerable control over admissions criteria, and this may result in admission of fewer disadvantaged students than charter school enthusiasts expect to see. Charter schools may not benefit those in the inner city who need them most. The achievements of charter schools have yet to be fully documented.

TRENDS AND IMPLICATIONS

In the nineteenth century Horace Mann promoted a vision of publicly funded, free, secular schools—then a new and radical idea in the United States. Do the innovations discussed in this chapter represent the beginning of the end of the common school he envisioned, the end of public education as we have known it for more than 150 years? Is decentralizing power an extenuation of democracy? Or do the racial politics involved in decentralization schemes reflect a breakdown of community? Do vouchers and tuition tax credits breach the wall of separation between church and state? Should public money be used for tuition to a religious school, or does that constitute an "establishment of religion"? Do charter schools give parents greater control of their children's education? Or are charter schools subject to the same abuses found in public education? Will these decentralization, choice, and charter schools bring greater equity to education? Or are these reforms evidence of a radical revolution that will change the face of public education? Will these transformations survive in the twenty-first century? Or will they soon be forgotten, evidence that nothing is as dull as an innovation in education past its prime. It is risky to speculate. It is, however, possible to draw four inferences from assumptions underlying these three educational transformations.

1. All three transformations challenge the assumption that consolidation of resources in education provides financial savings while expanding curricula. Decentralization is based on a rejection of consolidated bureaucracies, on a belief that smaller administrative units are by definition better. Choice is premised on the belief that a market economy is superior to the consolidation of resources that critics describe as a public school monopoly. Charter schools are by definition individualized, freestanding institutions with financial, albeit public, and curricular autonomy.

2. All three of these transformations are an attempt to provide parents with the tools of empowerment. The decentralization movement in New York City sought a remedy for ethnic and racial powerlessness by creating smaller administrative units subject to community control. Vouchers and charter schools, which are based on the expectation that parents are looking for educational options not currently available, promise parental empowerment in choosing an existing private school or in the creation of an entirely new educational structure.

3. All three of these reforms are based on a rejection of the education establishment. In decentralization innovations, this establishment represents distant, unresponsive power. To supporters of vouchers and charter schools, the bureaucracy is sometimes described as an educational monopoly. For some who support vouchers, the establishment also represents secular education, represents separation of church and state as this idea has evolved in the United States. For supporters of charter schools, the established bureaucracy may represent cumbersome state school codes and inefficient local school board oversight. This is both a philosophical and a structural rejection.

4. All three of these reforms promise greater equality of access to education resources in order to level the playing field, particularly for inner city youth. Decentralization promises equity through commu-

nity control. Vouchers promise equity through access to private and public schools of choice. Charter schools promise equity through creative structures free of bureaucratic control. Horace Mann's *12th Annual Report* provided a direction for public education in 1848 in which rich and poor could share a common experience. Does the advent of a market economy in public education signal the emergence of educational fragmentation in which a commonality of learning experience is lost? Are decentralization, vouchers, and charter schools evidence of new, but not necessarily better, equity goals?

NOTES

[1]"The powers not delegated to the United States by the Constitution, nor prohibited by it to the States, are reserved to the States respectively, or to the people."

[2]*De jure* segregation refers to legal restrictions on the enrollment of Caucasians and African Americans in the same schools and classrooms, a widespread practice in certain southern states prior to the Brown decision. *De facto* segregation in education refers to a pattern of school enrollment, usually a reflection of housing patterns, in which schools, while not segregated by race because of legal restrictions, are dominantly either African American or Hispanic or (in the wealthy suburbs) predominantly white. In the United States, inner city schools are likely to be predominantly populated by African Americans and Hispanics.

[3]The author has taught the cases cited in this article for many years and cannot therefore, except for recent cases, provide any one source. It is suggested that readers wishing to know more consult the text of each case. Full citations are provided.

REFERENCES

Barnes, Robin D. (1997). "Black America and school choice: Charting a new course." *Yale Law Journal* 106(8): 2375–2409.

Bauknight, Suzanne R. (1998). "The search for constitutional school choice." *Journal of Law & Education* 27(4): 525–550.

Brouillette, Matthew J., and Jeffrey R. Williams. (1999). *The impact of school choice on school employee labor unions.* Midland, MI: Mackinac Center for Public Policy.

Bundy, McGeorge. (1969). *Reconnection for learning. A community school system for New York City.* New York: Praeger.

Butts, R. Freeman. (1987). "A history and civics lesson for all of us." *Educational Leadership* 44(8): 21–25.

"Charter school closes amid allegations of fiscal mismanagement." (1999). *Managing School Business,* 4, no. 10 (July 29).

Chubb, John E., and Terry M. Moe. (1990). *Politics, markets, and America's schools.* Washington, DC: Brookings Institution.

Conant, James Bryant. (1959). *The American high school today: A first report to interested citizens.* New York: McGraw-Hill.

Cookson, Peter W. (1994). *School choice. The struggle for the soul of American education.* New Haven, CT: Yale University Press.

Cookson, Peter W., and Barbara Schneider. (1995). "Why school choice? A question of values." In Peter Cookson and Barbara Schneider (eds.), *Transforming schools*, 557–577. New York: Garland.

Corwin, Ronald G., and Robert A. Dentler. (1995). "Education Vouchers and Desegregation Programs: Prospects and Remedies." In Steven S. Goldberg and Kathleen Kelley Lynch (eds.), *Civil rights in schools*, 41–52. New York: AMS Press.

DeSpain, B. C. and Martha J. Livingston. (1996). "Roads to reform (Will charter schools, privatization, and vouchers lead to better schools?)" *American School Board Journal* 183 (July): 17–20.

"Divide and suffer." (1998, January 5). *Philadelphia Inquirer,* A10.

Finn, Chester E., Jr., and Rebecca L. Gau. (1998). "New ways of education." *Public Interest* 130 (Winter):79–92.

Fox, Jonathan. (1999)."Sending public school students to private schools. The untold story of special education." *Policy Review* 92 (January–February):25–29.

Friedman, Milton. ([1962] 1982). *Capitalism and freedom.* Chicago: University of Chicago.

Friedman, Milton. (1997). "Public schools: Make them private." *Education Economics* 5(3): 341–344.

Giroux, Henry A. (1999). "'Schools for sale' public education, corporate culture, and the citizen consumer." *The Educational Forum* 63(2):140–149.

Goldhaber, Don D. (1997). "School choice as education reform." *Phi Delta Kappan,* 79(2):143–147.

Hallowell, Anna. (1900). "Autobiographic notes." Unpublished typescript. Friends of the Historical Library, Swarthmore College.

"Hazards of making public schooling a private business." (1999). *Harvard Law Review* 112:695.

Henig, Heffrey R. (1994). *Rethinking school choice. Limits of the market metaphor.* Princeton, NJ: Princeton University Press.

House, Ernest R. (1998). *Schools for sale: Why free market policies won't improve America's schools, and what will.* New York: Teachers College Press, Columbia University.

Kneller, George F. (1971). *Introduction to the philosophy of education.* New York: Wiley.

Lewin, Nathan. (1999). "Are vouchers constitutional? Yes and here's how to design them." *Policy Review* 93 (January–February):5–8.

Loconte, Joe. (1999). "Will vouchers undermine the mission of religious schools?" *Policy Review* 93 (January–February):30–36.

Mahtesian, Charles. (1998, January). "Charter schools learn a few lessons." *Governing Magazine,* 24.

Mann, Horace. ([1848] 1957). "Twelfth Annual Report." In Lawrence A. Cremin (ed.), *The republic and the school. On the education of free man.* New York: Teachers College Press, Columbia University.

Manno, Bruno V., Chester F. Finn Jr., Louann A. Bierlein, and Gregg Vanourek. (1998). "How charter schools are different: Lessons and implications from a national study." *Phi Delta Kappan* 79:448–498.

Meyerson, Adam. (1999). "A model of cultural leadership. The achievements of privately funded vouchers." *Policy Review* 93 (January–February):20–24.

Nathan, Joe. (1996). *Charter schools. Creating hope and opportunity for American education.* San Francisco: Jossey-Bass.

Peterson, Paul E. (1999). "Vouchers and test scores. What the numbers show." *Policy Review* 93 (January–February):10–15.

Ravitch, Diane. (1974). *The great school wars. New York City, 1805–1973.* New York: Basic Books.

Ravitch, Diane. (1983). *The troubled crusade.* New York: Basic Books.

Ridley, Jennifer J. (1999). "Charting a new course for public education in Michigan. Charter schools: A significant step toward meaningful education reform." *University of Detroit Mercy Law Review* 76:607.

Rush, Benjamin. ([1786] 1965). "Thoughts upon the mode of education proper in a republic." In Frederick Rudolph (ed.), *Essays on education in the early republic,* 9–23. Cambridge, MA: Belknap Press.

Ryan, Jim. (1998). "School choice: School choice and the suburbs." *Journal of Law and Politics* 14:459.

Segal, Lydia (1997). "The pitfalls of political decentralization and proposals for reform: The case of New York City public schools." *Public Administration Review* 57(2):141–149.

Sianjina, Rayton R. (1999). "Parental choice, school vouchers, and separation of church and state: Legal implications." *The Educational Forum* 63, no. 2: 108–112.

Turekian, Karla A. (1997). "Traversing the minefields of education reform: The legality of charter schools." *Connecticut Law Review* 29 (Spring): 1365.

U.S. Department of Education. (1999). "The state of charter schools: Third-year report." Washington, DC: U.S. Department of Education, Office of Educational Research and Improvement.

Wells, Amy Stuart. (1999). "California's charter schools. Promises vs. performance." *American Educator* 23, 1 (Spring): 18–24.

Wong, Kenneth K. (1995). "Can the big-city school system be governed?" In Peter Cookson and Barbara Schneider (eds.), *Transforming Schools,* 457–488. New York: Garland.

DISCUSSION QUESTIONS

1. Is Diane Ravitch's critique of decentralization just? Why or why not?

2. What is meant by the market metaphor in education? To what extent is criticism of public education as a governmental function implied by these words? Is such criticism justified? Why or why not?

3. What are the constitutional issues involved in use of vouchers in denominational schools? Is such constitutional concern justified? Why or why not?

4. How do charter schools differ from public schools? Do these differences reflect strength or weakness in the movement?

5. Do decentralization, choice, and charter schools pose a threat to public education as it has evolved in the United States? Why, and why not?

CHAPTER 6

Changes in European Higher Education
A Response to Society's Needs

HANS LINGENS

European education institutions, and especially those of higher education, are undergoing changes in response to the changing needs of society. The challenges facing higher education are numerous. Increased enrollment, democratization, autonomy, efficiency, financing, and academic freedom are some of the important concerns. Europe is changing in economic, social, and political aspects to become an economic and political union. Education has to respond to these changes. Society asks for more transparency of research and teaching, and it also asks for the cooperation and specialization of universities to avoid duplication of efforts. These institutions are asked to provide explainable credits for studies, evaluation of research and teaching, and social responsibility through service to society and business.

EXPANSION AND ACCESS

Since the 1950s universities have changed from elitist institutions to mass institutions with a changed clientele. Over the last decades, probably since 1970, the number of students in institutions of higher education grew tremendously from about 12 percent of an age cohort to about 30 percent and more in some countries. For example, the number of students in Germany doubled from 900,000 to 1,800,000, twice as much as the capacity of the institutions of higher learning. From 1980 to 1996, the student population in France doubled from one million to two million. Similar situations exist in other countries. In Norway, the student population has increased by more than 50 percent since 1988 (Aamodt 1995). In the Czech Republic, similar growth has taken place since 1990 (Koucky 1995). In Spain, student enrollment has doubled every ten years (Mora, Palafoux, and Perez 1995). The number of students increased from 692,000 in 1982/1983 to 1,370,000 in 1993/1994 (Sánchez-Ferrer 1997). Since 1989, the number of students in Romania has doubled to about 20 percent of the age cohort, which is a dramatic growth for this country (Eisemon et al. 1995). In the Ukraine, new institutions were founded after gaining independence to support the increase in number of students. After 1991, private higher education institutions were founded, and their number was 130 in 1996 (Webler 1998). Many of the higher education institutions became mass institutions modeled after the United States where they were first developed after World War II.

In the United Kingdom, mass universities developed in the 1980s (Neave 1998), later than in other countries. A push for access to higher education came with the 1992 government decree that changed the thirty-six polytechnic institutes to universities. This was a move away from the traditional university to a more diverse institution. At the same time there was a push to attract more students, resulting in an increase of 71 percent from 1989/1990 to 1996/1997 (Tugend 1999). Now about 33 percent of an age group is in higher education, no longer the elite group of 17 percent ten years ago.

As shown by the examples above, enrollment in higher education has increased tremendously and is still on the rise. The competition for study places is fierce; in some countries, like Romania, twenty people compete for one place. In Germany, access to higher education is guaranteed to all that pass the *Abitur* (secondary leaving certificate). This leaves the system overtaxed, and some students are deferred to a later date.

The reasons for the increase are manifold, from the newly gained freedom in Eastern Europe to easier access to higher education in general. The expansion of democratic ideals, not only in Eastern Europe but also generally over the continent, has prompted an increase in student population to provide every young person a chance to receive the best education in secondary schools. Industry is looking for qualified workers, and institutions of higher education sort out potential employees by the qualification a student achieves. Many young people choose university training to achieve the best possible position in the job market. The threat of unemployment keeps students in universities even longer, with many studying for a second degree and with that a better chance to find a place to work. Others like to stay on in fear of the working world.

GOVERNMENTS' REACTIONS

Through changes in their policies and laws, governments are responding to society's and business's demands to improve the efficiency, effectiveness, and quality of higher education. With the increase in numbers and the demand for improvement, one would expect an expansion of facilities, an increase in the number of instructors, and a general increase in spending for higher education. This is not so. Governments do not have enough resources to pay for expansion and improvement. The increase in enrollment is too great, and the cost of higher education is escalating even more. There is also a feeling of uncertainty about the quality of higher education. Overall, governments still keep tight control on higher education through budget allocation and on how money is spent.

Higher education serves a wide variety of students and purposes. It has to accommodate the full-time student, the part-time student, the mid-career changer, and senior citizens (Meyer-Wolters 1998). High-level skills have to be taught for the complex workplace. At the same time it is expected that all students will succeed and become contributors to society. It is also expected that research have world-class standards.

Universities and institutes of higher education always wanted to be independent from outside influence, but they are not. Understandably, in the eastern countries of Europe, such as in Romania and the Ukraine, they were subjected to the governing regime (Eisemon et al. 1995; Webler 1998). In Western Europe, universities are supposed to be free to determine what is being learned and what is being researched, but they are financed by the state, and their budget is allocated and controlled by governments. Other institutions of higher learning have definite mandates and are organized to produce graduates who have practical knowledge and competencies to function in industry and business. In the following sections some examples of national development are outlined.

The United Kingdom

In the United Kingdom, higher education was traditionally free of government controls, quite independent, and elitist. The universities were run in a collegial way by professors, with the assistance of low-level administrators with their own governing board. They were independent and autonomous, but still supported by the state, in contrast to most continental universities.

With the decline of public financing and the increase of numbers of students from all social backgrounds, the role of the government increased, and the universities became more dependent on government aid. The universities moved into the public eye; their programs and teaching became more transparent, and the efficiency of their operation was scrutinized. Money was allocated according to department "earnings." The government was seeking ways for better distribution of money. After several changes in agencies, the Higher Education Founding Council was established, and since 1992 distributes funds to the universities as block grants (Thomas 1998). The use of the funds is up to the universities and department administrations. Heads of departments now need not only to have a good academic training but also good managerial skills to use the money allocated most efficiently and effectively. Departments have to attract income from sources other than government and compete for students and research opportunities to increase their income.

With the change in student enrollment, the elitist model of the university has changed. Only slowly do institutions of higher education accommodate nontraditional students (Tugend 1999). The dilemma is that greater access increases the number of students, which might result in declining standards. The debate is now whether traditional standards should be used to evaluate the performance of a university or, if not, what new standards should be employed. Control that was in the hands of professors in the mid–1980s passed to the state and the market (Kogan 1998).

Since fall 1998, British students have to pay the equivalent of $1,600 tuition. Students from households with less than the equivalent of $56,000 per year can receive some subsidy. Excluding needy and minority students, selection of students is according to their ability to finance their studies. Since the Thatcher years, when full-maintenance grants were cut, students have to pay for living costs or depend on their parents' support. More students are working now, and graduate students and part-time students have difficulty paying, resulting in a drop in these groups' enrollments (Tugend 1998).

Lifelong learning has become very important. No one is expected to hold one job throughout a career. Many people just need to know more and enjoy learning. For this reason, the government wanted more nontraditional students enrolled in higher education and provided several incentives, such as easing the tuition for students, financial incentives to universities to seek out disadvantaged students, money for two-year certificate programs, and incentives for the collaboration of higher education with other postsecondary institutions (Tugend 1999). Nontraditional students are still at a disadvantage since they cannot attend courses during the day, and the tuition is often too high. Institutions of higher learning in the United Kingdom are moving more toward the United States model and the free enterprise market. To really effect change to include all students, the structure of the institutions and management needs to change to accommodate the new reality (Thomas 1998).

Romania

In Central and Eastern Europe, higher education had to be restructured from the totalitarian regimes to democratic, decentralized systems in accordance with changes in the economy, society, and politics.

In the case of Romania (Eisemon et al. 1995), a revitalization of higher education took place after the collapse of the Communist regime. Romania had a chance to build a new independent system from the bottom up. The previous system was organized and manipulated by the government to meet the country's requirements in politics, command economy, and the workforce. The communist education included:

- political indoctrination,
- subordination of the education administration to the unique party,
- polytechnic education,

- police control of persons and institutions, and
- compulsory use of student labor for production (Birzea 1995).

The country has had to change its politics, economics, culture, and moral and psychological attitudes. Some of these can be achieved relatively fast; others related to culture and psychology will take a generation or more.

Birzea (1995) suggests four stages for the postcommunist transition in Romania: deconstruction, stabilization, restructuring, and counterreform. Deconstruction was needed to break from the severe communist ideology. The communist system and most institutions associated with it were disbanded. The universities were to receive autonomy so they could diversify and look for financial support in places other than the government. In addition to being free from government regulations, autonomy means that higher education institutions can determine internal organization, governance, distribution of resources, the generation of income from private sources, and recruitment of staff and, most important, have the freedom to research and teach (De Groof, Naeve, and Ševec 1998).

In the stabilization phase the changes were solidified through a legislative framework. The singular structure of higher education needed to be diversified so institutions could identify their own mission. Higher education was divided into short term (2 to 3 years), long term (4 to 6 years), postgraduate education (1 to 12 months), and postgraduate schools (1 to 2 years). The constitution, adopted in 1991, guaranteed autonomy for the universities. However, accountability of departments and a more efficient use of resources were requested.

In the fourth stage, the counterreform was led by old-time communists. This demonstrates the difficulties of quickly disbanding an ideology. Many former communist officials were in places of influence. Former professors believing in Marxism/Communism have formed private universities.

After the fall of communism, access to higher education was expanded to accommodate the many students wishing to enroll. Private nonaccredited institutions were established, and the number of public universities increased. In addition to a dramatic increase in the number of students, the number of institutions grew from forty-four in 1989/1990 to 56 in 1992/1993. The number of faculty more than tripled. But with the rising number of students there was still a shortage of facilities and teaching resources.

The first years of freedom from communist rules brought uncertainty and conflict into this nation's higher education system because many of the innovations were stalled by the still-present communists. In November 1996, a new president, Emil Constantinescu, the former rector of the University of Bucharest, was elected. As rector at the university, he initiated many institutional and curricular changes (Woodard 1997). In government, he surrounded himself with progressive educators to move forward with modernization. The new government dismissed officials who were against reform and is moving ahead with changes. Many have great hopes for improvement in education at all levels. Institutions of higher education became more independent and autonomous in administration, diversification, and their use of money. Government no longer controls curricula, and institutions can respond more quickly to local needs and demands from a still insecure labor market.

Mostly because of shortages of resources in 1999, a law was passed to distribute government funds to the academic departments directly, based on enrollment (Agovino 1999a). This increased competition for funds and should make higher education more efficient. In this time of economic downturn, officials in the universities did not have enough funds to pay their instructors because the funds allocated were not sufficient. Private institutions can compete for finances allocated by the state.

These were good intentions, and diversification of teaching was called for to meet the ever-increasing need of a growing and more diverse society (Eisemon et al. 1995). The 1998 revolution brought former high-level communist party officials to power. Subsequently, the central government still had control and seemed to stall innovation and failed to respond to immediate needs and the need for autonomy.

Teaching was and, in many instances, is considered rigid and outdated. It does not meet the needs of the quickly changing labor market. Studies needed to be diversified, and some general studies applicable to a range of subjects had to be added. The government encouraged changes in the structure of studies to deal with the increasing number of students, but they were only superficial. Older faculty held on to their positions and did not want to change (Agovino 1999a). Having no interest in modernizing, some have used the same books and strategies for many years, creating tension between younger, more forward-looking faculty and older members.

To ensure minimum standards, a national council on evaluation was established to accredit institutions of higher learning. Government agencies provide funds in the form of grants to institutions that agree to undergo an evaluation and accreditation process. The evaluation and the accreditation system gives some quality assurance and accountability, protects students from fraud especially in private institutions, and guarantees international competition and acceptance of courses and diplomas in Europe.

The financing of higher education became similar to the one developed in the United Kingdom (Thomas 1998). All public and private institutions have to raise funds from private sources. Some public universities charge tuition, allowed under the new law. Money received from research can be kept in the department. Greater flexibility in salaries according to performance and type of job was introduced. A higher education finance council has been established to implement and oversee these changes. However, it will take some time before the universities are free from the influence of government, if ever. These institutions have gained freedom from communist rule. Are they now free to do what they want or must they respond to their financial supporters, be they government or private sources?

In addition to the previous concerns, Romania has to deal with the issue of minorities. Romania has a Hungarian-speaking minority of two million. They were oppressed by the old regime. They had their own university in Cluj until 1959. Since then the Bolyai University was combined with the Romanian Babes University as a bilingual Babe-Bolyai University. Hungarians now want to reestablish their own university. Nationalist Romanians want to suppress all teaching in the Hungarian language.

The countries in Central and Eastern Europe have a chance to diversify postsecondary education to respond to the new demands of the new century. Higher education or tertiary professional/vocational education has undergone many changes in Romania, but like most countries in the region, it is planning many more to meet the needs of the population and to come closer to European Integration (Jigau et al. 1998).

Spain

Higher education in Spain was highly centralized before 1977 and was controlled by the central government's ministry of education. All important decisions were made at this level, from admission procedures, curricula, and budgets to appointments of rectors. The rector was the local agent of the state, controlling the institution according to government instructions. However, professors as civil servants had influence on the decisions made by central government officials and within the institutions enjoyed individual freedom, as there was no formal control over their teaching. Often they were part of the government bureaucracy through positions they held in government departments. Teaching was their main duty and research was only a marginal activity for most.

The increase in the number of students and the demands of students and society made it necessary to change from the rigid bureaucratic system to a more democratic, diversified, and inclusive system of higher education. In 1977, Spain became a democracy, and the government began the process of decentralization (Sánchez-Ferrer 1997).

The University Reform Act (*Ley de Reforma Universitaria* [LRU]) was passed after long negotiations in 1983. Institutions became more autonomous in managing their own activities and were no longer under tight control from the central government. The power of the central government became limited to general issues, basic legal rules, and rules of staffing since instructors were civil servants (Mora 1997).

Regional governments took responsibility for funding and management. This was very strongly supported by politicians in the autonomous regions of

Basque and Catalonia. Eighty five percent of the total budget is administered regionally (Mora, Palafox, and Perez 1995). Controlling the budget means also controlling the institution, but the influence on higher education is more diverse than it was before 1983, since more players are involved.

Decentralization for all regions was accomplished in 1996. To have some similarities among the regions and the universities, a national council, the Council of Universities, was established. It consists of representatives of the central and regional governments, higher education experts, and all rectors of universities. University policies and curricular reforms are discussed and initiated at this level (Sánchez-Ferrer 1997). Flexibility and efficiency to meet the needs of the individual, society, and individual regions should be the primary goals of the new institutions.

The universities are in charge of their internal organization, curricula, and appointments, and they can develop cooperative projects with private businesses. Decentralization also brought strength to the internal administration of higher education institutions. More power is vested in the rector and his board. They can make decisions of local importance and need to approve all decisions made by faculties, departments, and staff.

At each university a social council was established as an outside body to assist in bringing social needs and demands to the attention of the universities. Representatives from the larger community are members of the council. The role of this body, fashioned after the board of trustees in the United States, is not clear and therefore it has no real power. Most do not want to interfere in the universities' internal affairs (Sánchez-Ferrer 1997). Major decisions are to be made in an assembly consisting of faculty, students, and nonacademic staff. However, institutions are still not as democratic as envisioned because the leadership is still mostly in the hands of the academic senate where most important decisions are made, such as electing the rector.

The studies at universities are divided into a three-year short cycle and a four-year long cycle. The latter takes an average of seven years. Most students finish the short cycle in five years. The course requirements are so numerous that students cannot finish in the officially prescribed time. In both cycles the dropout rate is from 38 to 41 percent. After the long cycle the qualified student may enroll in a two-year doctoral program requiring a thesis (Mora and Garcia 1999). Only recently were the courses changed to semester courses with credits.

Access to higher education is open. Any restrictions are prohibited because they would prevent equality of access. The prospective students have to pass an examination to be eligible, and most do pass. The 1978 constitution established the right to an education by all citizens, and the 1983 University Reform Act reemphasized this right for access to higher education in a democratic society (Gil 1995). The enrollment increased to about 1.5 million, which is about 40 percent of an age group. The student population comes about half from worker families and half from families with higher income such as owners, employers, or managers, indicating a change from an elite to a mass institution (Mora and Garcia 1999).

The increase in the number of students was accompanied by a 50 percent per student increase in public spending on higher education between 1985 and 1993 (Sánchez-Ferrer 1997). Spain spends as much as 0.9 percent of its GDP on higher education, very close to other European states.

Students pay tuition, and most stay at home, with only 20 percent living in student housing. They are allowed to apply only to regional universities unless a subject they want is not offered in the region. Student aid is available for needy and academically qualified students.

Improving higher education in Spain was very important, but not much improvement can be observed (Mora 1997; Sánchez-Ferrer 1997). The intent of the reform plan was to increase university efficiency, standards of teaching, research, and student performance. It was hoped that a self-evaluation system would improve the quality of higher education and that the universities would respond to society's needs. But tradition is hard to overcome. There is hardly any mobility of students or professors, and modernization of courses is very slow and sometimes nonexistent. The structure of courses has changed to a credit system, but the teaching methods are still only theoretical.

Spain has made great efforts to decentralize and democratize higher education, but the results are not a reflection of these efforts. There is no accountability of performance or evidence of efficiency. Universities need not compete for professors and promote from within. The tremendous and fast growth in the number of students is one obstacle in developing quality programs and less bureaucratic institutions. The foundations for change are laid, and outside influences including the need to be competitive in Europe, will perhaps speed up the process.

Germany

As in Spain, the expansion of higher education in Germany has not been matched with an increase in funding. Higher education institutions accommodate twice as many students as their resources permit. In order to allow more students to enroll in higher education, more universities were founded, and a new institute, the *Fachhochschule* (college of higher professional training) was created.

Higher education is the responsibility of the sixteen federal states. The cost of these institutions is high, and state governments alone can not finance higher education. Therefore, the federal government stepped in to help finance and to streamline higher education, even though by law it had no authority. In the 1950s, the federal role was advisory, but its influence in policymaking expanded. To legitimize its competency, the federal government's

Basic Law was changed. Now, federal and state governments work cooperatively to finance and develop higher education. Eventually a Federal Framework Act for Higher Education was ratified by parliament and has been amended several times. Some may interpret this change as a move toward centralizing higher education or at least providing uniformity throughout the Federal Republic.

The newest reform efforts of the Framework Act for Higher Education stipulate many changes with regard to financing and educational processes:

1. Institutions should receive funds according to their performance.
2. An evaluation should take place on a regular basis to improve teaching and research.
3. The prospective student should gain a better insight into the institution he/she will attend.
4. The obligatory study time should be reduced.
5. An interim exam should be introduced to measure student progress.
6. A credit point system should be introduced to ease transfer to other institutions.
7. Bachelor's and master's degrees such as those accepted in Anglo Saxon countries should be introduced.

These reforms will make the universities and the *Fachhochschulen* more responsible for their work because their achievement will be scrutinized. Competition for students and funds among the institutions should make them more efficient. Including all members of the staff in the decision-making process should make these institutions more democratic.

Nevertheless, federal funds are short, and the federal government cannot promise extensive financing. This makes it necessary for the institutions of higher learning to function more efficiently. The desire of these institutions to have greater autonomy played into the hands of supporting agencies to provide a limited amount of money without detailed spending stipulations. Institutions can use the money as they see fit. This, however, is being tried with only a few institutions.

According to the framework, universities will compete for money from public sources and receive funds according to their performance. Since this will not be enough, they will also have to ask the private sector or foundations for support. Instead of obtaining complete financing from the government, universities will need to be involved in fund raising.

In 1999, the magazine *Der Spiegel* conducted a ranking of universities by about 12,400 students at eighty-one higher education institutions (Uni Spiegel 1999). The effects are not clear since this is the first attempt at such a large-scale survey. But it shows that universities are no longer isolated from the public eye. Probably students will seek out places to study where they find more attention by their instructors and where universities are not mass institutions.

The *Fachhochschule* is now part of higher education. It differs from the university in that it is more structured in course work and length of study. In some ways it may be compared with professional schools in the United States. It meets the requirement of industry to train highly qualified workers, who gain theoretical and practical knowledge, in a shorter period of time. Students are in courses designed for a specific line of professional work and have to have practical experience in their field. Some industries have established courses and professional colleges in their own facilities to train personnel. The diplomas or certificates are accepted for further training in other institutions.

The establishment of these institutions and *Fachhochschulen* is really a response to outside needs and is very much oriented toward using studies for practical purposes. Some fear that the academic freedom of higher education will be abolished in favor of the need to be efficient and bring quick results. In business and industry, 75 percent of the engineers and 50 percent of the industrial managers have graduated from *Fachhochschulen*.

The concept of *Fachhhochschulen* has been adopted by other European countries as well. In the United Kingdom the polytechnics are now universities and compete with older universities in subjects geared toward practical application. In the Netherlands, *Hogescholen* are similar to the *Fachhochschulen* but offer a broader spectrum of subjects, such as teacher training, social work, business administration, engineering, arts, and journalism. About two thirds of the students are enrolled. In France the *Instituts Universitaires Professionalisés* offer a four-year study program in engineering, which is interspersed with practical experiences.

Norway

Higher education in Norway has also expanded, due to the demand for more highly skilled workers and the shrinking labor market. By getting a better education, students try to improve their chances of getting a job. The government consciously increases funds to higher education to protect students from unemployment and to satisfy their desire for a better education. In this way, the central government controls both the labor market and the universities (Aamodt 1995).

In this country, too, new colleges opened up to accommodate the influx of students and to direct them away from the overcrowded universities. In these institutions, students can be trained as highly skilled professionals in engineering, teacher training, social work, and health education. The studies last two to three years. The student population is also larger than in the universities. In the universities, nearly all subject areas have admission restrictions, and the competition to get accepted is very intense. The government establishes each university's minimum capacity. The number of students accepted depends on the individual institution and the allocation of available funds. On the other hand, funding for universities is allocated according to the number of students. The Norwegian government is perceived as using higher education to influence the labor market or to better the unemployment rate of young people.

Universities are encouraged to look elsewhere for funding, especially for research. To raise funds, the University of Oslo is trying to use research as a service to business and industry. This is considered a partnership with industry. The university provides a service of research and knowledge. At the same time, the institution wants to stay independent of its clients' influence (Tjeldvoll 1997) and preserve its autonomy. Institutions support their programs in research and teaching and serve the community in providing knowledge and support through contractual agreements. They still believe they have enough freedom because their clients are many and no one dominates.

In summary, governments want to diminish their responsibility toward higher education because they cannot provide the monetary support, with the result that these institutions need to become more efficient by cutting costs, responding to the needs of business and industry, and competing for funds from both public and private sources. Higher education institutions seem to agree with these ideas and hope for greater autonomy. But they will need to show greater accountability for their performance in research, teaching, and making students successful.

HIGHER EDUCATION IN A EUROPEAN CONTEXT

From these few examples one can see that higher education in Europe has no uniform approach or easily comparable outcomes. The institutions try to move away from central control to autonomy to preserve their freedom and to manage their own affairs. Yet, most of them are dependent on financing from outside sources. In all countries the governments are responsible for providing and financing higher education, even though their own resources are no longer sufficient to sustain—let alone expand—higher education for very long under current circumstances.

Efficiency and evaluation have become important concepts in higher education. To become more efficient, universities need to specialize and cooperate. Not all programs can be offered at all universities. To accomplish greater responsiveness, universities and other institutions will combine their efforts and resources to work more efficiently to survive. An example of cooperation is the formation of the European consortium of Innovative Universities. Several public universities in Europe cooperate to apply science and technology in industry and business. Not only do these institutions work together, they also help to develop commercial enterprises in joint efforts (Bollag 1999).

European Union citizens can settle wherever they like. They can also study abroad for a period of time and receive their certificate or diploma from a university of their choice. Their diplomas and final examinations are to be recognized throughout Europe for further study and employment. Yet, every country in Europe has its own approach to higher education with course sequence, duration, examination, and certification.

It is hard, or rather, impossible, to make a comparison of studies and requirements, or to find equivalence of obtained qualifications. The German university education system is considered as having a solitary quest for knowledge (Girod de'Ain 1997). The student selects courses from many possibilities that may fit the requirements of the course of study. Attendance at lectures is not mandatory. Much independent work needs to be accomplished. Exams are given as a cumulative evaluation, usually with a thesis and an oral examination at the end of the studies. No units are counted, and all depends on the examination result.

British students have their first examination at an average age of twenty-one (similar to the bachelor's degree in the United States) and are ready for the labor market after a college-type education. Only a few students go on to postgraduate studies. They have to finish their studies in a set period of time, while German students' time is basically unlimited. Final examinations are somewhat like the ones in Germany in that they examine the acquired knowledge over the years of study. Here however, units of instruction, similar to the U.S. credit system, have been introduced in some universities (Girod de'Ain 1997) to make possible the transfer of credits. In France the course of studies is again different in that students can collect units and still have a final examination. They can finish their studies at age twenty-three. This includes graduate work.

It is difficult for students in this situation to transfer to an institution outside the country, since their transcripts may not be able to be evaluated, or the sequence of courses does not match. Similar problems exist throughout the region. The study time at German and Norwegian universities is considered very long in comparison to that of other European countries. When students join the work force at age twenty-seven and later, they are at a disadvantage in comparison to students from other countries.

Efforts are under way to make studies and exams equivalent by streamlining higher education throughout the European Union. Courses need to be equivalent and length of time needs to be agreed upon. The equivalence of degrees and certifications needs to be established. This also means that individual institutions could lose their unique character. The pressure to become competitive and cooperative in Europe is part of the policy and suggestions by the European Union, the Council of Europe, and to a great extent the Organization for Economic Cooperation and Development (International Association of Universities 1997).

The Council of Europe has established guidelines for cooperation among countries, universities, and other institutions of higher learning to provide acknowledgment of diplomas for admission, periods of university study, and recognition of higher education qualifications. These guidelines do not ask for equivalency of studies in member countries but rather for understanding of courses and diplomas.

Only three years of study leading to qualifying exams for the profession is required. If an employer in a member country determines that there is greater discrepancy in the training and education—such as too short a study time or missing courses—additional studies, professional experience, or an examination can be required, all of which fall within the framework of the European Convention.

In June 1999, in another attempt to bring better understanding, education leaders from twenty-nine European countries signed a joint declaration to move toward greater cooperation with the goal of achieving better compatibility and comparability in their systems of higher education (*The European Higher Education Area* 1999). The leaders realized the need to strengthen European "intellectual, cultural, social and scientific and technological dimensions." Europe is supposed to become an area of common knowledge and competencies for all its citizen to create and strengthen "stable, peaceful and democratic societies." The emphasis is on compatibility and comparability rather than uniformity. Through this process, the leaders believe, a "European area of higher education" and a "European higher education" will be created and become more competitive and attractive in the world. Key components of the declaration are:

- to establish easily readable and understandable degrees for better employability and competitiveness;
- to create a system consisting of undergraduate and graduate cycles wherein the degree after the first cycle should lead to better employability in the area, and the second cycle should lead to advanced degrees;
- to establish a credit system for better student mobility, which can include credits earned from non–higher education institutions;
- to promote quality assurance by using similar methods of evaluation; and
- to promote European dimensions through curricula and institutional cooperation and mobility of faculties.

Some universities have introduced the internationally recognized steps of examination, the bachelor's and master's degrees. The degree name may be the same but the contents of the instruction may vary widely. If this is indeed acceptable, then the course contents and units of instruction need to be comparable. For many countries this would mean a restructuring of the course of studies. For some it would mean that higher education would be more like school, *Verschulung* (Huber 1999). Introduction of other short cycle studies is another option.

The financial situation in most countries does not allow for great unchecked spending on higher education. In fact the spending on higher education has decreased substantially in many countries. An example is Finland, where the budget decreased by 16 percent over a two-year period (Lindquist 1998). Most Finnish universities are financed to 30 percent by nongovernmental sources. German higher education has lost 30 percent of its funding (Landfried and Lange 1998).

Whatever the approach to higher education will be, in all countries it has to become compatible and needs to be competitive not only inside a country but over all of Europe, eventually over the globe. While there are attempts for universities to cooperate in the European area, there are also attempts to forge partnerships across the globe. A most recent example is the founding of the International University Bremen in Germany. Rice University in Houston, Texas, and the University of Bremen, a state university, set up this independent private university for international students and faculty. It is considered an experiment to see whether a private independent institution can exist in Germany. The university, patterned after U.S. institutions, wants to remain independent of government funding and hopes to have an endowment of $130 million in ten years. In the quest to become independent from government rules and funds these institutions depend on private donors and will be accountable to them.

The idea of the classic university will continue to exist but will be available only for the few who will continue their studies and remain at the university to build the core of scientists who will be concerned with basic research and the search for truth. The greater number of students of higher education will look for education that has practical application in the job market and has immediate application for their responsibility in society. Universities and other institutions of higher learning will become accountable and more efficient, and the use of terms like productivity and output will be used more often.

CONCLUSION

Many forces are working on higher education, but changes are sporadic and slow. Institutions of higher education are steeped in tradition and the idea of autonomy and academic freedom. They can no longer cater to an elite group of students but must deal with greater numbers and a more diverse population. To ease the burden on the universities and to provide a highly trained professional work force, some countries have established new institutions that provide a more practical curriculum; other countries have included practical studies in higher education. Financial constraints and the increasing need to serve the community require a more efficient higher education system and the need to compete for public and private funds. This in turn requires an evaluation of higher education institutions and competition for funds and students.

To show more compatibility with outside institutions, country equivalencies of studies and diplomas need to be established. Some institutions try to introduce the unit system and the bachelor's and master's degrees to be more competitive. In all, today's universities in Europe serve a different purpose and a different clientele than previously, and it will require a great amount of effort and ingenuity to do this successfully.

REFERENCES

Aamodt, P. O. (1995). "Floods, bottlenecks and backwaters: An analysis of expansion in higher education in Norway." *Higher Education* 30(1).

Agovino, T. (1999a). "Romanian academics worry as reforms open universities to competition." *Chronicle of Higher Education* 45(34):A44.

Birzea, C. (1995). "Educational reform and educational research in Central-Eastern Europe: The case of Romania." Paper presented at the IBE International Meeting on Educational Reform and Educational Research. Tokyo, Japan (ERIC No. 392 667).

Bollag, B. (1999). "Some European universities are moving beyond reliance on state support." *Chronicle of Higher Education* 45(28):A50.

De Groof, J., G. Naeve, and J. Ševec. (1998). "University structures and institutional autonomy." *Legislating for higher education in Europe. Volume 2. Democracy and governance in higher education.* The Hague: Kluwer Law International.

Eisemon, T. O., I. Mihalescu, J. Vlasceanu, J. Zamfir, J. Sheehan, and C. H. Davis. (1995). "Higher education reform in Romania." *Higher Education* 30(2):389–406.

The European higher education area: Joint declaration of the European Ministers of Education. Report of conference held in Bologna, Italy, June 1999. (1999).

Gil, G. A. (1995). "Spain." In T. N. Postlethwaite (ed.), *International encyclopedia of national systems of education.* 2d ed. New York: Elsevier Science.

Girod de' Ain, B. (1997). "The future of the European universities: How should students earn their diplomas? Nine goals for renovation." *Higher Education Management* 9(1).

Huber, L. von (1999). *"Wer B.A. sagt muß auch C sagen: sollen flinke Retuschen vor echten Reformen schützen?" Die Zeit,* June 2, pp. 63–64.

International Association of Universities (IAU). (1997). *Analysis: The feasibility and desirability of an international instrument on academic freedom and university autonomy.* IAU working document. UNESCO. http://unesco.org/iau/fre/tfaf_feasibility.html.

Jigau, M., R. Mihail, E. Radulescu, and C. Olariu. (1998). "Romania." In M. A. Hennessey, O. Lampinen, T. Schröder, H. Šebkova, J. Setényi, and U. Teichler (eds.), *Tertiary professional and vocational education in Central and Eastern Europe.* Strasbourg: Council of Europe.

Kogan, M. (1998). "University-state relations: A comparative perspective." *Higher Education Management* 10(2):121–135.

Koucky, J. (1995). "Access to higher education in the Czech Republic: From central regulation to a balance of incentives." *Alma Mater* 5:121–134.

Lindquist, O. V. (1998). "Changes in Europe: The example of Finland." *Beiträge zur Hochschulpolitik, 3.* Bonn: Hochschulrektorenkonferenz.

Meyer-Wolters, H. (1998). "Zur Situation und Aufgbe der (deutschen) Universität." *Pädagogic* (2):181–196.

Mora, J.-G., and A. Garcia. (1999). "Private costs of higher education in Spain." *European Journal of Education* 34(1).

Mora, J.-G., J. Palafox, and F. Perez. (1995). "The financing of Spanish public universities." *Higher Education* 30(4): 389–406.

Neave, G. (1998). "Four pillars of wisdom." *The Unesco Courier* 51(9): http://proquest.umi.com/pqdweb.

Sánchez-Ferrer, L. (1997). "From bureaucratic centralism to self-regulation: The reform for higher education in Spain." *West European Politics* 20(3):164–184.

Shafer, S. (1988). "Polytechnic education in practice in the German Democratic Republic." Paper presented at annual meeting of the Comparative and International Education Society, Atlanta, Georgia.

Shafer, S. (1994). *New social studies teachers for Eastern Germany.* Unpublished manuscript.

Shafer, S. (1997). *Patterns in Eastern German schools.* Unpublished manuscript.

Thomas, H. G. (1998). "Reform and change in financial management: The need for an holistic approach." *Higher Education Management* 10(2):95–106.

Tjeldvoll, A. (1997). "The service university in the global marketplace." Paper presented at the Western Regional Conference of the Comparative and International Education Society, Los Angeles, CA.

Tugend, A. (1998). "British students adjust to paying tuition." *Chronicle of Higher Education* 45(3):A 47.

Tugend, A. (1999). "British universities struggle to serve non-traditional students." *Chronicle of Higher Education* 45(43):A37.

Uni Spiegel. (1999). "Uni - Ranking '99: Zum Studieren in den Osten." *Der Spiegel,* Nr 2, June 7. http://www.spiegel.de/unispiegel/nf/0,1518,imgid=8613-artid=17060,00.html.

Webler, W. D. (1998). "Evaluation und Akkreditierung von Hochschulen in der Ukraine, Erfahrungen als Berater in einem EU/Tacis-Project mit Reformen in einem ehemaligen Mitgliedstaat der GUS." *Das Hochschulwesen* 46(2):78–98.

Woodard, C. (1997). "Universities in Romania hope for improvements with an ex-rector as the nations' president." *Chronicle of Higher Education* 43(26):A43–A44.

DISCUSSION QUESTIONS

1. Should taxpayers pay for institutions that do not wish to be controlled by the public or by government mandates?
2. Should the university be an institution to prepare students for work, or should it be a place where freedom to teach and learn exists independent of the practical usefulness of the learning?
3. How much freedom do institutions have when they have to depend on outside financing?
4. Will institutes of higher learning become dependent on private sponsors? How can they avoid this situation and still be partners?

CHAPTER 7

Upper Secondary Graduates' Perceptions of School in Russia and Germany—A Comparative View

GERLIND SCHMIDT

For decades, school and pupils in both the Soviet Union and the new Russia were isolated from developments and research in the Western world and thus from those in Germany. As a result of perestroika more than fifteen years ago, and the subsequent collapse of the Soviet system, the situation is changing. In the new Russia there has been a growth of interest in examining its own education system with reference to issues and methods prevalent in the Western world. International comparison provides Russian educationists with an opportunity to ascertain what is specific and what is universally valid about their own education when compared to the countries of the Western world. It also helps develop a new identity for Russia and its society in the wake of the disintegration of the Soviet communist system. Such a comparative perspective provides new ideas for coping with the immense challenges resulting from the political and social upheaval with regard to reforming, or rather, transforming, the traditional Soviet system of education.

Comparative studies provide a chance for a reorientation of the German situation from an international perspective, and these have been encouraged during the past decade, although not with regard to the same issues. In Germany changes in schooling and education need to be examined against a background of new challenges arising from the processes of European unification and progressive globalization. In 1990 the unification of both parts of Germany presented new tasks for comparative research. It also provided contacts to and a growing amount of cooperation with Central and Eastern Europe. The necessity of carrying out far-reaching educational reform was not regarded as a consequence of this context, however. It was only in the middle of the 1990s that major economic problems would be partially resolved through cautious examination of educational policy reform.

The opening up of Germany in the direction of Eastern Europe resulted in numerous contacts and opportunities for cooperation, including educational aid. These opportunities arose at various levels of the education system and made relevant the issue of what the education systems of Germany and Russia did or did not have in common. The interest in a comparative review of Germany and Russia in all areas of the education system, including compulsory general education, increased. German educators, who, apart from a few specialists, were not acquainted with the educational situation in Russia, as a result of their differing political systems, generally had the impression, as did Russian educators, that there was undoubtedly a great discrepancy between the educational situation in the schools of the two countries. Among experts in both countries it was common knowledge that fundamental ideas concerning the German education system, such as those regarding universities and the *Gymnasium* (upper secondary school), indeed, the very way of organizing schooling and conducting teaching had influenced Russia and its education system during the time of the tsars. It was known likewise that these traditional elements in the educational systems of the two countries had survived the political upheavals of the twentieth century, to some degree without in-depth change. This aspect is becoming even more relevant now that educational traditions of the nineteenth and early twentieth centuries are actually being revived in Russia at present. The perceived discrepancy was obviously underlined by the fact that the Russian side ascribed to the Germans the task of providing encouragement, advice, and aid in the process of transforming the old Soviet system into a new system of education founded on the principles of democracy and the rule of law. Any transfer in the other direction was regarded as a secondary issue at the most, or even quite out of the question by both Germans and Russians.

Cooperation in research concerned with pursuing these issues with a view to clarifying the present need for reform has remained the exception between the two countries for various reasons of both a material and practical nature, which cannot be gone into in detail here.[1] It should also be stressed that unsolved problems arose concerning the concepts involved (Kirchhöfer 1995). In view of the prevailing difficulties it must be regarded as a stroke of luck that two small research groups in Germany (the German Institute for International Educational Research, abbreviated in German as DIPF) and in Russia (the Laboratory for Educational Sociology of the Russian Academy for Education, abbreviated in Russian as RAO) began long-term investigations in 1991/1992. They have compiled a wealth of promising empirical data for comparing the perception of schooling in the two countries. It was the aim of both research teams, neither of whom knew anything of the other's intentions, to focus their investigations on a survey of young people at the end of their school career. They wanted to compile information on pupils' attitudes and wishes concerning school content, and eventually to filter the information acquired back into the schools via the teaching staff and head teachers to influence the ongoing or envisaged processes of change. Their intention was also to achieve a qualitative improvement of schools and their work. The

Russian and German project groups drew up questions in their surveys that were very similar, sometimes even using the same wording. In both surveys the Russian and German teams received surprisingly similar answers from the pupils to a large number of questions.[2] This applies to three issues in particular: the statements on a widespread fundamental acceptance of school and the pupils' feeling of satisfaction with it from a number of essential aspects, but also their critical comments on certain points; criticism made concerning the unsatisfactory communication between teachers and pupils needs to be stressed, as do the comments on the lack of involvment of the pupils in the shaping of classwork and school life.

This noticeable correlation in the results is a reason for in-depth analysis if one considers how different the conditions are in which the young people grow up and follow their school careers, and how different the school systems and basic attitudes to education have been in the two countries until recently. It does, however, also cast doubts on the impression given by the survey results of the predominant feeling of alienation and aloofness in situations involving exchange and contact. Are they not the same functions that the schools in both countries have to solve, each according to its specific situation? Can a comparative analysis not lead to an understanding that is profitable for educational reform in Germany as well as in Russia?

The two studies provided a starting point for a comparative examination, but it was the similarity in the questions and answers that determined the actual point of departure. More ideas for a productive comparison are to be found in the closeness of the goals set and the educational premises that become evident when placed in the wider field of comparison already available in the international scene.

The studies found their particular background in the transformations that, in Germany, occurred following Unification and the inclusion of young people from East Germany[3] and, in Russia, following the change of political direction. In a wider context they were also concerned with international comparisons of educational achievement as well as with research on youth and on the quality of schooling. It is not, however, possible to assign the studies neatly to any one of these areas of research. The specific nature of the issues of the two projects and of their methodological approaches is that they both focus on central themes such as satisfaction, a feeling of well-being, and the ability to identify with school as the context for examining teaching, educational contents, attitudes to achievement, and pupil-teacher relations. One of the core points in both projects is communication. This goes hand in hand with the issue of pupils' personality development, an issue central to the educational task in that it is affected by the pupil-teacher relationship as well as by the relationships among the children themselves. The authors regard schooling as a significant part of the lives of the young people. It is, however, a part that conflicts with their present and future lives outside school, and it is assumed there is a dichotomy between school and life.

The starting point of these two investigations is characterized by the primary educational line of reasoning and the objectives. It is accompanied by their emphasis on the communication aspect and by their practical approach, as well. The educational concept has been formed by observations, experience, and convictions assembled in the context of everyday life at school. This provides a useful launching pad for channelling the results back into school life, to head teachers, teaching staff, pupils, and parents.

Following the example of international comparative educational achievement research by the International Association for the Evaluation of Educational Achievement (IEA), since the 1970s attention has been directed toward this context: "However, large-scale objective compilations of data and school methods—no matter how revealing—may give little or no idea of the 'inside feeling' of those being educated, or of the changing personal and social context in which vital educational choices are made." (King 1997, 87).

At the same time, attention was drawn to the problems produced by the great differences prevailing in different places and times when comparisons of the results from different countries were made. Since then, the question continues to arise as to what is peculiar to and what is generic in the specific national and cultural contexts. At the time, the question was posed from a comparative point of view and went hand in hand with the issue of the general change in the perceptions and needs of young people.[4] During a period of extended comparative educational achievements research, which is pursued with political emphasis both in Germany and Russia, this question has gained greater importance.

A fairly large number of systematic surveys had been carried out by youth research both in the Soviet Union and in Germany during the previous two decades. Their aim had been to provide information on the attitudes and behavior of young people about politics, the state, and society. Pupils from the upper secondary level were a particularly favored population for surveys since their special high social status distinguished them from young people in vocational education or in employment. In the Soviet Union, unlike in Germany, only those results reached the general public that corresponded to the state's ideological objectives. Interest in Russia is now focused on enquiring about the results of new socialization patterns after the upheavals and the term *sotsial'nyi portret* (social portrait) of young people was applied to describe the findings.

For a long period that lasted well into the 1990s, young people in the two countries were rarely regarded as the subjects of such research, but were primarily considered the objects of politics and social and family influences. In this context, school was regarded by youth research in both countries as a place of institutionalized education, as an "agency" or a subsection of the social system. It remained up to the educational sciences to deal with it from the point of view of educational change. However, when educational experts and research workers attempted, by means of empirical investigations, to discover what was actually happening in schools and how those concerned reacted, it was common practice to ignore pupils as self-determined, acting subjects, as "specialists in their own field" (Schefold and Hornstein 1993). The fact that pupils and learners—frequently termed "children," "kids," or at best "young people"—are likely to be underestimated in their maturity and attitudes to school affairs by teachers, head teachers, and administrators is only slowly and by no means all-embracingly changing (King 1997). It is the impetus to change this situation that is joining the German and Russian inquiries.

Finally, it also seems legitimate to compare the two studies from the point of view of methods. Neither of them is representative, and both of them stress the qualitative rather than the quantitative aspect. The questionnaires used were based on open interviews and the evaluation of pupils' essays. They included open questions in order to examine the wishes, needs, and expectations of the pupils in greater depth. In fact, the actual procedure was inductive.[5] In evaluating the questionnaires, the German and Russian teams based their work on the same methodological procedures required for empirical and quantative investigation in the social sciences. However, as far as the quantative results (percent information) are concerned, it is only possible to compare tendencies, not the actual figures, due to a different structuring of the survey questionnaires, including the types of answers.

The study carried out in Russia aimed at examining the situation in St. Petersburg for the sample. It has been repeated every two years since 1993 and has now been extended to other regions. Towns with a different social and cultural profile have been included alongside St. Petersburg (Novgorod as an "old" Russian provincial city and Tol'iatti as a "young" industrial town). In contrast, the German Institute's investigation explicitly included a widespread international comparison. It included a number of European countries (Denmark, England, Wales, France, Greece, the Netherlands), but not Russia.[6]

What results and ideas for our own German situation can be learned from a comparison to an already completed survey of German and Russian pupils? And what can be learned about the application of comparative procedures in similar cases? Our study should help to show how a comparative view will sooner or later make the differences become relative that are generally focused on when educators and those interested in education (the term being used in the broadest sense) meet and where academic work and cooperation are concerned. This applies to the aspect of the transformation of the political system, the social sphere and education politics, the everyday life at school, as well as the aspect of historical framework conditions for education.

DIFFERING CONTEXTS AND, IN FACT, SIMILAR PROBLEMS?

An overview of the common and differing conditions governing the educational systems that seem significant for an analysis of the two surveys must include the following aspects of the school system of the two countries.

Generally speaking, schools in Russia and Germany may be regarded as still closely related to the traditional view of schooling as a strictly regulated institution. In Russia, subject divisions in teaching are on principle aligned to the contents of academic subject disciplines, while in Germany this applies in particular to the classes preparing for the school-leaving certificate and university admission. In both countries teachers regard themselves, to a large degree, as representatives of the subjects they teach. In the course of their teaching careers, the professional aspect of providing specialized subject tuition increasingly conflicts with their tasks of acting as educators and representatives (agents) of the state and society. In both countries the tradition of the upper secondary school during the period of the German Empire and the tzars of being a school for "rote learning" or "swotting" continued with little check until after World War II in Germany and in the Soviet Union even until perestroika, leaving a very definite imprint on secondary education oriented toward university entrance. The legacy of the educational reform movement with its child-centered approach produced strained relations with this type of schooling. Yet, in many respects this situation has continued directly up to the present despite the changing political background, which, in the Soviet Union resulted in a complete break with such reform concepts during the Stalin era, ending only in the late 1980s.

In Germany the *Gymnasium* was able to retain its position as a preparatory school for university entrance within a traditional vertically structured school system, although its highly selective character has been clearly diminished.[7] In contrast, the general education school of the Soviet era, the tenth or eleventh grade middle school, which continued through to university entrance, was conceived of as completely egalitarian until the early 1990s. Its goal—never actually achieved—of awarding virtually every young person the right to university entrance has been rapidly abandoned in recent times in favor of reducing the length of compulsory education to nine years. Despite this policy, there has been no great drop in the large numbers hoping to gain the final certificate of so-called complete intermediate education *(polnoe srednee obrazovanie)*.

Privately run schools may currently present an alternative supported by some sections of the general public in both countries, but they are only slowly gaining ground in view of the tradition of state-maintained schools that prevails in Germany, and what used to be the only option in Soviet schooling. Despite the rapid changes involving the external and internal affairs of the

Russian school, it appears on the whole to be a stabilizing institution in the process of social upheaval. In German schools, on the other hand, where for years rigidity in the internal circumstances has prevailed (Graudenz and Randoll 1997), there are signs of a "painful and as yet undigested transition to a different kind of school" (Glowka 1995, 232).

GERMANY: ITS SPECIFIC CONTEXT

In Germany the changes in paradigms that could be observed in the political and social spheres in the postwar period produced several shifts important to education in the relationship between the generations until the late 1980s. Attention has focused on guaranteeing the political and economic achievements of the five decades following the end of Hitler's dictatorship and the prospects of being able to pass them on successfully to the younger generation. This situation was not greatly affected by the integration of East Germany, as this process occurred under the conditions of the existing political and social system in the Federal Republic. In a process evolving over a number of years, leading to changes in the formal and informal rights and independence of pupils who are already legally adults at eighteen (until the 1970s at twenty-one), it became inevitable that these young people should increasingly be granted a "subject position" in everyday school life as well as in the whole educational process. Following the riots among university and school students and the ensuing social reforms of the late 1960s and early 1970s, an emancipatory kind of education eventually became firmly established. Young people criticized the authoritarian nature of German school tradition. There is no doubt that schools changed quite fundamentally in the following decades, as far as content, the ways of teaching, and teacher-pupil communication are concerned. The obligatory subjects of the upper secondary level were replaced by a range of obligatory and optional course components, and, alongside the teaching of specialized knowledge and skills, attention has increasingly been focused on the acquisition of social skills, so-called key qualifications.

As in their social sphere, pupils behaved in many ways like young adults in the upper secondary classes at school. Teachers were of the opinion that they, in their turn, treated these young adults differently. Until the present day, however, schools legally hold "special powers" for dealing with young people, a situation causing some strain when thinking about the students' subject position. The special status of the school has its origins in the traditional role of the school as a state institution empowered to grant fundamental socialization as well as entitlements; it continues to affect teacher-pupil relations at a very basic level. The upper secondary school as the type of school leading on to university within a vertically structured system is still particularly strongly characterized by this.

This tension was increasingly accompanied by a realization among the public and some specialists that the needs and interests of business and society as well as those of young people were jeopardized rather than enhanced by an obvious lack of elitism, selectivity, and achievement orientation of German upper secondary schools. For the past two decades conservative circles have been criticizing low standards of teaching in conventional fields of knowledge and skills and demanding a return to the traditional educational tasks of promoting diligence and discipline as well as basic (conservative) value orientation. Very recently these opinions have been boosted by the comparatively poor results achieved by Germany in international achievement comparisons in the field of traditional knowledge as reflected in Third International Mathematics and Science Studies (TIMSS). At the same time an increasing weariness of reforms and a certain immobility and feeling of being burned out on the part of the not-so-young teaching population is becoming very apparent. The school situation is now regarded very critically by business and parts of society from the economic point of view of providing "manpower." This has provoked the opposition of a large number of educators who are trying to uphold the idea of a school directed toward the needs and interests of the pupils at their "here and now" stages of development, that is, of a school focused on education and upbringing. The young people themselves judge the situation from various angles and cannot be allotted precisely to either of the two positions, as the results of the present survey show.

RUSSIA: ITS SPECIFIC CONTEXT

After the upheavals of 1990/1991 the relationships between the generations in Russia altered drastically, and the young generation increasingly began to appear as an "agent" in business, (somewhat less) in politics, and in society. For young people the authority of adults that used to prevail in society and families has been shattered because the elder generation's wealth of experience appears to have lost its value as a result of the collapse of the system. The attitudes of young people to the reforms, to democratization, and to the introduction of the market economy have become a target for public interest, and sociologists talk of a newly socialized type of person. There are complaints about the considerable loss of values in the fields of social responsibility, moral steadfastness, and mental stability, emphasizing negative characteristics ranging from individualism, material orientation, moral decline, and roughness in interaction with others, to cynicism among young people. Yet, fairly positive comments can be heard, referring, for instance, to a "generation of realists" who view life quite soberly, occasionally joined by a few young pessimists (Vershlovskii 1994a). After the original uncertainty caused by the growth of an unregulated sphere of employment parallel to the customary state sphere of employment, education has increasingly come to be regarded as having great value in society. Since the middle of the 1990s this has concretely meant the gaining of the entitlment to university admission and a university degree. The acquisition of knowledge has enjoyed almost unswerving priority.

Unlike in Germany, Russian schools face a process of upheaval involving the whole political system as well as state and society.[8] In this situation, Russian schools had to achieve a "transition from an institution steered by ideology and a central power to one determining its own affairs and oriented towards democracy" (Glowka 1995, 8). Schools have been given a "school constitution" revealing far-ranging changes and adhering to the principles of de-ideologization, humanization (stressing individual and personal relations), democratization, and the introduction of variety and inner autonomy, as well as elements of a market economy. For the first time, each pupil has a wide choice of course contents and other options (free choice of schools and the path of education to be pursued, and course options).

Influenced by innovative teachers and head teachers, schools have experimented with paths and content, some of them completely new, in order to overcome the previous uniform regime of state schools. The uniform ideological and educational precepts governing the whole country, the largely standardized structure of the educational system, of educational contents, curricula, textbooks, and teaching methods, and the state-regulated transition to the world of work—all these belong to the past now. Teachers no longer have to relinquish their "social, ethnic and political [and religious] sympathies and antipathies . . . at the school threshold" (Vershlovskii 1994a, 9). For the first time teachers have been able to develop their skills outside the hierarchies of the profession. Their professional conscience, and identities have been endowed with a new prestige. At the same time, academics involved in education have been attempting to emerge from their isolated position regarding international educational discussions and the development of the educational systems.

In view of the slow pace of change in many basic structural areas, these innovations need time to become established, particularly since they involve the existing teaching body, socialized in the old system. State and society are currently affected by an unprecedented crisis regarding material needs and mental attitudes, a crisis that has not stopped at the school gates. As a result, doubts have rapidly appeared about Western patterns and examples in the field of education (as about "Western civilization" in general!). The chances for introducing democracy and "humanization" into schools have thus become far less favorable. The feeling of being socially secure that school used to impart to both teachers and pupils is tending to vanish, and these groups are facing excessive demands together with general mental stress. This likewise influences the way school as a place for practicing the new political liberties is regarded. The increasing economic and social pressure on young people that arose outside school is now also entering the classroom, a fact reflected in the students' different attitudes of behavior to one another. Calls to return to at least some of the "achievements" of the Soviet school are on the increase.

COMPARING THE RESULTS OF THE GERMAN AND RUSSIAN SURVEYS OF PUPILS AT THE FINAL EXAMINATION STAGE OF UPPER SECONDARY EDUCATION

To illustrate the two surveys of young people completing the upper secondary school, two summaries of the studies compiled by their authors are quoted in full. This should give the reader some impression of how extraordinarily similar they are.

Germany

Tätigkeitsbericht (1996) reports the following:

> For German pupils, school plays a major role as a place of communication with other pupils and friends. This aspect appears to make school attractive. The final examination group commented positively on certain subjects, individual teachers and particular events in school life. However, a number of other areas can be found where pupils have divergent expectations which do not correspond to the reality of school as they perceive it. Achievement for instance is important for pupils, but it is not the most important area. They want to be identified not only by their achievement but to be taken seriously as an individual. This, however, would involve a different teacher-pupil relationship. Teachers would have to be interested in the ideas and feelings of their pupils, show they understand their worries and fears and take time for the pupils' problems. The pupils ascribed psychological and educational skills to "only" a few teachers. In addition, they would like teachers to view their own behaviour in a critical manner; criticism should not be directed only at pupils' behaviour but should include the teachers' as well.
>
> Pupils would like to have a greater say in school affairs and more rights in the decision making process, including an influence on courses offered. Subject matter together with the way it is taught has a great influence on the pupils' motivation. The sense and function of subject matter needs to be meaningful to them, particularly so that they can grasp its relation to their world of experience outside school. This, however, many pupils are missing. It is also obvious that many pupils regard teachers' influence on e.g. their creativity, their motivation to learn, their feeling of well-being and their self-respect to be too unspecific or somewhat unfavourable. Teachers should be interested not only in extending pupils' range of knowledge but also in supporting their personality development. This should not be done

with admonishments (according to the opinion of their peers, 70 percent of pupils do not wish to be "told how to behave") but in a fair, open and reciprocal manner. The group in the survey did not appear to expect anything "unusual" of their teachers, that is to say they manage to cope fairly well with teachers' "flaws." There are, however, many signs in our results that they expect more credibility and authenticity from their teachers, in particular a more comprehensive perception of and respect for themselves as people—not just for their academic achievements. (74–75)

Russia

Vershlovskii gives the following account of the Russian study:

The school is life for pupils *(Shkola zhizni vypusknikov)*. The survey showed that the main sources for feeling satisfied were the presence of friends, the opportunity to communicate with them, exchange of ideas *(obshche-nie)* with some of the teachers, teaching in certain subjects, a friendly class atmosphere *(druzhnyi klass)* ... As we can see, one of the main factors determining young people's attitude to school is communication *(obshchenie)*.

... On the one hand young people's expectations with regard to school are growing—on the other, it is becoming increasingly difficult to meet their expectations. Roughly 50 percent are sad to leave school—nearly half of those surveyed declared they were satisfied with school. Young people's alienation from school does not arise because schools have become "worse," but because they are so slow to change. And that is enough to produce negative effects. Young people are anxious about losing their status as pupils. Growing up is linked to the norms and cultural attitudes of a young peoples' sub-culture and the classroom becomes a meeting point for the reference group (Clique; *tusovka*).

... For many of them it [school] is "a large hospitable house," a "part of their lives, indeed a very important part," etc. At the same time the assessments are dominated by a critical note ... "School doesn't teach what's important any longer ... How to live, how to go on living in this almost unimaginably difficult world" (a sixteen-year-old girl) ... The children *(deti)* are strangely alienated from school ... because it is so slow to change and finds it so hard to part from its accustomed academic approach. (1994b, 9)

Pupils continue to appreciate teachers who are good at their subjects and know how to teach them ... Young people have a definite feeling of their own dignity and of individual insecurity. They strive for independence and are not capable of dealing with it. These feelings arouse a need for a well-intentioned atmosphere at school which is protective and supportive. Tolerance and the capacity for cooperation, the teacher's attentiveness are characteristics which are appreciated together with professional skills. These are typical remarks: "The atmosphere at school has literally become more like that at home. Of course we have our disagreements. But what family doesn't? Our teachers often take our side in these conflicts, they try to find compromises" (sixteen-year-old girl). However, different opinions kept appearing in the essays and interviews: there are controls instead of cooperation, evaluation instead of attentiveness; force is used instead of tolerance . . . communication with teachers is not possible at our school: We simply don't understand one another." [Teachers' and pupils'] inability to understand one another removes all sense from the educational process and makes teaching results shrink to virtually zero. One of the most painful issues is marking. Pupils complain teachers award marks according to their moods, that they have their "favourites" . . . that a pupil who starts off on the wrong foot has virtually no chance to correct the situation. It becomes apparent that one of the serious factors leading to pupils' alienation from school is the humiliation involved in getting marks . . . Nonetheless 37 percent of those surveyed mentioned "communication with some of the teachers" among the factors they find satisfactory. The materials make it possible to state that a new kind of communication is gradually gaining ground in the schools, characterised by respect of the individual and his or her right to their own opinions and ideas. (1994a)

A comparison of the results of the German and Russian studies reveals the following noteworthy parallels:

1. A relatively large number of pupils appreciate school not just as a place for learning but also as a place for communicating with their peers, and they pronounce themselves satisfied with school for this reason.
2. What pupils expect from teachers with regard to both teaching and support in personality development (including the need for understanding, help, and support) is met by only some of the teachers; a partnerlike relationship is not often achieved between teachers and pupils.
3. Among the majority of the pupils, their influence on the teaching process and their involvement in shaping school life is very underdeveloped.

TENSIONS TOWARD SCHOOL "REALITY" AND STUDENT PERSONAL REALITIES AS A CREATIVE GAP FOR EDUCATION

How are the similarities in the results of the two investigations related to the circumstances that they do and do not have in common in the educational systems and to their present situations? How do they fit into the educational policies and special subject areas in the two countries that are placed in such different historical situations?

I will focus on three aspects among these issues that reach far beyond the comparison of survey data:

1. the "duality" of the realities with respect to political education;
2. the question of pupils' opportunities for becoming involved in and influencing school affairs;
3. the "social" aspect of school connected with the emotional needs of pupils for encouragement of personality development, attention, and affection.

The duality of the normative level and that of school reality, of the institutional and "life at school" aspects (*obraz zhizni v uchebnom zavedenii*, i.e., the kind of life in the school) (Vershlovskii 1996, 46) are among the themes of the St. Petersburg study. From the Russian point of view they are described in an essay by one of the pupils as a kind of "let's pretend" in the way teachers behave while teaching and the way pupils behave while learning; in this context an "alienation of pupils towards school" (Vershlovskii 1994a, 9) can be perceived in the colloquial sense of the phrase, as well as in the philosophical sense found in the early writings of Marx. Similar observations on their school are described by the Russian authors in the German-Russian survey (see Note 1): "A strange, unspoken agreement among pupils and teachers . . . is described . . . The teachers appear to teach and the pupils behave as if they were learning and everyone is aware of the artificial nature of the agreemeent. We have noticed particularly characteristic examples for this "agreeeement" in classes in the humanities. Any challenge of this tradition on the part of the pupils leads to a conflict situation" (Glowka 1995, 211f). This study also mentions the "dual standards" apparent in pupils' behavior at German schools (217). It appears in the shape of a greater degree of "social self-organisation of German pupils who hide . . . their involvement in affairs behind signals indicating aloofness." In contrast to the situation describing Russian pupils, German pupils definitely seem to be personally involved even though this is not actually shown. This corresponds to the German Institutes results, as well as the pupils' statements complaining that teachers lack authenticity and credibility.

The expressions of duality described could be addressed from a number of different aspects, including a psychological approach, but at this stage they will be examined from the point of view of political education. In the case of Russia, the change in the systems must be borne in mind. With the upheavals it became possible for the first time for Russian teachers to introduce their "social, ethnic or political sympathies or antipathies" into the classroom. This is not unproblematical. For a period following the upheavals, in a "general atmosphere of permissiveness . . . for the pupils to be included in the teachers'

personal preferences became a matter of the teachers' professional conscience. At times the still susceptible minds of young people are directly
threatened by the exertion of mental force and manipulation on the part of a
teacher with his [or her] religious and ethnic prejudices and political sympathies" (Vershlovskii 1994a, 9). In a different context, this problem arises in
German schools, too, meeting with a similar feeling of discontent among
pupils: 69 percent of the German pupils in the survey regret to some extent
that "socially relevent themes (e.g. peace, disarmament, threat of atomic
warfare, environment) [do] not receive enough attention in the classroom"
(Graudenz and Randoll 1997, 50).

In this respect Russian teachers still seem to be affected by the example
of the Soviet teacher who was supposed to put across the "most important
'ideological' ways of approaching interpretation" in the humanities, and the
"basic ideas of science" in mathematics and the natural sciences (Glowka
1995, 186, 210). Glowka writes about the "authority" of the subject matter in
Russian schools. For teachers at German schools the terms of reference and
the means of implementing them have changed quite fundamentally since the
end of Hitler's dictatorship, in other words, a long time ago. There is a commitment to political education in the field of civic education at school. Generally the teaching staff carry this out with "political correctness" without any
conflict with the limits set on the influence of personal political opinions at
school even in a democratic society. According to the comments of German
pupils, their need and wish for teachers to discuss socially relevant—that is to
say, political—themes is by no means satisfied. In other words, teachers tend
to avoid tricky subjects like peace, disarmament, and atomic warfare, which
rouse pupils' interest (Graudenz and Randoll 1997, 50). Does this not reflect
the inner aloofness with which teachers regard their overall task, in this particular case the task of providing political education?[9] The lack of credibility
among their teachers in this area mentioned by the pupils in the survey concerns political education, too; the circumstances outlined here in the field of
political education fit in with the manifestation of duality already described.
A further idea is indicated here: as a school in a totalitarian regime, the Soviet
school produced a very obvious duality, as may be inferred from the situation
already detailed, but even in a school functioning as an institution in a democratic and constitutional state, a teacher is required to put aside part of his or
her own personal political and other convictions, attitudes, and preferences,
in favor of the requirements set by regulations of school as an institution of
state and society. In doing this, a teacher has to constantly walk a narrow path
if he or she wishes to remain credible and accessible as a person while—following educational tradition—setting an example. At this point a comparative
view must pose the question: Is it at all possible to imagine a school that
avoids the dualism described, and should not all calls for such a school rather
be regarded in the sense of a utopia to take behavioral bearings by?

What conclusions may be drawn from a comparison of the opportunities for influencing school affairs of German and Russian pupils? The German pupils are apparently less exposed to adult influence although the fact that they are older than the Russian examination group—18.9 years on average (Graudenz and Randoll 1997) compared to age sixteen to seventeen for the Russian pupils—must be regarded as a modifying factor. As mentioned earlier on, openly authoritarian attitudes at German schools have been noticeably reduced since the student movement of 1968. This applies to the formal rights of pupils whereby arrangements for pupils to have a say in school affairs had officially been introduced long before this. A large number of teachers, particularly in the humanities, do attempt to take account of pupils' interests and preferences in selecting material; the opportunity to choose options has become one of the main features of pupils' activities with regard to subject matter, making this a matter of principle in schooling. The situation of Russian pupils has been quite unlike this in the past decades. At the start of post-Soviet reforms there were very few signs of a tradition of formally based options as far as the significant decisions about education in pupils' lives were concerned. Any influence pupils had in the Soviet schools was closely connected to activities of the Communist Youth League, the youth organization in the Communist Party, and did not really achieve a profile of its own within the schools. As far as the pupil-teacher relationship goes, observers from Germany have frequently pointed out the teachers' authoritarian style in the way they treat pupils in Russian schools.

Despite the differences between the two countries, pupils' answers in both surveys correspond in that their ideas have as yet scarcely been put into practice and their scope for action is, on the whole, perceived to be restricted. In the German survey it is suspected that a feeling of resignation and lack of enthusiasm are the reasons why pupils do not go to greater efforts to influence the course of school processes within the scope available to them (Graudenz and Randoll 1997). These kinds of attitudes and behavior can likewise be deduced from the remarks of the Russian pupils. Here, too, it seems obvious to conclude that in both countries school is an institution where the needs and rights of pupils to have a say and to shape school affairs should be addressed again and again in the sense of a striving to achieve Utopia. There is no lack of evidence in the two countries that pupils' activities in this field will be reduced to a "let's pretend" level. However, it should also be remembered that the duality ascribed to the schools of the Soviet education system was caused by an adherence to the monistic political and ideological system. This explains why it reached different quantative and qualitative dimensions than was the case in the pluralistic framework of Germany's democratic system and its school.

CONCLUSION

It should be emphasized that both groups of pupils express a need for support, care, and affectionate attention, although the Russian group expresses this in a more emotionally colored guise than the German pupils do; for example, 50 percent of the Russian pupils left school with a feeling "of sadness" (Vershlovskii 1994b, 9). For both groups of pupils it is true to say that according to their own comments, their emotional needs—in particular those of a specifically "private" nature that are situated outside school life—are not sufficiently met by their teachers. The sphere of life at school that this touches on comprises a number of different aspects, including the relationship between school and family that has been shaped differently in the two countries. The remarks made by the groups confirm the assertion that even in the present circumstances Russian schools play "a greater role than German in providing a 'second home' to pupils . . . schools' function as a 'place of safekeeping for children' [is given] a positive dimension" (Glowka 1995, 227).

In the Russian study, one of the girls made a comment about putting school and family on an equal footing. In contrast to the tradition created in the Soviet Union, school in Germany would be regarded by pupils as a public sphere quite separate from the private sphere and would thus be perceived as having a different quality.[10]

An additional influence on pupils' desire for support, care, and affectionate attention will have been introduced by the female dominance in schools, the teaching staff being largely women. From a comparative point of view it should also be stressed that, unlike in Germany where the father was traditionally represented as the head of the family, it is "a Russian tradition for the woman to dominate the educational events in the family" and for the teacher to accept "the role of motherhood" at school and in the classroom, including the "right to take decisions concerning the children" (Glowka 1995, 228).

Against the background of rapid change in Russia it is, however, debatable whether a statement like "school welcomes us all" will continue to apply to Russian schools without reservation, even though pupils clearly wish this to be the case. Teaching staff are still influenced by the Soviet view of the teacher, one of whose tasks was to try to integrate all pupils in the classroom community from the point of view of achievement and social behavior. Under the recent political circumstances, it has become evident that schools are already becoming increasingly selective with the introduction of competition among schools, and parents are prepared to pay for extra educational opportunities. This could soon alter the attitude of the teaching staff toward egalitarian education and upbringing. The first objections can already be heard criticizing the fact that schools no longer fulfill their job of being "places of social integration."

The Russian pupils in the survey already miss "warmth and affection" and express the wish to be accepted "just as I am." This applies particularly to young people from broken homes or one-parent families who comment positively on the support for their personal development at school (*Social'nyi protret* 1995, 21, 22). Do German pupils not wish for definite interest to be taken in their thoughts and feelings, for understanding of their worries and fears? This is a sphere where they are distinctly dissatisfied with teachers.[11] In view of the "aloofness" of their behavior, should German pupils not be urged to take a close look at their own contribution to the situation? Their peers in Russia appear to have fewer problems and to be more accustomed to making their emotions heard at school.

It is especially with respect to the emotional quality of life at school that the studies from Russia and Germany are able to produce impressive rewards from the comparative point of view. This should, once again, be regarded from the point of view of a behavior-oriented utopia. The pupils' need of a "good" emotional atmosphere at school is only met in a spontaneous fashion at schools where the pupils are really still children. Only here is the need taken seriously enough by teachers, a situation that definitely does not apply only to Germany. Older pupils, including those who are in fact adults, clearly agree with these demands and expectations, but they claim that very few teachers are prepared to or are capable of doing justice to the needs of students in this field. Once again it must be concluded that at the brink of the twenty-first century, school as an institution embedded in state and society cannot do full justice to the life expectations of pupils due to the inbuilt institutional limitations. It is an issue for all those concerned with school to keep renewing these demands at a time of changing political and social conditions.

NOTES

[1]Mention should primarily be made of the only comparative study carried out jointly in all respects by German and Russian educationists, which entailed compiling school portraits and a (small) survey of pupils based on differential school research (Glowka 1995).

[2]A remarkable correlation to the pupils' survey is to be found in the German/ Russian investigation carried out in the same period, for which Detlef Glowka was responsible (Glowka 1995).

[3]A special survey of East German students from 1992 finally was not included in the survey of the German Institute because of obvious theoretical and practical problems of interpretation.

[4]"Or are generic changes of perception and need taking place? If so, how can an investigation be mounted to reveal what is specific, what is generic . . . ?" (King 1977, 87).

[5]This makes it possible to include some of the results of the school comparisons in the anlaysis so as to widen the interpretation (Glowka 1995).

[6]The comparative studies on Germany-Denmark, Germany-Netherlands, and Germany-Greece have now been published (Graudenz and Randoll 1998, Graudenz, Randoll, and Brouzos 1998).

[7]Currently 24.4 percent of students each year pass the final school leaving exam *(Abitur)* in Germany as a whole; in large cities (especially city states like Hamburg and Berlin) the percentage is nearly half of the age group (Graudenz and Randoll 1997). In Russia the percentage of young people who passed "complete secondary education" exams *(attestat zrelosti)*, which were proclaimed to be compulsory (but never realized) in the late Soviet era, severely declined in the post-perestroika period. In the early nineties about half of the age group changed to this type of general education after finishing compulsory schooling.

[8]During perestroika this was preceded by an educationally motivated "teachers' movement" from the bottom up; some politicians involved with education even refered to the school reform then getting underway as a "pacemaker" for perestroika.

[9]This trend is strengthened by the fact that length of service tends to go hand in hand with a growing concentration on subject matter by teaching staff (Graudenz, Randoll, and Brouzos 1998).

[10]The long-term influence of the Russian and Soviet tradition did not allow such a clear distinction between the private and the public sphere to arise in the way it did in Germany. This would also have affected school as a state institution (Simon 1998).

[11]According to information from 64 percent of the pupils, very few teachers are at present able to project themselves into the minds and feelings of their pupils (Graudenz and Randoll 1997).

REFERENCES

Glowka, Detlef. (1995) *Schulen und Unterricht im Vergleich. Rußland/Deutschland* [Comparing schools and teaching: Russia/Germany]. New York: Waxmann.

Graudenz, Ines, and Dirk Randoll. (1997). *So deutsch wie nötig, so dänisch wie möglich* [German as much as necessary, Danish as much as possible]. Cologne: Böhlau.

Graudenz, Ines, and Dirk Randoll (eds.). (1998). *Internationale Befragung von Oberstufenschülerinnen und -schülern über Schule, Lehrer, Unterricht. Niederländische Befragungsergebnisse* [International survey of young people's perceptions of school, teachers, and teaching: Results of the Netherlands survey]. Translated by Karen Hosper and Wilma Vollebergh. Frankfurt am Main: Deutsches Institut für Internationale Pädagogische Forschung.

Graudenz, Ines, Dirk Randoll, and Andreas Brouzos. (1998). *Schule im Urteil deutscher und griechischer Oberstufenschüler/innen. Eine vergleichende Betrachtung* [German and Greek students' views of schools. A comparative investigation]. Frankfurt am Main: Deutsches Institut für Internationale Pädagogische Forschung.

Khazard, Dzh., and S. G. Vershlovskii. (1992). "Cennostnye orientacii sovetskikh i amerikanskikh uchitelei" [Value orientations of Soviet and American teachers]. *Pedagogika* 3/4:102–106.

King, Edmund. (1997). "A Turning Point in Comparative Education: Retrospect and Prospect." In Christoph Kodron et al. (eds.) *Vergleichende Erziehungswissenschaft. Herausforderung – Vermittlung – Praxis. Festschrift für Wolfgang Mitter zum 70. Geburtstag.* Vol. 1, 81–90. Cologne: Böhlau.

Kirchhöfer, Dieter. (1995). "Alltagsorganisation Moskauer Kinder" [Organization of children's everyday life in Moscow]. In Hans Merkens and Folker Schmidt (eds.), *Lebenslagen Schuljugendlicher und sozialer Wandel im internationalen Vergleich,* 79–84. Baltmannsweiler: Schneider Verlag Hohengehren.

Schefold, W., and W. Hornstein. (1993). "Pädagogische Jugendforschung nach der deutsch-deutschen Einigung" [Educational research about youth after the German unification]. *Zeitschrift für Pädagogik* 39(6):909–930.

Simon, Gerhard. (1998). *Welchen Raum läßt die Geschichte für die Modernisierung Rußlands?* [How much space does Russian history leave for the modernization of the country?]. Bundesinstitut für ostwissenschaftliche und internationale Studien. Cologne: Berichte des BIOST.

Sotsial'nyi portret vypusknika Sankt-Peterburgskoi shkoly 90-kh godov. Vypusknik— 95 [Social portrait of the Saint Petersburg school leaver in the 90s. School leavers '95]. (1995). St. Petersburg: Centr pedagogicheskoj informacii.

Tätigkeitsbericht. 1993 bis 1995 [Progress report 1993 to 1995]. (1996). Frankfurt am Main: Deutsches Institut für Internationale Pädagogische Forschung.

Vershlovskii, S. G. (1994a). "Uchitelia i ucheniki. Edinstvo i protivostoianie" [Teachers and pupils: Agreement and opposition]. *Uchitel'skaia gazeta* 24 (May 31):9.

Vershlovskii, S. G. (1994b). " 'Vypusknik—93,' Rezul'taty issledovaniia" [School leavers '93. Results of an investigation]. *Informacionnyi biulleten* 1:8–10.

Vershlovskii, S. G. (1995, August 25). " 'Nasha zhizn'—ogromnyi strashnyi poezd' " ["Our life is a big terrible train"]. *Sankt Peterburgskie vedomosti,* 7.

Vershlovskii, S. G. (1996). *Lichnost', sem'ja, shkola* [Personality, family, school]. St. Petersburg.

Vershlovskii, S. G. (ed.). (1999). *Na poroge vzroslosti.* St. Petersburg: Institut obrazovanija vzroslych Rossijskoj Akademii Obrazovanija.

DISCUSSION QUESTIONS

1. Discuss the cooperation problems in the field of educational research between Germany and Russia. What are the main reasons for each to study education in the other country?

2. Why do you think pupils' perception of schooling has been neglected in the field of comparative education? Is this a transitory problem?

3. Discuss whether students have better chances to discuss topics of politics at school in a transitional state, such as the Russian Federation, or in a country of the "Western democracy" pattern, such as Germany?

4. What do you think about the attention (or lack) of students' personal and relational aspirations in German and Russian schools compared to your own experience in American schools? Will school be able at all to satisfy young people's expectations in the way that the family is sometimes considered to do?

CHAPTER 8

Education for Democratic Citizenship in Central and Eastern Europe in the Mirror of Globalization and Transformation

WOLFGANG MITTER

EDUCATION IN THE MIRROR OF GLOBALIZATION AND TRANSFORMATION

Democracy and Education

In his fundamental study *Democracy and Education,* John Dewey stated that the "devotion of democracy to education is a familiar fact." To explain this statement he identifies "voluntary disposition and interest" among the citizens as an important feature of political coherence within the commonwealth that extends beyond the rules of the political system in its capacity as a societal subsystem (to use system-based terminology). "Voluntary disposition and interest," he argues, "can only be created by education." The "deeper explanation," however, he finds in the essential quality of democracy as a "mode of associated living, of conjoint communicated experience" (Dewey [1916] 1980, 93). Education "to personal initiative and adaptability" appears in Dewey's conclusion as a necessary prerequisite for the viability of democracy (94).

A clearer understanding of Dewey's conceptual approach is obtained by examining his earlier study *The School and Society,* in which he focused his attention on the structure of the societal system within which education and democracy can interact successfully: "If our education is to have any meaning for life, it must pass through an equally complete transformation . . . To do this means to make each one of our schools an embryonic community life, active with types of occupations that reflect the life of the larger society." When the school trains "each child of society into membership within such a little community," Dewey concludes, "we shall have the deepest and best guarantee of a larger society which is worthy, lovely and harmonious" (Dewey [1899] 1976, 19–20).

It is not my intention to continue this interpretation of Dewey's fundamental thoughts. In particular, I do not want to discuss, in this context, the specifically *American* background of his argumentation and the transferability of his model to countries or regions with economic, sociopolitical and cultural conditions, others than those of the United States. However, a generalizing interpretation flows into my focal thesis that *there is* an interrelation between democracy and education to be based on two assumptions:

- Education is understood as an undeniable base for freedom, including freedom of political participation and decision making;
- Democracy is understood as a community focused on the acknowledgment and practicability of human dignity and human rights.

The core of Dewey's statement containing the irrevocable interdependence between *education* and *democracy* has been reflected in many constitutional and legal documents and also in many theoretical discourses in the fields of philosophy, political science and education, though in diversified contexts and formulations. This interrelation is rooted in the emergence of the *modern state* and its amalgamation with the concept of nation-building in its European configuration in the eighteenth and nineteenth centuries. That means that this interrelation was born in the period of *absolutism* and, therefore, is older than modern democracy. It can be derived from the basic idea that the modern state has always needed formally educated and trained citizens who were (and are today) loyal subjects or citizens and are able to contribute to the economic welfare and sociopolitical stability by exercising their knowledge as well as their working skills and social attitudes.

The wider range of this interrelation comes forth, in an exemplary way, in John Stuart Mill's words: "A general state education is a mere contrivance for moulding people to be exactly like one another; and, as the mould in which it casts them is that which pleases the predominant power in the government, whether this be a monarch, a priesthood, an aristocracy, or the majority of the existing generation, in proportion as it is efficient and successful, it establishes a despotism over the mind, leading by natural tendency to one over the body" (Mill [1859] 1977, 302).

In political concerns, beyond this trans-systemic approach, John Stuart Mill's statement seems to be stimulating and at the same time alarming, for it relates state education to *any* predominant government—from the monarchy to one that represents the majority of the existing generation. It is true that this interpretation, at least implicitly, includes democracy, but it differs from John Dewey's aforementioned optimistic view nevertheless.

The comparison between Dewey's and Mill's approaches to state education is suited to exemplify the ambiguous nature of education for democratic citizenship. In Mill's definition it appears as a medium of policy and governance from the top, which is mirrored in countries with centralized and hierarchical power structures, as demonstrated by France. In Dewey's concept, however, it is based on a model of educational policy starting from the bottom. Its primary function can be determined by enabling children and adolescents to gain experiences in the everyday reality of schools provided with self-government and participation structures, as are indicated by the educational concepts in the United States as well as in Denmark and the Netherlands. In France the Napoleonic concept has laid the foundation of the French education system, which has proved its vitality all over the various political periods toward the constitution of the democratic state, regardless of some recent approaches to decentralization. This is why there is no objection to arguing that *both* models of educational policy have been developed and defended as manifestations of "education for democratic citizenship." Each of them has to cope with an optimum balance between centralized responsibility and self-government at regional and local levels, and both are subject to modification and change, according to the continuous process in the "greater society," to quote Dewey again. Needless to say, communal "public" as well as "private" schools (in the broadest meaning) have been, though to various extent, included in both models, affirmed by constitutional and legal provisions.

The more the duality of the models of educational policy approaches the reality of the modern state, in its nation-based configuration, the more its typological nature is being replaced by specific national manifestation. The variety concerning curricular and pedagogical designs of education for democratic citizenship can be identified as an essential proof of the openness of democracy as idea and reality. Yet, it should also be taken into account that historical evidence warns not to neglect the bias-oriented implications inherent in the nationalization of education for democratic citizenship with regard to its top-based as well as to its bottom-based roots. In particular, we have to ask whether the young generation is to be educated to a form of democracy that allows for diversity, or whether the target of educational efforts is determined by a specific type of democracy with precisely demarcated qualities to be derived from national peculiarities, including religious and cultural components. As Erwin Epstein observes, the "state's interest in teaching children to be loyal is so compelling that it cannot allow schools merely to teach objective knowledge. Consequently, schools mix myth with facts to ensure that children gain a favorable view of the national culture. However, democratic states also claim as a hallmark that their citizens are freer both to express themselves and to choose what knowledge professed by others to accept. Unfortunately, the democratic aim of ensuring unfettered access to knowledge is undermined by the universal need of nations to gain political legitimacy and social and economic stability" (1997, 43). Consequently, education for democratic citizenship ends up in rather a restricted form, especially when linked with nationalistic drives.

To include these introductory thoughts under a broader theoretical range, the following considerations are based upon the hypothesis that education in democratic societies can be placed within a square whose corners are defined by the state (with its legal and administrative institutions and instruments), the market (with its mechanisms), the civil society (in its organizational and sociocultural framework), and the individuals concerned (students, teachers, parents, etc.). In principle, there is interdependence among the four corners, whereas the degree of interdependence indicates a wide range of manifestations that are rooted in history and distinguished by contemporary socioeconomic and cultural peculiarities. In any case, education is involved in all these manifestations, namely as conditioning and supporting power.

All over the world the *state* is constitutionally and legally defined as the exclusive or, at least, predominant school provider. As Mill's argumentation suggests, in this function the democratic state has retained an inheritance that traces back to the emergence of the modern state in terms of comprehensive administration, jurisdiction, and military force. It would be stimulating, in this context, to draw a line from the monarchic and the succeeding constitutional to the democratic configurations and to compare the developments among individual states to be exemplified by the nation-state of France on the one hand and by the multinational and multicultural empires in Central and Eastern Europe on the other, in particular the Hapsburg Empire and Czarist Russia. This exploration would be worthwhile, the more so as the political and education systems of Central and Eastern Europe, which the subsequent sections of the present chapter will concentrate on, are the heirs of those multinational models. The democratic state, as the youngest offspring of the modern state, looks upon education, and particularly upon curriculum and pedagogy, as an essential instrument for economic, social, and political progress.

As far as the market is concerned, international educational comparisons call our attention to worldwide trends that reveal approaches to market-driven educational reforms (Mitter 1996). Information on respective trends or, more precisely, innovative projects and proposals, is available from all continents. In this context there is striking evidence that such thoughts and desires are put forward just in countries whose education systems only a few years ago were governed and controlled by mechanisms focused on state monopoly and planned economy. Thus it does not seem to be surprising that calls for market-driven reforms are distinctly articulated in the postcommunist countries of Central and Eastern Europe, and that with special respect to education. They are supportive of democratizing processes, as long as they are in accordance with progressive trends within the civil society.

There are various definitions of what a *civil society* is and how it operates. To quote Michael Walzer, the "word 'civil society' names the space of uncoerced human association and also the set of relational networks—formed for the sake of family, faith, interest, and ideology—that fill this space" (1991,

293). Ralph Dahrendorf emphasizes the institutional and legal components by stating that "the civil society involves institutions which are autonomous in that they are not state run, are not subject to the whines of kings and tyrants, but are sustained by citizens endowed with rights and the wherewithal to make use of them" (Dahrendorf 1990, 142; Glenn 1995). The current debates on civil society indicate a revival of previous philosophical efforts. In this context Adam Smith's considerations about the "impartial spectator" as an institutional model mediating between state and market comes into the picture (Osterwalder 1993, 85–108). It was Smith who identified education as that societal subsystem that mirrors the complexity of the four-square relationship and its impacts on people's needs and desires. This question has often been neglected by authors focusing their attention only on the relationship between state and market and their impacts on education. Therefore there is continuity from Smith's thoughts to the current debates. These are, finally, rooted in the acknowledgment of individual freedom and human rights as fundamental values and in the democracy as their institutional home and protector.

The individuals directly concerned occupy the most important corner, since they are the genuine subjects of the education and learning processes, whereby the mutual stimulation of educator and educand has to be considered as a basic law of education in democratic countries. Under nondemocratic or authoritarian conditions, let alone education under totalitarianism, teachers and students are deprived of these fundamental rights. Even the history of fascist and communist education, however, allows for a great number of examples showing that pedagogically committed teachers and educators, in their daily work, were dedicated to the fundamental values of human rights, tolerance, and democracy below or even against the imposed norms of intolerance and ideological narrow-mindedness. Yet, in their daily practice they were forced to ignore alternative and even contrasting value codes in their students' families, peer groups, religious communities, and other apolitical groups.

Coming back to the illustrating square, I should point to comments whose authors allocate a fifth corner to the family as the traditional nucleus and root of society and, therefore, the basic conveyor of values to the growing-up generation (Rau 1991, 31). Without invalidating such a placement, I prefer including the family in the corner of the civil society, as regards its position in the education system. To give an example, parents have increasingly become social agents, in particular as members and chairpersons of parents' committees and comparable organizations. If we, moreover, reserve a special place to families in our scheme, why should we not do the same with churches and other religious communities that share with the families their predemocratic origin? On the whole, however, concrete arrangements of interrelationships always need references to the context in which they are devised.

The four corners are both interrelated and at the same time related to the center of the square, which is occupied by education systems, individual schools, and the sphere of nonformal education. To live up to the claim to be democratic, they need educational concepts comprising codes of goals, contents, rules, and values to be focused on philosophies. They also need legal provisions protecting them against arbitrary decisions at the top by state governments and bureaucracies, but also by local authorities, principals, and other officeholders. Concepts and legal provisions constitute the framework of each school. Whether and how its internal space is filled with what deserves recognition as education for democratic citizenship depends, however, on all the persons concerned: principals, heads of departments, teachers, and students, who are challenged to practice democracy in their everyday individual attitudes and actions as well in their collective interactions and decisions. In the wider context this challenge appeals to parents and the committed citizens in the community. Summing up, the democratic quality of education depends on the existence of a school culture or, to apply usual synonyms, school ethos or school chemistry. As a result of this historically determined requirement, all the partakers of the educational business must be provided with an optimum degree of freedom to be legally embodied in the code of human rights. Given this supposition, the reality only reveals democracies in progress, or in regress. Therefore, in this concrete case, the end of the path will always be open.

Education and Globalization

At this point the scene of our observation flows into the overarching process of globalization. In our considerations this notion must be related to its multidimensional range including not only economy, labor organization, and communication technology, but also politics, social order, and culture. There can be no doubt that education becomes more and more included in this worldwide process in its capacity not only as a reinforcing, but also as a stimulating force (Ramirez 1997; Spring 1998).

The German sociologist Ulrich Beck speaks of "second modernity" in order to emphasize the "irreversibility of globality" as a fait accompli that the "first modernity" had wanted (1997, 29). Among the focal components of second modernity, the decreasing power of the nation-state has been identified (McGinn 1997, 41–54; Green 1997). The dominant position it has held for two hundred years is relativized from two sides. On the one hand we get aware of the emergence of a world market with transnational production and service processes as well as management structures, and of the formation of political unions or communities with international or even supranational status. These trends at the upper level of the globalizing processes are essentially reinforced by people's migrations in the widest meaning of this notion; it covers the broad range from emigration, immigration, and temporary change of residence, to various forms of traveling, including the growing exchange programs among young people. In this context the ambivalence of globalization comes into the picture, as regards its appraisal as a step toward progress or regress in people's efforts to find the optimal balance between freedom and equity in their mutual relations.

This worldwide globalization process, including the move toward transnationality, is, on the other hand, counterclaimed by people's search for homes offering them protection and support against the challenges of globalization, which are perceived as threatening. There may be a controversial approach to the question concerning the reactive or independent character of this countertrend. In any case there is a growing revival of ethnic, religious, and social identity, based on regional and local cohesion, and there are various manifestations of this revival in the form of community activities, regardless of their open or segregational tendencies. Having analyzed both trends, globalization and the "clash of localities," Roland Robertson (1992) has proposed the new notion of globalization.

Until now, the interdependent challenges have relativized, but not essentially contested, the nation-state in its historical existence and its prospects; it remains open where this process may end after all, taken into special consideration the persistence or even renaissance of nationalism in several regions of the world, for example, in Eastern and South-East Europe or Eastern Asia. In any case, the "devotion of democracy to education," (Dewey 1980) is necessarily affected by the relativized association between democracy and nation-state with its impacts on the self-awareness of democratic citizens. This change of paradigm, in the tension between myth and fact (Epstein 1997, 43), and resulting from the changing position of the nation-state within the continuing globalization process, distinctly affects education for democratic citizenship, as regards the levels of identification.

In its pluridimensional range, globalization indicates an overarching process that is mirrored in the reality of people's lives. This essential feature makes it stand against virtual reality, so well illustrated in Goethes's *Faust* (Part 1), where a few townsmen have a chat "in front of the gate about war and murder far behind, far away in Turkey." The actuality of that scene is given by Goethe's ironic view—two hundred years ago! At present, globality confronts us with the reality of a global society. In its pluridimensional range, globalization, with its manifestations and trends in the education system, challenges both the theory and practice of educational science.

As regards the goals of globalization, however, one has to make a distinction between short- and middle-term objectives whose realization, though more or less exactly, can be predicted, and long-term designs ending up in utopia. This two-tier orientation can be exemplified by a comparison of contents and trends inherent in recent publications of the big world organizations. On the one hand, the *World Education Reports* of the United Nations Educational, Scientific, and Cultural Organization and the reports of the Organization for Economic Cooperation and Development (OECD) (e.g., *Education at a Glance* 1996) document the realistic view of the world.

On the other hand, the Report of the International Commission on Education for the Twenty-First Century, published under the title *Learning: The Treasure Within* (1996), while also containing a great deal of data and information, casts a forward glance to the "necessary Utopia," as Jacques Delors has appropriately summarized the long-term goal of learning (1996, 23–35). Yet, the glance at the "good Utopia," implied in this prospect, should not mislead educators to neglect the dangers that have been identified by the theory of the "world risk society" (Beck 1997, 168). This theory includes, at least implicitly, the perspective of a bad utopia, for the risk is not only inherent in the ecological component of globalization, but ultimately shows up in the question about people's ability and readiness (including their limits) to meet the challenges enforced by globalization. Taking Delors's appeal seriously, however, educators can build a bridge between the risk and the perspectives of a good utopia. Therefore they are incited to accept the challenge by participating in the globalization debate and by examining and reflecting globality in its two-tier range: as reality and desideratum.

Education and Transformation

Realizing that, in their dialectic association, globalization and localization exercise growing influences on the cohesion of nation-state-based democracies, this hypothesis seems to be both logical and legitimate: Democracies in radical transformation are affected by these worldwide processes to an exceptional extent. In them the promotion of democratic citizenship must be coped with under double or (if we regard globalization and localization as trends of their own) triple pressure.

Although the relevance of transformation to education in general and to education for democratic citizenship in particular has recently attracted growing interest among educationists (Schriewer 1999), it seems legitimate to devote some overall considerations to the current debate on theoretical criteria of transformation research within its pluridisciplinary dimension. The following approach to a rough classification results in identifying these seven levels (Sandschneider 1994).

First, the definition of the notion of *transformation* is, in principle, complicated by its competition with the notion of *transition*. It is true that there have been attempts at demarcating the contexts of both notions against each other. While, accordingly, transformation is related to processes revealing an act of volition, conceived and exercised by leading political powers (in the widest meaning of this term), transition emphasizes processes that are produced and effected within a given society, without indicating any distinct act of volition (Schröder 1995, Sandschneider 1995). Yet, there is no evidence allowing the assumption that this demarcation has gained uncontested acceptance.

Second, there is wide agreement in the debate on the essential targets of transformation processes: market economy, civil society, democracy. In more discriminating classifications this basic view is broadened toward the addition of further targets: constitution (or restitution) of a middle class; cultural change, concerning, among others, status, use, and dominance (or minor position) of languages in public life; religious revival; plurality of genres in literature, music, architecture, and fine arts; renaissance (or emergence) of national identities; changes of individual life and value patterns (as mirrored in attitudes to family, property, work, and age); changes of elite structures; and finally, changes in the education system (as societal subsystem) with its formal and nonformal components.

Third, the debate on the structures of transformation processes is focused on the revealing acceptance of the *five-phases model* to describe the process as such. The first phase is characterized by the political upheaval whereby disagreement has arisen on the applicability of the notion of revolution in this connection. Vaclav Havel (1992) has enriched and at the same time modified this debate by using the term *velvet revolution* to interpret the collapse of the communist regime in Czechoslovakia (1989) as peaceful event; his version has been generalized in various analyses on the turns in the whole region of Central Europe (Mitter 1992). The following phases comprise the decline or collapse of the old societal system: the introduction of new political, economic, and social structures; the (more or less successful) stabilization of the new system; and finally, the consolidation of its structures, related above all to its self-regulating ability.

Fourth, in the comprehensive context of the debate the "dilemma of simultaneousness" (Offe 1991, 279–292) has claimed paramount attention, focused on the rank of economic modernization and political democratization within the globalization process. Claus Offe argues that "market economy gets into its stride only under predemocratic conditions. In order to promote it, democratic rights must be pushed back. It is only a developed market economy which produces sociostructural conditions for stable democracy and enables the building of compromise" (286). His view, being in distinct favor of the "dilemma" argument, differs from those that set priority to democratic government and, even more so, to the emergence of a civil society, according to Dahrendorf's aforementioned definition. Affirming his view on the precedence of civil society in principle, he concludes that "the point simply is that an economy moving from force and total planning to incentives and elements of the market needs free and empowered citizens as much as a political community that is moving from one-party to democracy. Civil society is the key to any successful transition" (Dahrendorf 1990, 142). Giuseppe di Palma (1991), to quote a further prominent voice, even attributes the focal place to the civil society when commenting the causal factors of the collapse of communism: "Civil society has turned out to be the surprising protagonist of the East European countries—surprising for two reasons. First, recent transitions from Western dictatorships show civil society most often taking a secondary role of democratization, which has originated instead within the dictatorship itself. Second, since the notion of a civil society is fundamentally antagonistic to communist doctrine, communism, unlike Western authoritarianism, should supposedly leave no space for civil society" (63). Retrospective views on statements made in the latest phase of the communist systems in the Soviet bloc are worth including in this debate, insofar as they call attention to the historical roots of the transformation, exemplified by the case of that region (Huntington 1984; Young 1986).

Fifth, since the collapse of communism, the debate on the nature of transformation has concentrated on the former Soviet bloc, with South Africa as a second exemplary case. This seems to be plausible in view of the radical range of transformation in both regions, indicating changes of the sociocultural order in its totality, including not only politics, but also economy on the forefront and, behind it, social relationships, individual life, and value patterns. Understandable though this concentration is, it does not exclude the extension of the applicability of the notion of transformation to partial changes of sociopolitical or economic structures (Sandschneider 1994). In this context the cases of Spain, Portugal, and Greece, with the collapse of their authoritarian dictatorships as merely political upheavals, show up. Extending the dimension further, the decolonization processes in the southern hemisphere throughout the second half of the twentieth century are open to analyses in the framework of transformation research.

Sixth, the current transformation research can be considered as part of the pluridisciplinary efforts, centered round the notion of modernization and its reflection in societal reality. It is true that this debate, initiated in the framework of globalization, has modified these efforts, but it has not made it obsolete. In this approach modernization is treated as a teleological category, substantially rooted in assumptions of a global (or regional) progress toward a better world, as expressed by market economy, civil society, and democracy. In this view, however, transformation research has to face the question of how to deal with changes that indicate a political act of volition and allow applications of the five-phase model, while it does not transcend the applicability of the notion of modernization beyond its teleological commitment, either entirely or at least partially. Examples for an alternative, such as transteleological application of transformation could be ascertained with the October Revolution (1917) or the Nazi takeover (1933), since neither of them can hardly be, in principle, subsumed to the requirement of progress to a better world.

Finally, transformation research is involved in the tension between the historical and the social science approaches. While the former is determined by singular, nation- or region-based, processes, the latter is focused on theoretical models that are developed to provide foundations for comparability (with regard to analogies and differences). With transformation research continuing, it seems there is approximation of both approaches in sight, aimed at the recognition of the complementarity of both and stimulated by the classical research on totalitarianism. It should be added in this connection that transformation research has been recently enriched by designs based upon social and cognitive psychology, derived from growing interest in the changing life and value patterns of individuals and groups.

EDUCATION FOR DEMOCRACY IN CENTRAL AND EASTERN EUROPE

Progress of Democracy in the Twentieth Century

The twentieth century was, on the whole, characterized by the rise or, at least, quantitative increase, of democratic states. At the threshold of the twenty-first century this statement holds true even if we include the considerable number of democracies that disappeared from the map with the rise of totalitarian and authoritarian dictatorships. Rising democracies have, therefore, essentially contributed to the sociopolitical picture of the twentieth century, whereby, in the individual case, the causes and concomitants of the emergence have given birth to specific manifestations. In Africa and many regions of Asia democracies have been the outcome of decolonization and liberation, the special case of South Africa with its peaceful transformation from apartheid to freedom as a unique exception. On the other hand in Latin America and Europe the young democracies have risen from the collapse of dictatorial regimes of the aforementioned variations. This is the point where we have to localize the postcommunist countries of Central and Eastern Europe as the chosen case of this discussion. In this context we could start a long and controversial debate about the eastern and southeastern borders of Europe. Instead, let us choose a pragmatic approach and join the present range of the Council of Europe comprising the whole of Central Europe, the Baltic republics, Southeastern Europe (as far as it concerns former communist countries including former Yugoslavia and Albania, but, of course, neither Greece nor Turkey), and, finally the Slavonic states of Eastern Europe, including the Eurasian Russian Federation, where Europe and Asia merge. The Transcaucasian republics, for the time being applicants to the Council of Europe, remain outside for their current transitional position.

Rising Democracies

In what respect can the term "rising democracies" be assigned to the countries of this large and heterogeneous region? This is a crucial question indeed, insofar as the answer gives rise to investigate the specific features, problems, and troubles characterizing the particularities of each subregion, if not of each country. This is the outcome of a rough classification:

1. The first subregion consists of countries for which the assignment of rising democracies is entirely legitimate, because they are void of any democratic past, namely, the countries of Eastern Europe in its proper sense: Russia (including its Asian components), Ukraine, and Belorussia (Belarus). This statement takes into regard the very short interruptions of "starts for democracy" between the collapse of czarist autocracy and the victory of the new Bolshevik masters from the second to third decade of the twentieth century.

2. The second subregion, being the largest and, in itself, most heterogeneous one, is formed by countries whose history is marked by democratic periods, in particular in the years immediately following World War I. It covers the wide range from Estonia to Bulgaria, where in the 1920s or 1930s rising democracies were overthrown by authoritarian or semifascist régimes of different structural and ideological nature.

3. In the whole region there remained only *one* country with an intact democratic constitution and, according to the aforementioned prerequisites, democratic reality: the first Czechoslovak Republic (1918–1938). It was not void of internal conflicts with special regard to handling its minority issues. Viewed on the whole, however, manifold sources show that, for instance, the spirit of interethnic tolerance in the field of education and the will to cooperate were comparatively greater than elsewhere (Mitter 1990), let alone the permanently operating constitutional and legal foundation on the whole.

While the emerging democracies in Eastern Europe can be meaningfully classified as "rising," the answer concerning the two other subregions is more complicated. In an overview it may be stated nevertheless that the rather short-lived, though atrocious, Nazi occupation and the more or less immediately following Soviet hegemony were aimed at extinguishing the existing or surviving elements that had formed cultures of democratic education—partially—with remarkable qualities. As far as their outward appearances are concerned, the communist educational policies with their indoctrinating methods were not entirely ineffective. Moreover, they suggested a picture of success that the governments presented to the outside world—and also to their own people. Moreover, the impacts of indoctrination have certainly left some traces in the thoughts and attitudes among the offspring of communist school education. Yet, views have been expressed that communist education as an ideology-bound enterprise geared to the creation of a "new man" had been a failure from its start. This opinion seems to be on solid ground, insofar as the radical changes having resulted from the collapse of the Soviet Bloc have brought to light how little effect the Marxist-Leninist doctrines and their educational components have had on the minds of the majority of adolescents in terms of those young persons' political and ideological commitment. However, the question of how and to what extent this picture must be modified by inquiries into the deeper dimensions of people's behaviors and attitudes is more intricate; as first evidence shows, the question cannot be dismissed by reference to the merely visible level of utterances and activities. Needless to add that in any case the prerequisites underlying the "start" or "return" to democracy must be clarified in comparative analyses. Furthermore, the sectional initiatives in the 1980s toward relativizing, or even undermining, the stability of the communist power structures with regard to ideological orthodoxy and political uniformity must be paid appropriate attention, in particular in the cases of Poland and Hungary in that period.

Allow me to materialize these theoretical reflections by quoting from my own report on my pedagogic journey to Poland in the spring of 1983. The following comment was written down immediately after the end of this journey (Mitter and Muszynski 1997):

> In details, the people's attitudes seem to indicate a broad range: acceptance of understanding, linked with the readiness of collaboration [with the régime] for the sake of one's own existence and the country's future; collaboration with reservations mirroring tokens of uncertainty, but also arrangement in the everyday life; skeptic utterances to be heard above all from young people bearing witness of verbal resistance at least; finally; the cross of flowers in front of Saint Anne's Church in Warsaw with slips of papers attached, filled with words of sympathy and accusation signalizing protest against the death of the young student who had been arrested by the militia shortly before. Below this whole surface there is the level which cannot be easily ascertained, when, for instance, teachers and principals speak of 'political troubles' in their schools. The situation in the schools seems to be frequently characterized by a striking solidarity between teachers and pupils which . . . becomes evident when pupils are protected from formal punishment (e.g. exclusion from the school). Besides, I was told of cases, in which pupils were depriving an (for political reasons) unpopular teacher of doing his job by permanent silence, like the visitors of a play in a Warsaw theater who prevented a "collaborating" actor from getting a hearing and from acting by permanent knocking. (6)

Of course, this question must be completed by the explanation that these observations were made in Poland as, like Hungary, the communist country with a comparatively tolerant education system in the aftermath of the first *Solidarnosc* action of 1980–1981. I am sure that I could not have made such observations in the Soviet Union or in the German Democratic Republic.

Present-Day Trends

The start (or revival) of education for democratic citizenship in the present situation must be seen as a remarkable component amid multifarious approaches to innovations and reforms in the education systems of the Central and Eastern European countries. In the course of the past ten years there has been a development that indicates consolidation as regards the legal provisions at various levels. In particular, mention has to be made of the educational acts that have been passed by the parliaments of all the countries concerned. Furthermore, efforts have been made in introducing new curricula; among these attempts the publication of the "National Core Curriculum" in Hungary deserves particular attention. Of course, this process must be divided into national and subregional processes that mirror the diversity of transformation in Central and Eastern Europe, viewed as a whole. Rooted in the historical particularities that have been tackled already, it comes forth in the current policies with their changing parliamentary majorities and governments; there is not one government, let alone one minister of education, that has held its office for a whole decade since the upheavals of 1989 and 1990. On the other hand this diversity reflects the scope of the transformational changes that have seized the political, social, and economic frameworks related to the education systems.

Despite the provisional progress in consolidation of the education systems, uncertainty is still a significant criterion at present, which has been, as even concerns the most progressive education systems of Hungary, Poland, and the Czech Republic, affirmed by the recent reviews undertaken by the OECD. Taking this open situation into special consideration, we must refrain from offering any definite analysis. By constantly observing the scene, however, we feel encouraged to draft some contours that intimate a few trends, whereby our attention concentrates on their relevance to the building of a culture of education for democratic citizenship. In this limited view the following list of items should be understood only as a selective approach. It does not only allow revisions and extensions, but even postulates them instead.

1. The innovative approaches have been focused on the removal of all indoctrinating pressures to which the socialist education systems were subjected by means of political power and ideological totalitarianism. It goes without saying that the opening toward democratic and pluralistic self-awareness of education is highly dependent on the aforementioned degree of political democratization. The state of the change has become, for example, manifest in the closing down of university institutes and chairs that were devoted to one-sided investigation and transmission of Marxist-Leninist ideology (or, when this was thought to be possible, in their transformation into institutes of

sociological research, etc.), in the elimination of formerly ideologically structured civics and in the purification of curricula and syllabi in general and of susceptible subjects in particular, such as history and national literature. Thus, teachers have had to tackle emergency situations in their everyday practice; in some countries this process has not come yet to an end at all. In all the countries it started with canceling certain syllabi and with withdrawing, or at least selecting, application of hitherto valid textbooks. The latter procedure still prevails in a good number of cases because of the difficulties of having new textbooks available, let alone obstacles in the material production sphere. In many schools old textbooks are still used, with "offensive" papers or passages eliminated. In their turn, all these troubles have affected the introduction of new regulations with special regard to examinations (in particular secondary school leaving examinations and graduations in higher education).

2. The attainment of intellectual freedom and plurality is closely connected with a new way of handling the steering mechanism of the education system and therefore with the role of the state in the educational policy. It should not raise any astonishment that the removal of such pressures exercised on students, teachers, and parents by bureaucracies that were ideologically disciplined and hierarchically structured has entailed particular weight with regard to calls for autonomy. The recent innovative steps, taken by legal and administrative provisions, have demonstrated various ways of new concepts of self-government that can and should be implemented in educational policy and, moreover, in the classroom with regard to content and scope. Generally speaking, such innovations are often distinguished from similar approaches in Western Europe by the radicality of the models and propositions that can be discerned as a widespread criterion in transformation processes.

The most significant example is presented by the development in Hungary. In 1985 the Hungarian parliament, still under the control of the socialist United Labor Party, enacted an Education Act that included features of reform. In particular, it confirmed first steps toward decentralizing the network of responsibilities in the education system that had been initiated already in the late 1970s; on the other hand, the Act stressed the need for granting internal autonomy to individual schools, as well as to teachers and students. The sociopolitical changes in 1989 seemed to lay foundations for promoting this process, now in the framework of democratic policies. However, the trends toward autonomy—with regard to local self-government as well as managerial and curricular self-regulation within the individual schools—has not been linear since then, due to two substantial changes in the composition of the governmental coalitions. As concerns the entire region, one can observe a certain, though diversified, departure from far-reaching autonomy designs, as preferred in the period of euphoria immediately following the collapse of the communist regimes, such as the election of principals (as practiced, for instance, in the Russian Federation) and 50 percent proportions of students in decision-making processes at universities and other higher education offices (e.g., in the former Czechoslovakia). The recent changes, therefore, signal disillusions with unfulfilled expectations and, moreover, call attention to arguments saying that school autonomy and local self-government have to be in congruence with the responsibility of the state in matters of nationwide requirements and needs. In regard to recent developments in Eastern Europe, it seems indeed that this issue had been often neglected in debates, legislative initiatives, and pilot projects.

3. The third issue deals with innovations in the curricula, within the given thematic framework, having already resulted in various pilot projects. They are first of all characterized by the reduction of the former overload of the syllabi and the revision of instruction methods that are focused on replacing the conventional forms of receptive learning and authoritarian teaching with open forms based on dialogue and communication—and that in close linkage to the principle of education for democratic citizenship. Considering that reforms aimed at open forms of teaching and learning have to overcome traditional attitudes and expectations among teachers and administrators as well as among parents everywhere in the world, it goes without saying that attempts at generalizing experiences of pilot projects necessarily collide with resistance in the current period of the post-communist education systems.

4. All the basic trends outlined in this chapter are based on the idea of maintaining the state monopoly concerning responsibility for the education system. On the other hand, the development, though only in view of quantitative proportions at the margins of the reform spectrum until now, reveals efforts aimed at the establishment of private schools. We can observe a wide range of such alternative innovations. First, they concern the restitution or establishment of schools run by the big religious communities. In Poland and Hungary this sector has never disappeared from the scene in spite of extensive restrictions, while in the rest of Central and Eastern Europe entirely new initiatives have become known in this field. Second, the recent development in the whole region, including the Russian Federation and other republics of the Commonwealth of Independent States (CIS), give evidence of the emergence of "private" initiatives (in the

narrower sense), either aimed at the restitution of traditional school types or aimed at the reemergence of ideas that are commonly labeled as "progressive education" or "reform movement in education" *(Reformpaedogogik)*. For the time being, it has to remain open whether this attractiveness of private education offers is only a symptom of radical response to the former rigid state monopoly, and therefore perhaps a fashion, or if this trend will continue, thus following the increased interest such schools have also gained in Western countries. In any case, it seems that the private sector is likely to occupy an alternative place beside the state or public sector. Higher education has been especially affected by this trend, as the establishment of a good number of private universities indicates.

5.   The collapse of the Soviet bloc has entailed the revival, or, in some cases such as Moldavia, the emergence of nationalism and ethnocentrism all over Eastern Europe, exercising great influence on organizational structures of the education systems and on curricula. This trend has become manifest from the level of legal and administrative provisions down to the grassroots of individual schools and classrooms. This issue is too complex to be more than outlined in this present context (Mitter 1997, 1998). Among the curricular foci concerning the curriculum on the whole, mother tongue and multilingual education are worthy of being given particular weight, since they have (re)gained highest relevance within the educational policies. Needless to add that education for democratic citizenship has turned out to be another essential field mirroring the new trend. Solutions are in most places complicated by the fact that ethnic and linguistic demarcations rarely coincide with national (or regional) boundaries. Education for democratic citizenship, therefore, is necessarily involved in conflicts of expectations, goals, and contents, wherever the norms and value systems of the state and the nondominant group(s) collide. This texture of conflicts has an immediate impact on the grassroots level of the school system, insofar as it affects attitudes of students and teachers as well. The relevance of this problem also concerns the political cohesion of the state which presupposes the loyalty of all its citizens, including those whose "ethnocultural" loyalty is not congruent with that of the "dominant" group.

6.   Teachers have to cope with overcoming their own communist past in their day-to-day professional practice. They must adjust to the demands of the new democratic education system. This is an urgent task, the more so as they have to teach and educate an increasing number of students who have no immediate remembrance of the communist past at all. Success or failure of such adjustment is dependent on the socioeconomic circumstances as well as the quality of

initial and in-service training. It seems, however, that in most countries the involvement of teachers appears to be the weakest link in the chain of measures to transfer reform programs and political declarations to legal provisions and, moreover, to the day-to-day practice. The current crisis characterizing the situation of the teaching profession and teacher education is, furthermore, reinforced by two special components. On the one hand, providing trainees and acting teachers with those qualities needed in Central and Eastern Europe nowadays necessitates the demand for respectively qualified teacher trainees to be available in universities, colleges of education, and other training institutions. At this stage, however, the mental confusions in which teachers are involved appear again. On the other hand, teaching in Central and Eastern Europe is predominantly a task for women. Their everyday overload resulting from the troubles to link professional and private responsibilities under poor economic conditions, has not ended with the collapse of the communist regimes; on the contrary, it has rather been increased by the challenges of the new ways of life under the conditions of the market. This, of course, weakens motivations for innovative commitment. Moreover, mostly women suffer from dismissal measures.

Education for Democratic Citizenship in the Curriculum: The Hungarian Case

Education for democratic citizenship must be identified as a complex task to be implemented in this four-tier context:

- as a clearly defined school subject appearing within the curriculum under various names, such as social studies, civics, community instruction, etc.;
- a pluridisciplinary principle of instruction pervading the whole curriculum, though focused on an inner circle with civics, history, and geography in the core, extended by national literature as well as foreign languages and literatures;
- a pedagogic principle including curricular and socializational requirements and activities on the one hand, as well as cognitive and affective qualities on the other; and
- a pedagogic principle to be implemented in teaching and learning processes inside and outside the formal school system, consequently as a principle of lifelong learning.

As far as schools are concerned, the aforementioned Hungarian National Core Curriculum (issued in 1995), comprising the compulsory grades one to ten, is presented as a noteworthy example, since it signals the complexity of the task as a whole in the clearest and most elaborate way, compared with concurrent initiatives in the region. This "basic document in public education" (Setenyi 1996, 15) has not been conceived as "a curriculum in the traditional sense, but a basis for local curricula and teaching subjects" (15), in this case "history and social studies, economics and civics" (including geography) within the "cultural domain," called man and nature. The objectives of the individual subjects are interlinked under the umbrella of "common (cross-curricular) educational objectives of the cultural domains" (20). Education for democratic citizenship appears under the headings of homeland and integration into Europe and the world. To underscore the exemplary rank of the Hungarian document, the two relevant paragraphs are quoted.

> Homeland. Every student should become acquainted with characteristics of our national heritage and the traditional values in our nation's culture. They should learn about the work and achievements of great Hungarian politicians, scientists, inventors, artists, writers, poets, and sportsmen. They should be well-informed about our country's geography, literature, history, and everyday life. Students should become adept at individual and social activities and knowledge, resulting in understanding and respect for their homes, local communities, their country and its peoples. They should know the traditions and features of urban and rural life. Furthermore, students should be open to know and appreciate values and achievements of other nations and ethnic groups within Hungary and in our neighboring countries. Studying Homeland assists students in living in harmony with their natural and social environment as well. These studies provide a foundation of national consciousness, and deepen patriotism. In addition, they induce students to discover the historical, cultural, and religious heritage of their local and broader environment. Finally, such studies encourage students to engage in individual and social activities and at preserving and developing their heritage.
>
> Integration into Europe and the World. Students should adopt a positive approach towards the common European values. They should respect the achievements of European development, including Hungary's role and contribution. Students should be interested in European culture, habits, lifestyles and traditions, especially in those of our neighboring countries and peoples. They should realize the importance of strengthening European unity, the potential contradictions involved, and the role these aspirations play in Hungary and its people's lives. Students should know the most important and influential achievements of universal human culture. They should be open and understanding towards different habits, life-styles, cultures, and religions and show respect for them. They should be well-informed about global problems, especially those directly affecting Hungary; know about international cooperation aimed at tackling such problems. They should be interested in understanding the complexity of these problems and in finding solutions to them. Schools and their students

shall strive to participate directly in the development of international cooperation. (20–21)

The National Core Curriculum has been in effect only since the 1998/1998 school year. This is why there is not yet any information available on implementation and its outcomes. Considering its decentralized structure of decision making and its orientation toward cross-curricular objectives, the National Core Curriculum can be appraised as an ambitious project, with education for democratic citizenship included as an important component. Special attention should be paid to the authors' endeavor to integrate national and cross-national (European and global) concerns.

CONCLUSION

Present-day developments in the education systems of the former communist countries with all their approaches to reforms and innovations, do not yet allow any definite predictions. At this moment the whole region is still involved in transitional processes, whereby education must be seen in close relation to the comprehensive socioeconomic, cultural, and political transformation process in its transnational dimension. Remembering the enormous troubles on the economic scene, one can conclude that the march into the future is far from being consolidated at all. The internal attitudinal problems in all East European countries aggravate the crisis probably even more than the economic and financial austerity as such. In this context one has to consider two significant obstacles. On the one hand the prevalence of a "perverted" market ideology that is void of the liberal code of values primarily associated with Adam Smith and John Stuart Mill comes by its evil effects through Mafiatype attitudes and actions. On the other hand the majority of countries have to cope with multinationality issues resulting from their precommunist inheritance and, in the successor states of the former Soviet Union, from the enforced migration policies, and having been revived by the postcommunist wave of nationalism and ethnocentrism. The dissolution of the Soviet Union and the warlike collapse of the former Yugoslavia have proved to be reinforcing factors in both problem areas.

Moreover, the general societal crisis is aggravated by the combined effects of transformation and globalization. It is true that adjustment in Western countries to the challenges of globalization is demanding enough to overcome, in spite of their developed industrialized and market structures. However, in the countries of Central and Eastern Europe this challenge must be met under the force to reshape the societal systems with *all* their subsystems. On the other hand, it should be noted that the necessity to cope with the complexity of the adjustment has set in motion surprisingly remarkable initiative and creativity in the economic as well as the educational subsystems, especially among members of the "unencumbered" younger generation.

Education is directly involved in the totality of the problem of how people as individuals and citizens experience such radical transformation in the framework of globalization. In this context, Václav Havel, the current president of the Czech Republic and leader of the velvet revolution in his country, states:

> The return of freedom into a society, in which all moral standards were entirely dissolved, has led to the explosion of all kinds of evil human attitudes. Although it seems that this was inevitable and therefore to be expected, the extent is, in a disproportional way, greater than any one among us could have imagined before. It seems that the various problematic or at least ambiguous human inclinations, inconspicuously cherished in the society over years and, at the same time, inconspicuously included in the services of the day-to-day course of a totalitarian system, have been suddenly liberated from this strait-jacket and thereby reached their full display in the end. The definite order—if one can define it as such—given them by the authoritarian regime (which thereby legalized it), has collapsed, but a new order which defines these attitudes, instead of utilizing them, namely an order of freely accepted responsibility to the whole and for the whole, has not emerged yet and cannot have done so, because such a responsibility grows in the course of many years and must be cultivated. (125–126)

This message was written in 1992; in 1999 it did not seem at all that it should have lost its significance. On the contrary, some totalitarian attitudes have come to the foreground again after the end of "euphoria." While the communist ideology postulated the "new man," which has turned out to be a utopian claim from the beginning, the postcommunist democracies are confronted with challenges that can be called comparatively modest, as they appeal to ordinary people in their never-ending imperfectibility, yet, at the same time they are pretentious, insofar as they include the claim to educate people to an ameliorative, though imperfect world. It is true that within this framework of uncertainty, differences among the individual states and communities are obvious, as has been outlined. The challenge per se, however, can be related to the whole of the postcommunist region.

Schools have to overcome enormous internal difficulties, let alone the troubles caused by the overall societal crisis. They must cope with structural stagnation and with curricular contents that have become obsolete. Among the overall structural and curricular issues, democratization and autonomy can be identified as basic concerns indeed. However, case studies that have been published in recent years have given evidence of admirable efforts among school reformers, in particular at the "grassroots" of "pedagogic islands," such as in schools with creative teachers and pupils in their centers (Mitter and Muszynski 1997, 105–108). Of course, illusory expectations must give weight to realistic appraisals indicating that many problems can only be solved by continuous efforts. Therefore, warnings against hasty and unreflected borrowing of Western examples have gained great relevance. They concern the overestimation of certain structural and curricular achievements of Western education systems. Frequently the Eastern counterparts do not take special regard of the conditions under which those examples have been developed. In particular, such search for borrowing neglects the long and hard experiences *before* such achievements have been reached—and, moreover, the fact that they are often far from being consolidated in the West, too. As regards the relationship between the education system and the labor market, the communist experiences, though based upon the principle of merging training, research, and production, are unlikely to be helpful for developing future-oriented models in a market-driven and civil society–based democracy. Such models must follow the idea of free partnership between educational institutions, in particular at the vocational and higher levels, and firms, wherein transitional solutions are inevitable, although to be reviewed against the background of short-term free market euphoria.

Whether education for democratic citizenship is able to take its expected and necessary role in the desired societal progress of the Central and Eastern European states will depend on how and to what extent a balance between initiatives, continuous efforts, and realistic expectations will be gained and maintained. At this point the scene must be opened again to the global dimension concerning the interrelation between democracy and education in the framework of the comprehensive transformation processes. In this sense I hope to have given some food for discussing comparable problems in other transformational regions of the world. Expressing this hope I am fully aware that comparability is not congruent at all with identity.

The challenge is on the agenda, but so are the troubles concerning its transfer to educational theory and educational politics as well as to the everyday school practice. The existing problem can be summarized by referring to the following considerations expressed by Fodor Gabor, the former Hungarian minister of education (in November 1995). They are directly related to the issues of school autonomy, but can be legitimately extended to education for democratic citizenship in general: "I know perfectly well that not the entire teaching community, and not every local government education committee can meet these expectations and challenges. There are people who have grown tired of everyday battles, given up their ambitions and broken into the daily routine, or who simply cannot shape up to the tasks assigned to them. But I trust that improving the system of extension training and with consistent effort we shall be able to strengthen the progressive processes and to make our schools provide their students convertible knowledge that will enable them to match steps with the more advanced part of Europe" (Szabó 1995, 40).

REFERENCES

Beck, Ulrich. (1997). *Was ist Globalisierung? Irrtümer des Globalismus—Antworten auf Globalisierung* [What is globalization? Errors of globalism—Answers to globalization]. Frankfurt am Main: Suhrkamp.

Dahrendorf, Ralph. (1990). "Transitions. Politics, economics and liberty." *Washington Quarterly*, 13 (3): 133–142.

Delors, Jacques. (1996). Learning: The treasure within. Report to UNESCO of the International Commission on Education for the Twentieth-first Century. Paris: United Nations Educational, Scientific, and Cultural Organization.

Dewey, John. (1976). *The middle works 1899–1924, vol. 1 (1899–1901)*. Carbondale: Southern Illinois University Press.

Dewey, John. (1980). *The middle works 1899–1924, vol. 9 (1916)*. Carbondale: Southern Illinois University Press.

Education at a glance: OECD indicators/analysis. (1996). Paris: Organization for Economic Cooperation and Development.

Epstein, Erwin H. (1997). "Filtering democracy through schools: The ignored paradox of compulsory education." In Christoph Kodron, Botho von Kopp, Uwe Lauterbach, Ulrich Schäfer, and Gerlind Schmidt (eds.). *Comparative education: Challenges—Intermediation—Practice: Essays in honour of Wolfgang Mitter on his 70th birthday*, 32–45. Cologne: Weimar/Wien.

Glenn, Charles L. (1995). *Educational freedom in Eastern Europe*. Washington, DC: Cato Institute.

Green, A. (1997). *Education, globalization and the nation-state*. London: Macmillan Press.

Havel, Vaclav. (1992). *Sommermeditationen* [Summer meditations]. Berlin: Rowohlt. Originally published as: *Letni premitani*, Prague: Odeon, (1991).

Huntington, Samuel P. (1984). "Will more countries become democratic?" *Political Science Quarterly* 99, (2): 193–218.

McGinn, Noel S. (1997). "The impact of globalization on national education systems." *Prospects* 27(1):41–54.

Mill, John Stuart. ([1859] 1977). "On liberty." In *On liberty: Essays on politics and society*, ed. John M. Robson (Collected Works of John Stuart Mill, 18) 213–310. Toronto: University of Toronto Press.

Mitter, Wolfgang. (1990). "German schools in Czechoslovakia 1918–1938." In Janusz Tomiak et al. (eds.), *Schooling, educational policy and ethnic minority*, 211–233. New York: New York University Press.

Mitter, Wolfgang. (1992). "Education in Eastern Europe and the former Soviet Union in a period of revolutionary change: An approach to comparative analysis." In David Phillips and Michael Kaser (eds.), *Education and economic change in Eastern Europe and the former Soviet Union*, 15–28. Wallingford: Triangle Books.

Mitter, Wolfgang. (1996). "State and market in education: Opponents, competitors, partners? A historical and comparative approach." In Chinese Comparative Education Society Taipei (ed.), *Educational reform from tradition to postmodernity*. Taipei: Shi Ta Publishers.

Mitter, Wolfgang. (1997). "Divergent and convergent trends in multicultural education in Russia and its neighbouring countries." In Keith Watson, Celia Modgil, and Sohan Modgil, (eds.), *Educational dilemmas: debate and diversity,* vol. 3, 221–228. London: Cassell.

Mitter, Wolfgang. (1998). "Changes in the relations between centres and peripheries: Consequences of the collapse of the Soviet Union." In Andreas Kazamias, and Martin G. Spillane (eds.), *Education and the structuring of the European space,* 251–268. Athens: Siros Editions.

Mitter, Wolfgang, and Heliodor Muszynski. (1997). *Pädagogische Reisen in Polen 1989–1995* [Pedagogic Journeys in Poland 1989–1995]. Cologne: Böhlau.

Offe, Claus. (1991). "Das Dilemma der Gleichzeitigkeit. Demokratisierung und Marktwirtschaft in Osteuropa" [The dilemma of simultaneousness: Democratization and market economy in Eastern Europe]. *Merkur* 4:279–292.

Osterwalder, Fritz. (1993). "Schule und Unterricht im ordnungspolitischen Konzept der klassischen und neo-klassischen Ökonomik" [School and instruction in the political concept of the classical and neo-classical economic theory]. *Zeitschrift für Pädagogik* 39(1): 85–108.

Palma, Giuseppe di. (1991). "Legitimation from the top to civil society." *World Politics* 44(1): 49–80.

Ramirez, F. (1997). "The nation-state, citizenship and educational change: Institutionalization and globalization." In W. K. Cummings and N. F. McGinn (eds.), *Handbook of modern education and its alternatives.* Oxford, UK: Elsevier Science.

Robertson, Roland. (1992). *Globalization: Social theory and global culture.* London: Sage.

Sandschneider, Eberhard. (1995) *Stabilität und Transformation politischer Systeme. Stand und Perspektiven politikwissenschaftlicher Transformationsforschung* [Stability and transformation of political systems. State and perspectives of transformation research in political science]. Opladen: Leske and Budrich.

Schriewer, Jürgen. (ed.). (1999). *Comparative perspectives on the role of education in democratization. Part 1. Transitional states and states of transition. Part 2. Socialization, identity, and politics of control.* Frankfurt am Main: Peter Lang.

Schröder, H. H. (1995). "Die richtungslose Transformation. Zum politischen und gesellschaftlichen Wandel in Rußland" [Transformation without direction: Concerning political and societal change in Russia]. *Blätter für deutsche und internationale Politik* 8:936–945.

Setenyi, Janos. (ed.). (1996). *National core curriculum.* Budapest: Ministry of Culture and Education.

Spring, J. (1998.) *Education and the rise of the global economy.* Hillsdale NJ: Lawrence Erlbaum Associates.

Szabó, Mária. (ed.). (1995). *Conference book: Local autonomy and shared responsibility in managing schools, 6–12 November 1995.* Budapest: Hungarian Educational Managers' Association.

Walzer, Michael. (1991). "The idea of civil society." *Dissent* 38:290–303.

Young, Oran. (1986). "Regime dynamics: The rise and fall of international regimes." *International organization* 36(2):277–297.

DISCUSSION QUESTIONS

1. How does national diversity in curriculum contribute to democratic citizenship? How does diversity limit democracy, and what is the impact in societies undergoing transformation?
2. How does teacher autonomy contribute to or limit democratic participation by all partners in the educational process?
3. What pressures are increased as a result of globalization and localization for democracies in radical transformation?
4. Has the increased number of so-called democratic states in the world during the twentieth century led to the demise of authoritarian or totalitarian forms of government of a more long-term nature? What is the evidence?
5. What are the current demands on and challenges for teachers in Central and Eastern Europe?

PART III

Educating Democratic Citizens
The Challenge for Civic Education

CHAPTER 9

Democracy, Worker-Consumer-Citizens, and Teacher Education
Theoretical Musings with Findings from Research in Mexico

MARK B. GINSBURG

> *Politics is a kind of profession, a profession engaged in by*
> *citizens. . . . [S]ome . . . may be poorly prepared . . . but*
> *this doesn't mean that nothing higher is practicable.*
> —WHEELER 1971, 10–11

Few would deny that education, including teacher education, is part of the problem—and part of the solution—of poorly prepared citizens. The significance of this problem is especially felt in democracies. This partly helps to explain why Elshtain (1994) and Lasch (1994) express serious concerns about the vitality of institutions in societies characterized as democracies, at the same historical moment that there are reports of "universal enthusiasm for democracy" (Giddens 1994) and a "global resurgence of democracy" (Diamond and Plattner 1993). However, these different appraisals also reflect different meanings of the term *democracy*, as well as different conceptions of the implied role for citizens within democratic political economies. In this chapter I first discuss different ways of conceptualizing democracy (and citizenship, a related concept), and then illustrate some of the issues based on data gathered from students in a preservice teacher education program in Mexico.

CONCEPTUALIZING DEMOCRACY AND CITIZENSHIP

Many contemporary (and historical) treatments of democracy focus on *procedural* entitlements of citizens, that is, the right to vote or to otherwise directly or indirectly determine government decisions. For many, this is the sine qua non of democracy: there is no democracy without fair elections and open channels of communication between citizens and government officials. However, some analysts highlight a substantive notion of democracy (focusing on the distribution of material and symbolic resources), either substituting it for or combing it with a procedural notion of democracy (Copp, Hamilton, and Roemer 1993). For example, Highland (1995) states that democracy exists to the extent that "all those who are subject to the decisions have equal effective rights in the determination of decisions to which they are subject" (67); he clarifies that having equal effective rights necessitates "both procedural entitlements to participate in a decision-making process *and* adequate access to a wide range of resources [e.g., shelter, food, healthcare, education, money] that would enable a person to utilize her or his procedural entitlements" (2).

Paralleling the emphasis on the procedural aspect in discourses on democracy is the focus on individuals functioning in relation to the political system in the literature on citizenship. For example, Ramirez and Rubinson (1979, 79) note that "citizenship is that social status which confers membership in the state" (see also Green 1997). However, building on Marshall's (1964) notion of citizenship having a "social" element—"the rights to a modicum of economic welfare and security, to share in the full social heritage and to live the life of a civilized being according to the standards prevailing in the society" (72)—we might conceptualize citizenship as pertaining to individuals' and groups' relation to the economy (i.e., their roles as workers and consumers) as well as their relation to the polity (see also Barbalet 1988; Compton 1993; Turner 1993).[1] More appropriately, we may consider citizenship in relation to the political economy—the union of what often are treated as separate systems: political and economic (Clarke 1996). Indeed, Polyani (1944) observes that it was only with the emergence of laissez-faire liberalism in the latter half of the nineteenth century, particularly in the United States, when the idea took hold that market relations should be free from steering mechanisms of the state, that "the institutional separation of society into an economic and political sphere" became part of the dominant ideology (71).

WORKER-CONSUMER-CITIZENS[2]

Work entails "the creation of material goods and services, which may be directly consumed by the worker or sold to someone else" and "includes not only paid labor but self-employed labor and unpaid labor, including that of homemakers" (Hodson and Sullivan 1995, 3). *Workers* create these goods and services through their physical/manual, mental, or emotional labor (Hochschild 1983; Willis 1997). They labor not only in relation to direct and indirect consumers, but also to other workers, who are vested with varying degrees of power and status, as well as (in the case of paid employment) to employers, to whom they sell their labor. This clarifies that the social relationships of work have a political as well as a technical dimension to them (Ginsburg 1995b): "the employment relationship involves the exercise of power" (Bowles and Gintis 1993, 375) and "social relations of production . . . can be cooperative and egalitarian . . . or hierarchical and unequal" (Hodson and Sullivan 1995, 4).

Citizens have an important relationship with the economy beyond that constituted by the work they do within public and private spheres. This is their role as *consumers,* which Sarup (1996) suggests has become a "mode of being," a way of gaining identity, meaning, and prestige (see also Hall 1988). As Gilbert (1997) explains, "postmodern lifestyles are seen increasingly to focus on consumption as people's most direct and conspicuous connection with the economy" (68–69). Drawing on the ideas of Miller (1995), Gilbert suggests that consumerism is "the vanguard of history" (69), in which the rhetoric of consumer choice can be a progressive force if people are empowered to use it to arbitrate the moralities of institutions that provide goods and services." That is, consumers—at least when they operate collectively—can have a conservative or transformative influence not only the nature of products available for consumption, but also the conditions under which such goods and services are produced and distributed. For instance, imagine consumption decisions being based not only on utility—physically and socially—(Barber 1995; Fine 1995), price, and aesthetics, but also on whether the workers and the environment are seen to be enhanced (versus exploited) in the production and distribution processes.

GLOBALIZATION, MULTICULTURALIZATION, AND THE WITHERING OF THE STATE[3]

Such a broad conception of citizenship, attending to people's relationships to the national economy as workers and consumers as well as their relationships to the national political system or nation-state, may still be limited given two dynamics that have reduced the importance of the nation-state and national level analyses. The first dynamic *globalization,* which has two components: "economic globalization" and the "growth of supra-national and regional political organizations" (Green 1997, 9; see also Gunsteren 1998; Habermas 1995; Orzack 1992; and Ward 1990).[4] With respect to the first component, Gilbert (1997) concludes that "globalization, deregulation, privatization, and post-Fordist production [and disorganized capitalism][5] interfere with the contractual relations of state and corporation which have underpinned the economic significance of the state" (66). In terms of the increasing import of international political organizations, Gilbert notes that the "legitimacy of national governments is put in question when their decisions can be challenged in international forums, and their authority over their citizens is similarly weakened" (71) (see also Crook, Pakulski, and Waters 1992).[6] We should note, moreover, that some of the international political organizations (International Monetary Fund, World Bank, the World Trade Organization, the European Union, and the North American Free Trade Agreement [NAFTA]) are explicitly focused on efforts to steer the global economy.

Even as the political economic globalization undermines the potency of the nation-state and, potentially, its primary focus for citizen activity (Clarke 1996; Heater 1990), a different dynamic, *multiculturalization,* is having a similar effect on the state and its relationship to its citizens. As Turner (1993) explains, our conception of "citizenship will have to develop to embrace both globalization of social relations and the increasing social differentiation of social systems. The future of citizenship must therefore be extracted from its location in the nation-state" (15) (see also Green 1997). By multicultural-ization I mean the process of enhancing the racial and ethnic diversity of members of nation-states through both the new immigration of "culturally different" peoples to a given society, and through the rebirth or intensification of "different" racial/ethnic identities of groups involved in previous waves of immigration or groups based in contiguous territories that had been gathered together under a nation-state (Gilbert 1997; Habermas 1995).

Thus, our conception of worker-consumer-citizens must take into con-sideration not only racial/ethnic groups but also social classes (Hodson and Sullivan 1995; Marshall 1964) and gender groups (Crompton 1993; Reskin and Padavic 1994). These groups not only function as collective actors within local, national, and global political economies, but they also serve as impor-tant sources of identity for individuals (Gunsteren 1998). Moreover, by attending to cultural (and structural) differences among groups, while not ignoring similarities, we can hopefully avoid the problem that

> the ideal of the public realm of citizenship as expressing a [universalistic]
> general will, a point of view and interest that citizens have in common and
> that transcends their differences . . . imposes a homogeneity that suppresses
> group differences . . . and in practice forces the formerly excluded groups to
> be measured according to norms derived from and defined by the privileged
> groups. (Young 1995, 178–81)

As Pateman argues with respect to gender groups: "Democratic theorists have not yet confronted the implications of the patriarchal construction of citizen-ship . . . It is taken for granted that for women to be active, full citizens they must become like men . . . although women have demanded for two centuries that their distinctive qualities and tasks should become part of citizenship" (Foster 1997, 55). The point is that there are likely to be identity and praxis differences among worker-consumer-citizens that result from culturally shaped differences in the extent and nature of physical, mental, and emotional labor (in the private and public spheres), consumer behavior, and other politi-cal activity. At the same time we should remember that individuals are mem-bers of many groups and thus "individuals—the substrata of citizens—have become bouquets. They compose their own mixed identities out of the vari-ous connections and bonds" (Gunsteren 1998, 22).

EDUCATING WORKER-CONSUMER-CITIZENS

Education plays a key role in the development of the world views, values, knowledge, skills, attitudes, and identities of worker-consumer-citizens. The literature on education's role has tended to focus separately on citizenship, worker, and consumer education. With respect to the first category, Heater (1990), for example, argues that "education for citizenship is not an optional extra, but an integral part of the concept" (319) (see also Albala-Bertrand 1996; Laski 1937). And Bendix (1964) observes that "education [is] the only 'right' of citizenship that was actually a duty" (Ramirez and Rubinson 1979, 79). Similarly, Green (1997), drawing on Hobsbawm (1977), comments that schooling was "'the most powerful weapon for forming . . . nations.' . . . National education helped to construct the very subjectivities of citizenship, justifying the ways of the state to the people and the duties of the people to the state" (14).

Citizenship education was initially a primary purpose of government or public schooling, in that the origins of state systems of education tended to coincide with the creation of nation-states in the nineteenth century in Europe and North America and in the postcolonial period of the twentieth century in Africa, Asia, and Latin America (Ramirez and Rubinson 1979). However, in many societies, the emphasis in educational goals has changed, moving from a primary focus on creating citizens to a concern with developing workers (Sehr 1997) and consumers (Gilbert 1997). As Spring (1980) observes,

> nineteenth-century goals for developing systems of modern schooling . . . which included the development of patriotism, nationalism, and good citizenship, have not disappeared from the educational system [of the late twentieth century] but they have become secondary in importance to the economic goals of schooling. (ix)

In conceptualizing how workers are "produced" in education, of course, we note that the "concept of human capital has been important in supporting arguments for increased investment in education in the welfare state. . . . The idea of human capital considers human being as objects to be improved, like machinery, for the more efficient operation of the industrial system" (48).

Extrapolating from Gilbert's discussion of "citizens" (1997), I suggest that any consideration of education of worker-consumer-citizens "needs to acknowledge the role of consumption . . . whereby people find pleasure, identity, and forms of expression as well as utility" (69).[7] Through messages transmitted via the formal and hidden curriculum of schooling and teacher education (as well as via mass media), young people are not only exposed to various products and services that they can—or need—to buy, but they are also socialized about the normalcy of individualist versus collectivist and passive versus active strategies of consumer behavior. For example, one powerful message transmitted through the hidden curriculum, at least in the contemporary era, is that education, itself, is "a matter of [private,] individualized consumption in a market of differentiated educational products. . . . Education as a public, collective and social process disappears" (Green 1997, 8).

EDUCATING FOR ACTIVE/PASSIVE AND INDIVIDUALIST/COLLECTIVIST STRATEGIES

We should keep in mind that the process of constructing worker-consumer-citizens in education involves empowerment as well as the social control of individuals and groups (Bowles and Gintis 1975; Spring 1980), with the latter function being accomplished, at least in part, "through its role as the primary mechanism legitimating the economic and political allocation of individuals • in society" (Ramirez and Rubinson 1979, 79–80). Thus, in analyzing how worker-consumer-citizens develop, we need to consider whether they are becoming oriented to change or to conserving existing social arrangements, as well as whether they are being prepared to function—*individually* or *collectively*—as active or passive worker-consumer-citizens (Spring 1980; Heater 1990).

The contrasting conceptions of *active* or *passive* citizens is derived, at least in part, from what have been termed, respectively, "public" and "privatized" notions of democracy (Turner 1993). The ideas behind *public democracy*, which implies active citizen involvement, come from Jean Jacques Rousseau, while privatized democracy and the passive view of citizenship come from John Locke.[8] In the "public" notion of democracy, according to Sehr (1997, 34), the common people are "the only ones who could guarantee that the government would not be corrupted,"[9] and thus their active involvement in governing was essential. Otherwise, the political system would be corrupted by those who would seek only to preserve their own privileged positions (Heater 1990). For Rousseau ([1762] 1985), it was people's "avid thirst for profits" (140), that is, their "tendency to pursue private interests at the expense of their participation in public affairs . . . [that constituted] a serious threat to the well-being of democratic government" (Sehr, 40). In contrast, *privatized democracy,* which implies passive forms of citizenship and was based on writings of John Locke (1963), is grounded on the belief "that people come together in political society for protection against constant exposure 'to the invasion of others.' In this way, people effect the 'mutual preservation of their lives, liberties, and estates,' all of which Locke referred to by the general name, 'property'" (Sehr 1997, 32).[10] And as Sehr continues, "these ideas . . . encourage 'antipathy toward direct democracy' . . . [in part because of] fears about the people's ability to govern itself, without threatening established property relations" (32).[11]

The references to property relations—as part of the rationale for active and passive forms of citizenship—remind us of the shortcomings of conceptualizing too strong a distinction between citizen and worker-consumer, and between the polity and the economy. Workers and consumers as well as citizens can be educated to be active or passive and collectivist or individualist in their relations with the political economy, with implications for whether change does or does not occur.

TEACHERS, TEACHER EDUCATION, AND WORKER-CONSUMER-CITIZENS

The issues about democracy and citizenship discussed in the preceding sections are germane to all segments of the population. Focusing on teachers, though, is compelling for a number of reasons. First, although often discussed as if they were apolitical, teachers engage in actions in classrooms, educational institutions, unions/associations, homes, and communities that sustain or alter existing relations of power and distributions of material and symbolic resources (Ginsburg 1995b). Second, in many societies teachers constitute a sizable proportion of the middle class, which Lipset (1960) and Stephens (1993) argue have played and will continue to play a "pivotal role" in developing and sustaining democracy.[12] While important reasons for focusing on teachers, the two identified here pale in comparison to the third reason: teachers constitute one of the major socializing agents of all worker-consumer-citizens. Teachers perform this role by what they do and do not say during lessons in classrooms, but they also may serve as role models by what they do or refrain from doing in the school as a workplace, in their unions/associations, in their homes, and in local, national, and global communities. Thus, teacher education is more than a technical activity; it involves the political construction of worker-consumer-citizens who in turn play a role in socializing other worker-consumer-citizens (see Ginsburg and Lindsay 1995).

ILLUSTRATIONS FROM A TEACHER EDUCATION PROGRAM IN MEXICO

This section of the chapter draws on data I collected as part of a four-year ethnographic study (1989–1993) of the political socialization of students attending *a licenciatura* program offered by the Facultad de Pedagogia at the Universidad Veracruzana (for related studies, see Ginsburg 1994 and 1995a; Ginsburg and Tidwell 1990). The program, which was designed to prepare students for professional roles as schoolteachers, career counselors, and educational administrators, had two sections (day and evening), each of which was divided into eight class groups of students who remained together during their four-year program, and whose classroom was visited by instructors during a given semester as they delivered the various courses included in the curriculum. My research focused on two class groups, one in the day and one in the evening sections. The day section class group, which took classes between 8:00 A.M. and 2:00 P.M., consisted of thirty-three students: 85 percent females, 100 percent "traditional-aged" students (nineteen to twenty-three years old in 1990), 33 percent whose fathers and 45 percent whose mothers had no more than six years of primary education, 12 percent involved in paid work roles, and 6 percent having their own children. The evening section class group, which took classes between 4:00 P.M. and 10:00 P.M., consisted of twenty-five students: 84 percent females, 24 percent "non-traditional-aged" students (twenty-five years old or older in 1990), 60 percent whose fathers and 75 percent whose mothers had no more than six years of primary education, 28 percent involved in paid work roles, and 8 percent having their own children.[13]

As part of the effort to understand how students preparing to be educators understood their current and future roles as worker-consumer-citizens, I used a self-administered survey that consisted primarily of open-ended questions and was included in the annually administered questionnaire. Data presented in this chapter are from responses to the following items:

- Do you believe that teachers can or should be agents of social change? Why and how? (This question was asked in 1990.)
- Please indicate two major economic, political, or social problems that we must try to resolve. For each problem (mentioned above) describe what things you try or would try to do to resolve them in your work . . . [and] outside of work. (This question was asked in 1991.)
- Describe the things, if there are any, that you would try to do in your work . . . [and] outside of work to promote important social changes. (This question was asked in 1992.)

After briefly summarizing the types of problems the students identified, I focus on (a) the kinds of actions they did or did not plan to take in seeking to address these problems and (b) the constraints they perceived to becoming more actively involved in collective strategies for dealing with these problems.

Perceived Societal Problems

The students were most likely to mention some type of economic problem (23 of 33 for day and 19 of 25 for evening programs). When specified, the economic problems mentioned included lack of jobs or unemployment, foreign debt, and the anticipated negative consequences for Mexico of the North American Free Trade Agreement.[14] Some of these students focused their attention on poverty, uneven development, low salaries and living standards, reflecting a view of society in which economic problems are perceived to affect differentially some groups. For example, Elena, (one of the respondents from the day program) emphasized gender group differences, that women tend to have "submissive and self-sacrificing" roles and have a "lack of chance to participate" equally in the economy (1991).

Education problems were a close second to economic problems (18 of 33 and 17 of 25 for the day and evening program, respectively). Often students reported system-wide problems, such as "low quality of education," "poorly trained teachers," inappropriate curriculum, and outcome failures (e.g., illiteracy or dropouts). However, some students (4 of 25 in the evening program only) focused on inequalities in education as the problem, particularly calling attention to the disparities between schooling in urban and rural areas. For example, Margarita (from the evening program) criticized "the low level of importance the government gives to education in the marginalized or rural areas" in addition to lamenting the problem of Mexico's "dependency on educational methods and theories from capitalist countries," especially the more urbanized, industrialized power to the north, the United States (1991).[15]

Political problems were cited next most often (6 of 33 and 10 of 25 in the day and evening program, respectively). These problems were generally described in terms like "lack of democracy," "government corruption," and "electoral fraud." Two female students in the day program highlighted gender inequalities—women's "lack of chance to participate" (Elena in 1991) and "low [rate of] participation" (Iris in 1992)—in politics as a problem.

Students also identified other problems, which while clearly related to problems in the economy, polity, and education, were labeled by the students as "social problems." Three students in the evening program identified the following such problems: overpopulation, urban migration of *campesinos*, and a housing shortage. Among day program students, six called attention to environmental or ecological problems, often described as "contamination"; five other students mentioned health problems, including alcoholism and unsanitary hygiene, especially in rural communities; three students referenced overpopulation or a housing shortage; three students cited children with special needs, that is, physical or mental challenges; three students focused on young people who had psychological problems, were living on the street, or were delinquents; and one student identified street maintenance and lack of community-based cultural programs.

We can see that students involved in these preservice education programs perceived a variety of different societal problems that required some efforts by individuals and groups to resolve them. Thus, we can say, these students are aware, to varying degrees, of matters on which they as worker-consumer-citizens should or could focus their energies. The interesting question is how they might seek to address these problems, to what extent they would do so through strategies that varied in terms of their being passive/private versus active/public, and collective versus individualistic. I organize the discussion next in terms of the location for such strategic activities: within work or outside work.

Within-Work Strategies

Students' responses to the questionnaire items identified above were grouped into four major categories of within-work strategies: [16]

1. enhancing educators' knowledge, skill, and effectiveness;
2. developing students' and parents' knowledge, skills, and habits;[17]
3. raising students' consciousness and orienting them to collective action; and
4. collaborating with colleagues.

While all four of these types of strategies signal potential action on the part of these future educators, the first two types are more privatized and individually focused forms of engagement as worker-consumer-citizens. Developing individuals' skill and knowledge—whether these individuals be students, parents, or educators—involves less public and collectivist forms of action than raising consciousness for collective action and acting in concert with colleagues.

The first two strategies, which were more often mentioned (respectively by 24 of 33 and 22 of 33 of the day program students, and 12 of 25 and 12 of 25 of the evening program students) might be seen as fitting easily into a narrow view of the work role of teachers. For example, when Gilberto (from the day program) responded to the question about teachers as change agents, he said that they are:

> not so much agents of social change but agents facilitating teaching. Since social change implies many structures, ideological and material, [teachers] can't make changes at one time or from one day to another. But teachers have a specific field of work [e.g., transmitting knowledge to students] toward which they have to dedicate themselves. (1990)

The latter two strategies, which were less likely to be mentioned (respectively by 13 of 33 and 12 of 33 of the day program and 15 of 25 and 6 of 25 of the evening program students), reflect action that might be seen as stretching educators beyond the technical dimension of their work roles. For example, Ines (from the day program) noted that she viewed teachers as "change agents" because "they are the ones who give children diverse ideologies about the type of society that we can have . . . if we are interested in their ideals, we can put them into practice" (1990). In 1991 Ines explained how she would deal with the economic, political, or social problem she identified, the "low participation of women in the political arena: I would stimulate female children as well as adults in my community to be aware of the problem and encourage them to participate in elections and other political activities." And a year later she expressed a commitment to promoting social change at work through "achieving better human relations with and higher participation by students in school, helping them to not be afraid to ask questions or express their own ideas and encouraging them to be interested in being active in dealing with problems in the real world."

Strategies Outside of Work

Students' responses to the questionnaire items were sorted into the following categories:

1. transmitting knowledge, skills, and attitudes;[18]
2. improving one's own capacity and increasing personal effort;
3. raising community members' consciousness and promoting collective action;
4. participating in community projects; and
5. voting, lobbying, and public speaking.

The first two categories of strategic action entail more of a privatized and individualized form of worker-consumer-citizen activity, emphasizing the need to change individuals. The latter three forms of strategic action are more public and collective in nature.[19] The differences in forms of worker-consumer-citizen activity are illustrated by day program student Josefina's responses to the 1991 questionnaire. She describes a privatized, individualistic strategy when she notes that she would seek to solve the country's "economic crisis" by "developing myself as a professional to gain more investment for the state" and "get a good job and do my best to be productive." She also suggested a more public, collectivist strategy when stating that to deal with the "problem of human rights violations" she would "learn [with others] more about the laws and join with others to demand and defend our rights" and "link up with people suffering from human rights violations to see if I can work with them to put an end to such violations."

There are interesting differences between students in the day program and those in the evening program with respect to level of anticipated participation in these two different sets of strategies. For example, more than two-thirds (24 of 33) of the day program students mentioned that they would engage in transmitting knowledge, skills, and attitudes as a strategy for dealing with social problems; this was the case for fewer than one-third (7 of 25) of their evening program counterparts. Similarly, the day program students (15 of 33) were more likely to refer to more individualistic efforts to increase their own capacity and productivity than the evening program students (6 of 25).

With regard to the more public and collectivist strategies, in contrast, evening program students tended to anticipate being more active than did their day program counterparts: (a) 10 of 25 evening program students versus 5 of 33 day program students mentioned that they would promote consciousness raising of community members; (b) 15 of 25 evening program students compared to 16 of 33 day program students mentioned that they would become involved in or initiate community projects; and (c) 12 of 25 evening program versus 11 of 33 day program students identified voting, lobbying, and speaking out on issues as a means of dealing with economic, political, and social problems.

If we examine how these students responded to my questions in 1992 about their interest, involvement in the campaign, and plans for voting with respect to the governor's election, we observe similarly that evening program students were more likely to report that they planned to vote than day program students. Among students who answered the question, approximately one third (9 of 31) of the day program students indicated that they did not plan to vote, while only 15 percent (3 of 20) of the evening program students projected that they would not vote. Table 9.1 summarizes the students' responses indicating whether or not they planned to vote and for which party—the more centrist Partido Revolucionario Institucional (PRI) or the more leftist Partido Revolucionario Democratico (PRD)—they planned to vote in the 1992 election for governor of the state of Veracruz. Note also that none of the students projected voting for the other major party contesting in this election, the more rightist Partido Accion Nacional (PAN), and among those voting, the evening program students were equally oriented to vote for the PRI or the PRD candidate (6 of 17), while the day program students disproportionately gave their support to the PRI candidate (11 of 22) over the PRD candidate (3 of 22).

Although we will not seek to explain fully the differences between the two programs in students' projected forms and levels of activity as worker-consumer-citizen behavior, the following would represent good starting

Table 9.1

Program	PRI	PRD	Which party	Does not plan to vote	No answer
Day	11/33	3/33	8/33	9/33	2/33
Evening	6/25	6/25	5/25	3/25	5/25

Note: PRI, Partido Revolucionario Institucional; PRD, Partido Revolucionario Democratico.

points in that effort: (a) the evening program students tend to have grown up in families with less formally educated parents (and thus are likely to have a more working- versus middle-class cultural context); (b) the evening program students tend to be at a different life stage (older and employed); (c) there were observed differences in the background, experience, and degree of university integration of the instructors; and (d) there were observed differences in content of class sessions, partly because of the input of instructors and partly because of the nature and frequency of contributions from students.

Constraints on Collective Action As Worker-Consumer Citizens

In the previous two subsections I summarized the varying degrees (and forms) of in-work and out-of-work strategies for dealing with social problems identified by *Facultad de Pedagogia* students at the Universidad Veracruzana (UV). The general disinclination toward public forms of citizen involvement among UV pedagogy students may be attributable to the fact that the large majority are females. As noted above, girls and women tend to be socialized away from involvement in the public sphere, and their current or anticipated private sphere responsibilities make such participation more difficult. However, we observed that some students (female and male) anticipated being more active than others, particularly when it came to participating in public life.

In explaining why they did not plan to be (and were not now) more active, particularly in those tasks normally associated with their future work roles, some students in the day program just offered general statements, such as things were "difficult to change" (5 of 33 students), they had "no time" (4 of 33 students), or they had "no interest" in politics and elections (5 of 33 students). For example, Roberto expressed his cynicism and resignation to the status quo when he noted that he could not do anything outside work to address the problem of centralization in the economic and political systems: "I cannot participate outside of work since although I could do something with my colleagues and friends, it would have no consequence" (1991). None of the evening program students remained at such a general level when explaining why they anticipated limited or no involvement in "politics."

Whereas the day and evening program students specified their reasons for not being actively involved in promoting social change, UV students focused on the nature of the existing government and/or the dominant political party (PRI) as the constraint.[20] Other students (8 of 33 day program and 5 of 25 evening program) explained their noninvolvement in electoral politics in terms of their cynical belief that the results would be manipulated or somehow the dominant party, PRI, would win regardless of whether or how people voted.[21] The following quotes from a variety of students obtained during the 1992 interview illustrate this view:

> I will not vote for any candidate, because the one [party] in power always wins and they don't take us [citizens] into account. (Carla, day program)

> I'm not going to vote because . . . I already know [which party] is going to be in the government; all is manipulated and our votes are in all manner nullified. (Iris, day program)

> I may vote, but I'm not going to participate in the campaign of any party. . . . There is so much corruption in our country that the one [party] that is going to win has always won. (Celia, evening program)

When discussing perceived constraints on their ability to be active in their future roles as worker-consumer-citizens beyond voting, some students signaled similar cynicism—as well as criticism—about the working of the government between elections. These students (8 of 33 in the day program and 6 of 25 in the evening program) made references to the "system not being open" or the government "stifling participation" and being "corrupt." For instance, in discussing how she would deal in work with the problem of Mexico's external debt, Lena (evening program) stated that "I know that I won't influence much of what occurs since the government does what it wants" (1991).

If the government and the dominant party (abbreviated in Spanish as PRI) were viewed by students as a constraint to their becoming active collectively as a worker-consumer-citizens, what about the national teachers' union, *Sindicato Nacional de Trabajadores de la Educacion* (SNTE)? What in some contexts might be seen as a base for collective action to deal with social problems, the union for educators was viewed by 10 out of 33 students in the day program and 13 out of 25 in the evening program to be a part of the problem, rather than the solution.[22] This conception of SNTE being a part of the problem was evidenced when students discussed in 1990 "what they thought about the teachers' movement" that was prominently featured in both in the national as well as Veracruz and Xalapa press in the years preceding my interviews. Sometimes they responded by criticizing the SNTE or teachers' organizations generally, and sometimes they did so by applauding the accusation of the independent teachers' movement (CNTE) of a "lack of democracy" within the SNTE. The following responses are illustrative:

> Each time the [SNTE] leaders acquire more power, and then there are more problems for the members. (Margarita, day program)

> The teachers' movement is very important. It is having a great influence on the sociopolitical development of the country. It is good that they have formed the CNTE in order to challenge the corruption of the leaders of SNTE. (Linda, evening program)

> The independent [teachers'] movement [CNTE] is aimed in general to achieve an improvement in salaries and to confront the corrupt leaders [of SNTE]. CNTE is a vanguard group of the rank and file. CNTE does not

have leaders [determined] by the hierarchy but by representatives of the collective interest. (Benito, evening program)

The UV students' perception that the government, the party, and the teachers' union were undemocratic, corrupt, and/or blocking efforts to address economic, political, and social problems was not the only factor influencing students' plans for their forms and levels of participation as worker-consumer-citizens. Because government, party, and union officials were understood to be gatekeepers for job opportunities, students' desire to obtain (and maintain) employment after graduation also weighed heavily in how they projected their activity as worker-consumer-citizens—but in contradictory ways.

It was clear from observations of and conversations with students that they were concerned about their employment prospects (as were many workers—university educated or otherwise—in Mexico during this time). Moreover, in 1990, 1991, and 1992, when responding to my question, "What do you think you will do after completing your degree program, 9 out of 33 day program and 8 out of 25 evening program students stressed the problematic nature of anticipated job searches. For example, Martha (day program) replied, "work, if I can find a job" (1990) and "search for a job . . . knowing that it will be difficult because there are not many opportunities; [education] is a very saturated field" (1992).

Their concern about getting jobs (over which party, government, and union officials exercised considerable control) and their perception that existing institutionalized forms of collective action were unsavory and unproductive (with respect to solving social problems) led some students to project that they would avoid being involved in political party activities (including electoral campaigns), and union business, and what they generally described in pejorative terms as "politics." For instance, in discussing what he would do to deal with the problem of "the political, social problems occurring because democracy is not functioning," Marco (evening program) commented that he "would leave to others the realm of political activity" (1991) at work at least. In contrast, some UV students saw becoming involved in organized forms of politics as a way to meet—and, perhaps, ingratiate—the people who could help them in their job search. For example, Alicia (day program) explained that to deal with the problem of unemployment she would use her potential "connections with a union leader who could aid people she recommended in getting a job" (1991). Similarly, Benito (evening program) explained that although he has since switched his political party allegiance to the PRD, he had earlier obtained "a position . . . as a coordinator of pedagogy in the popular youth organization of PRI . . . because I wanted to get employment for myself" (1992).

CONCLUSION

I began this chapter with a quote from Wheeler (1971) that "politics is kind of profession . . . engaged in by citizens" (10–11). After exploring a variety of issues related to conceptualizing democracy and citizenship, particularly examining procedural and substantive notions of democracy and highlighting citizens' relationships to the economy and the polity, I suggested that it may be appropriate to amend the statement by referring to politics as the profession (or activity) engaged by worker-consumer-citizens. The data derived from my research with pedagogy students at the Universidad Veracruzana illustrate how such a broader conception helps us to understand political identities and orientations of students involved in a program designed to prepare future educators. Their concerns about economic problems (including inadequate salaries and conditions of employment for *workers* as well as *consumers'* inability to purchase enough goods and services to sustain a sufficient quality of life) as well as political problems and their anticipated strategies for dealing with these problems stretch beyond the narrower conceptions of democratic citizenship. While these pedagogy students made little, if any, reference to consumer behavior in their discussion of anticipated strategies for dealing with economic, political, and social problems,[23] a variety of within-work and community-based strategies were identified.

All of these pedagogy students showed evidence of developing as worker-consumer-citizens—being aware of societal problems that needed attention and thinking of strategies they might pursue to address such problems. Many of the students, however, seemed to be oriented primarily toward a "privatized" model of democratic citizenship. Although some students discussed plans along the lines of a "public" model of democratic citizenship, involving collective action within existing or emerging organizations or social movements, the majority's anticipated strategic engagement could be characterized as individualized activity designed to change individuals' (including the students' own) ideas and behaviors. My point is not to criticize students' choice of models for democratic citizenship, but to shed light on why they may have come to prefer a privatized versus a public model.

As noted, students often indicated that they would avoid playing an active role in collective political action because they perceived leaders of political parties, unions, and the government to be selfish and corrupt and to be likely to block needed social change initiatives. Of course, this is a reasonable position to adopt. How can we expect them to become active worker-consumer-citizens themselves, let alone encourage future students to be active, if they are alienated from the political system of governance and from existing organizations, including those self-styled as democratic alternatives (PRD and CNTE, respectively) to the dominant political party (PRI) and teachers' union (SNTE)?

However, we need to ask why and how they come to hold these negative views of organized or collective political action. Such views are shaped in part by the formal curriculum of their university program as well as by the hidden curriculum. With respect to the formal curriculum Heater's (1990) portrayal of the self-fulfilling prophecy of the "conservative/elitist" model of citizenship, which underlies some education programs, seems accurate in representing the experience of pedagogy at the Universidad Veracruzana:

> Teach about constitutional machinery and not about political controversies because the former is dull and safe. Because it is dull and safe, it will be uninteresting. Because it is uninteresting, young people will turn away from their role as citizens and leave political matters to an élite who "know about these things."

In the hidden curriculum of the pedagogy program the students learn about politics—and develop cynicism as a result of the perceived corruption of leaders and organizations—through their direct observations of, for example: (a) student "party" organizations that operated in relation to the student (and university) governance system, and (b) faculty and staff unions at the Universidad Veracruzana (for details, see Cordova and Ginsburg 1998). However, their views were also (mis)informed by media accounts of the activities of these groups as well as the functioning of political parties and unions more generally.

While not wanting to argue the (indefensible) case that Mexican and other societies' political institution are corruption-free, I do want to suggest that media messages that highlight the "corrupt" nature of some political actors and actions may function ideologically to characterize all politics as corrupt and alienating. Note that "the issue of corruption can be used as a ploy in the game of politics" ("Report on corruption" 1993, 11) and that the tarnish of "political corruption" can undermine the "legitimacy" of a political system (Diamond and Plattner 1993, xviii–xix). We need further investigations of the conditions under which the delegitimization of "corrupt" political institutions would lead teachers (and their students) toward cynical acceptance of the status quo or toward public democratic forms of collective action to transform the political economic system.

NOTES

[1]Marshall (1964) also identifies political and civil entitlements of citizenship. In relation to social entitlements, he states that trade unionism is a "secondary system of industrial citizenship parallel with and supplementary to the system of political citizenship" (94). Like Marshall (1964) and Highland (1995), Gunsteren (1998) suggests that full "social equality—that is the elimination of differences of standing and power in the social sphere—is not required . . . [but only that] unequal social relations not be allowed to prevent any individual from having reasonable chances of access to political equality" (26). However, I question whether political equality can obtain in the presence of any degree of social inequality.

[2]While the concept of worker-consumer-citizen has been derived from many sources, Joel Spring's (1980) book, *Educating the Worker-Citizen: The Social, Economic, and Political Formation of Education*, is an important influence on this discussion.

Democratizing Education and Educating Democratic Citizens

[3]While Lenin predicted the "withering away of the state" as a part of the transition from socialist to communist society, here I am appropriating the expression to refer to the weakening of the nation-state that currently stems from the globalization of capitalist economic relations, the expansion of the role played by international organizations, and the increase in cultural diversity of national populations.

[4]Green (1997) stresses, however, that the political economic changes are ideological as well as structural. He states that "the resurgence of neo-liberal politics and *laissez-faire* economics has undermined the leading role which Keynesian welfarism formerly assigned to the state in the direction of and regulation of the economies and societies" (9).

[5]"Disorganized capitalism involves the geographical dispersal of production and distribution through the globalization of markets and industrial deconcentration" (Gilbert 1997, 66).

[6]Others counter or at least qualify the conclusion about the withering away of the state stemming from the growth in international organizations, arguing that the "state is not being dismantled, nor even disaggregated, but rather reconfigured" (Callaghy 1997, 392) and that "the announcement of the death of the sovereign state . . . has been exaggerated" (Heater 1990, 230).

[7]Gilbert (1997) also cites Wexler (1990), who cautions that there may be "an illusory sense of self-determination in the act of consumption" (68), to the extent that people's consumption behavior is shaped by corporate-owned media, and people act as isolated individuals in their consumption of corporate-produced goods and services.

[8]The views of Rousseau and Locke, however, can be contrasted with Aristotle's notion of *zoon politikon,* that " 'by nature man is a political animal' "(Hogan 1997, 27) as well as with Dante's concept of *politizare,* that "to live a fully engaged life is to live politically. . . . In a significant sense to be is to be political" (Clarke 1996, 23). Neither Rousseau nor Locke view humans as naturally socially and politically active, but rather primarily oriented to protecting their physical selves and material possessions. However, unlike Locke, Rousseau "sought to derive a logic participation from the logic of protection" (Hogan 1997, 38). Note, moreover, that Locke's vision of democracy is based on a concern to protect individual economic elites from the masses, while Rousseau's view is focused more on protecting the individual non-elites from economic elites.

[9]We should note that, at various times in various societies, human beings who did not own property, people of color, and women were excluded from this conception of "people" (Crompton 1993, 139; Habermas 1995).

[10]Similarly, Heater (1990) distinguishes "participatory/democratic" and "conservative/élitist" models of citizenship. He explains that the élitist model, based on the assumption that the masses are "slothful and ignorant," views the government as "a device to keep them apathetic lest their propensities to selfishness and violence undermine communal life. . . . The conservative élitist would rather emphasize the right of the individual to exercise his [or her] freedom *not* to participate. His [or her] ideal is the private, not the public citizen" (214–215).

[11]The references to property relations—as part of the rationale for active and passive forms of citizenship—remind us of the shortcomings of conceptualizing too strong a distinction between citizen and worker-consumer, between the polity and the economy.

[12]While agreeing with Lipset (1960) that the middle class contributes in significant ways to the development of democracy, Stephens (1993) concludes, based on his quantitative and qualitative historical research, that it is the "organized working class" that is the "key actor in the development of full democracy . . . [However,] because the working class nowhere was strong enough to push through democracy alone, the middle class assumed a pivotal role in the development of democracy" (436–437).

[13]Note that evening program students, compared to their day program counterparts, tend to: (a) be older (24 versus 0 percent being of nontraditional age), (b) be involved in paid work (28 versus 12 percent), and (c) have parents with less formal education (66 versus 33 percent having fathers with no more than six years of primary schooling, and 75 versus 45 percent having mothers with no more than six years of primary schooling).

[14]The references to "foreign debt" and to NAFTA (the negotiations for which received substantial media attention during this period, leading up to its implementation in January 1994) point to the students' understanding of the global context in which they were functioning as worker-consumer-citizens.

[15]Note the more globally oriented perspective.

[16]The next most frequently cited in-work strategies for dealing with social problems were (a) making curricular changes, mentioned by three day-program and four evening-program students; (b) promoting cultural activities, mentioned by four day-program students and 1 evening-program student; and c) finding a good job for oneself, mentioned by four day-program students only.

[17]This category includes a focus on "knowledge" in general as well as more specific forms of knowledge, such as that concerning birth control, hygiene, the electoral process, the importance of education for children's futures, and how to choose a career. Conduct refers to things like punctuality, studying, maintaining hygiene in the home, and not littering.

[18]In this category, projected efforts focused on developing literacy, knowledge about health, hygiene, and drug and alcohol abuse, vocational skills, and a positive attitude toward formal education as a means for children and adults acquiring the knowledge and skills needed to gain employment.

[19]Note, however, that while voting is usually considered to be a public form of political action, by itself it represents a more individualistic, privatized form of activity.

[20]The issue here is not merely a question of agreeing with the party's platform, although this also discouraged and encouraged some students' participation. For example, Javier (of the evening program), one of the few students who reported being a party activist, explained, "I had participated actively in the PRI, but dropped that because this party did not live up to my ideological aspirations" (1992). Javier reported that he subsequently became active in the PRD because "I sense a confrontation of ideas and a feeling of political struggle" (1992). In contrast, for 3 of 33 day program students and 2 of 25 evening progam students, PRI served to motivate their involvement in electoral politics. As examples, Juanita (day program) stated that she was attracted to vote for PRI because it sought to "improve the welfare of my state and above all the education . . . of the youth" (1992) and Irma (evening program) explained: "I'm going to vote for PRI because I consider it the best. . . . I can't imagine how our country would be when this party is not in power" (1992).

[21]It is interesting that this view of the inevitability of a PRI victory, however fraudulent, was expressed at a time when local and state elections in other states brought members of both PAN and PRD into office. However, PRI electoral dominance had not been successfully challenged in the state of Veracruz. The students' views were thus accurate, if at the same time part of a self-fulfilling prophecy that enabled PRI to win the 1992 election for state governor.

[22]Note that 7 of 33 day program and 13 of 25 evening program students indicated some degree of support for collective teacher action, for salaries and/or democratic rights as workers. However, 10 of 33 students in the day program and 7 of 25 students in the evening program either did not respond or stated that they did not know enough about the teachers' movement to offer a view. The reported lack of knowledge, of course, signals limited attention to, and interest in, a significant "political" dynamic within the professional arena for which they were preparing themselves.

[23]The students' lack of attention to consumer behavior may be a result of the way the issues were posed on the questionnaire as well as a function of not having much emphasis in their school or university curriculum on the "political" dimension of individual and collective consumer action. Since NGOs engaged in mobilizing consumer boycotts, and so on, to address economic, political, and social problems have yet to be stained with the brush of "corruption," this aspect of worker-consumer-citizen action may be easier to mobilize on a collective basis.

REFERENCES

Albala-Bertrand, Luis (ed.). (1996) "Citizenship and education: Towards meaningful practice." *Prospects* 26(4):645–778.

Alexiadou, Nafsika, and Colin Brock (eds.). (1999). *Education as a commodity.* Great Glenham, England: John Catt Educational Limited.

Aristotle. (1981). *The Politics* (rev. ed.). T. J. Saunders (ed.). Harmondsworth, UK: Penguin.

Barbalet, J. (1988). *Citizenship: Rights, struggle and class inequality.* Minneapolis: University of Minnesota Press.

Barber, Benjamin. (1995). *Jihad vs. McWorld.* New York: Times Books.

Bendix, R. (1964). *Nation-building and citizenship.* Berkeley: University of California Press.

Bowles, Samuel, and Herbert Gintis. (1975). *Schooling in capitalist America.* Boston: Routledge and Kegan Paul.

Bowles, Samuel, and Herbert Gintis. (1993). "A political and economic case for the democratic enterprise." In David Copp, Jean Hamilton, and John Roemer (eds.), *The idea of democracy,* 375–399. Cambridge: University of Cambridge Press.

Callaghy, Thomas. (1997). "Globalization and marginalization: Debt and the international underclass." *Current History* 613 (November):392–396.

Clarke, Paul. (1996). *Deep citizenship.* Chicago: Pluto Press.

Copp, David, Jean Hamilton, and John Roemer. (1993). "Introduction." In D. Copp, J. Hamilton, and J. Roemer (eds.), *The idea of democracy.* Cambridge: Cambridge University Press.

Crompton, Rosemary. (1993). "Citizenship and entitlements." In *Class and stratification: An introduction to current debates,* 138–165. Cambridge: Polity Press.

Crook, S., J. Pakulski, and M. Waters. (1992). *Postmodernization: Change in advanced society*. London: Sage.

Diamond, L., and M. Plattner. (1993). *The global resurgence of democracy*. Baltimore, MD: Johns Hopkins University Press.

Elshtain, J. (1994). *Democracy on trial*. New York: Basic Books.

Fine, Ben. (1995). "From political economy to consumption." In Daniel Miller (ed.), *Acknowledging consumption: A review of new studies*. London: Routledge.

Foster, Victoria. (1997). "Feminist theory and the construction of citizenship education." In Kerry Kennedy (ed.), *Citizenship education and the modern state*, 54–64. London: Falmer Press.

Giddens, Anthony. (1994). *Beyond left and right: The future of radical politics*. Stanford, CA: Stanford University Press.

Gilbert, Rob. (1997). "Issues for citizenship in a postmodern world." In Kerry Kennedy (ed.), *Citizenship education and the modern state*, 65–81. London: Falmer Press.

Ginsburg, Mark (1994). "Aprendiendo a ser actores politicos: La educación de maestros en México." *Punto y Seguida* 7:17–20.

Ginsburg, Mark (ed.). (1995a). *The politics of educators' work and lives*. New York: Garland.

Ginsburg, Mark. (1995b). "Contradictions, resistance, and incorporation in the political socialization of educators in Mexico." In Mark Ginsburg and Beverly Lindsay (eds.), *The political dimension in teacher education: Comparative perspectives on policy formation, socialization, and society*, 216–242. New York: Falmer.

Ginsburg, Mark, and Beverly Lindsay (eds.). (1995). *The political dimension in teacher education: Comparative perspectives on policy formation, socialization, and society*. New York: Falmer.

Ginsburg, Mark, and Monte Tidwell. (1990). "Political socialization of prospective educators in Mexico: The case of the University of Veracruz." *New Education* 12(2):70–82.

Green, Andy. (1997). "Education and state formation in Europe and Asia." In Kerry Kennedy (ed.), *Citizenship education and the modern state*, 9–26. London: Falmer Press.

Gunsteren, H. (1998a). "Deep groups under a multicultural surface." In *A theory of citizenship: Organizing plurality in contemporary democracies*, 59–66. Boulder, CO: Westview Press.

Gunsteren, H. (1998b) "Theories of citizenship, old and new." In *A theory of citizenship: Organizing plurality in contemporary democracies*, 11–30. Boulder, CO: Westview Press.

Habermas, Jürgen. (1995). "Citizenship and national identity: Some reflections on the future of Europe." In Ronald Beiner (ed.), *Theorizing citizenship*, 255–281. Albany: State University of New York Press.

Hall, Peter. (1989). *The political power of economic ideas: Keynesianism across nations*. Princeton, NJ: Princeton University Press.

Heater, D. (1990). *Citizenship: The civic ideal in world history, politics and education*. New York: Longman.

Highland, J. (1995). *Democratic theory: The philosophical foundations*. Manchester, England: Manchester University Press.

Hobsbawm, E. J. (1977). *The age of capital, 1848–1875.* London: Abacus.

Hochschild, Arlie. (1983). *The managed heart: Commericialization of human feeling.* Berkeley: University of California Press.

Hodson, Randy, and Teresa Sullivan. (1995) *The social organization of work,* 2d ed. Belmont, CA: Wadsworth.

Hogan, David. (1997). "The logic of protection: Citizenship, justice and political community." In Kerry Kennedy (ed.), *Citizenship education and the modern state,* 27–53. London: Falmer Press.

Lasch, C. (1994). *The revolt of the elites and the betrayal of democracy.* New York: W. W. Norton.

Laski, Harold. (1937). *A grammar of politics,* 4th ed. London: Allen and Unwin.

Lipset, Seymour. (1960). *Political man: The social bases of politics.* Garden City, NY: Doubleday.

Locke, John. (1963). "Second treatise on government: An essay concerning the true original extent and end of government." In John Somerville and Ronald Santoni (eds.), *Social and political philsophy.* Garden City, NY: Anchor Books/Doubleday.

Marshall, T. H. (1964). "Citizenship and social class." In *Class, Citizenship, and Social Development,* 65–122. New York: Doubleday.

Miller, Daniel. (1995). "Consumption as the vanguard of history: A polemic by way of an introduction." In Daniel Miller (ed.), *Acknowledging consumption: A review of new studies,* 1–57. London: Routledge.

Orzack, Louis. (1992). *International authority and the professions: The state beyond the nation-state* (EIU Jea Monnet Chair Papers). Badia Fiesolana, Italy: European University Institute.

Pateman, C. (1989). "The fraternal social contract." In C. Pateman (ed.), *The disorder of women,* 1–20. Cambridge: Polity Press.

Polyani, Karl. (1944). *The great transformation: The political and economic origins of our time.* Boston: Beacon Press.

Ramirez, Francisco, and Richard Rubinson. (1979). "Creating members: The political incorporation and expansion of public education." In John Meyer and Michael Hannan (eds.), *National development and the world system: Educational, economic, and political change, 1950–70,* 72–82. Chicago: University of Chicago Press.

"Report on corruption: The politics of corruption and the corruption of politics." (1993). NACLA *Report on the Americas* 27(1):11–12.

Reskin, B., and I. Padavic. (1994). *Women and men at work.* Thousand Oaks, CA: Pine Forge Press.

Rousseau, Jean Jacques. ([1762] 1985). *The social contract.* New York: Penguin Books.

Sarup, Madan. (1996). *Identity, culture and the postmodern world.* Edinburgh: Edinburgh University Press.

Sehr, David. (1997). *Education for public democracy.* Albany: State University of New York Press.

Spring, Joel. (1980). *Educating the worker-citizen.* New York: Longman.

Stephens, John. (1993). "Capitalist development and democracy: Empirical research on the social origins of democracy." In David Copp, Jean Hamilton, and John

Roemer (eds.), *The idea of democracy,* 409–446. Cambridge: University of Cambridge Press.

Turner, Bryan. (1993). "Contemporary problems in the theory of citizenship." In B. Turner (ed.), *Citizenship and social theory,* 1–18. London: Sage.

Ward, Kathryn. (1990). "Introduction and overview." In K. Ward (ed.), *Women workers and global restructuring,* 1–22. Ithaca, NY: ILR Press/Cornell University.

Wexler, Philip. (1990). "Citizenship in the semiotic society." In Bryan Turner (ed.), *Theories of modernity and postmodernity.* London: Sage.

Wheeler, Harvey. (1971). *Democracy in a revolutionary era.* London: Penguin.

Willis, Paul. (1977). *Learning to labour: How working class kids get working class jobs.* Westmead, England: Saxon House.

Young, Iris Marion. (1995). "Polity and group difference: A critique of the ideal of universal citizenship." In Ronald Beiner (ed.), *Theorizing citizenship,* 175–207. Albany: State University of New York Press.

DISCUSSION QUESTIONS

1. What are the implications for different groups in society of defining democracy mainly in terms of procedures, that is, not taking into consideration the substantive notion of democracy?

2. What are the advantages and disadvantages, with respect to our understanding and pursuit of democracy, if we consider people's economic roles (as workers and consumers) as well as their political roles (as citizens)?

3. If globalization and multiculturalization are reducing the importance of worker-consumer-citizens' relationship to the nation-state, should the school curriculum continue to stress nationalism and patriotism?

4. Should educators encourage their students and/or their colleagues to be active/collectivist or passive/individualist worker-consumer-citizens, and if so, how should they do so?

5. How similar or different are the orientations of the *Facultad de Pedagogia* students in Mexico to your own orientations or others you know or have read about?

CHAPTER 10

Teaching Democratic Values in Teacher Education Programs in Canada, Mexico, and the United States

NORMA TARROW, RATNA GHOSH, AND
AURORA ELIZONDO

In this chapter, we assume that values are the fundamental basis of any civil democratic society and that their transmission is one of the fundamental purposes of education. While in previous eras this responsibility rested primarily with the family and church, the complexity of the contemporary world turns the spotlight on the formal educational system and its role in the transmission of values of democracy and citizenship. Ethnic conflicts, international migration, issues related to social inequities, globalization of the economy, and the diminished influence of the family and organized religion lend a sense of urgency to the questions of what values are being conveyed and by whom. The doctrine of the separation of church and state and the failure to realize that democratic values may include but supersede particular religious beliefs resulted in hesitancy to deal with values issues in the secular public school domain.

Today, many are calling for the public schools to address again values issues. Thus, a morally responsible position on the part of those entrusted with the preparation of teachers in democratic societies mandates attention to the development and maintenance of democratic values and good citizenship. Failure to integrate these values into teacher education programs would be an abrogation of the professional responsibility of faculties of education in the preparation of teachers for social realities at the dawn of the twenty-first century.

Therefore, we will provide an overview of the context in which the values discourse is taking place in the three democratic societies of North America. This is followed by a discussion of theoretical and philosophical perspectives related to values, democratic values, and education, and the place of values in

Appreciation is extended to Rose Gibbs for her assistance with the review of the literature.

teacher preparation. We will close with a brief review of the findings of a comparative study of values in teacher education programs in the three countries—Mexico, Canada, and the United States.

THE VALUE QUESTION: WHAT IS A VALUE?

Although there exists a proliferation of definitions of the concept of values, the operational definition of values we use in this chapter is based on the work of Garcia and Vanella (1992):

> Values are conscious and unconscious preferences, accepted by the majority of members of the society and are socially regulated. They arise during a particular moment of history and transcend that epoch, as ideas of values— not definitive in themselves, but maintained by consensus even when not put into practice. Since a value implies a decision, it requires an act of autonomous reflection and prioritization. This prioritization derives from one's vision of individual life or society or the world and guides one's actions and life. (87)

What is a value? The concept surrounding the word originated with the Stoics who used this term for that which is good for us, thus giving it a moral and subjective connotation. On the other hand, we recognize that the notion of value is universal, so the concept has a Kantian element of objectivity. From this perspective, a value comprises that which is valued and "ought to be." It is an ideal to strive for but is not often realized in fact. It is the medium through which we make judgments or assign attributes to things. In order for something to have value, there must be someone who recognizes it as valuable. Therefore, value connotations change throughout history and differ depending on the physical and geographical context. Values, then, must have a historical and cultural context.

This recognition of the universality of the value notion as well as its dependence on a historical and cultural context creates some difficulty. Values are neither real nor tangible and do not exist on their own. They are not things, but are the characteristics that we assign to different things, and they tend to be prioritized. This perspective, as suggested by Frondizi (1962) allows for a better understanding, but it does not resolve the inherent contradictions related to subjective judgments and relativistic differences in sociohistorical contexts. On the one hand, values are the creation of men and women. They vary and are transformed through the course of history in a manner that is essentially subjective. On the other hand, at the same time, values serve as a basis for action and are social constructions. Values have a subjective characteristic that becomes their essence. Thus, one cannot say everything has value. However, although our values precede us, in the sense that we inherit them, based on our time and place in a historical and cultural context, this does not preclude the possibility of us creating something new and distinct.

Habermas's theory of moral consciousness and communicative action is helpful here. For Habermas (1983, 1991), the contradiction we have outlined cannot be resolved solely through analysis because the question of values rests on the notion of praxis, that is, it involves an understanding of both theory and reality. In this way Habermas recognizes the hermeneutic dimension, the element of interpretation essential to human interaction. Habermas recognizes three cognitive elements underlying the way in which knowledge is conceptualized. These are "the shared lifeworld," "the objective world," and the "subjective world." "It is this reference system of precisely three worlds that communicative actors make the basis of their efforts to reach understanding" (177). In other words, in order for human beings to come to a shared understanding they need to bring together these three points of reference. Habermas sees communicative action as involving individuals acting in specific situations and taking responsibility for those actions, as well as being influenced by the cultural or social environment of which they are a part.

These concepts lead us to assert, in agreement with Garcia and Vanella (1992) that values are conscious and unconscious preferences with which the majority of people in any society comply. Values are socially determined. Values are construed as such in a particular moment in the history of humanity. They remain with us, not in an immutable form, but as ideas of value, not defined in themselves, but maintained by consensus even when not put in practice.

THE CONTEXT OF THE VALUES DISCOURSE IN NORTH AMERICA

As part of the worldwide movement toward a global interactive society, the three countries of North America have joined forces under the aegis of the North American Free Trade Agreement (NAFTA) in economic, sociocultural, and educational spheres. Yet, to understand significant differences in the history, social structure, and responsibility for the transmission of societal values, it is important to consider the following:

- the sociocultural context of these multilingual, multicultural societies;
- government and educational policies related to democratic values and citizenship;
- the role of educational institutions in imparting societal values; and
- instructional practices utilized by educators charged with the task of creating responsible citizens for a democratic society.

The next section provides a brief overview of the value orientations guiding policy and practice in Canada, Mexico, and the United States.

Canada

The literature on values originating in the United States and Canada has a somewhat different and less theoretical emphases than the Mexican literature. Although Dror (1993) points out that moral education and values education lack comprehensive theories, it must be pointed out that, indeed, there are multiple theories. Bélanger (1993) comments that a conceptual framework for studying the way values are imparted is lacking. He goes on to posit his own theoretical perspective and identifies three dimensions of moral education (mode, intent, and preparation) that can provide the structure for observing, discussing, and planning for the imparting of values. *Mode* addresses the delivery of values through both content and process of educational settings. *Content* refers to knowledge, skills, and attitudes imparted relative to values within different subject areas. Even the selection of facts, examples, and emphases is based on value judgments on the part of the teacher. Values questions are inherent in every area of education. *Process* refers to experiences selected by the teachers and the values inherent in these practices. *Intent* refers to the degree to which the educator reveals to the learner the values imparted. This may either be explicit or implicit. *Preparation* connotes the mental set of the educator before the values learning experience. It forms a continuum, from proactive through reactive to unaware.

Education in Canada as a whole has been imbued traditionally with the values of the two "founding nations," the French and the English. The English, or Anglo-Saxon, viewpoint and values have tended historically to have the greatest influence in the country as a whole. However, in the province of Quebec since the Quiet Revolution of the 1960s, French Quebecois traditions and values are being asserted throughout the state. The population statistics for the province of Quebec help to explain this trend. The 1991 census indicated that out of a total population of 6,896,000 people, 81 percent were described as being of French origin. In contrast, only 9 percent were of British origin. People of native origin comprised 1 percent of Quebec's population and 9 percent are people who described themselves as "other" or "of mixed origin" (Ghosh et al. 1995). The current policy statements for the province of Quebec in the area of education reflect, in many instances, the dominance of French culture and values.

The document *The Schools of Quebec: Policy Statement and Plan of Action* (1979) lists the values that should be reflected in the schools of Quebec. The individual curriculum and curriculum guide in each subject mentions specific values while referring to this base document. Values are discussed in the document within a broad section titled "The Aims of Education." In the segment "The Values of Education," the document specifies the government's position:

Education is based on a certain number of values and, more precisely, on a series of general and instructional objectives. These values must be reflected everywhere, at the primary and the secondary level, and especially in the objectives of the course of study. In the schools they are still quite frequently the subject of research and discussion. Nevertheless, they point out goals, the pursuit of which will encourage young people to realize their potential for development. Values are categorized as follows (in no special order of importance):

- intellectual values
- emotional values
- aesthetic values
- social and cultural values
- moral values
- spiritual and religious values

It is the responsibility of each school to identify the values necessary for its educational project and to effect choices that reflect the aspirations of the community (*The Schools of Quebec* 1979).

As regards moral education, Quebec has taken the lead when one looks at its initiative in this area compared to what has taken place in the other provinces of Canada. Quebec has legally entrenched its position on moral and religious education in the school system. Bill 107 provides for freedom of choice within the parameters of Catholic, Protestant, or moral instruction. Students must be exposed to one of these in their schools. The number of hours to be given to one of these areas of instruction is also specified. In the elementary school it is sixty hours. The Quebec documents also indicate that students are expected to use a moral perspective in discussing controversial topics (Cochrane 1992).

In the area of multicultural policies and values, the Quebec government and respective school boards have undertaken several initiatives. As French grew in importance as the main language of the government and of business, programs were instituted in the schools to aid in the process of integration of immigrants. Special programs for newcomers were started in schools in the 1960s to hasten their acquisition of French. These were the *classes d'accueil,* or welcome classes. Heritage language programs were also started about the same time (McAndrew 1994).

In Quebec, school boards have traditionally been organized by religious affiliation according to the British North America Act of 1867, which made education a confessional system. The Protestant School Board of Montreal and the Montreal Catholic School Commission were the two largest boards.

The Schools of Quebec specifies the spiritual and religious values that should be taught in schools. However, recent changes in the structure of school boards have made linguistic affiliation rather than religious orientation the basis on which schools are organized. This took effect in September 1998. The linguistic boards have, for the moment, been superimposed on the religious divisions. Despite the traditional emphasis on organization of the educational system along religious lines, the recent Proulx Report (1999) has prompted a major debate on the place of religion in schools. The Report recommended the elimination of Catholic and Protestant schools, thus de-emphasizing the place of religion in the public school system. Now under-discussion, the report has brought considerable opposition from the Catholic sector. The report's secular approach would lead to a neutral place for reli-gion in all public schools, and would encourage schools to offer studies of all the world religions as cultural expressions, rather than the promoting of any one doctrine.

The changes in the school population in several school boards in Quebec, especially in the Montreal region, illustrate the need for special attention to be given to issues of diversity. The now defunct Montreal Catholic School Commission, once the largest school board in Montreal, saw its French-speaking student population decline from 83.5 percent in 1984–1985 to 69.8 percent in 1988–1989. During the same period the allophone population, (students whose first language is neither French nor English), increased from 15 percent to 28.4 percent.

Bill 101, instituted in 1977, legally requires that all immigrants to Que-bec send their children to schools that operate in French. The implementation of Bill 101 means that immigrants have no choice but to enroll their children in French schools. Previously, in the Montreal area for example, immigrants tended to flock to Protestant schools, the majority of which operated in En-glish. Catholic and French-speaking students tended to go to French schools that were run primarily by the Montreal Catholic School Commission. The main goals of Bill 101 have been summarized as follows: (a) to make French the primary language and to protect the French language and culture, (b) to foster the integration of immigrants into Quebec society, and (c) to make the use of French mandatory for progress in the Quebec society (Ghosh et al. 1995).

Bill 101, therefore, drastically changed the demographics in schools in Montreal. There, some city schools are often used to illustrate the dramatic changes in makeup of the school population in terms of cultural heritage. In some schools there are as many as eighty-five different cultures represented, and close to 90 percent of the students speak a language other than English or French at home (Ghosh 1995).

There is some divergence between the way intercultural education is in-terpreted in the traditionally French Catholic sector and the way it has devel-oped in the Protestant English sector. The French sector focuses, to a large extent, on the promotion and enhancement of French language and culture. So, its attempts at integration center on the integration of the "other" ethnic groups into the French milieu. The earliest attempts of the now defunct Mon-treal Catholic School Commission to acknowledge and manage diversity were the *classes d'acceuil,* of which integration is the stated purpose. The emphasis on language learning is predominant.

The traditionally Protestant sector has, since 1988, given the most attention to the development of a multicultural education policy. In one of its reports, the Protestant School Board of Greater Montreal (PSBGM) points out: "In a fundamental sense, the purpose of a multicultural/multiracial approach to education is to address the problem of racism" (3). When racial and cultural tensions developed in its school communities in the 1970s and 1980s, the response of the PSBGM was to establish ad hoc committees.

By 1984, a comprehensive multicultural approach was being considered by the PSBGM. A task force to explore this approach was set up in 1986. Its findings have been formulated in a paper entitled "A multicultural/multiracial approach to education in the schools of the Protestant School Board of Greater Montreal: Report of the task force on multicultural/multiracial education" (1988). In a section on Curriculum and Learning Resources this report states:

> Through an examination of the existing curriculum, it is clear that students are expected to acquire an awareness of the cultural richness and diversity of the peoples around the world and of Canadian and Quebec societies. In a multicultural/multiracial approach to education, ongoing curriculum evaluation must ensure that biases are removed, omissions corrected, stereotypes eliminated and positive values of all cultures imparted through careful curriculum planning. Also inherent in this approach is the recognition that multiculturalism/ multiracialism and a human rights perspective is a necessary preparation for all students and not just for recent immigrant students; that the curriculum, both the formal and the "hidden," is an important vehicle through which values, attitudes and beliefs are learned and the self developed. (17)

To sum up, concern with values issues are reflected in Quebec and school board policy documents. However, insofar as multicultural issues are concerned there is some contradiction between the needs of a diverse population and the ideological position on culture held by the Quebec government and supported in the French sector.

Mexico

Mexican educational philosophers concerned with values and their implications for educational institutions include Barba (1990) and Daniel (1995), who review the categories and elements involved in the teaching of values; Cortes (1995), who discusses different philosophical perspectives on education and suggests that what is needed is the building of an educational axiological model for the well-being of everyone; Huerta and Ezcurra (1997), who propose a taxonomy of the stages of moral psychosocial development;

Flores (1994), who proposes an open values education that avoids defining values unilaterally; and Ribeiro (1996) and Yuren (1995), who each propose values typologies.

Recognizing that the change process and modernization create a crisis for the country, not only in the legal and administrative domains, but in the ethical domain as well, several Mexican authors place the problem of values education in the current economic-political context. These authors include Amezcua (1984), Benavidez and Gonzalez (1990), Carrizalez (1990), Muñoz (1991), and Yuren and Vela (1985), as well as those participating in the International Summit on Education (Cumbre Internacional de Educación 1997) and the researchers of *Los mexicanos de los noventas* (Mexicans of the Nineties) (Instituto de Investigaciones Sociales 1996). In these works we can distinguish two different perspectives. The first describes the framework of educational norms and objectives in the political dimension and the second analyzes values implied by political action.

In the first category are those whose point of departure is the political significance of educational norms and goals. There are critical and theoretical discussions of a variety of topics, such as the lack of achievement of national values (sovereignty, equality, democracy, justice, self-determination), the value orientation of industrial societies (the focus on consumerism and ownership), the exclusion of large segments of the society from economic and political globalization, and a challenge to the belief in the neutrality of the curriculum.

The second category, the implications of political actions, is exemplified by the work of *Los Mexicanos de los noventas,* in which the values and attitudes predominant in recent social and political changes are analyzed. Those that stand out include preferences in the economic and political spheres—for example, nonacceptance of the rules of the market economy (i.e., there is nonacceptance with respect to privatization and price regulation in the free market). In the political realm the idea of democracy predominates (i.e., the institutions and practices of formal democracy are valued).

In the cultural arena, these writers observe that trust, friendship, and loyalty constitute permanent values, so that there is a rejection of behavior that reflects corruption, cronyism, and nepotism, the opposite of emerging social values of equality under the law. These writers support the thesis that the characteristics of an open, modern society, such as equality, tolerance, and respect for differences, are linked to deinstitutionalization in the religious sphere as well as in that of family and sexual relationships even though the tendency toward change is not universal. With respect to the family, they acknowledge the positive associations of union, children, love, home, well-being, parents, and understanding. The family is perceived as an economic unit and this signals the valuing of the work of women outside the home. In the responses of the participants in these studies, we can observe an identification with, or at least, an expressed preference for, the new values derived from the emerging sociopolitical and cultural conditions of the country. Finally the writers in this category analyze the extent of communication between those who agree and those who disagree with changes in the model of the Mexican state.

In Mexico, for much of the twentieth century, discussions relating to values were, for the most part, circumstantial, considered apart from social duty, and one might say, considered out of place. Not to discuss this subject was, on most occasions, the best option. This was so for various reasons deriving from the constitutional process and the dynamic based on the secularization of education, which generated a schism between the moral (conceived from a religious standpoint) and the political. To speak of values and morals was considered inappropriate for people with a sense of political or social/scientific duty. These topics were considered the domain of the church and the family. With this scenario, ethical education was seen as something distinct from the school, to which was assigned responsibility for civic education. The latter constituted a combination of rituals and ceremonies that ignored what it means to be a good citizen and its relationship to political duty. The citizen was more a patriot dedicated to national symbols than a political actor capable of influencing government policy. With this approach, there was a void in the political and ethical aspects of the social function of the school (Cullen 1997).

Today the schools have opened the value debate, a topic that has enormous force and has expressed itself in the creation of new curricula and programs that add ethics to the notion of civic education, approaching the gamut of values from the negative sphere (sexuality, drug addiction, etc.). A series of questions arises from this debate, such as: What type of citizen is desirable? What norms and types of behavior should be promoted and how? Are science and politics competitive areas without a relationship between them? What is the relationship of both of them with ethics? How do we determine the selection of values we want as a society? Can the schools maintain margins of autonomy in this determination? How do we balance tradition and modernity? This combination of questions has infused the educational system with a process of change.

The 1995–2000 plan of educational development (Poder Federal Ejecutivo 1995) proposed reducing the quantity of information in the curriculum for elementary schools. Instead, emphasis was placed on reinforcing values and attitudes that permit optimal development, as well as on strengthening interest and appreciation of scientific and technical knowledge. In a parallel form, it proposes inculcating values and attitudes that yield authentic, democratic conduct and that contribute to the respect and preservation of human rights in all aspects of life. At every educational level, special attention is given to encouraging the participation of women, to help them overcome conditions that explain their lack of progress, and to expand the role they can play in all fields of human activity free from prejudice and discrimination.

In response to global ecological deterioration, the plan seeks to create a consciousness of the gravity of the problem and the necessity of adopting behaviors that support the equilibrium and improvement of ecology. In addition, it urges that school experience be adequate for the acquiring of ethical values to develop attitudes fundamental to a healthy personality, and for learning social relations based on respect, mutual support, and legality. Within the life of the school, it proposes reinforcing self-respect, respect for others, tolerance, freedom of expression, a sense of responsibility, cooperative attitudes, rationally accepted discipline, and a desire for learning. It is based on the belief that practice and example consolidate values such as democracy, honesty, appreciation of work, the reason for working, and a sense of its value to a nation with a proud history and culture.

It claims that civic participation requires knowledge of rights and duties, as well as respectful attitudes toward others and the law. Further, it requires the power to locate history in the development of humankind, the conscience to live on a planet with limited and fragile resources, concern for the natural environment, and encouragement of international understanding and acceptance of diversity. It also proposes promotion of curiosity, a capacity for observation, ease in imagining explanations, and love of nature. Civic participation should stimulate the ability to understand questions of special significance for the quality of life, preserve health and development of personal equilibrium, appreciate diverse forms of art, express artistic sensibility, and promote physical activity. Finally, it places emphasis on personal maturation, sexuality and reproductive health, and combating addiction to toxic substances that generate dependency.

This policy faces a number of difficulties—an economic crisis in which the education sector has suffered a budgetary cut and a crisis in the power exerted at different levels with political motives predominating over the planning of services.

United States

Historically, the United States has been seen as a nation whose government and policies are founded on the principles of justice and democratic ideals. Nineteenth-century educational pioneers, realizing that America was to be a very diverse multicultural nation, saw the need for a school system that would "teach the civic virtues necessary to maintain our novel political and social experiment" (Ryan 1993, 16). Attention to "universal" democratic and civic values was considered especially relevant due to the increasing number of immigrants who would have the opportunity to become true Americans and part of a larger "melting pot" society through the process of schooling with attention to these universal values.

Twentieth-century critics considered these "universal values" to be relative in nature, defined by the opinions of various ethnic, racial, and religious groups and/or by school personnel. Therefore, attempts at dealing with values in the schools were seen as indoctrinating. It was believed that a truly heterogeneous society could not support the teaching of a single set of values. Teachers shied away from issues of moral significance entirely. It was felt that the responsibility to influence the child's moral and civic formation resided with home and/or church. By the mid-twentieth century, any consensus on the importance of values education was replaced by an attitude that all things, including morality, are in a state of perpetual flux. Even civics education went by the wayside. The celebration of the autonomy of the person elevated individual rights above responsibility. Such forces as increasing cultural diversity, alternative lifestyles, family structure, secularization, and commitment to the doctrine of separation of church and state all influenced the schools to reduce or eliminate their previously central role in the transmission of values (Lickona 1993).

In the 1970s, the Values Clarification approach of Kirschenbaum and Simon (1973) and the Just Community Efforts of Kohlberg (1975) enjoyed a brief period of popularity before they fell victim to conservative political, religious, and ideological forces that demanded that schools abstain from values education. Kohlberg's response to these critics fell on deaf ears:

> Education in the public schools should be restricted to that which the school has the right and mandate to develop: an awareness of justice, or of the rights of others in our Constitutional system. While the Bill of Rights prohibits the teaching of religious beliefs, or of specific value systems, it does not prohibit the teaching of the awareness of rights and principles of justice fundamental to the Constitution itself. (169)

The content of both formal and informal curriculum and instructional practices is never value-free. As Etzioni points out, "there is no way of teaching subjects without teaching values—every teaching act has a moral dimension" (Bereth and Scherer 1993, 12–13). According to Leming (1993), values develop within a social web or environment. The nature of that environment, the message it sends to individuals, and the behaviors it encourages and discourages are important factors.

Therefore, all schooling entails the imparting of societal values held by teachers who mostly mirror the mainstream society. Their value orientation may differ from that of diverse student populations and their communities. This is an especially critical issue in schools that have had a dramatic shift in demographics of the student population that has not been reflected in the demographics of the teaching staff.

In California, the state's population growth, like that of much of the nation, has been both dramatic and diverse. Since 1950 the state has more than tripled from ten million people (or one out of fifteen people in the U.S.)

to over 33 million (or one out of every eight U.S. residents) in 1998. California educates about 12 percent of all students in the United States, kindergarten through grade twelve. California's student population is increasingly more diverse than that of the nation as a whole, and as such is a harbinger for educational challenges yet to unfold throughout the nation. For example, between 1997 and 2007, the percentage of white students is expected to decline by 16 percent while other groups will increase by the following percentages: Hispanic, 35 percent; Pacific Islander, 30 percent; and Asian 15 percent. One out of five students was born outside of the United States. These trends reflect population changes throughout the state where, by the turn of the century, no ethnic group was expected to constitute a majority of California's population (California Department of Education 1999).

The ever-changing demographics of the United States has posed a critical demand for qualified, competent teachers who are better prepared to address the multifaceted needs of diverse student populations. The needs of racially, linguistically, and culturally diverse students go far beyond the obvious academic areas of language development and acquisition of core content knowledge. Students with diverse backgrounds also face a multitude of challenges, both in school and in the wider community. Without an understanding of how to build on the values of family and community, teachers are seriously hampered in their ability to provide meaningful learning environments and opportunities for culturally and linguistically diverse students. Cummins (1989) emphasizes the need for quality instruction with qualified practitioners who advocate for the needs of culturally, racially, and linguistically diverse students and who view primary languages and cultures as assets and strengths. This happens more readily, however, when teachers share values and cultures.

Thus, with both the rising awareness of cultural diversity and the emphasis on multicultural education in the last two decades of the twentieth century, attention has once more been directed at the issue of values and the role of the schools. Commenting on current efforts at transformation of the educational process, Gay (1999) notes that "the most fundamental and deeply engrained values, beliefs, and assumptions, which determine all educational policies, content, procedures, and structures will be revolutionized by being culturally pluralized" (354).

The last two decades of the twentieth century, however, were also characterized by a growth in troubling trends that affect the relationship between values and the role of the schools. Lickona (1993) identifies the following:

- rising youth violence
- increasing dishonesty (lying, cheating, stealing)
- growing disrespect for authority
- peer cruelty

- resurgence of bigotry on school campuses from preschool through higher education
- decline in the work ethic
- sexual precocity
- growing self-centeredness and declining civic responsibility
- ethical illiteracy
- increases in self-destructive behavior (9)

To this last trend, we can unfortunately add destruction of others—through massacre of classmates and teachers, and acts of cruelty based on race, religion, and sexual orientation. Hate crime legislation at both federal and state levels is being implemented and many parents are opting for enrollment in private or parochial schools that focus on the values they want imparted to their children. In the public schools, within the constraints of separation of church and state, the pendulum is swinging back to the notion of teaching as a moral endeavor after decades of attempts at "value-free" education. Kohlberg's Just Community, Kirschenbaum and Simon's Values Clarification, Josephson's Character Education program, Tappan and Brown's narrative approach to moral education, the American Bar Association's Law-Related Education program, the Anti-Defamation League's World of Difference program, the Southern Poverty Law Center's Teaching Tolerance program, and many others are currently being looked to as antidotes to some of the negative aspects of modern society. As Lickona so elegantly articulates:

> We are recovering the wisdom that we do share a basic morality, essential for our survival. That adults must promote this morality by teaching the young, directly and indirectly, such values as respect, responsibility, trustworthiness, fairness, caring, and civic virtue; and that these values are not merely subjective but that they have objective worth and a claim on our collective conscious. Such values affirm our human dignity, promote the good of the individual and the common good, and protect our human rights . . . they define our responsibilities in a democracy, and they are recognized by all civilized people and taught by all enlightened creeds. Not to teach children these core ethical values is a grave moral failure. (9)

The challenge has been issued to those institutions charged with the preparation of teachers. While most have made efforts to include issues related to cultural pluralism in their programs, little or nothing has been done in preparing teachers to deal with moral or civic issues. This response, or the lack of it in the curriculum of teacher education programs, is the subject of the research undertaken by the authors on values education, and carried out in teacher education programs in California, as well as in Mexico and Canada, and is summarized in the final section of this chapter.

TEACHER EDUCATION AND THE TEACHING OF VALUES

While there are different routes followed in the preparation of teachers in reference to values education in Mexico, Canada, and the United States, researchers in each country voice some common concerns. It appears that in reference to values and teacher preparation the Mexican literature is primarily theoretical and moves from the macro or general societal level, giving limited attention to the specifics of values education. On the other hand, in Canada and the United States, the reverse is true—with emphasis on specific and practical issues involved in transmitting values, while still concerned with determining universally acceptable values. Thus, in these two countries the movement appears to be from the micro to the macro level.

Mexican literature is primarily concerned with the concept of values and the understanding of the impact of educational policy in the formation of notions of nationalism and citizenship, and the form in which the social mores are reflected in the schools. From the sociocultural context the Mexican literature then moves to the classroom. It is from this perspective of the whole sociocultural context that it then looks at educational institutions and teaching-learning practices. There appear to be more studies dealing with the hidden curriculum and institutional power games than with specific curriculum and civic participation. The central themes relate to the need to create a more democratic and equitable society. The school would become a more democratic space, permitting the development of autonomous citizens with problem-solving and critical thinking abilities.

In Canada and the United States, however, there is extensive literature focused on the micro level—concerned with the teaching-learning process in relation to teacher training and the teaching of values. It is from *this* perspective that attention is directed back to the societal level. Problems arising from the construction of multicultural education have made explicit the necessity of giving more attention to injustice and inequality. The school is charged with rethinking the proposals of John Dewey in order to promote democratic practice and critical citizenship, as well as the ideas of Giroux and McLaren (1986) in viewing teachers as "transformative intellectuals" in this practice.

The role of the individual classroom teacher in promoting values education is considered paramount in Mexico. For this reason, researchers have typically looked at the hidden curriculum in order to understand classroom interaction and have given less attention to content and methodology in the delivery of values education. In contrast, the American literature points out that in the United States, the teacher is primarily concerned with cognitive processes and the self-esteem of the students. In Mexico, the term "moral education" has been viewed with disfavor, and values are dealt with as "civic education," in contrast to Quebec where moral education has a substantive place in government policy statements as well as in mission statements of educational institutions. In the United States there has been a void for a long time in both moral and values education. Today one can observe a renewed concern with values issues that has brought with it a series of specific educational proposals, such as the previously described Just Community Approach, the narrative approach, and character education.

The Mexican literature highlights the rejection of "capitalist" ideas in favor of the theme of democracy as a concern. Loyalty, friendship, and truth appear as current and significant values together with respect for the family (which functions in Mexico as an economic unit). In the schools, one can identify an authoritarian system that prioritizes concepts such as respect, subordination, reverence for ideas of courtesy, and rituals and ceremony that place more emphasis on form than meaning. American research highlights values such as self-esteem and personal integrity, short-term and medium-term consequences for behavior, and the development of social abilities within the child's immediate environment. Intensive attention has been directed at conflict in various situations within the school, above all multicultural situations that emphasize recognizing differences arising from race, class, gender, and national origin.

Mexican researchers recognize three influences on values education: educational legislation, pedagogical theory, and day-to-day school practices, the latter being the most significant. With a resurgence of specific curricula related to values education in the United States and Canada, researchers in both these countries focus on the need for introspection, genuine dialogue, and discussion of issues relevant to diverse democratic society and social change. In Canada, official multicultural policy provides additional emphasis. Researchers in all three countries agree that school is part of society and as such it incorporates a process of replication of the values existing in the larger society, and that democratic values should play a more significant role in the education of teachers.

A COMPARATIVE STUDY OF VALUES IN TEACHER EDUCATION: CANADA, MEXICO, AND THE UNITED STATES

A tri-national study was conducted from 1996–1999, in the three NAFTA countries, on the "Construction of Values in Elementary Teacher Education" by Elizondo, Ghosh, Tarrow, and Quezada (1999). In Mexico, the research was conducted at the Universidad Pedagogica Nacional (UPN) in the degree program in elementary education, Mexico City, and in a cooperative degree program in bilingual/bicultural education offered by UPN (Mexicali campus) and California State University (Long Beach). In California, the research involved faculty and students in Cross-Cultural Language and Academic Development (CLAD) credential program, and Bilingual Cross-Cultural Language and Academic Development (BCLAD) credential program for elementary teachers. The former program is offered at Long Beach and the latter is offered there and in a system-wide program in cooperation with UPN at the Mexico City campus. In Canada at McGill University (Quebec) the research was conducted in programs of Bachelor of Elementary Education and Bachelor in Second Language Education.

The research was carried out in two phases in the above locations with a total population of 200 students. The main goals of the research project were:

- to develop a schema of values considered most important by students in elementary teacher education programs in all three countries; and
- to encourage teacher education programs in each of the three countries to focus on helping future teachers learn how to reflect on how their values and those of their students affect schooling and society.

This would mean helping teachers understand that every decision they make in educating students is based on their own implicit values and that teachers must take into consideration cultural values and areas of value conflict in all of their dealings with students and their families. Given these objectives and the characteristics of the research team—a group from three distinct research traditions, different sociocultural contexts and three working languages—the choice was made to have a qualitative research design that permitted comparative analysis.

In Phase I, interviews were conducted with teacher educators and students to identify the values deemed most important in the teacher education program. As a result of this process, a list of 71 values was generated. In Phase II, faculty and students rank ordered the values identified in Phase I to determine the top 8 to 10 values in each of the three countries. Utilizing a semantic net technique, the meaning attached to each of the top values was clarified. A paradigm was then developed, and the identified most significant values were classified according to this paradigm.

The schema of the values considered most important by future teachers in all three countries indicated that while there were common values articulated, each country had very distinct ways of conceptualizing and describing their most significant values. Ethical values identified by teachers in all three countries highlighted interpersonal relationships and effective communication. In all three countries teachers articulated the need to stress *honesty, respect for human beings, respect for difference/diversity,* and *respect and strengthening of human rights.* These values emphasize the need to form inclusive classrooms where diversity is valued and democratic ideals are central to the school program.

There were common concerns shared by the participating countries about the values that are critical to the education of diverse student populations. In Mexico, prospective teachers emphasized values of family and community, whereas the data on values from the United States and Canada recognized that prospective teachers held more individualistic values. Thus, Canadian and U.S. participants, while emphasizing the importance of community, articulate value constructs emphasizing individual responsibility.

In the ethical sphere, individual-communal differences arise again. All three countries mention *honesty* as an important element with an emphasis on *truth* and *respect*. However, while Canadian and U.S. teachers relate honesty to individual integrity, Mexican teachers stress group integrity based on fraternity and love. The welfare of the group appears to come before individual success at the expense of their peers or any abstract principle.

For the Canadian participants, the important attributes of the value respect for differences and diversity, were *acceptance, open-mindedness, multiculturalism, understanding* and *tolerance*. Mexican subjects emphasized *respect for human rights* by using defining words such as *love, justice,* and *honesty*. The U.S. participants emphasized attributes such as *empathy, respect, courtesy,* and *kindness* in regard to the value *respect for human beings*. Thus while all teachers in all three countries identify respect as a significant value, it is clear that the attributes of the word *respect* highlight these differences. While in Canada and the United States *self-respect* and *autonomy* appear to be emphasized, in Mexico the focus is on respect for *authority* (the family, the community, and the state).

Values related to democracy appeared in the ethical sphere in Canada and the United States. In Mexico's case these values appeared in the political sphere, a category not even addressed by Canadian and U.S. teachers. The values articulated by Mexican teachers related to a sense of patriotism or nationalism not articulated in the responses given by U.S. and Canadian teachers. While Mexico has its heroes, its history is replete with examples of change brought about almost totally by communal effort. The deemphasis on individualistic values by Mexican teachers may reflect their historical as well as political reality that it takes a whole community to effect change.

Another hypothesis as to the significance accorded the political category in Mexico and the absence of this category in the Canadian and United States relates to an entrenched political system, which, while espousing democratic principles, is only now beginning to effectively utilize democratic structures. Thus, for Mexicans both the functioning of democratic processes and the impact of the individual on that process are relatively new concepts.

Canadian or American teachers working with Mexican families often have difficulty understanding that what may appear to be lethargy in relation to participation in government or to social activism beyond the local level may actually reflect the individual Mexican perception of powerlessness to change a traditionally entrenched political system. It may also be that the sense of powerlessness reflects the perception that an individual can make very little difference, yet change is indeed possible by working within and as a community.

CONCLUSION

In this chapter we examined the issue of what is meant by a "value" and gave an extensive review of the context of the values discourse in the three countries of North America. We reviewed philosophical and political issues related to values education and focused on the roles of educational institutions and teacher education in reference to the teaching of democratic and civic values. Finally we presented a brief summary of the comparative findings of a three-year tri-national research project related to these values.

There appears to be unilateral agreement among educational theorists and practitioners that education and multicultural relations in the contemporary world demand a morally responsible position in the development and maintenance of democratic values and good citizenship. Yet, there appears also to be a still largely unmet need for those charged with the training of teachers in every society to examine and/or revise their programs to assure that the teachers they produce examine their own values, develop an awareness of value differences in diverse societies, and are prepared to deal with values issues in the classrooms and communities in which they teach. Failure to integrate values and value conflicts into whatever treatment is given to issues of race, language, and culture would be an abrogation of the professional responsibility of teacher educators to prepare teachers for the reality of our changing society in the twenty-first century.

REFERENCES

Amezcua, J. (1984). *Hacia los fundamentos axiológicos de la educación media.* Tesis de maestria. Escuela Normal Superior. Mexico City.

Barba, B. (1990). "Valores y educación. Introducción los enfoques teóricos, pedagógicos y de investigación educativa." In *Reportes de Investigación educativa,* 7–8. Mexico City: Universidad de Aguascalientes.

Barcena, F., F. Gil, and G. Jover. (1993). "The ethical dimension of teaching: A review and a proposal." *Journal of Moral Education* 22(3):241–252.

Bélanger, W. (1993). "Imparting values: A multidimensional perspective." *Journal of Moral Education* 22(2):111–123.

Benavidez, L., and A. Gonzalez. (1990). *Valores en la educación.* Mexico City: Instituto Nacional de Educacíon de Adultos.

Bereth, D., and M. Scherer. (1993 November). "On transmitting values: A conversation with Amitai Etzioni." *Educational Leadership,* pp. 12–15.

California Department of Education. (1999). *Language Census Report.* Demographics Unit. Sacramento: California Department of Education.

Carrizalez, C. (1990). "Obesiones pedagógicas de la modernidad." *Modernidad y posmodernidad en educación.* Mexico. City: Universidad Autónoma de Sinaloa y Universidad Autónoma del Estado de Morelos.

Cochrane, D. B. (1992). "The stances of provincial ministries of education towards values/moral education in Canadian public schools in 1990." *Journal of Moral Education* 21(2): 125–137.

Coles, R. (1986). *The moral life of children.* Boston: Atlantic Monthly Press.

Cumbre Internacional de Educación. (1997). *Nacional de Trabajadoresde la Educación.* Mexico City: Author.

Cummins, J. (1989). *Empowering minority students.* Sacramento: California Association for Bilingual Education.

Daniel, M. (1995). "El aprendizaje indirecto de los valores a través de la enseñanza moral. Ponencia presentada en el Foro Internacional Educación y Valores. México 1994." *Revista Mexicana de Pedagogía* 6(21):17–23.

Dror, Y. (1993). "Community and activity dimensions: Essentials for the moral and values educator." *Journal of Moral Education* 22(2):125–137.

Durkheim, E. (1989). *Educación y Sociología,* 2d ed. Mexico City: Colofón.

Elizondo, A., R. Ghosh, N. Tarrow, and M. Quezada. (1999). *Construcción de valores en programas de formación docente en educación basica: México, Canada y Estados Unidos.* Mexico City: Colegio de México.

Flores, R. (1994). "Educar en los valores y para los valores." *Foro Internacional: Educación y Valores.* Mexico City: Instituto de Fomento e Investigación Educativa.

Foucault, M. (1983). *La verdad y las formas jurídicas.* Trans. by Enrique Lynch. Mexico Editorial Gedisa.

Frondizi, R. (1962). *Qué son los valores?* Mexico City: Fondo de Cultura Económica.

García, S., and L. Vanella. (1992). *Normas y valores en el salón de clases.* Mexico City: Siglo XXI.

Gay, G. (1999). "Bridging multicultural theory and practice." In A. C. Ornstein and L. S. Behar-Horenstein (eds.), *Contemporary Issues in Curriculum,* 2d ed. Needham Heights, MA: Allyn and Bacon.

Ghosh, R. (1995). "New perspectives on multiculturalism in education." *McGill Journal of Education* 30(3):231–238.

Ghosh, R., R. Zinman, and A. Talbarie. (1995). "Policies relating to the education of cultural communities in Québec." Canadian Ethnic Studies.

Giroux, H., and P. McLaren. (1986). "Teacher Education and the politics of engagement: The case for democratic schooling." *Harvard Educational Review* 56(3): 213–238.

Goodlad, J. (1990). *Teachers for our nation's schools.* San Francisco: Jossey-Bass.

Habermas, J. (1983). *Conciencia moral y acción comunicativa.* Barcelona: Península.

Habermas, J. (1991). *Moral Consciousness and Communicative Action.* Trans. by Christian Lenhardt and Shierry Weber Nicholsen. Cambridge, MA: MIT Press.

Huerta, I., and M. Escurra. (1997). *Desarrollo de valores y régimen de verdad en el niño Mexicano.* Mexico City: Centro de Investigaciones Educativas, Universidad Nacional Autónoma de Mexico, and Instituto de Fomento e Investigación Educativa.

Kirschenbaum, H., and B. Simon (eds.). (1973). *Readings in values clarification.* Minneapolis, MN: Winston Press.

Lickona, T. (1993). "The return of character education." *Educational Leadership.* 51(3):6–11.

McAndrew, M. (1994). "Ethnicity, multiculturalism, and multicultural education in Canada." In R. Ghosh and D. Ray (eds.), *Social Change and Education,* 3d ed. Toronto: Harcourt.

Ministère de l'Education du Québec. (1979). *The Schools of Québec: Policy Statement and Plan of Action.* Quebec: Author.

"A multicultural/multiracial approach to education in the schools of the Protestant School Board of Greater Montreal:" Report of the Task Force on Multicultural/Multiracial Education. Montreal: Author (1988).

Muñoz, B. (1991). "La transmisión de los valores y la orientación educativa." Ponencia presentada en el Primer Simposio, Valores y Educación. Normal Superior de Toluca. Mimeo. México City.

Poder Federal Ejecutivo. (1995). "Programa de Desarrollo Educativo, 1995–2000" (Federal Executive Power. Educational Developmental Program). Mexico City: Department of Communication, Office of the President.

Proulx Report. (1999). *Religion in secular schools: A new perspective for Québec.* Quebec City: Gouvernment du Quebec, Minstère de l'Éducation.

Ribeiro L. (1996). *Los valores de acceso y la practica docente.* Mexico City: Plaza y Valdèz.

Ryan, K. (1993). "Mining the values in the curriculum." *Educational Leadership* 51(3):16–18.

The Schools of Quebec: Policy Statement and Plan of Action. (1979). Gouvernement du Québec, Ministère de l'éducation.

Tappan, M., and L. Brown. (1991). "Stories told and lessons learned: Toward a narrative approach to moral development and moral education." In C. Witherell and N. Noddings (eds.), *Stories Lives Tell.* New York: Teachers College Press.

Tappan, M., and L. Brown. (1996). "Envisioning a post-modern pedagogy." *Journal of Moral Education* 20:101–110.

Yuren, M. T. (1995). *Etnicidad, valores sociales y educación.* Mexico City: SEP-UPN.

Yuren, M., and M. Vela. (1985). "Los valores y la teoría del desarrollo curricular." *Serie Desarrollo Curricular,* Mexico City: SEP-UPN.

DISCUSSION QUESTIONS

1. What are the major arguments for and against the inclusion of values education in the curriculum of public schools?
2. What do you consider the role of the teacher in relation to values education?
3. What should be the role of teacher education programs in relation to values education?
4. What sociocultural characteristics could account for differences in values in the three North American countries?
5. Design a teacher education program to prepare teachers to deal with values issues in multicultural societies.

CHAPTER 11

Education for Democracy in Pluralistic Societies
The Case of Israel

YAACOV IRAM

Political scientists estimated that out of 130 independent U.N. member states in 1990, 59 states (45.4 percent) were democratic. However, in 1973, out of 122 states only 30 were democratic (24.6 percent). Indeed in the 1980s and 1990s there was a growing tendency toward democratization not only in Europe, particularly in the former Eastern Bloc, but also in South America, Africa, and Asia. Most of the democratic states are divided primarily into ethnic or national groups, and a secondary division might include religion, language, socioeconomic status, and political power (Huntington 1981). Democracies might be classified as Liberal or Consocial (Lijphart 1977). Israel represents a unique blend of both types of democracies (Lijphart 1994).

Education plays an important role in pluralistic societies such as Israel; education for democracy means more than teaching about a political system or a form of government. It is a process that involves imparting a way of living, and belief in individual and group worth and rights, guided by the practice of social equality and solidarity. It is also expected to impart cooperation out of mutual respect, tolerance, and diversity.

In this chapter I will present various programs of education for democracy in Israel, and ways to cope with socioeconomic, political, ideological, and national divisions in Israeli society in the wake of recent heightened tensions. A specific program of education for democracy to preservice teachers will be analyzed.

THE STATE OF ISRAEL: HISTORY, GEOGRAPHY, DEMOGRAPHY, ECONOMY, AND GOVERNMENT

The area of Israel within its 1949 armistice borders measures 20,700 square kilometers. In addition, Israel controls administered territories of about 7,500 square kilometers, occupied since the 1967 Six Day War, that include territories of Syria, Jordan, and Egypt. They are administered by military government according to regulations in force prior to the occupation, and part of these territories have been relinquished to the emerging Palestinian entity. Since the Oslo agreements in 1993 and 1995, more territories are being transferred. Israel is bounded on the north by Lebanon, on the northeast by Syria, on the east by the Hashemite kingdom of Jordan, as well as by the emerging Palestinian autonomous area in the West Bank, and on the southwest by the Gulf of Aqaba/Eilat and the Egyptian Sinai Desert (*The Middle East and North Africa* 1996, 530).

Israel's total population in December 1994 was 5,462,300, of whom 82 percent were Jews and 18 percent were non-Jews. The non-Jewish population is comprised of 14.2 percent Muslims, 2.3 percent Christians, and 1.7 percent Druze and others (Circassians and Ahmadis) (Central Bureau of Statistics 1995). The Jewish population is predominantly urban, while the Arab minority is rural.

One of Israel's most striking characteristics is the rapid increase in its population. The main source of the growth of Israel's population is immigration, accounting for 58 percent of the yearly increase between 1948 and 1977, and for 30 percent of the yearly increase in the total population, and 46.2 percent in the Jewish population between 1948 and 1988 (Central Bureau of Statistics 1989). The ethnic composition of Israeli society changed according to the source of immigration. In 1948 the ethnic division according to parental origin was 80 percent Ashkenazim, 15 percent Orientals, and 5 percent Israeli born. Mass immigration from countries in the Middle East and North Africa caused an "orientalization" of Jewish society in Israel. Thus, ethnic origin division in 1989 was 38 percent Ashkenazim, 42 percent Orientals, and 20 percent Israeli born. Half a million Jewish immigrants who arrived from the former Soviet Union countries again changed the ethnic mix to 40 percent Ashkenazim, 37 percent Orientals, and 23 percent Israeli born (Central Bureau of Statistics 1994).

In the early 1990s, Israel remains a migrant society. Of 2,315,900 Israeli-born Jews, only one-third (33.9 percent) are second-generation Israelis. Of the total Jewish population, only 21.5 percent are second-generation Israelis (Central Bureau of Statistics 1994, 83). The large waves of immigration in the early 1990s, which arrived mainly from Russia but also from Ethiopia, resulted in a further cultural and social diversification of Israeli society. This precipitated major problems in economic absorption, social integration, and education. Special programs were introduced to teach the Hebrew language and to impart Israeli culture to new immigrants.

Israel is also a pluralistic society. Nationally there exists a Jewish majority and a non-Jewish, predominantly Arab, minority. Linguistically, there are two official languages: Hebrew and Arabic. As a result of national, religious, and linguistic pluralism, separate educational systems emerged: Jewish, Arab, and Druze (Mari 1978).

The Jewish majority is diversified ethnically, religiously, culturally, and educationally. From an ethnic perspective, in the sense of country of origin, there are *Ashkenazim*—Jews who originate from Eastern and Central Europe; and *Sephardim* or "Orientals"—Jews from the Mediterranean Basin and other Arab and Muslim countries (Ben-Rafael and Sharot 1991). Israeli Jews are also divided into "religious" and "nonreligious" categories (Liebmann 1991). From a cultural perspective, diversity arises from the different ethnic groups who brought from their countries of origin different customs, ceremonies, attitudes, values, and ways of life. In terms of education, differences in religious observance have resulted in the emergence of three Jewish school systems: state education, state-religious education, and the independent education of ultraorthodox Jewry.

Israel's economic development was affected by objective difficulties. These hardships included a heavy defense expenditure (absorbing 25 percent of the budget) as a result of the continuous Arab-Israeli conflict and the need to absorb immigrants, about half of whom came from underdeveloped, semifeudal, and traditional societies in the Middle East and North Africa, and who lacked formal education and skills required by a modern industrially oriented economy. Israel's economy was also adversely affected by a scarcity of water and natural resources. Despite these difficulties, during the years 1951–1972 the Gross National Product (GNP) and constant prices rose by an annual average of 10 percent. From 1973 onward the rate of growth decreased considerably to 1.3 percent in 1976 and 1977, increased to 4.7 percent in 1978, and registered as static in 1982. The rate of growth increased by less than 1 percent in 1983 and 1.6 percent in 1988, and expanded by 5.9 percent in 1991, 6.6 percent in 1992, and 6.5 percent in 1994. Defense takes the largest share of the annual state budget, more than 20 percent, while allocation for education amounts to 7.5 percent of the state budget in 1993–1994 (Central Bureau of Statistics 1994).

Israel's government and politics share basic democratic principles and practices derived from, and associated with, Western parliamentary democracies. Israel essentially is a parliamentary democracy. Elections are held every four years. National and local elections are strictly proportional, reflecting multiparty competition. No single party has been able so far to secure a majority of seats in the 120-member Knesset (Parliament). As a result, all governments are formed by coalition between political parties. The Arab and Druze citizens of Israel enjoy full rights of citizenship and formal equality, including equal rights in education (Beilin 1992). However, in recognizing the identity of its non-Jewish citizens, the state provides a separate Arabic system of education with Arabic as the medium of instruction at all levels, except for higher education. Unlike other levels of the educational system, which are administered directly by the government, the higher educational system is largely autonomous, in spite of governmental funding of 60 percent to 80 percent of its budget.

THE ISRAELI EDUCATIONAL SYSTEM—
AN OVERVIEW

The modern educational system dates back to approximately fifty years before Israel gained independence. Many of the foundations laid during the early years are still evident. The system includes kindergartens, primary schools, secondary schools (including vocational and agricultural secondary schools), teacher training institutions, postsecondary schools for continued and vocational studies, and colleges and universities. Hebrew language and culture comprise the basis for studies. The school year is approximately ten months long, from September through July; the study week is thirty to thirty-five hours. Studies take place in homeroom classes staffed by homeroom teachers, who are responsible for class studies and social activities. In the lower grades the homeroom teacher teaches most of the studies, while in the higher grades specialized teachers are employed to teach subjects. Schools maintain close contact with parents, and most classes have a parents' committee. In addition to formal studies, there are an extensive range of extracurricular activities (informal education) inside and outside of school.

The state educational system includes separate schools for Arab and Druze students. The structure of the Arab school sector is similar to that of the Jewish sector. The main differences are in the language of instruction (Arabic), and in the curriculum, which is designed to reflect the unique culture and history of the various Arab populations (Muslim, Christian, and Druze) (Al-Haj 1995).

Israel's educational enterprise is a centralized system financed by the state and directed by the Ministry of Education, Culture, and Sport. It is subdivided into Jewish and Arab schools, which implies that it is a bilingual system embracing Hebrew and Arabic. The Hebrew-speaking schools are divided into two tracks: state schools (*mamlachti*-state) and state religious (*mamlachti-dati*) schools. Parents have the right to choose between religious and nonreligious schools. Schooling is free and compulsory between ages five to sixteen, and free but not compulsory between the ages three to four and seventeen to eighteen. The educational system is ideologically oriented and performs a dual mission. First, it fulfills the social mission of providing equal educational opportunities to disadvantaged children, mainly of Oriental origin. Second, in recent years it performs the national mission of integrating the various groups of immigrants (i.e., Russians and Ethiopians) into the fabric of Israeli society.

The educational system in Israel copes with dilemmas and conflicts inherent in its historical and sociocultural conditions: tradition and modernity, nationalism and universalism, uniformity and pluralism, elitism and egalitarianism, centralization and decentralization. These dilemmas characterize all spheres of public life and institutions, but they have a particular effect on education.

EDUCATION OF MINORITIES

Problems

Minority groups can be defined in various ways: by region, ethnic background, language use, socioeconomic status, religion, gender, educational attainment, lifestyle, and more. These diverse definitional bases are not all of equal political importance, if we define political importance as measured by "the extent of conflict in society regarding who exercises power over whom" (Thomas 1986, 399). Furthermore, the political importance (and power-status) of a particular minority group varies from one society to another and from one time to another within the same society.

Education of ethnic minorities is closely related to issues such as cultural diversity and equality of educational opportunity to all. As the problems of ethnicity and migration continue to provoke conflicts at home, and to become global in scope involving people of many different backgrounds, it becomes incumbent upon educationists to seek proper ways to deal with these problems, and upon educators to better prepare young people with the knowledge, perspectives, willingness, and skills that will enable them to be willing to live with and become more effective in collaborating with people different from themselves. Such an education is referred to by negative names such as *anti-bias-education* and *anti-racist education* (Taylor and Bagley 1995), or by titles with positive attributes: *multicultural education, intercultural education,* and *international/global education.* Unfortunately most of these ideas and programs have not been implemented in most schools. However, if we want to live in societies that encourage the participation, and welcome the perspectives, histories and contributions of all its members, if we wish to create ultimately a society that rejects oppression, discrimination, xenophobia, and racism, we must redouble our efforts in all levels and structures of education from kindergarten to university, to promote and implement existing programs and to continue new and more effective means.

Low academic achievement of ethnic minority children (which in many countries is synonymous with newly arrived immigrants) is related to issues such as: (1) racism in teachers and in the school system; (2) cultural bias in the curriculum and educational materials; (3) racial and cultural factors in the training of teachers; (4) hiring and promotion problems in regard to ethnic minority teachers and administrators, and (5) wider cultural, racial, and socioeconomic problems (Male 1986). We, as both educators and educationists, do not have an easy task. Our challenge and mission is to prepare future teachers and to reeducate in-service teachers with the knowledge and skills that will enable them to work effectively with students from a wide range of backgrounds. This knowledge and these skills must be transferred to students—most of whom will live most of their lives in highly interdependent intercultural or multicultural societies, whether in the United States, Russia, England, France, and Germany (Tulasiewicz and Adams 1995) or in newly reestablished countries such as Bosnia- Herzegovina (Bosnians, Serbs, Croations). The task is to transform attitudes from monoculturalism to multiculturalism—namely the process through which a person develops competence in several cultures (Johnson 1977). In pluralistic societies, multiculturalism is imperative in order to be able to communicate with, understand, and participate in a cultural context other than one's own, within the same sociopolitical framework. Schools must be the major locus of efforts to teaching multiculturalism in the spheres of language, culture, and intergroup relations (Masemann and Iram 1987).

In some cases, multicultural education might lead to intercultural education, namely "an attempt to generate a cultural synthesis [and not just a coexistence]: the production of new cultural models grafted onto the existing base of national cultures which, while remaining in place, themselves become enriched as a result of the process" (Tulasiewicz and Adams 1995, 265).

The task of equality or equity in the education of ethnic minorities is not easy in light of what we know about the ways by which people learn about cultures other than their own, and about reluctance of governments to act decisively both in legislation and provisions and, finally, in the implementation of declared policies. Nevertheless, we are obliged to fulfill this task, given the time, place, and circumstance in which we now live. Forward-looking education cannot ignore such vital, crucial, and moral issues.

Promises

The issue of minority education is, of course, part of the larger question of how various groups are to be treated and whether they are to have access to the mainstream society while retaining their group identity, regardless of whether that identity is based on religion, race, color, or language. The problem was treated in a special issue of a respected journal (*Education and Urban Society* 1986) that was devoted to "Policy Issues in the Education of Minorities: A Worldwide View." The countries chosen for analysis were Australia, Canada, England, (West) Germany, India, Israel, Japan, and Malaysia. These countries were selected because they represented factors such as race, color, caste, religion, nationality, immigrant status, and worldview (traditional versus modernism).

Countries differ in the extent to which role their national governments, courts, civil right groups, and teachers' unions play in minority education. They differ also in the means they employ to cope with issues such as busing, quotas, multicultural education, and racial balancing of pupils and teachers.

It is both reassuring and discouraging that most countries continue to struggle with questions relating to the education of minorities, suggesting that the slowness in solving problems of education of minorities is not only due to ineptness, but also to the basic difficulties inherent in the issue of minorities. We might be discouraged because racism, unfairness, discrimination, and lack of equal educational opportunity for minorities continues in many countries, and in others, such as the former Yugoslavia, instances of these difficulties have risen.

Many societies, it seems, are increasingly subject to multinational migration, whether of ethnic workers or refugees. This modern migration across geopolitical borders and cultural fences in pursuit of economic needs and political interests assumes the guarantee of cultural identity and equality. It does not assume the superiority of dominant cultures, nor the insult of rejection that accompanies dominance. Cultural equality, let alone socioeconomic equity, must be legislated. However, de facto multiculturalism does not assure the promotion of unity and harmony, but it can be integrative or divisive depending on how it is conceptualized and legislated.

Legislated multiculturalism is based on the premise of respect for individuals and cultures. This respect does not require that we believe each culture is equally acceptable by each and every individual, but that we respect each culture equally, that we value the rich *mosaic* of individual and cultural difference within our national boundaries and beyond them, that we recognize the right to a unique identity for both individuals and groups, and that we guarantee equality of educational opportunities.

The experience of human migration and resettlement shows that respect for cultural differences is not achieved by the willingness to tolerate the customs, beliefs, languages, and social structures of other cultures at a distance, or from a position of dominance. Distance and dominance restrict the obligation to understand and appreciate the others.

To really understand cultures other than our own requires thoughtful, systematic inquiry of the similarities and differences of meaning, organization, and practice of other ethnocultural groups. And as a result, it requires acceptance and assurance of cultural and political rights. A liberal society can be distinguished by the way it treats its multiple cultures (minorities), assuring individual rights to dignity, nationality, free speech, and due process— without discrimination based on race, origin, color, ethnicity, religion, gender, or age. These characteristics of authentic identity protect both individuals and cultural groups from assimilative tendencies of dominant cultures.

Multicultural education implies *multilingual* teaching whenever necessary. Multilingual competency enables cross-cultural dialogue. It requires, always, *cultural sensitivization,* that is, sensitizing ourselves to the point of recognizing the substance of others' beliefs, claims, habits, practices, and needs. This is not a process of relativizing one's cultural beliefs, identity, and perceptions, rather it allows for a dialogue of recognition, intercultural understanding, and equality of participation.

Most nations today are pluralistic and multicultural societies. They have one or more minority groups, depending on the definition of minority. For the purpose of this article, minority status does not necessarily imply numerical inferiority. It refers rather to "the quality of power relations between groups" (Ogbu 1983, 169). Thus, a population is defined as a minority "if it occupies some form of subordinate power position in relation to another population in the same society." According to this definition, many groups may rightly claim the status of minority group, employing criteria such as their percentage in the total population or their share of power, prestige, or wealth.

As none of the prevalent typologies or classifications of minority groups (Ogbu 1978) fit social diversity in its totality, it will be more useful to apply, with some modifications, a conceptual framework that deals with modes of interaction between dominant (or majority) groups and subordinate (or minority) groups in pluralistic societies (Smolicz 1985). Three modes of pluralism that can be used to analyze intergroup relations in any given society are assimilation, multiculturalism and separatism. *Assimilation* implies that the minority group adopts the language, traditions, mores, and values of the host society (in case of immigrants) or of the dominant group (usually the majority), up to the point of abandoning its original language and culture. At the opposite pole of intergroup relations is *separatism,* a rejection by one or both sides of any attempts at desegregation or integration, thus adopting a position of mutual exclusion, whether by *indifferent side-by-side* existence, or worse, conflictual existence and no cultural transactions whatsoever. *Multiculturalism* implies adjustment of all groups, minority and majority alike, and resorting to *intentional coexistence* out for willingness for mutual adjustment and acceptance (Bhatnager 1981; Iram 1987).

Prospects

Based on a previous comparative study of Canada and Israel by Masemann and Iram (1987), I would like to offer the following conclusions in regard to prospects for future policy development in regard to education of minorities.

First, it seems that constitutional provisions are not necessarily a guarantee of equality or equity, particularly when there is disparity in status among ethnocultural and linguistic groups, and even more so when groups occupy dominant and subordinate status within a national framework.

Second, it is difficult to measure or assess the success of multicultural development and human rights, because the qualities of tolerance and intercultural understanding are so evanescent, and may actually be threatened if cultural retention rather than cultural sharing is the outcome of programs for cultural development, or if political events such as warfare consistently present a negative picture of intergroup relations.

Third, multicultural development may be difficult to foster by government decree, if its foundations are not already laid in the history and social structure of a country.

Fourth, official language policy is an important part of multicultural development, and the educational framework of such policies demonstrates the degree of commitment to linguistic and cultural equality.

Fifth, the political realities of overt hostility to, or subordination of, groups may far outweigh the harmonious wishes of policymakers or educators.

Sixth, there have been significant steps made in multicultural programming and ideas in the educational systems of many countries, but in the vast scale of things these programs are only the beginning.

Finally, there is a clear policy needed in countries to assess demographic trends and to plan for a future in which the rights of minorities and multiculturalism development are safeguarded.

The years ahead will demonstrate how well various policies, such as providing economic justice, strengthening cultural unity, and maintaining peace among the ethnic groups by providing equal (and not favored) educational and economic opportunities to all, will indeed promote economic and educational parity among ethnic groups and achieve the cultural unity and the peaceful social coexistence desired.

I would like to conclude my discussion of the prospects with a few words of caution or rather realism, quoting the American author and critic Henry Louis Mencken (1880–1956). These might add some perspective to the situation we presently face and to the changes that we look forward to. Mencken stated, "for every complicated problem there is an answer that is short, simple, and *wrong*." There are indeed no short and simple answers to the problem of education of ethnic minorities, we must take the long and hard way of working to transform the manner in which we conceive education in these intensive interdependent societies and intense multicultural times.

EDUCATION FOR DEMOCRACY IN PLURALISTIC SOCIETIES—THE CASE OF ISRAEL

In multicultural societies education for democracy is expected to stress social relationships and interactions between individuals and groups that reflect such qualities as mutual respect, cooperation, tolerance, and encouraging diversity.

Education Toward Democracy Program

I will conclude this chapter by introducing a specific program that was adapted to teach "a world of difference" in the Israeli society in the wake of heightened political-ideological tension. The program was introduced to pre-service, prospective teachers to train them in awareness of stereotypes and to cope with prejudice toward individuals and groups by modifying conceptual and attitudinal biases.

The Education Toward Democracy and Tolerance workshops conducted at Bar-Ilan University, are the only university-sponsored workshops of their kind in Israel. These workshops are an adoption of the Anti-Defamation League's (ADL) A World of Difference (AWOD) Program. The focus of these workshops is stereotypes and biases.

The university framework brings with it a number of advantages: the workshops are under academic supervision; they were prepared mainly by faculty members expert in educational theory and technique; and they can be scientifically monitored as to their effectiveness, both in the immediate and long-term perspectives. A central part of the workshops, from the university's point of view, is the monitoring and evaluation of *implementation* and *effectiveness* of the learned materials and exercises in the classroom by teachers who participated in the workshops. It is important to underline the defining principles of the academic democracy tolerance workshop as it eventually emerged at Bar-Ilan University.

The primary purpose of the School of Education course, as it developed, was to examine the principles of democracy and tolerance, and, secondarily, to examine how these mesh with Jewish traditional teachings. The workshops not only conducted activity sessions and encouraged introspection as a teaching technique, but also incorporated theoretical study of educational approaches and "value orientations" to tolerance, group discussion based on selected reading materials, and qualitative and quantitative assessment.

The incorporation of Jewish cultural and religious elements in the curricular materials in the workshops adds a unique value orientation to the new program—one that is usually absent in other educational exercises of this nature. Discussions involving reactions to stereotypes (such as attitudes toward sexual preference), for example, included consideration of viewpoints in Jewish tradition on this matter. This is in addition to the consideration of personal reactions to the stereotype, as the AWOD Program would suggest. The Bar-Ilan workshops add special dimensions that will prove central in successfully instituting the curriculum into Israeli schools, especially the traditional ones.

The new product, a pilot curriculum, is a blend of prejudice-reduction introspection exercises and techniques developed by AWOD, with a theoretical base of educational approaches to value orientations and tolerance, and an approach to traditional Jewish viewpoints on these issues, as well as Christian and Muslim attitudes, introduced by non-Jewish students of the workshops.

The student population in these workshops represent the multicultural, multiethnic, and the socioeconomic fabric of the Israeli society: Jews and Arabs, religious and secular, Easterners and Westerners, veterans and newcomers, in particular, recent immigrants from the former Soviet Union republics, and from Ethiopia.

THE WORKSHOPS

Rationale

Contemporary Israeli society copes with issues relating to its social and cultural character. In this struggle different identity groups of Israeli society take part: religious and secular, Westerners (Ashkenazim) and Easterners (Orientals—Sephardim), Jews and Arabs, rich and poor, immigrants and veterans. Opportunities for dialogue among these groups are few and mainly through the media and the political system.

Stereotypes, though unconscious, are prevalent and hinder dialogue among the groups. The individuals who participate in these dialogues see themselves as representatives of their groups, and therefore relate to their counterparts in generalizations that diminish the capacity to listen and to form a personal relationship.

Such a dialogue between individuals who see themselves as representing distinct groups prevents bridging differences and creating personal relationships, which is essential in the formation of a tolerant and pluralistic society.

On the basis of a strong conviction about the feasibility and necessity of keen dialogue between individuals belonging to different groups, the Chair in Education for Human Values, Tolerance and Peace, initiated the workshops on Education for Tolerance: On Stereotypes, Prejudice and Tolerance. These workshops are based on the ADL's program A World of Difference. The program was adapted to the unique characteristics of the Israeli society, Bar-Ilan University, and its sociocultural diverse student body that represents the diversity of the Israeli society.

Aims of the Workshops

1. to provide a framework for meetings and personal dialogue between students from diverse groups in Israeli society
2. to identify meaningful different identity groups that are useful to the participants of the workshops
3. to form a framework that enables tracing and learning about individual and group stereotypes that exist in each of them
4. to deepen the awareness of the participants in these workshops to the existence of stereotypes and extremism in both the affective and cognitive domains, and also in our thoughts, behavior, and action
5. to experience and experiment in effective and open interaction while identifying stereotypes that hinder effective and meaningful interaction

6. to discuss and analyze the concept and meaning of tolerance on the personal and group level in light of the universal-humanistic values and Jewish tradition.

Structure

The workshops consist of fourteen semistructured meetings of an hour and a half each. Each group includes fifteen students who belong to different groups of Israeli society. The dynamic interaction in the workshops reflects in microcosm Israeli society. The group interaction that occurs "here and now" serves as a basis for discussion and analysis. The activities within the workshops are mainly in the affective domain and are based on personal and group experiences that are presented by the workshop facilitator (instructor). Within each workshop there are group discussions about the processes that occur in the particular meeting, based on theoretical relevant material.

Topics

Identity. The identity unit exposes the participants to the social groups that are most meaningful to them and presents cultural, symbolic, and modes of behavior that are most meaningful to their group. They also analyze prevalent attitudes within their group on other groups.

Stereotypes. In this unit the participants learn to identify their own stereotypical thinking about others, and to explore their feelings when others think of them in stereotypes. The students read articles on the roots and formation of stereotypes and analyze their group stereotypes as they face individuals of other groups.

Tolerance. In this unit, tolerance is dealt with in the affective domain: the individual's conception of tolerance and its boundaries. An attempt is made to distinguish between pragmatic tolerance and tolerance as a human value that views differences and diversity as an asset.

The issues of tolerance are dealt with also from the Jewish (and in some groups also Moslem and Christian) traditional perspective and its ramifications.

The starting point of the workshops is defining self-identity, realizing that awareness of the individual's social and cultural heritage is a precondition for acceptance of one's self and of one another. Probing the self-identity of the other groups lays the foundations for mutual respect among the individuals from the diverse groups who participate in the workshops.

People immediately tend to think in categorical and generalizational forms. There is need for both cognitive and affective efforts to identify one's own stereotypic thinking and to understand the emotional and group needs that have caused their formation. Following the understanding of individual and group identity one might understand why and which stereotypes have been studied in this group. The next stage provides opportunities to confront our stereotypes of the other group in the face of our personal acquaintance with them.

The aim of the workshop is to widen the role of tolerance in our world-view and to minimize the unconscious existence of stereotypes and prejudices. The facilitators of the workshops meet regularly to discuss the group processes and individual conceptions.

REFERENCES

Al-Haj, M. (1995). *Education, empowerment and control: The case of the Arabs in Israel.* Albany, NY: State University of New York Press.

Beilin, Y. (1992). *Israel: A concise political history.* London: Weidenfeld and Nicolson.

Ben-Rafael, E., and S. Sharot. (1991). *Ethnicity, religion and class in Israeli society.* Cambridge: Cambridge University Press.

Bhatnager, J. (ed.). (1981). *Educating immigrants.* London: Croom Helm.

Huntington, S. P. (1981). *American politics: The promise of disharmony.* Cambridge, MA: Belknap.

Iram, Y. (1987). "Changing patterns of immigrant absorption in Israel: Educational implications." *Canadian and International Education* 16(2): 55–72.

Johnson, N. B. (1977). "On the relationship of anthropology to multicultural teaching and learning." *Journal of Teacher Education* 28(3):10–15.

Liebman, C. S. (1991). *Religious and secular: Conflict and accommodation between Jews in Israel.* Jerusalem: Keter.

Lijphart, A. (1977). *Democracy in plural societies: A comparative exploration.* New Haven, CT: Yale University Press.

Lijphart, A. (1994). *Electoral systems and party systems: A study of twenty-seven democracies, 1945–1990.* Oxford: Oxford University Press.

Male, G. A. (1986). "Policy issues in the education of minorities—England." *Education and Urban Society* 18(4): 477–486.

Mari, S. K. (1978). *Arab education in Israel.* Syracuse, NY: Syracuse University Press.

Masemann, V., and Y. Iram. (1987). "The right to education for multicultural development: Canada and Israel." In N. B. Tarrow (ed.), *Human rights and education,* Oxford: Pergamon Press, 101–119.

The Middle East and North Africa. (1996). London: Europa Publications.

Ministry of Education, Culture, and Sport (1996). *Facts and figures.*

Ogbu, J. U. (1978). *Minority education and caste.* New York: Academic Press.

Ogbu, J. U. (1983). "Minority status in plural societies." *Comparative Education Review* 27(3): 168–190.

Smolicz, I. J. (1985). "Multiculturalism and an overarching framework of value: Education responses to assimilation, interaction and separatism in ethnically plural societies." *Bildung und Erziehung* (Supp. 2), pp. 245–267.

Stanner, R. (1963). *The legal basis of education in Israel.* Jerusalem: Ministry of Education and Culture.

Taylor, M. J., and C. A. Bagley. (1995). "Multicultural antiracist education." In Y. Iram, Z. Gross (eds.), *The role and place of the humanities in education for the world of the 21st century.* Proceedings of the 11th International Congress of the World Association for Educational Research, Ramat-Gan, Bar-Ilan University and WAER, 251–262.

Thomas, R. M. (1986). "Policy issues in education of minorities—Malaysia." *Education and Urban Society* 18(4): 399–411.

Tulasiewicz, W., and T. Adams. (1995). "Multicultural classrooms and intercultural education in the European community." In Y. Iram, Z. Gross (eds.), *The role and place of the humanities in education for the world of the 21st century.* Proceedings of the 11th International Congress of the World Association for Educational Research, Ramat-Gan, Bar-Ilan University and WAER, 263–270.

Yifhar, Y. (ed.). (1984). *Laws of education and culture.* Jerusalem: Ministry of Education and Culture.

DISCUSSION QUESTIONS

1. There are different types of democracies. What might the implications be for education? Would you suggest different strategies in education? Be specific.
2. Most democratic states are diverse. What could the impact of diversity be on education toward democracy as a way of life and not just as a political system?
3. Issues of minorities pose a challenge to every society and to democracy. Countries and societies differ in their approach to these issues. How is/could that be reflected in your educational system?
4. How is Israel's multicultural diversity reflected in its complex educational system? In what way is it similar/different from your own and other educational systems. Can you suggest alternative approaches to those that were adopted by Israel?
5. This chapter presents a program in Education toward Democracy. Do you agree/disagree with its rationale, aims, and methods? To what extent is a similar program applicable to your own education system?

CHAPTER 12

The Purposes of Schooling in France
Liberty, Equality, Fraternity, and Dilemmas of Individual Responsibility and Social Control

LESLIE J. LIMAGE

THE REVOLUTIONARY VISION OF EDUCATION IN FRANCE: 1792

The following is from the *Report on the General Organization of Public Instruction* presented by Condorcet, deputy from the Department of Paris, on 20 April 1792 to the National Legislative Assembly, as quoted by Allaire and Frank (1995, 25–26):

> Offrir à tous les individus de l'espèce humaine les moyens de pourvoir à leurs besoins, d'assurer leur bien-être, de connaître et exercer leurs droit, d'entendre et de remplir leurs devoirs; assurer à chacun la facilité de perfectionner son industrie, de se rendre capable des fonctions sociales auxquelles il a le droit d'être appelé, de développer toute l'étendue des talents qu'il a reçus de la nature; et par là établir entre les citoyens une égalité de fait, et rendre réelle l'égalité politique reconnue par la loi: tel doit être le premier but d'une instruction nationale; et sous ce point de vue, elle est, pour la puissance publique, un devoir de justice . . .
>
> La première condition de toute instruction étant de n'enseigner que des vérités, les établissements que le puissance publique y consacre doivent être aussi indépendants qu'il est possible de toute autorité politique. . . . il résulte du même principe qu'il faut ne les rendre dépendants que de l'assemblée des représentants du peuple, parce que de tous les pouvoirs, il en est le moins corruptibles . . . il est dès lors le moins ennemi du progrès des lumières . . .
>
> Ainsi, l'instruction doit être universelle. . . . Elle doit être répartie avec toute l'égalité que permettent les limites nécessaires des dépenses. . . .
> Enfin, aucun pouvoir public ne doit avoir ni l'autorité, ni même le crédit, d'empêcher le développement des vérités nouvelles, l'enseignement des théories contraires à sa politique particulière ou à ses intérêts momentanés.

The views expressed in this chapter are solely the author's.

The preceding may be translated as follows:

> To offer all individuals of the human race the means to see to their needs and ensure their well-being, to know and exercise their rights, to know and fulfill their obligations; to offer everyone the possibility to improve his skills, to be capable of fulfilling the social responsibilities for which he may be called upon, to develop all potential talent received by nature and to establish equality of condition between citizens and real political equality recognized by law: these should be the first goals of a national system of instruction (schooling); and seen from this perspective, this goal is a duty of justice for the state (public power) . . .
>
> Since the first condition of all instruction is to teach only truths, institutions established by the state (public power) must be as independent as possible of any political authority. . . . that independence is best ensured by the assembly of representatives of the people, because it is the least prone to corruption . . . and the least likely to be an enemy of enlightenment and progress than any other power . . .
>
> Thus, instruction should be universal . . . It should be distributed with all the equality that available resources allow. . . . No public institution should have the authority or even the possibility to prevent the development of new truths, the teaching of theories which contradict its particular policies or its short-term interests . . ."

THE NEW LOOK AT VICHY: 1997–1998

As far back as the French Revolution, all the issues that currently surround the role of education in France have been present and consciously debated. The text cited of an early report presented by Condorcet to the revolutionary National Legislative Assembly goes on to address freedom of expression in education, the role of the family, the Church, and the State, secularism *(laïcité)* and neutrality; girls' education, the social role of each level of schooling, obligatory attendance, the right of all citizens to instruction, the distinction between education and instruction and their place in schools. It makes concrete proposals for the organization of public schooling at all levels. It speaks of both rights and responsibilities in the spirit of the times, and the necessary form of democracy that might best ensure that all citizens are actually able to know and exercise their political and social rights and responsibilities. "Liberty, equality, fraternity," the founding principles inherited from the Revolution, become the measure against which all successive policies concerned with schooling and education in France are evaluated with historic lapses, particular interpretations, and inherent unresolved dilemmas.

While the revolutionary proponents of universal education were convinced of the importance of instruction (as distinguished from education) to promote democracy, they would have been hard pressed to foresee all the effects of a highly centralized state apparatus with schooling dispensed by civil servants. I will examine only two issues that echo daily in public debate in France but which stop at all school gates: individual responsibility and social control.

For the first time in fifty years, the general French public is confronting its role and that of the Vichy government under German Occupation during World War II through the much-delayed trial of Maurice Papon, former high-level Vichy civil servant in the Bordeaux region and high-level minister in the Giscard d'Estaing government, who was convicted of crimes against humanity. By and large, the issue of collaboration and the responsibility of civil servants was quickly dismissed by General De Gaulle as he returned to form a postwar government with the argument that national unity and reconstruction took priority (Greilsamer 1997b, Paxton 1982, Weisberg 1996). From autumn 1997 until the end of March 1998, most French media covered this trial on a daily basis. It was the trial of individual responsibility in the civil service when faced with orders to facilitate genocide. Such a public debate would have been unheard of in earlier years. Such debates have not taken place in most European countries, such as the Netherlands, whose civil servants zealously undertook the deportation of Dutch Jews. This debate has been public in France, with positions taken by numerous political, intellectual, religious, and social actors from former President Valéry Giscard d'Estaing to current President Jacques Chirac (Kauffman 1997). The trial included long testimonials by virtually all the eminent historians of the period as well as victims and families of victims (see sample of testimonials reported in newspaper articles in bibliography). But World War II was not taught during the year of the trial in French history classes in secondary schools. No part of the centralized curriculum is devoted to what Anglo-Saxons call "current events," "social studies," or "civics" in this broader sense in schools.

In his summing up for the plaintiffs he represented in the Maurice Papon trial, Arno Klarsfeld described the trajectory of a civil servant who has committed crimes against humanity. Referring to Papon (Dumary 1998e, 9), he stated:

> Il n'y a pas de volonté haineuse"chez Maurice Papon. "Il a eu le souci de servir ses intérêts immédiats. Il s'est toujour efforcé d'être du côté du pouvoir et des honneurs . . . Il n'est ni un antisémite farouche ni hitlérien. Il a accepté {la délégation d'autorité} sur le service des questions juives parce qu'il pense que l'Allemagne va gagner la guerre, qu'il a une place dans cette nouvelle Europe dirigée par les nazis, parce que c'est un poste de responsabilité." . . . "Maurice Papon est un homme qui ne voulait pas la mort de ses victimes, à la différence de Barbie ou Touvier. Un homme qui n'irait pas brutaliser un enfant en raison de sa religion. Un homme éduqué, policé, qui n'est pas sanguinaire. Maurice Papon, élévé dans la direction du bien et de l'intérêt général, a trahi. On ne lui demandait pas de s'opposer, mais de ne pas participer . . . Comment se rend-on complice de crime contre l'human-

ité? En croyant que céder sur les petites choses ne prête pas à conséquence. Tout finit par s'amasser, brindille par brindille, compromis après compromis. On se retrouve à la croisée du chemin entre le bien et le mal. On accepte, on accepte. On cède à soi-même. On s'abrite derrière son absence de haine peut-être derrière un sentiment anti-boche. On fuit tout contact avec la réalité. On oublie l'homme qu'on a été, l'homme qu'on devrait être. On se dit spectateur alor qu'on est déjà protagoniste. Et c'est tout naturellement qu'on accepte l'irréparable.

Maurice Papon a été Maurice Papon, un homme qui avait tout et qui a choisi d'accomplir le pire". Me Klarsfeld s'adresse enfin aux jurés, à qui, selon lui, 'incombe la tâche de fixer les repères pour les générations à venir afin que soit définitivement condamnée une administration toujours prête à apporter son concours aux pires ignominies, du moment qu'elles se trouvent couvertes par les instructions de leur hiérarchie.

Klarsfeld's argument may be translated as follows:

Maurice Papon was not motivated by hatred. He straightforwardly sought to serve his own self-interest. He always managed to be on the side of the powerful and those who could bestow honors. . . . He is neither a ferocious anti-Semite nor a fervent supporter of Hitler. He accepted the delegated authority for the Jewish Affairs Section because he expected that Germany would win the war, that he had a place in this new Europe led by the Nazis, because it was a post of responsibility . . . Maurice Papon is a man who did not actively wish the death of his victims, as opposed to Barbie or Touvier. Nor a man who would brutalize a child because of its religion. Maurice Papon, an educated, disciplined man with no blood-thirsty tendencies, raised to promote good and general well-being, was a traitor. No one expected him to actively resist, only not to participate. . . . How does one become an actor engaged in crimes against humanity? By believing that giving in on small matters doesn't count. These acts, in fact, add up, little by little, compromise after compromise. One finds oneself at the crossroads between good and evil. One accepts more and more. One lets oneself go. And one excuses oneself because there isn't really any hatred behind the acts or maybe one is actually anti-German. One loses all contact with reality. One forgets the man one used to be or should be. One calls himself a spectator when one is already a protagonist. And then, one naturally accepts to commit irreparable harm.

Maurice Papon was Maurice Papon, a man who had everything and chose to commit the worst crime known to mankind. Mr. Klarsfeld then turned to the jury to ask them to "definitively condemn an administration which was always ready to assist with carrying out the worst horrors, as long as they were covered by instructions from their hierarchy."

With such history and civics lessons going on in a courtroom in Bordeaux and daily transmitted by the mass media in France, how is it that the classroom remained out-of-bounds in 1997 and 1998? (A selected few secondary school classes did actually watch the retransmission of a day's trial sessions in Bordeaux but they were the exception). Then, in 1999, across France another related debate was opened as a result of this first one: the French government's lack of reparation for the pillaging of all property (homes, art collections, businesses, etc.). Across Europe, beginning with a look at Swiss confiscation of bank accounts held by Jewish clients and a thorough examination of the extent of Swiss collaboration with Nazi Germany, international conferences and negotiations have been taking place. Again, there has been little reflection of such debates within schools.

Most recently, in 1999 and especially in the first part of 2000, another dimension has been highly mediatized: violence in and around schools. The measures taken by the Minister of Education, Claude Allegre, announced in January 2000 are all of a repressive nature (Blanchard 2000). Schools will be open to police presence, and more stringent sanctions to exclude children and adolescents from school will be available to school disciplinary councils. The already marginal class on civics given in the second year of lower secondary schooling will attempt to address violence. There is no discussion about the institutional violence of the school and relations between pupils and teachers, or between teachers, the administration, and parents, other than the traditional ones that respect be one-sided, that is, parents and pupils toward teachers. In such a climate of inability to look at any other kinds of relations to educate young people into a culture of "civility," to use the French expression, the question must be raised as to why there is a fairly uniform view across French society of the problem and the possible answers. Who is responsible, and for what?

A partial answer lies in the conception of the role of public schooling in France and the responsibility and rights of each of its major partners: the republic/nation, the state and its civil service/teachers and administation, and civil society including parents and children. It also lies in an unresolved dilemma: the meaning of equality of opportunity.

A CENTRALIZED SYSTEM INTENDED TO PROMOTE EQUALITY: THE FIRST DILEMMA

The highly centralized French school system has always been perceived as offering the best means to promote equality and national unity. The notion of the state in the Enlightenment sense began to take form with the French Revolution in 1792 (Furet 1978). The France of the late eighteenth century was a linguistically and culturally diverse collection of regions and divergent interests. And the France of 1998 remained fundamentally diverse in spite of two hundred years of centralization, imposition of the French language, and enormous efforts to promote a unified notion of equality in a single state, administered in a superficially equal manner (De Certeau, Julia, and Revel 1975).

It has long been thought that only a highly centralized system could and would effectively redistribute the nation's wealth to reduce regional disparities and special interests. This view extends, of course, well beyond France and in centralized countries/systems of schooling is only marginally challenged from within. While globalization, the expansion of multinational corporations, and the movement toward a more politically and economically united Europe proceed at one level, the basic principles upon which the French state was founded, and the school system that it built to support those principles, continue fairly untouched by outside influence.

Social science research of the 1960s and 1970s such as that of Pierre Bourdieu demonstrating the social reproduction role of this centralized system has had virtually no long-term impact on how French schools are administered, how French teachers teach, or how schooling is organized. Other research demonstrating that the school system straightforwardly contributes to wastage and underachievement by arbitrarily creating failure at an early age *(échèc scolaire),* such as that of Baudelot and Establet (1989), still has little impact on how equality of opportunity is best defined. Even very recent studies about the actual disparities between resources allocated by the central state school system to different regions has little effect on philosophical debate about the role of schooling. The fact that schools in Paris have better-qualified teachers than do those of other cities; that the material conditions of teaching and learning vary from one part of the country to another; and that, in spite of basic principles, an inequality of resources dominates school provision in France all have little impact on how decision makers, intellectuals, trade unions, and the school administration see matters. Parents and pupils are rarely heard (Gurrey 1997).

A recent definition of equality and the newer concept of positive discrimination by a member of the National State Council *(Conseil d'Etat),* François Stasse, states the position as clearly as possible (Stasse 1997). Stasse finds the origin of the notion of equality before the law in the "Declaration of human rights and those of the citizen of 1789" in the statement that all men are born and remain free and equal under the law. The notion of equality progressively comes to mean that all citizens confronted by a similar situation should be treated *identically* under the law. This means that no distinction can be made between citizens on the basis of race, religion, or origin.

This critical definition has a basic weakness. The concept of equality before the law has had little impact on reducing economic, social, and cultural inequalities in France (or elsewhere). The State Council recognizes the weakness of the simple principle of equality before the law and begins to address equality of opportunity as a form of social solidarity. Most of the social welfare measures of the post–World War II period and those currently under debate or criticism today have been developed with this second concept in mind. And even more recently, equity as equality of condition enters the arena of political debate. The implications for schooling are critical but the response is extremely hesitant.

On the one hand, the overriding principle that equality should mean providing everyone with the same instruction or knowledge (with respect to schooling) does little to address the issue of inequality of ability or interest in taking advantage of that body of knowledge or instruction. The French school system was founded in the latter part of the nineteenth century on the principle of equal access to the same education for all at the first stage (primary school). But it has taken nearly a century for the notion of positive discrimination to gain any ground. Educational priority areas *(zones d'éducation prioritaires)* based on the British model have been developed on the model that more educational resources need to be provided to particularly disadvantaged areas.

But these measures are seen as temporary and fraught with the risk of further stigmatizing or marginalizing the populations they are meant to serve. The argument in France remains that special measures must lead back to the mainstream view of equality, the ability to participate on the same footing with all other young people, regardless of socioeconomic origin in the same access to the same body of knowledge.

An understanding of this philosophical position is critical to understanding why and how French schools actually operate, and the contours of debate about schooling. It plays a critical role in the experience of children of immigrant origin in French schools and explains considerably the discourse concerning "integration" of populations of differing religions, geographic origins, socioeconomic status, and so on.

A TEACHING FORCE THAT IS CIVIL SERVICE AND UNACCOUNTABLE BEYOND HIERARCHICAL RELATIONS: THE SECOND DILEMMA

Most teachers in France are civil servants. It has long been a corollary of the basic principle that the state is responsible for providing equal instruction for all, and that the best way to ensure that responsibility is through a civil service. The civil service is viewed as the best status for teachers to ensure that they remain independent of outside pressures, be they of passing political views, the voices of families, or children, or religious positions. The French primary school teacher of the late nineteenth century was seen as a moral authority to promote the republican ideas of liberty, equality, and fraternity in an atmosphere of secularism and complete neutrality. And if we return to the quotation from Condorcet at the beginning of this chapter as he addressed the National Legislative Assembly in 1792, the roots of this view of teachers is already present. Condorcet referred to a system of instruction free of all outside influence in which all have access to a body of knowledge based on the truth as it is understood in a specific historic context. There was no doubt at that time that there was a single truth to instruct, nor that that truth would evolve over time. But the school system and its teachers will remain the best neutral judges of what is best to include in the body of knowledge to be conveyed.

French teachers fairly readily agree with this view and have done so consistently over time. It frequently makes it difficult for those from decentralized systems and Americans, Canadians, Australians, and others to understand why French teachers do not behave in the same way nor value the same priorities that they do.

The history of French unionization of teachers reflects this very particular perspective. Initially, teachers did not have the right to organize but as they did begin to do so, many tendencies of a political nature arose to distinguish between different views of what it meant for civil servants to unionize. While I cannot go deeply into the history of unionization of French teachers, at least a few critical points need to be made. According to André Robert (1995), early forms of organization have simply been intended to protect and promote better conditions of service, rather than to question in any way the content of education or its transmission. This was not a difficult decision, as a strong distinction has long been made between what constitutes school-based knowledge and instruction and a larger role that has *not* been that of the school, namely, to educate.

French teachers have rarely questioned the basic principle that they hold the knowledge to be transmitted and that knowledge is based on official instructions and decisions about what is to be taught, where, and how. French teacher unions all question salary and working conditions, allocation of positions in different parts of the country, insecure conditions and violence, attempts to ask them to take on additional tasks that are not purely instructional, and any non-formalized contact with parents or pupils. They do not take on pastoral care or organize clubs, for example, as do teachers in many other countries with few exceptions.

Parents are organized in separate bodies. The two principle parent associations in France are the Fédération des Parents d'élèves de l'enseignement publique (PEP), which is fairly conservative, and the larger Fédération des conseils des parents d'élèves (FCPE), which is more progressive. In both cases, however, parents associations are welcomed solely to support teachers in their demands for better conditions of service and are in no way considered as partners to what goes on within the classroom. Parents and teachers, as well as pupils have been united in major demonstrations in very recent times on maintaining a secular school system. In the 1980s there was a confrontation between greater control over private essentially Catholic schools and in the mid-1990s against an attempt by the conservative government to allow state resources to be spent on improving private school buildings, again essentially Catholic in France. In 1995 and again in 1997, teachers, parents, and pupils went on strike to protest violence in schools. During the same period, a similar solidarity but of a more complex nature surrounded the restrictions placed on Islamic girls whose families wished them to wear a head covering in school. The great debate about the *"foulard islamique"* led to the exclusion of children who insisted on or were obliged to wear this head covering. The basic principle of French schools as free of such religious symbols or pressures also made for unanimity across teacher, parent, and student organizations (Allaire and Frank 1996, Glenn and de Jong 1996, Limage 2000).

In several surveys and analyses of the teacher union press and policy statements by André Robert (1995), teacher preoccupation remains resolutely the same over time. No teacher union asks for or considers parent or pupil participation in any classroom issue. Teachers "instruct." Parents "educate." Pupils receive, successfully or otherwise, "knowledge."

Teachers are accountable only to their hierarchy, as in most civil service contexts. There is virtually no possibility for a teacher to be censured except for the most flagrant abuse of pupils, and even these cases are very difficult to prosecute. Results on examinations or performance in class are resolutely the child's fault or the parents' lack of support. Teachers are in no way accountable.

A recent consultation held by the current Minister of Education, Claude Allègre (Blanchard 1998) asked teachers and pupils separately for their views on a range of educational matters. A direct consultation by questionnaire has no precedent. The resultant response about pupils by teachers especially at secondary level is precisely the same response that has been given for over a century (well recorded in Baudelot and Establet's study of 1989). Teachers reported that pupils are lazy, don't have any intellectual curiosity, do not have the level or standards of former times, aren't motivated, come to secondary school with limited reading and writing skills, and are unable to assimilate the large body of knowledge they are expected to cover in lower secondary school *(collège)* or other forms of upper secondary school. The only indication that schools (not teachers) might have some responsibility in the matter comes out in the replies when teachers refer to overcrowded classrooms, lack of material resources, or violence overflowing from disadvantaged neighborhoods into the schools.

Allègre has managed to alienate virtually the entire teaching and national education administration community as well as a number of intellectuals. He began his administration as minister by denouncing teacher absenteeism and by threatening to reduce the size of the administrative apparatus of the national school system. He referred to the sacred *"education nationale"* as a mammoth that needed to be put on a diet *("dégraisser le mamouth")*. He immediately became unpopular across the board with teacher organizations while official reports were produced that teachers are responsible for the loss of classroom instruction for pupils up to about 10 percent of yearly hours but that it was not actually their fault. Teachers were simply not replaced when absent for illness, maternity leave, or further training in very many instances. (All in-service training for teachers takes place during classtime, thus creating a real problem for pupils to achieve continuity in their schooling).

An interesting recent criticism of Allègre's efforts to undertake what are viewed as American decadent reforms—more parent participation and consultation of pupils, opening the school to the community, and so on—came recently from a famous left-wing intellectual, Régis Debray, comrade of Che Guevara during the revolutionary movements in Latin America in the 1960s. Débray denounced Allègre for attempting to let the vox populi (meaning parents and children) into discussion of what should be taught and how. He denounced the very notion that anyone other than teachers might decide what should be taught and how. His discourse places him in the mainstream of the very long tradition of what schooling is all about (Debray 1998).

SCHOOL-BASED KNOWLEDGE AS THE EXCLUSIVE DOMAIN OF THE STATE AND ITS TEACHERS: THE THIRD DILEMMA

Since school-based knowledge remains exclusively the domain of the state and is dispensed by teachers, a number of dilemmas occur, including the ones central to this discussion. History and civics education are the content areas in a highly compartmentalized system of disciplines that are of particular interest in this context. The syllabus for each year of schooling is strictly decided by the Ministry of Education, and teachers' choice is limited to selecting the books that their pupils must purchase for their classes (books are free at primary and lower secondary level but still selected by teachers based on a national syllabus).

Given the strong traditional commitment to utmost neutrality and secularism in the French tradition, the teaching of history and civics is subject to great caution. An interesting example occurred during the breakup of the former Soviet Union. Since historians consider they must have some distance on an event to evaluate it, and all the more so when referring to school textbooks, the response in French secondary schools was to simply eliminate the post–World War II Soviet Union from the syllabus.

Similarly, and for no apparent reason, while a major educational event has been taking place in the courtrooms in Bordeaux, France, since the autumn of 1997 around the long-delayed trial of Maurice Papon (Secretary General of the Prefecture of the Gironde Region under the Vichy government of the Occupation), World War II was not on the secondary syllabus that year. To be fair, however, it would be necessary to point out that the internal situation under the Occupation and the role of the Vichy government has not figured prominently in the history syllabus in any case in France. Similarly, across Europe, few countries have addressed their own roles during this period in any critical manner in their schools as evidence from Sweden, Switzerland, Belgium, the Netherlands, and others is now making for numerous documentaries and media reporting.

In the French case, there are least two explanatory dimensions. The first is the long tradition of deciding what is appropriate to instruct in classrooms and what is the subject of political moods or trends. The second is the larger social issue of the place of individual and collective responsibility in the course of human events. If this issue is not addressed in history or philosophy classes in France, why does it not appear in civics education either?

For the past fifteen years or so, successive ministers of education, from Jean-Pierre Chevènement to François Bayrou, wanted to give civics education a real place in secondary school programmes. At present, civics education is hidden at the lower secondary level in a short course on the institutions of the Fifth Republic and general moral principles of the secular French system of government. But the content of a renewed and enlarged program has beaten each minister.

Initially, Jules Ferry, founding father of obligatory state primary schooling, saw civics education as inculcating respect for the values of the Republic in children from an early age. These basic principles, according to Ferry, were attachment to secularism, respect for public institutions, and active and responsible citizenship in full knowledge of one's rights and responsibilities. The former minister, Claude Allègre, and the minister for schools, Ségolène Royal, proposed that civics education have a place throughout all schooling and that it be based on the principles of tolerance, responsibility, respect for rights and obligations, secularism, solidarity, and courtesy. And since no one can be opposed to these generalities, the problem lies in how one takes a step from general principles to a syllabus. The shadow of political pressure or non-neutrality remains omnipresent to each minister (ministers being political nominees, while the civil servants of the National Ministry of Education remain as guarantors of this "impartiality").

Civics education has consistently been the most difficult content area to define in French schooling for these reasons. There is no question of American style "social studies" or "current events" periods. The only non-controversial content has been the study of the institutions of government in a fairly formalized manner. Another major stumbling block is already inherent in the institutional context of schooling. There is no space for the practice of democracy in the school as institution, the classroom in particular. Parent bodies, as already mentioned, are outside the school and negotiate from outside. Parent representation on school councils that meet several times a year only exist as such since the Haby Reform of 1975. These councils in no way allow parents or their representatives to discuss pedagogical matters.

Similarly, student representatives on these councils, and student organizations, are simply formally present to ask polite questions and receive decisions
taken by teachers about their classmates. They are not the site of dialogue.

The practice of democracy and participation has virtually no place in the
institutions where children spend so much of their time from the age of three
to sixteen (if not longer). In schools, pupils receive sanctions that vary from
one teacher to another and from one school to another. It is quite customary
for teachers to insult their pupils of all ages with vague accusations of how
stupid they are and how incapable. School report cards in the French tradition
frequently note: "doesn't have the level *(niveau);* lazy, unmotivated, incapable, needs to make a greater effort" and teachers are not accountable for
these vague comments that follow a pupil throughout his or her school career.
Again, the impunity of teachers and the school administration makes it very
difficult to envisage a civics education based on a shared view of individual
and collective responsibility. The imbalance of power is too flagrant. The
only response possible to many young people is to retreat into indifference or
insolence (Gurrey 1997).

EQUALITY THROUGH EXAMINATION-BASED SELECTION:
A FOURTH DILEMMA

Another major constraint to developing a sense of individual and collective
responsibility in French schools has to be mentioned, though not fully developed, here. The French system is an examination-oriented system of education. Although overt selection after primary schooling has been eliminated,
orientation and instruction at the secondary level are bound and structured by
the examinations pupils will take in different forms of post-lower-secondary
schooling. While the syllabus for all schooling is decided centrally, so too, the
examination system dictates what will be taught and how it will be taught. As
long as a particular form of writing is critical to success in the philosophy
examination, at the baccaluareate examination, or another in the French language examination, all instruction focuses on those formalized rituals.

The goal remains in terms of equality to offer pupils equal opportunity to
learn how to express themselves successfully in terms of a highly codifed
means of expression at oral and written examination time. The form of
expression is considerably more important than the content, and outside
knowledge that has not been transmitted by the teacher (or obtainable in the
families of middle-class households) is anathema *(hors sujet).*

Similarly, the content of what is taught is homogenous and allows for
now-critical debate. As this book goes to press, the first European government since World War II to include a neo-Nazi party, has been named in Austria. While protests are formulating throughout Europe, Israel, and the United
States, it is unclear that the lessons of history and the meaning of democracy

have been learned. For example, the official French textbook for history for the last year of secondary school for the academic year 1998–1999 included the following definitions that students would need to learn by rote memory for the baccalaureate examinations:

> La *démocratie* est un régime dans lequel le pouvoir émane du peuple (démos en grec). Elle est née à Athènes au Ve siècle avant J.C. (mais seule une minorité d'Athéniens, les citoyens, y participent.
>
> Une *démocratie libérale* est un régime qui garantit les libertés individuelles (de pensée, de religion, d'expression, etc) et le pluralisme politique. Les élections sont libres et s'effectuent au suffrage universel.
>
> Une *démocratie populaire* est un régime dans lequel l'organisation sociale, économique et politique est dominée par un parti unique, le parti communiste, prétendant représenter la classe ouvrière et détenir la verité. Les autres partis politiques sont interdits. Une "démocratie populaire" n'est donc pas une démocratie au sens propre du terme. (Lambin 1998,180)

The translation is as follows:

> *Democracy* is a regime in which power comes from the people (from the Greek *demos*). It was created in Athens in the fifth century B.C. (but only a minority of Athenians, those who held citizenship, could participate).
>
> A liberal democracy is a regime that guarantees individuals freedoms (thought, religion, expression, etc.) and political pluralism. Elections are based on freedom and universal suffrage.
>
> A popular democracy is a regime in which the social, economic, and political organization of society is dominated by a single party—the communist party—that maintains that it represents the working class and is invested with the truth. Other political parties are forbidden. A "popular democracy is not, therefore, a democracy in the strict meaning of the concept."

These three definitions, as with all information contained in the official textbooks, are intended for assimilation without question. Grades on the baccalaureate examination are based on the uncritical reproduction of this knowledge or truth. In such a manner, a country such as France, with a Communist Party in its own government, holding important ministries, still maintains that a "communist" party by definition is not capable of democracy in the liberal sense of the term. There are a number of reasons discussed here as to why French schooling involves very particular notions of what constitutes knowledge and culture and what should be excluded. It should be pointed out, however, that French schooling, as defined by political leadership and growing European Union influence, specifically sought to define democracy in particular ways in view of enlargement of the EU to include postcommunist Central and Eastern European countries. On the other hand, as this book goes to press, France and the rest of Europe are confronting the first example of national socialism or neo-Nazi participation in one of their constituent governments in Austria and have not taken into account in school-based knowledge or governmental or intergovernmental institutions the impact of such an unexpected development.

PRINCIPLES OF SECULARISM, NEUTRALITY, AND EQUALITY THAT ARE DEFINED TO EXCLUDE DIVERSITY: A FIFTH DILEMMA

While the philosophical foundations of French society and schooling are intended to offer equality before a body of knowledge, they in no way allow for diversity. There is little acknowledgment of the cultural and linguistic diversity that makes up the school populations of France and French society in general. Since the French Revolution, the effort to impose the French language on all other dialects and languages has been seen as the best way to convey republican principles and to develop national unity. The languages and cultures of immigrant populations of first, second, and third generations as well as the regional languages of France have little place in schools. For a very long period, the latter were actually forbidden even on the school playground. The terms "multiculturalism" or "preservation of cultural identities" have no place in schools, other than the occasional look at recipes or songs or folklore of other cultures at primary level. Foreign language instruction at the secondary level is usually restricted to traditional English, German, Russian, Spanish, possibly Greek, Latin, and Portuguese. Students wishing to study to examination level Arabic or less often spoken languages may do so with special authorization by taking outside or distance education courses only (Limage 1987).

The emphasis on the French language as the only vehicle of equality also appears in the history of the recognition of literacy problems in France (Limage 1975, 1986). Until the early 1980s, no basic skill difficulties were recognized among French nationals. Illiteracy *(analphabétisme)* was a term applied to immigrants who in fact did not master French as a foreign language. And when basic skill difficulties were identified with the re-discovery of widespread poverty and youth unemployment in the early 1980s, a new term was coined to describe the illiteracy of French nationals who had been through all or part of the French school system who could not effectively use reading and writing—term *"illettrisme."* A large body of research and discussion of this distinction between "them" and "us" is beyond the scope of this discussion but must be mentioned in a discussion of the thorny hidden issue of diversity.

PARENTS, CHILDREN, AND THE OUTSIDE WORLD: A SIXTH DILEMMA

While parents are not simply intruders in the French school system, they are not partners either. The child is "educated" by its parents and community and "instructed" by its teacher. Outside knowledge, experience, and aspirations stop at the school door. And yet, France has one of the liveliest and most diverse political, social, and cultural arenas of any country in the world. There is more real diversity of political affilliation and activism than readily found elsewhere. France's socialist and communist parties are the strongest in Europe and are truly French. At the same time, its extreme right wing party, the Front National, has had electoral success in parts of the northeast and in certain Mediterranean municipalities of the south.

While the economic situation has continued to degenerate across Europe, new forms of solidarity have sprung up in France still based on the activism of a democratic society. Most recently, associations of the unemployed have taken to demonstrating and acting in an organized fashion to demand a minimal living standard for all. On the other hand, most other countries have not simply reduced social spending but have begun to call once more for charitable bodies and so-called partnerships with private industry to take up the challenge as in the nineteenth century. The former minister of education, Claude Allègre, was at his most controversial in relation to intellectuals and teachers' unions alike when he appeared to try to "privatize" on the American or International Monetary Fund/OECD/World Bank model and talked of "partnerships" with industry and so on (Roux 1998).

There is a very real sense of commitment to basic principles when these challenges are denounced. At the same time, there is a very real inability to take a step toward an acceptable form of dialogue between all "social partners." The school needs to recognize the "new truths" of the end of the twentieth century, but it still wants the monopoly through its civil service and the state on identifying those truths.

WHAT ARE THE PROSPECTS FOR ANOTHER IDEA OF SCHOOLING TO INCLUDE EDUCATING FOR DEMOCRACY AND PARTICIPATION?

This dilemma leads to a first assessment of prospects for another idea of schooling that might enlarge what is currently basically learned outside schools: democracy and participation. This chapter opened with quotations from Condorcet and from the Maurice Papon trial, notably by the well-known lawyer Arno Klarsfeld, whose parents, Serge and Beate Klarsfeld, have led the search for and prosecution of Nazis and other criminals of the Holocaust. Klarsfeld actually described the step-by-step itinerary of a civil servant who constantly maintained he was only obeying orders. The civics lesson in individual and collective responsibility in this particular courtroom is also being played out in the tribunal for crimes against humanity for ex-Yugoslavia and Rwanda, while atrocities go on around the world.

The two approaches to this dilemma in France have been to turn a blind eye (De Gaulle in forming the government after the war and in most other European countries) or to see individuals and nongovernmental organizations insisting that a civics lesson includes a serious understanding that everyone is responsible for his or her acts. There is no such thing as neutrality in the real world. At present, the prospect for integrating this lesson in French school programs or its practice in the daily life of schools looks fairly remote. The debates about violence in schools with further recourse to repressive measures to contain rather than rethink its origins; the first presence of a neo-Nazi or national socialist party in power in Austria; and the cancellation until a later date of a reform of the judiciary that would give the legal system independence from political power, all lead to a serious concern that collective and individual responsibility, lessons from history, have been learned.

REFERENCES

Allaire, Martine, and Marie-Thérèse Frank (eds.). (1995). *Les politiques de l'éducation de la France de la maternelle au baccalauréat.* Collection: Retour aux textes. Paris: La documentation Française.
Baudelot, Christian, and Roger Establet. (1989). *Le niveau monte. Réfutation d'une vieille idée concernant la prétendue décadence de nos écoles.* Paris: Editions du Seuil.
De Certeau, Michel, Domnique Julia, and Jacques Revel. (1975). *Une politique de la langue. La Révolution française et les patois.* Paris: Gallimard.
Education nationale, Ministère. (1999). *Baccalauréat général. Session de 1999. Histoire–Géographie, Séries.*
Furet, François. (1978). *Penser la Révolution française.* Paris: Gallimard.
Glenn, Charles L., and Ester J. de Jong. (1996). *Educating immigrant children: Schools and language minorities in twelve nations.* New York: Garland Publishing.
Lambin, Jean-Michel (ed.). (1998). *Histoire terminales* [History Textbook]. Paris: Hachette Education.
Lequin, Yves, Jean Baubérot, Guy Gauthier, Louis Legrand, and Pierre Ognier. (1994). *Histoire de laïcité.* Besançon: Centre Régional de Documentation Pédagogique de Franche-Comté.
Limage, Leslie. (1975). *Alphabétisation et culture.* Unpublished doctoral dissertation, Paris.
Limage, Leslie. (1984). "Young migrants of the second generation in Europe: Education and labour market insertion prospects." *International Migration* 22(4): 367–387.
Limage, Leslie. (1986). "Adult literacy policy in industrialized countries." *Comparative Education Review* (30)1: 50–72.

Limage, Leslie. (2000). "Islamic identity and education: The case of France." *Comparative Education* 36(1):73–94.

Paxton, Robert O. (1982). *Vichy France: Old guard and new order, 1940–1944*. New York: Columbia University Press.

Robert, André. (1995). *Le syndicalisme des enseignants*. Series: Systèmes éducatifs. La documentation Française, Paris.

Stasse, François. (1997). *"Egalité et discriminations positives."* Regards sur l'actualité. La documentation Francaise. Paris. Mensuel No. 232, June, pp. 19–25.

Weisberg, Richard H. (1996). *Vichy law and the Holocaust in France*. New York: New York University Press.

NEWSPAPER ARTICLES

Allègre, Claude. (1998). "Ce que je veux." *Le Monde*, 6 February, pp. 1, 14.

Blanchard, Sandrine. (1998). *"Les profs jugent le lycée."* Le Monde, 6 March, pp. 1, 13.

Blanchard, Sandrine. (2000). *"La multiplication des violences renforce les attentes à l'égard du plan Allègre."* Le Monde, 27 January 2000, pp. 1, 8, 9.

Blanchard, Sandrine, and Nathalie Guibert. (2000). *"Face aux violences, M. Allègre veut renforcer la discipline scolaire."* Le Monde, 23–24 January, pp. 1, 7.

Gurrey, Béatrice. (1997). *"Introuvable éducation civique."* Le Monde, 2 December, pp. 1, 20.

Kauffmann, Sylvie. (1997). *"M. Chirac explique Vichy aux Français."* Le Monde, 6 December, pp. 1, 6, 18.

Klarsfeld, Serge. (1997). *"TPI: Jacques Chirac doit corriger le tir."* Le Monde, 19 December, p. 16.

Roux, Jean-Paul. (1998). *"Ce que la démocratie exige de l'école."* Le Monde, 11 February, p. 13.

DISCUSSION QUESTIONS

1. How do differing definitions of equality affect policy measures for schools? How does the case of France differ from that of any of the other countries examined in this volume?
2. What are the dangers and advantages of open discussion of political, social, and economic issues in the classroom? How do definitions of what is actually considered knowledge or the truth at a particular time in history influence an analysis of those dangers and advantages?
3. Is there a developing debate about individual or collective responsibility as a result of the globalization of such issues through the creation of international courts of justice or attempts to render justice for crimes against humanity across national frontiers in the late 1990s and early twenty-first century? Consider the attempt to bring the former dictator of Chile, Augusto Pinochet, to justice by the Spanish judiciary and other human rights organizations during his stay in the United Kingdom, for

example. Is there any debate in schools in the countries with which you are familiar?

4. What are some lessons to be learned from centralized curriculum planning as well as decentralized planning? Compare, for example, critical issues that have arisen in the United States by states and local school boards to define knowledge in relation to the situation in France.

CHAPTER 13

Education for Citizenship in the United Kingdom—Caught or Taught?

MARGARET B. SUTHERLAND

The idea of education for citizenship produces mixed responses in British educators. Possibly because they were horrified by the authoritarian definition of citizenship in Nazi Germany and in totalitarian states since then, they have been reluctant to make citizenship an explicit part of the curriculum of schools, in case it would impose conformity to a rigid set of rules, determined by one political party. Or possibly because of a feeling that citizenship is too complex a matter to be defined as a school subject, or that patriotism is too sacred a feeling to be explicitly talked about (Kipling illustrated this in *Stalky & Co.,* by boys' horrified reaction to a talk on patriotism by a "jelly-bellied flag-flapper"), schools have generally confined themselves to teaching the more traditional subjects. And as a further reason for not teaching citizenship there is the belief that it is not something that *can* be taught, it is rather something to be learned through experience, and perhaps by imitating other people. Consequently, for a long time, many British educators have affirmed that "citizenship is caught not taught." They have trusted that the society in which the younger generation is developing is one in which learning of the right values and qualities will take place by osmosis. So citizenship education, or civics education has—in the vast majority of British schools—been given no formal place in the curriculum.

At the same time, it can be claimed that there have been *indirect* approaches to citizenship education within the curriculum of schools. While explicit "civics education" has been absent, schools have been engaged for some time in other teaching that does have relevance to citizenship, for instance (a) religious education; (b) new and old parts of the curriculum, notably Personal and Social Development, and history; and (c) informal activities. It is useful to survey these before noting the very different developments that have taken place in England and Wales, and in Northern Ireland, in the last decade and that seem to show divergent attitudes toward this sort of education.

SCHOOL-CENTERED PROVISION

Religious Education

This part of school education has probably reinforced the belief that no specific civic education is required. Historically, schools in the countries of the United Kingdom have provided for the teaching of the Christian religion. Before the introduction of a national curriculum for England and Wales in 1988, people in other countries found it amusing that although the school curriculum was not officially prescribed, there was one subject that schools were obliged to teach—religion. (This did not mean quite such an absence of centralization as might be expected, for although there was this apparent freedom of choice for individual local authorities, or independent schools, in deciding what subjects to teach, or which parts of subjects, the existence of external examinations, conducted by a small number of Examining Boards, meant that in secondary schools the curriculum was normally constructed to prepare pupils for the requirements of these examinations in various subjects. Consequently schools tended to follow much the same curriculum. But citizenship was not a subject for which examination syllabuses were set, though various aspects of British history, and study of the British Constitution, were among the available optional subjects.)

Obviously, religious education is not coterminous with civic education: it does not include study of the constitution and laws of the country or of the specific duties and responsibilities of the citizen: and it may well be argued that such study and knowledge are essential to citizenship education—they could be described by the recently popularized term "political literacy." Nevertheless, forming certain values and attitudes is the other major aspect of citizenship education. Many of the virtues advocated by Christian teaching have much in common with those proposed for citizens, notably, perhaps, concern for the well-being of others. So it could be assumed that when religion was taught in schools with a view to inculcating belief in the Christian religion, young people of the United Kingdom were receiving explicit teaching that was intended to produce characteristics of good citizens.

But the place of religious education in the curriculum of the ordinary schools in Great Britain has altered dramatically in recent decades. No longer is its purpose seen as inducing acceptance of a given religious faith; the aim has become not to inculcate religious beliefs but to give young people an understanding of what religious beliefs are, and introduce them to a range of religious beliefs held by the people of the world. Such a change seemed particularly necessary in some parts of the country where children of different ethnic groups attend school together. A multicultural approach to religion in the major cities of England, and especially in some districts of these cities, has seemed essential. It has been extended to the United Kingdom as a whole, though multiculturalism has a much less direct impact on the experience of children in rural parts of England, or in Scotland, where ethnic groups from other countries form less than 2 percent of the population.

Consequently, while religious indoctrination may in the past have contributed to forming the character of good citizens, the new objectives of religious education do not give the same support. It is doubtful whether the effects of this new direction in religious education were foreseen; possibly, of course, there was cynicism as to whether religious education had in fact had much effect in forming virtuous individuals. In France, on the other hand, when religion was expelled from state schools in the late nineteenth century, educators did realize the need to substitute an alternative (Halls 1965): lessons on morality were made part of the primary curriculum—and, admittedly, the defeat of France in the Franco-Prussian War had made educators very well aware of the duty of the public schools to produce staunch citizens. But as Britain experienced not a *withdrawal* of religious education but a change in its nature, the possible creation of a gap in moral education was not obvious.

Looking at the present guidelines on the teaching of religion in schools in Scotland (Scottish Office Education Department [SOED] 1992), we may see illustrated the present trends and the overlap there may still be with inculcating civic virtues. These aims are "to help pupils to develop a knowledge and understanding of Christianity and other world religions and to recognise religion as an important expression of human experience: appreciate moral values such as honesty, liberty, justice, fairness and concern for others: investigate and understand the questions and answers that religion can offer about the nature and meaning of life: develop their own beliefs, attitudes, moral values and practices through a process of personal search, discovery and critical evaluation" (SOED 2). Yet while moral values are still mentioned they are no longer firmly based on the authority of a chosen faith (Sutherland 1981). In higher secondary school classes, the study of Christianity is paralleled by a study of Hinduism or Islam or Judaism. Liberal as this approach to religion may be in encouraging the development of individual judgment, it apparently gives less support to moral standards important for the well-being of society than to the former teaching of religion.

We must, of course, recognize that in the United Kingdom there are still some schools committed to the explicit transmission of one religion. In England especially, at primary level, in addition to 11,831 nondenominational schools under local authority control, there are 4,562 Church of England, 1,767 Roman Catholic, 27 Methodist, and 20 Jewish schools; at secondary level, in addition to 2,829 nondenominational schools, there are 198 Church of England, 364 Roman Catholic, and 4 Jewish schools. Among the "other" schools there are 105 at primary level and 172 at secondary. There are a very few Islamic schools (Government Statistics 1998). In such schools, teaching of moral obligations can retain the benefit of divine authority, but it does not equate with preparation to be citizens of the United Kingdom. Here we see the contrast between British denominational schools and schools in countries where the state has an explicitly religious foundation, as, for example, Iran. In the latter case, teaching children their religion also means teaching them the laws by which life in their society is regulated.

Personal and Social Development

Continuing a survey of modifications of the traditional laissez faire approach to citizenship, we find that in fairly recent years time has been set aside in schools for a subject known in England as Personal and Social Education (PSE) or Personal, Social, Health Education (PSHE) and in Scotland as Personal and Social Development (PSD). This teaching varies according to the policies of individual schools: it certainly is intended to develop some qualities that are readily recognizable as those of good citizens, but the methods chosen differ considerably. Some schools may provide classroom lessons only, others may combine these with projects that bring schools into contact with the local community or give pupils the chance to observe politicians at work—a clearer indication of the relationship with civic education.

Aims set out by the Scottish Central Council for the Curriculum (1995) for such Personal and Social Development teaching are to produce "respect and caring for self, respect and caring for others, a sense of social responsibility, a commitment to learning, a sense of belonging." To achieve such aims, schools, it is emphasized, should have "a positive whole school climate and ethos, positive approaches to learning and teacher assessment," and "consider PSD in and across the curriculum"(5). The Scottish schools also have posts of special responsibility for Guidance teachers who may well be concerned with some aspects of individual pupils' development as members of society.

So some British schools take experiential as well as cognitive approaches to personal development. Their programs actively bring pupils into contact with their local environment. For example, pupils may decide that the derelict condition of a local park needs to be changed, and through working to clear it and make it a social amenity they learn a great deal about people in the neighborhood of the school, about local regulations and bylaws, and about the value of working as a good member of a team. But in many other schools, only cognitive learning may be provided.

Even so, the authority structure of the school may be part of a hidden curriculum with relevance to citizenship education. The Scottish Guidelines referred to the importance of the whole school ethos in personal and social development. In the United Kingdom there are generally rather large differences between schools whose own regulations or rules are affected by pupil participation in decision making and where pupils feel they are recognized members of a community, and those whose structure is authoritarian, leaving little responsibility to the pupils—and to junior members of staff.

The Teaching of History

This long-established part of the school curriculum has obvious links to the education of the citizens of a country. They need to know how the society of which they are members has come into being, what important events have shaped it in the past, what its status is in international terms. For many decades, most countries found the teaching of history to be straightforward; there was concentration on military history, and the interpretation of events was from a nationalistic point of view. More recently, in Britain as in other countries, history has been taught with more concern for social conditions in the past, and teachers have come to recognize, and to point out, that other countries' interpretations of events have not been identical to those held in their own country. The problem of the relationship between the teaching of history and young people's feeling of national identity has been more sharply realized in various countries since World War II. As the experience of Japan shows, the question of how past events are to be presented in school text-books is difficult to answer, since what seems to some educators a balanced account is seen by others as presenting elements of anti-Japanese propaganda. As educators in East and West Germany discovered in the years when Germany was divided, while it is important to give future citizens full knowledge of the past actions of their country, there is the danger that too much concentration on past errors may produce in some young people an excessive feeling of guilt and unworthiness because of their country's past actions. More recently still, history teaching about slave dealing in earlier centuries has tended to attribute guilt to a number of countries, reducing the pride that citizens might earlier have felt concerning the past of their country.

Another problem in the United Kingdom nevertheless has important implications for history teaching in general—which country's history is to be taught? Should it be the history of Scotland, of Ireland, of Wales, of England? Will the creation of the Scottish Parliament and the Welsh Assembly in 1999 mean that more attention is given to Scottish and Welsh history in the schools of these two countries? And if that history includes accounts of hostilities between, for example, England and Scotland, or if it concentrates on the distinctive development of the Welsh people, will the concept of being a British citizen be weakened or lost? Furthermore, concern for the multi-cultural dimension in the school curriculum has raised the question of whether schools should also give immigrant children, or the children of immigrants, knowledge of the history of the country from which they, or their parents, came.

The interpretation of historical events has of course differed in the past in individual European countries—a trivial example is the recent suggestion in the media that the name of Waterloo Station in London, commemorating what is seen as a glorious victory for the British, but that could be offensive to

French travellers who may thus be reminded of the sad defeat of a national hero, Napoleon. History teachers in different countries have welcomed the development of history books written as a collaboration among different countries to give a balanced presentation of events, and the European Council has encouraged the development of teaching materials for use within the European Community (Ryba 1994). Although learning about the history of *all* their fellow European citizens seems a daunting task, new interpretations of history may produce future citizens who will be less chauvinistic, and less arrogant in their attitudes toward their own and other societies.

A relatively minor, but practical, complication has also affected history as part of citizenship education in the United Kingdom. With the greater number of options offered to secondary school pupils, it has become increasingly possible for them to drop the subject of history after the age of fourteen, by which point they may be only poorly informed—in television quizzes for school pupils, many otherwise highly intelligent young people show amazing ignorance even of the century in which past monarchs or important personages lived. Moreover, the teaching method of presenting "topics" in history rather than a chronological account has left many learners without any impression of the continuous development of their country. These trends result from unwillingness to overload young learners by presenting them with too many subjects to learn or, within the subject of history, a long list of reigns and events. But recently, prescriptions in England for history teaching have aroused fury because they have seemed to leave the next generation with insufficient knowledge of their country's past, and to omit events and personages who are regarded generally as an essential part of the country's historical heritage.

Overall, the changing and uncertain state of history teaching in British schools at present makes its contribution to citizenship education rather problematic.

INFORMAL EDUCATION

We must note again that in addition to school-centered lessons and projects, there is informal education through youth organizations of various kinds, some of them with a strong religious background like the Boys' Brigade founded in 1883 (Springhall, Fraser, and Hoare 1983), and others catering to young people of a variety of faiths. A most obvious example is that of the Scouts and Guides (with their associated provision for younger children). The Scout movement was founded in 1908 (Rosenthal 1986) in response to perceived weakness in British society, and its linking of character building and citizenship training was further noted in America in the mid–twentieth century (Nicholson 1940). Even in today's painstakingly updated version of the Guide promise, recruits commit themselves to service to the Queen *and country,* and to "helping others."

Another aspect of informal education that is traditionally valued in England is the possible contribution of team games to developing civic virtues, notably the realization of the need to cooperate with others (those on the same side, of course), and to sacrifice individual comfort and glory to the wellbeing of the team. English enthusiasm for cricket is often cited as an important part of informal education, so may be the more plebeian sport of football—though, despite some recent feminist advances (Elsworth 1999), these games have the disadvantage of bias toward the male half of the population. And although hockey and netball, which girls do play at school, might be held to inculcate team spirit equally well, these games have not enjoyed the same prestige as more celebrated sports as a way of teaching civic values. It has also been remarked recently that the standards of sportsmanship, and so the examples set to the young, are apparently deteriorating—the cult of adoration of individual players similarly may conceal the value of good team work. And on the practical side, unhappily, the provision of facilities for sports has declined in some areas where school playing fields have been sold off for economic reasons—to such an extent that government action has now tried to put limits on such sales (Lightfoot 1999)—and disgruntled teachers are said to be less willing than before to volunteer to devote some of their hard-earned leisure to supervising games practice and games outings. Moreover in the spring of 1999, the government reformed the curriculum in England and Wales so that team games are no longer to be compulsory beyond the age of fourteen, pupils being offered alternative choices such as athletics, dance, swimming (Times Educational Supplement 1999).

In the matter of informal education, it would seem reasonable to include the experience of playing in an orchestra as one in which the value of cooperation and coordination of individual efforts with those of others is very clearly evident. But schools' provision for such activity is rare, so orchestral playing is not usually recognized as possibly contributing to civic education.

Changes in Recent Years

In these complex and often confusing circumstances, with different attitudes and beliefs about citizenship, with half-hearted efforts by some schools and a calm disregard in other schools—possibly in the majority of schools—successive British governments are apparently coming to recognize that clearer provision for citizenship should be made in the schools' curriculum. These provisions have differed for the different educational systems of the United Kingdom; they have been less strongly defined in Scotland than in other parts of the United Kingdom, so attention will be given now to what has been proposed, and what has been happening, in England and Wales, and in Northern Ireland. We find in these two systems good illustrations of the traditional dichotomy between formal classroom teaching of citizenship and the attempt to produce appropriate civic values by informal education.

Developments in England and Wales. After the passing of the Education Reform Act of 1988, much effort was expended in England and Wales in defining the components of each curriculum subject and the level of attainment to be reached by pupils at succcessive ages. But although the Act defined "core" subjects (English, math, and science, with a modern language at secondary school level) and "foundation" subjects of the traditional type, and these were carefully provided for in subsequent directives from the central curriculum authority, no specific part of the curriculum was to be devoted to citizenship education. Such education was rather to be a "transverse theme," that is, something that would be taught incidentally as part of the teaching of compulsory subjects such as in English, history, and geography. The not-surprising consequence, as schools have tried to cope with the plethora of instructions on the teaching of the core subjects, has been that the citizenship theme, like other transverse themes, has mainly been crowded out and lost sight of. Supportive teaching through Personal and Social Development lessons or sports and team games has been unequally spread: schools' resources for such teaching, and, as we have noted, their concern to carry it out, vary considerably.

Consequently, more positive action has increasingly seemed necessary. In 1997 the Secretary of State for Education and Employment appointed an Advisory Group on Citizenship, chaired by Professor Bernard Crick. The outcome of the group's deliberations was to be "a statement of the aims and purposes of citizenship education in schools." Consideration was to be given on how such education "can be successfully delivered" through a variety of approaches, developing personal and social skills.

The Advisory Group, whose chairman had for many years written authoritatively on civic education and values, produced its final report in September 1998. It recommended that "citizenship education be a statutory entitlement in the curriculum and that all schools should be required to show they are fulfilling the obligation that this places upon them" (22). The report further recommended how this requirement should be gradually introduced, how learning outcomes should be defined and assessed, and how information be given to all concerned in education as to "what is meant by citizenship education and their central role in it." As the key concepts of this education, the report listed "democracy and autocracy, cooperation and conflict, equality and diversity, fairness, justice, the rule of law, rules, law and human rights, freedom and order, individual and community, power and authority, rights and responsibilities." Longer lists were provided to define "values and dispositions, skills and aptitudes, knowledge and understanding," including, for instance, the values of "concern for the common good," "belief in human dignity and equality," the skill "to make a reasoned argument both verbally and in writing," and "a critical approach to evidence put before one and ability to look for fresh evidence." Among other aspects of political literacy were included "Britain's parliamentary political and legal systems at local, national, European, Commonwealth, and international level, including how they function and change" (44).

The report also offered admirable comments on such vexing questions as neutral, balanced, or committed chairing of controversial discussion topics. It recognized the importance of the school's own ethos. And very important, it emphasized that future teachers must receive guidance concerning methods of providing citizenship education since "the key to effective education for citizenship, as for all other areas, lies in recruiting the highest quality of entrants to the profession and ensuring that training is well targeted to meet the needs of teachers" (30).

Possibly with a faint echo of traditional concerns about the wrong kind of interpretations of citizenship—that is, biased, undemocratic teaching—the report referred to the "political sensitivity" of what was being proposed, and suggested the creation of a Standing Commission on Citizenship Education to monitor its progress, and when necessary to recommend amendments. The Commission was to include, among other members, "cross-party representation." The "political sensitivity" of such education was soon demonstrated by a report from a Methodist Church working party (Cassidy 1999c) that firmly warned against the dangers of political indoctrination in citizenship classes in schools.

Clear proposals were thus made for the introduction of formal lessons on citizenship as part of the curriculum in schools in England and Wales. The Crick recommendations, probably in a modified form, are to be put into practice. In May 1999, the government announced changes to the overloaded curriculum of recent years and, in some ways slimming it down, decided that citizenship education must indeed be compulsory. By the year 2002, in schools in England and Wales, lessons on citizenship are to be part of the school curriculum and should be allotted 5 percent of curriculum time (a percentage that has caused some despairing reactions from teachers who already find their timetables overcrowded). The government tried to allay teachers' fears by saying that to a considerable extent schools are already giving the kind of teaching intended, but apparently this response did not silence the protests from teachers and their unions (Cassidy 1999b).

The new teaching will include many elements that are already being taught under the heading of PSHE. The new statements of the curriculum will try to make clear to schools which elements of their teaching are essential to citizenship education. They will make it clear what secondary school pupils will be expected to know regarding citizenship and what, as citizens, they must be able to do. Such knowledge must include "the basics of the criminal justice system, central and local government, the electoral system and diversity of national, regional, religious and ethnic identities in the UK." Future citizens must be able to state their views and discuss them formally (*Times*

Educational Supplement 1999). In primary schools, citizenship will not be recognized as a separate subject, but will be included in the existing PSHE programs.

Developments in Northern Ireland. While prescription by the central government agencies has determined what subjects schools must teach in England and Wales, the prescription of the curriculum in Northern Ireland has not been ensured by a formal Act of Parliament like the 1988 Education Reform Act for England and Wales, nor by Guidelines in the Scottish style. Because of the absence of a Northern Ireland Parliament in the late 1980s, this educational change was introduced by an Order of the Privy Council in 1989. Prescriptions very similar to those proposed for England were made. As in England, the curriculum structures included "transverse themes," that is, topics to be presented through various ordinary subjects of the curriculum (Northern Ireland Curriculum Council 1989). As we have noted, such themes have received relatively little attention in England since schools have been so greatly preoccupied with adjusting to directions concerning teaching the traditional assessed subjects.

But the Northern Ireland situation, where the population has been subjected to various forms of terrorist violence for some thirty years, and an acceptable form of government has been sought without success, has given urgency to proposals to help young people develop qualities of good citizenship. Citizenship is difficult to cultivate when people have different attitudes toward the society in which they live and feel loyalty toward different organizations and different faiths. In Northern Ireland the problem of conflicting loyalties, and conflicting attitudes toward the constitution of the country, is long established. Questions about citizenship receive different answers from members of the Northern Ireland population. Some happily assert that their nationality is British—they are and want to remain British citizens. Others, the minority, consider themselves Irish and would wish to be citizens not of the United Kingdom of Great Britain and Northern Ireland but of a united Ireland. There are also some—perhaps a relatively small group—who would wish to retain and enjoy both a British and an Irish identity.

The situation is further complicated by religious affiliations. While absolute generalizations cannot be made, in the majority of cases Protestants support being part of the United Kingdom while Catholics have preferences for reunification of Ireland. It may be recalled that the "partition" of Ireland in 1921 resulted from recognizing the rights of a mainly Protestant minority in the North to remain British. But even earlier, the provision of education in this part of the world was bedevilled by the division of schools into those providing for Protestant children and those providing for Catholic children (Sutherland 1988).

Common citizenship in a dual system of schools? Since early in the nineteenth century various efforts have been made to develop a feeling of unity in the whole population of Ireland by enabling all children to attend the same schools. This attempt at National Schools in the nineteenth century failed because of the unwillingness of extremists on either side of the religious divide to agree on the correct presentation of religious education. So, unhappily, schools became divided into those mainly catering to children of Protestant parents and those catering to the children of Catholics. This situation persisted with the division into the Republic of Ireland and Northern Ireland in 1921. The dual system has thus remained one of the problem areas of education in Northern Ireland. Formally, though, the public schools of the country are open to children of all religious denominations and are regarded as essentially Protestant schools. Children from Catholic families have normally attended the schools set up under the auspices of the Roman Catholic Church. Occasionally, some children may attend schools of the "other" denomination, if, for example, those living in rural areas find travel to the nearest school of their faith too burdensome. At secondary level, some of the fee-paying schools have a tradition of accepting some pupils who are not of the religious background of the majority of their pupils, and this mixing normally seems to work well. From the financial point of view, increasing improvements in the latter part of the century have meant that Catholic schools receive practically the same support from public funds as do the schools under the control of the local authorities for education. But there is obviously the danger of producing or maintaining deep divisions in society, such as being unable to educate for shared citizenship or having two diametrically different sets of schools for the children of the country.

This danger has been recognized by educators in a number of countries, since it seems doubtful that a common loyalty and a feeling of common interests in society can develop among young people who have little chance to become acquainted with peers of a different religious outlook. The danger of ignorance leading to hostility or bigotry seems very real—though of course much depends on the opportunities for the young to meet with others of different faiths out of school, or possibly to attend during some stage of their education schools or colleges where there is not a separation according to religion—a point well recognized some time ago by Greeley and Rossi (1966), though ultimately that research indicated home life as having a much greater influence than the type of educational establishments attended. Certainly, in Northern Ireland some students have commented that it is only when attending university that they have had the opportunity to get to know "the other side" and have been somewhat astonished to find these others remarkably like themselves. Even so, in Western societies the competitive spirit often encouraged in the first levels of schooling may well help to develop a belief in the superiority of the kind of education the individual happens to receive during these formative years, and could inculcate animosity toward "outsiders." This kind of division may well be strengthened if, despite studying the same curriculum of school subjects and sitting the same exams, pupils of different schools engage in different sports—rugby, for example, or Irish football—and enter sporting contests run by different authorities. Such ingrained divisions are likely to be the stronger if schools, while sharing the common subjects of the traditional curriculum, make different choices in language learning. In Northern Ireland it is almost always the Catholic schools that offer pupils the opportunity to learn the Irish language, and that encourage them to participate in musical festivals using that language (Sutherland 1988).

For whatever reasons, with however perceptive or unperceptive an understanding of such factors, it has been the case that since the mid–twentieth century in Northern Ireland public opinion polls have tended to show that most people—of both religious affiliations—regret this separation into different schools and would prefer a unified system. But such preferences are not enough to effect major change, so future citizens remain largely divided during their school years.

Integrated schools. Nonetheless, in recent decades a remarkable innovation has been the experiment of creating schools that bring together, in roughly equal percentages, children from Catholic and Protestant backgrounds, and that ensure the same mixture of religious outlooks in the staffs of these schools. This experiment was made possible by the Education (Northern Ireland) Act of 1978 "to facilitate the establishment in Northern Ireland of schools likely to be attended by pupils of different religious affiliations or cultural traditions." This act defined the ways that schools can become recognized as integrated schools and, indeed, how parents can elect to change the nature of the school their children are attending. The practical introduction of integrated schools began on a small scale with a school opened in Belfast in 1981, but their numbers have gradually increased.

We can regard the existence of these schools as evidence of good citizenship on the part of parents and staff. They seem to demonstrate a belief in the values of informal education, of catching the good qualities of citizenship by working together with other members of society who have different views on religion and politics. But we have to recognize that there are other aspects of citizenship that militate against a great expansion of integrated schools, notably, the feeling of disloyalty that might worry some Catholic parents if they sent their children to such a school instead of to a school that is part of a Catholic system that church authorities and other Catholics have worked for and supported. There are, of course, other considerations, as, for instance, the rumor that the academic standards reached in the integrated schools are not as high as those in the ordinary schools, and doubt as to whether teachers in them could subsequently find employment in Northern Ireland schools of the usual kinds (Morgan et al. 1994).

In assessing the good results that integrated schools may have in producing liberal-minded future citizens, it would be necessary to take into account the fact that parents who choose to send their children to such schools are already demonstrating considerable open-mindedness, so the good effects on their children could be attributed to the home background rather than to the school experience. Some critics have also suggested that many parents using these schools are atypical because they are in a "mixed marriage," so the school is less a straightforward choice than a refuge from an otherwise difficult situation. Correspondingly, there is the fear among parents that attending an integrated school might enourage young people to proceed later into "mixed" marriages—that is, with partners of the other faith, for in some areas of Northern Ireland, the situation of such marriage partners is far from easy— indeed, as events such as a blast bomb thrown into a house have sadly shown, partners in such a marriage are more likely than other citizens to be the object of violent attacks.

Nevertheless, the fact that there has been government support for integrated schools would seem to indicate that politicians see some merit in such experiential learning of civic education. But, for a variety of reasons, the part of the pupil population so far affected by experience of this kind is very small—less than 5 percent in 2000.

Education for mutual understanding. For the majority of children in Northern Ireland, therefore, school education is likely to take place in an environment defined as either Protestant or Catholic. But, given this situation, the planners of the curriculum reform in 1989 introduced proposals that were to lead to a great variety of educational strategies, using both formal classroom education and informal, out-of-school education. The main focus of this part of curriculum reform was Education for Mutual Understanding (EMU), a "transverse" or cross-curricular theme (Northern Ireland Curriculum Council 1989).

Against the background of years of disruption in the life of society, and the repeated evidence of conflicting views about citizenship, this new construction of the curriculum stated that pupils should learn "to respect and value themselves and others, to appreciate the interdependence of people within society, to know about and understand what is shared as well as what is different about their cultural traditions, and to appreciate how conflict may be handled in non-violent ways." Among other objectives, pupils were to "know about and understand the interdependence of the different religious and cultural communities within Northern Ireland and the consequences of their integration and segregation; know about and understand the interrelationship between Northern Ireland, the rest of Ireland and the rest of the United Kingdom and have explored these within an international context" (16).

Complementing these aspects of citizenship came also the cross-curricular theme of Economic Awareness where the pupils were to learn, among other things, about "the purposes and effects of government taxation, spending and legislation on individuals, firms and on the community in general; the ability of local, central and European governments to influence the allocation and efficient use of scarce resources in the natural and the man-made environments" (18). It is worth noticing that the proposals did not portray citizenship as narrowly national, but recognized the growing importance of participation in Europe. Similarly, the cross-curriculum theme of Cultural Heritage, while emphasizing the need to learn about, and appreciate other British and Irish cultures, introduced "awareness of the international and transnational aspects of today's society" and "the role of some major international and transnational organizations and pressure groups."

For EMU a range of activities was indicated, including classroom discussion of controversial issues, talks from visitors, visits to other schools or to common ground, exchange of materials with other schools "using all forms of communication systems" (18), joint work that could extend to international contact.

Each of twelve traditional subjects of the curriculum was analyzed to show how the teaching of that subject could also contribute at the different "key stage" age levels—ages 7, 11, 14, 16—to the learning of the six cross-curricular themes. EMU figured prominently in the teaching of English, history, and geography and to a respectable extent in art and design, music, and drama, but to an understandably lesser extent in maths, science and information technology, and physical education—and not at all in language studies (i.e., study of modern languages, in secondary school up to age 16)! EMU did, however, make an appearance in the twelfth subject also: Irish—for schools teaching through the medium of Irish (a very small number).

These then were the prescriptions for school teaching that should contribute to forming good citizens and improving the state of society in Northern Ireland. The teaching of religion was not outlined in the proposals of the Curriculum Council, but of course we must remember that such teaching has been continuing in the schools of the dual system and may also be developing aspects of personality necessary for good citizenship.

To what extent have these prescriptions for EMU contributed to civic education in Northern Ireland? This cross-curricular theme has certainly received considerably more attention and has survived to a much greater extent than transverse themes in the education system of England. It is indeed difficult to survey all the attempts, large and small, that have been made by schools, teachers, and others in Northern Ireland to ensure better communication and better understanding. Some lasted for only short periods of time;

many have not been publicly reported. But it has to be recognized that EMU has been supported by a number of official interventions, by, for example, conferences bringing together authorities and teachers to discuss this part of the curriculum (Department of Education Northern Ireland 1990). Considerable attention has been given its development and effects, and some schools have duly held in-service days devoted to EMU.

But we have also to note the very large number of initiatives to improve intergroup relations made by individuals and groups of schools in the years before EMU was formally introduced—indeed, since the early 1970s, for already in 1970 there was the Schools Community Relations Project, based in Queen's University, Belfast; followed there by the Schools Curriculum Project; and in 1974, the (then) New University of Ulster began the Schools Cultural Studies Project. Some of these early ventures have been illuminatingly described in the report "Chocolate, Cream, Soldiers" (Jenkins et al. n.d.), showing in particular the difficulties that teachers may encounter in dealing with controversial matters in class. While such teachers may be unwilling to adopt a directive style, they may yet be horrified to discover how strong is the prejudice that pupils have already developed against those of "the other side." At the same time, it should not be assumed that all teachers are on the side of the angels. Some teachers—a small minority, it may be hoped—manifest prejudices as strong as any of the most bigoted members of the population.

During the years of "the troubles" (the typically low-key term for civic disturbances and terrorist outbreaks in Ireland) many schools have arranged meetings with schools of the other main religious affiliation. Various voluntary organizations have also organized interdenominational school camps or visits to other parts of the United Kingdom. The impression given by reports of these activities is that children can indeed meet each other with great friendliness on such occasions. But it has also appeared at times that many children are aware that on return to their home environment, friendship and companionship with someone of the other faith will not be possible—it will not be socially acceptable and, in some areas of Belfast and Londonderry, even visiting the territory of the other side may be inadvisable.

The school teaching of EMU has also been criticized from various points of view (Smith and Robinson 1992), for example, that it has been concentrating on what can be superficially interesting school visits and failing to come to grips with the controversial issues involved in the problems of citizens. It is said to have relied more on activities than thoughtful classroom discussions. A conference on Education for Civic and Social Responsibility in 1998, attended by the Secretary of State for Northern Ireland, indicated that "EMU could be strengthened to address the more contentious issues which often divide society in Northern Ireland and many of these relate to social justice and political themes" (Northern Ireland Council for the Curriculums, Examinations and Assessment 1998).

Nevertheless, it is clear that much good has resulted for many individuals from this plethora of educational efforts. Similar attitudes of goodwill have been evident in the formation outside the schools of various peace movements, uniting, especially, children or women. Even if such efforts have so far been unsuccessful in affecting the whole of society, it has to be recognized that they have at least created pockets of goodwill and mutual understanding, important for the lives of individuals if not yet for all the population. It might indeed be argued that in the many spontaneous projects to improve relationships and in the good behavior of the great mass of the people during what have been very troubling and difficult decades, we have proof of a remarkably strong and commendable spirit of citizenship. While some of this continuing peaceable willingness to live with others of different views can be attributed to some of the religious teaching received in the early years of education, it does seem plausible to argue that it is a kind of citizenship that has been "caught" rather than taught. If we were trying to assess the relative merits of teaching citizenship by formal lessons, or teaching it by letting it be "caught," the Northern Ireland example would seem to indicate that the evidence favors the latter method, even if, unhappily, the Northern Ireland situation also offers examples of the undesirable kind of citizenship being "caught."

Other Factors Relevant to Citizenship Education

Some factors relevant to education for citizenship are affecting not only education in the United Kingdom but that of a great many other countries, especially European countries, at present. There is the problem of conflicting loyalties to a nation-state or to smaller groups within that state; individuals, too, may feel their values threatened by the standards set by the society they are living in and so may resist and encourage their children to resist civic education provided by the public authorities. So it is important to recall some of these competing claims and to remember that citizenship education is a matter studied and debated in many countries.

Education for the wider citizenship of Europe. Possibly the foregoing discussions of citizenship have been clinging to an already outdated way of thinking, for nowadays it is increasingly evident that future generations should feel part of a larger society than that of their own nation. British politicians subscribing to the agreements of the European Union have indicated their acceptance of the need to introduce the European dimension to the schools of their country. But apart from vague hopes that this may be achieved incidentally by the teaching of such subjects as geography and history, there seems to have been no positive action to bring about this change. For example, even though the importance of knowing more than one European language has been officially recognized, there is little in the curriculum as prescribed by the Education Reform Act of 1991—and by the Scottish Guidelines and the Northern Ireland Order in Council—to encourage such learning. While a European language is to be learned in secondary schools up to the age of sixteen (and at present in Scotland such learning begins in primary schools), learning more than one such language, and continuing language study after the end of compulsory schooling, has not been made easy or attractive.

It must of course be recognized that the other, less formal, approach is being used to some extent to produce good Europeans. The European Commission has done a great deal by giving money to support projects that have ensured exchanges of students, teachers, and pupils traveling from one country to another and so assimilating knowledge of their fellow citizens in Europe (Smith 1988, Palomba and Bertin 1993). Schools' preparations for such visits—and even school projects that enable children to communicate on the Internet with their peers in other countries—must further be regarded as ways that parents are drawn into the learning experience, toward European citizenship. At the same time, we have to recognize that these experiences do not always contribute to the formation of friendly attitudes toward the people of other countries. Sometimes a badly planned visit—or the accident of unfavorable circumstances—may produce feelings of complete hostility and a firm conviction that one's own country is infinitely to be preferred to that of foreigners'. Again, informal education of this kind is unevenly distributed through British schools.

More positive action seems to be called for as there is some doubt as to whether pupils in schools in England are taking on the concept of being European. Some research, admittedly on a limited sample in a number of countries (Convery 1997), found that while 90 percent of a group of pupils from the Netherlands thought of themselves as European, 39.8 percent of the English group did not feel themselves at all European, 41.6 percent felt themselves partly so, and only 18.6 percent felt totally European! For young people in some European countries, dual citizenship—of their own country and of Europe—was readily accepted: 94 percent of the Netherlands group thought of themselves also as belonging to their own country. But the English group apparently was less clear about such an identity, for only 70.3 percent thought of themselves as totally English, and 25.7 percent felt "partly so" (the inclusion of some pupils of non-English ethnic origins did not seem to be the reason for these attitudes).

Possible resistances to schools' teaching of citizenship. Those British educators who have contentedly adopted the tradition that citizenship is caught, not taught, have apparently assumed that the environment the young live in offers only one kind of citizenship to be caught—and that that kind is good. But in today's conditions there is obviously more than one citizenship that young people can assimilate, and as we noted for Northern Ireland, the attitudes to be assimilated may in certain circumstances be far from good.

Two major sources of conflicting loyalties affecting the status of citizens, and education toward that status, may be noted. First, in many countries at present, the movement of populations has introduced large immigrant groups whose feelings of national identity are not those of the indigenous population, even if the children of such immigrants may gradually change to other concepts of their national identity. Second, there is also the question of indigenous minorities and alternative national traditions. Recent changes in the United Kingdom—creating a Scottish Parliament and a Welsh Assembly—seem likely to enhance consciousness of dual citizenship, even if, for the majority, it has long been possible to accept being both Scottish and British, or Welsh and British (though for both these groups, attribution of English citizenship has been far from acceptable). But for speakers of an indigenous minority language—Welsh, Scottish Gaelic, Irish Gaelic—the important national identity may be that of the language group, so that feelings of solidarity with people who do not know that language will be slight or nonexistent. And of course the home language of immigrant groups may cause similar feelings of not belonging to the same society as nonspeakers of that language. It may indeed create feelings of greater solidarity with people in other countries.

Even if some countries (the United Kingdom, for example) already can accept quite contentedly that some citizens hold more than one passport, the recent controversy in Germany about the dual passport issue has offered an interesting demonstration of how difficult it may be to cultivate feelings of common European citizenship where a clear division of loyalties between markedly different ethnic groups may be present. For example, an immigrant's possible possession of both a Turkish and a German passport has seemed unacceptable to a number of German citizens.

Associated with the problem of divided loyalties and good citizenship is the question of conflicting cultural values. In countries where one group of the population does not want its children to share the moral values of the majority, members of the minority group seek to have separate schooling incorporating their value system. This can raise very tricky questions concerning the rights of children as distinct from the rights of their parents.

Culture clashes of this kind tend to center more on the education of girls than on that of boys—though parents may be concerned for the morals of both gender groups. And, oddly enough, women may be generally considered to be in various respects better citizens than men—at the very least in their relative crime rate. An obvious example of special concern for girls' education, and a potential division within society, is the furor recently created in France when some girls opted to wear a head scarf to school, which was interpreted as a departure from the ideals of the common, secular school for all

French citizens (Coutty 1999). Similar, less publicized incidents have occurred in British schools, though they have been dealt with individually rather than made an issue for central government to rule on. But the culture clash goes further than matters of dress, since it would appear that in Muslim schools for girls the view is propagated that the role of men and women in society is different, and that women should concentrate not on involvement in public affairs but on the home. Such a view seems to be in clear opposition to British and other societies' affirmations of equal rights and equal access to positions of authority for both genders. Can a democratic society allow some of its future citizens to be educated to accept what appear to be nondemocratic principles? This possible conflict, and the duty of the school system to face the problem of parent groups who try to inculcate principles contrary to some of society's basic tenets, was recognized as far back as 1978 in Denmark in a report by the Danish Ministry of Education, Central Council of Education, titled *U90: Danish Educational Planning and Policy in a Social Context.* Or can educators hope that day-to-day living in a society, even when the home sets barriers to much participation, will transmit knowledge of principles that are not being respected in the young person's more immediate environment?

Admittedly, it could be said that in some respects the British environment in general scarcely exemplifies equality, so the young people "catching" notions of citizenship from it may come to accept various inequalities as natural, or different groups of young people will form different concepts of citizenship according to their social environment. This is no new thing, though possibly brought into sharper relief by modern conditions. In the nineteenth century Disraeli (1845) recognized the existence in England of "two nations"—"between whom there is no intercourse and no sympathy; who are as ignorant of each other's habits, thoughts, and feelings, as if they were dwellers in different zones . . . who are formed by a different breeding, are fed by a different food, are ordered by different manners, and are not governed by the same laws . . . The Rich and the Poor."

International comparisons. Because many countries have in fact for some time included civic education in the curricula of their schools, it might have been hoped that clear guidance would come from a study of their results. Various international comparisons have been made, but it is doubtful whether other countries' experiences give adequate answers to the questions regarding citizenship as "taught or caught," and whether the problem of conflicting loyalties within a society has been solved. Research on the effects of citizenship education in different countries (Torney, Oppenheim, and Farnen 1975)—given the official policies of not including civic education as a required subject, British schools have tended to be omitted from such surveys—has tended more to test pupils' knowledge (political literacy) and their attitudes toward certain behaviors than to discover to what extent they have resulted in the formation of good citizens. Valuable as these international comparisons are, there still remain some problems of separating school influences from the influences of various environments.

And, on the common sense level, in most countries instances of those who are "bad citizens" are normally not attributed to failure to give due attention to formal lessons in school; we are much more inclined to attribute delinquency or more adult vices to environmental influences.

CONCLUSION

Such considerations may bring us, however reluctantly, to the view that indeed school education has to give explicit teaching about citizenship. Such teaching could at least develop more adequate knowledge of government structures and the formal rights of citizens, more knowledge too of international relationships and organizations. At the same time, we are left with rather convincing evidence that the "caught" methods seem more effective than formal teaching. So not only are methods of informal education to be fostered and the ethos of schools reviewed to discover whether schools give experience of good citizenship in miniature, but for effective civic education the larger society also needs reform so that it becomes an environment in which good citizenship can be acquired by example and by participation.

REFERENCES

Cassidy, Sarah. (1999a, May 14). "Citizenship heads for secondary schools." *Times Educational Supplement* (London), p. 6.

Cassidy, Sarah. (1999b, May 21). "Unions challenge 'bogus' debate." *Times Educational Supplement* (London), p. 16.

Cassidy, Sarah. (1999c, July 11). "Methodists warn of politicised citizenship." *Times Educational Supplement* (London), p. 2.

"Citizenship Heads for Secondary Schools." (1999, May 14). *Times Educational Supplement* (London), pp. 6–7.

Convery, A., M. Evans, S. Green, E. Macaro, and J. Mellor. (1997). *Pupils' perceptions of Europe.* London: Cassell.

Coutty, M. (1999, May). "Le voile de Marianne." *Le Monde de L'Education,* 270, pp. 46–47.

Crick Committee. (1998). Final report of the Advisory Group on Citizenship. *Education for citizenship and the teaching of democracy in schools.* London: Qualifications and Curriculum Authority.

Danish Ministry of Education, Central Council of Education. (1978). *U90: Danish Educational Planning and Policy in a Social Context at the End of the 20th Century.* Copenhagen: Schultz Forlag.

Department of Education Northern Ireland. (1990). *Education for mutual understanding.* Belfast: Education and Training Inspectorate, DENI.

Disraeli, B. (1895). *Sybil, or the two nations.* Book 2, Chap. 5. London: Macmillan.

Education Reform Act 1988. Chapter 40. London: Her Majesty's Stationery Office.

Education (Northern Ireland) Act 1978. "An Act to facilitate the establishment in Northern Ireland of schools likely to be attended by pupils of different religious affiliations or cultural traditions." London: HMSO.

Elsworth, C. (1999, May 9). "Football set to beat netball as women's favourite sport." *Sunday Telegraph* (London), p. 19.

Greeley, A. M., and P. H. Rossi. (1966). *The education of Catholic Americans.* Chicago: Aldine.

Halls, W. D. (1965). *Society, schools and progress in France.* Oxford: Pergamon Press.

Jenkins, David, et al. (n.d.). "Chocolate, cream, soldiers." Final evaluation report on the Rowntree Schools Cultural Studies Project. Occasional Papers, the New University of Ulster, Education Centre, Coleraine, Northern Ireland.

Kerr, David. (1998 October). "Citizenship education and the revised national curriculum." NFER Annual Conference.

Kipling, Rudyard. ([1929]—reprinted edition). "The honour of their country." *Stalky & Co.* London: Macmillan.

Lightfoot L. (1999, June 8). "Playing field sell-off rules 'too weak.' " *Daily Telegraph* (London), p. 9.

Morgan, V., S. Dunn, G. Fraser, E. Cairns. (1994). "A different sort of teaching, a different sort of teacher? Teachers in integrated schools in Northern Ireland." *Comparative Education* 30(2):153–163.

Nicholson, E. (1940). *Education and the Boy Scout movement in America.* New York: Teachers College, Columbia University.

Northern Ireland Council for the Curriculum, Examinations and Assessment. (1998). *Developing the Northern Ireland curriculum to meet the needs of young people, society and the economy in the 21st Century.* Belfast: CCEA.

Northern Ireland Curriculum Council. (1989). *Cross-curricular themes.* Belfast: NICC, Stranmillis College.

"Of inventors and pioneers." (1999, May 14). *Times Educational Supplement* (London), pp. 6–7.

Palomba, D., and Bertin, N. (eds.). (1993). *Insegnare in Europa* [Teaching in Europe]. Milano: FrancoAngeli.

Rosenthal, M. (1986). *The character factory: Baden-Powell and the origins of the Boy Scout movement.* London: Collins.

Ryba, Raymond (1994, June). "On progress in the development of the European dimension in education." *CESE Newsletter,* pp. 1–6.

Scottish Consultative Council on the Curriculum. (1995). "The heart of the matter—Education for personal and social development." Edinburgh: SCCC.

Scottish Office Education Department. (1992). *Religious and moral education 5–14.* Edinburgh: HMSO.

Scottish Office Education Department. (1993). *Personal and social development 5–14.* Edinburgh: HMSO.

Smith, A. (1988). "The ERASMUS programme of the European Community—Some implications for international exchange and co-operation." *Higher Education Policy* 1(4):51–52.

Smith, A., and A. Robinson. (1992). *Education for mutual understanding: Perceptions and policy.* Coleraine, Northern Ireland: University of Ulster.

Springhall, J., B. Fraser, and M. Hoare. (1983). *Sure and steadfast—A history of the Boys' Brigade 1883–1983.* London: Collins.

Sutherland, M. B. (1981). "Foundations of moral education: A comparison of possibilities." *Compare* 11(2):199–206.

Sutherland, M. B. (1988). "Religious dichotomy and schooling in Northern Ireland." In W. Tulasiewicz and C. Brock (eds.), *Christianity and educational provision in international perspective,* 38–60. London: Routledge.

Torney, J. V., Oppenheim, A. N., and Farnen, R. F. (1975). *Civic education in 10 countries.* International Studies in Evaluation no. 6. Stockholm: Almqvist & Wiksell, John Wiley & Sons.

DISCUSSION QUESTIONS

1. If teachers are to be trained to teach citizenship education, what should that training consist of?
2. For what reasons have British educators been unwilling to include citizenship education in the curriculum of schools?
3. What seem to be the advantages and disadvantages of integrated schools in Northern Ireland?
4. In what ways can the teaching of history contribute to citizenship education?
5. What conflicting loyalties may make it difficult for the education system to define good citizenship, and may complicate learners' responses to citizenship education?

CHAPTER 14

Institutional Constraints on Promoting Civic Education in Hong Kong Secondary Schools
Insights from International Educational Achievement Data

LEE WING-ON AND LEUNG SAI-WING

Civic education has been an academically interesting and a practically pressing issue for Hong Kong since the signing of the Sino-British Joint Declaration in 1984 that determined the transfer of sovereignty from the British to the Chinese government in 1997. One year after the appearance of the Joint Declaration, the government issued the *Guidelines on Civic Education in Schools* (1985). The *Guidelines* became the first document that mentioned the need to know more about being proud of China, and being prepared for becoming Chinese citizens. However, 1985 was too early to attract any public attention for the change of sovereignty that would take place thirteen years later. The government was still operating in its colonial mode, though with gradual attempts to put Chinese into higher administrative position, and a gradual introduction of certain elected seats in the Legislative Council. The interval from 1985 to 1990 was a relatively quiet period of colonial transition. However, entering the 1990s, the political climate began to change markedly. Elected seats in the Legislative Council were increased from twelve to eighteen in 1991, and to twenty in 1995. Five political parties were established during 1990, and political debates became more intense with the approach of 1997. In sum:

> ... the turn of the 1990s marked the change of Hong Kong's political scenario from one that was depoliticized to one that was politically sensitized. It demarcated the end of consensus politics. Also, it witnessed the end of the narrow politics that was government sponsored or concerned only with influencing administrative functions and the beginning of mass politics in Hong Kong. (Lee 1999, 314–315)

The later period of colonial transition was then characterized by disputes and confrontations, causing distrust and, to some extent, hatred, between the people, between the Chinese and British governments, and even between the

Hong Kong people and the two governments. In 1997, Hong Kong ended her colonial status by reunifying with China.[1] This political reunion has not solved the issue of Hong Kong people's political and cultural identity in relation to the mainland. The situation of post-1997 Hong Kong is therefore similar to many of the postcolonial nations that have found difficulties "in trying to socialize young people to national consciousness and loyalty in a nation which to many people is nothing but a name" (Sigel 1970, 591).[2]

This issue, accompanied by a debate on whether civic education after 1997 should put more emphasis on the inculcation of national identity or on the cultivation of a democratic personality.[3] Hong Kong society was quite split in terms of what political orientations the territory should adopt. For example, the liberal camps argue that Hong Kong's political future lies in the pace of its democratization, and such a pace of development will very much depend on the provision of democracy education in schools.[4] For the patriotic camps, re-engineering civic education toward the reunification with China and upholding nationalistic education should be the only direction for its civic education. Of course, there are many other views as well. Some argue for a cultural citizenship approach, others for integrating the liberal and pro-China views, yet others even rejecting being both anticolonial and antinationalistic, pushing for an entirely open approach in its citizenship inquiry. However, whatever stance people take in suggesting the direction of civic education in post-1997 Hong Kong, all parties admit that the great majority of adolescents who were born in Hong Kong "have no special allegiance to some geographical point in China" (Cameron 1978, 259). The difference in their platform concerning revision of civic education simply indicates the difference in their aspiration of "one country, two systems." For the patriotic camps, the value of the formula lies in emphasis on "one country," but for the others, "two systems." Needless to say, many of the conflicts between national interest and Hong Kong's interest are much more possible in the future in relation to the issue of national identity. As Johnson (1986) aptly describes: "a distinct form of society was created that was once Chinese, but not *of* Chinese" (239).

As a macro phenomenon, the discussion of civic education in Hong Kong helps us to discern the possible ideological differences between state and society, the confrontation between different political parties and interest groups, and the power politics between government departments and school systems. As a micro phenomenon, the implementation of civic education in Hong Kong schools helps us to delve into the dynamics of a school as an institution, and into the institutional constraints on this implementation. The unfolding of these institutional constraints not only helps to shed light on the political disintegration of society and education in Hong Kong, but also on the political culture of the younger generation. In light of this context, Hong Kong's experience in implementing and launching reform in civic education will certainly become a significant case in civic education and political socialization literature.

INSTITUTIONAL CONSTRAINTS: INSIGHT FROM OLD INSTITUTIONALISM

Leung (1995) adopts an old institutionalist's theoretical stance to explore how the implementation of civic education was depoliticized and trivialized by the institutional arrangement of Hong Kong secondary schools. The notion of social institution is conceptualized as a set of rules, shared by the members of the relevant community or society, that structure social interactions in particular ways (Knight 1992). Educational practitioners are not free to act. Formally and informally, there are rules governing their roles and their interactions, and, in turn, their share of power in the educational hierarchy. To put it in another way, the choices of action for these practitioners are patterned, or say, limited, and they are induced, through socialization, reward system, affirmation of identities, and satisfaction of need, to choose the approved choices (Stinchombe 1975). If these educational practitioners' choice of action for the implementation of civic education is limited by the implicit rules and norms of the school system, or the assumed active role in implementing civic education is incompatible with their passive political role in daily life, or the active part played in implementing civic education would not receive as much reward as that played in preparing students for the open examination, then it is unlikely that civic education can have much space for development in the present institutional arrangement.[5]

Leung (1995) argues that civic education in Hong Kong secondary schools could only be seen as that of depoliticization and trivialization:

> How were the *Guidelines* [*Guidelines on Civic Education in Schools*] implemented? Teachers clearly play a critical role. However, on the one hand their subjective political culture makes them water down the political content of the *Guidelines* and emphasize moral education instead; on the other hand their insurmountable workload in company with the educational ethos of longing for success in examination and students' poor academic standard compel them to treat civic education as something unimportant or even dispensable. The result is a depoliticization and trivialization of civic education by teachers. (292)

These institutional constraints are the result of the government's lack of support for civic education. As a colonial government, the Hong Kong government tried hard to depoliticize Hong Kong society in the 1950s, 1960s, and 1970s. On the one hand, it minimized the government's intervention in society and made use of the appointment system and committee system to absorb local elites (Lau 1982; King 1981). The appointment of local elites has been found to be a very effective measure in pacifying the people. Governance then involved local leaders who were also eager to support the government. On the other hand, it played down the role of civic education in secondary schools. Before the publication of the *Guidelines* in 1985, civic education was taught in various subjects, namely, civics, social studies, and economic and public affairs.[6] The publication of the *Guidelines* did not mean that the government began to take an active role in civic education. In fact, the *Guidelines* retained its depoliticized nature (Leung 1995). The lukewarm attitude of the Hong Kong government toward civic education helped to explain why the government and the Education Department never accorded any substantial resources to an area that was important in developing citizenship in Hong Kong. The negligence, or more correctly speaking, the deliberate downplaying of civic education by the government, has also posed great difficulties for the schools to implement civic education. The policy negligence is therefore transformed into institutional constraints for the schools that wish to play a role in citizenship education.

This logic of theoretical argument clearly follows the basic tenets of old institutionalism. According to this school of thought, participants' preferences are shaped by institutional norms, and newcomers to an institution must undergo socialization, which leads to "internationalization" of organizational values. Institutional constraints refer to normative constraints on the behavior of newcomers, implementation of new programs, and introduction of new ideas to an institution (DiMaggio and Powell 1991a, 14–15). These normative constraints come from a relationship pattern in which norms, values, and preferences are shared by actors in the institution. Empirically speaking, whenever and wherever newcomers, new programs, or new ideas meet regular resistance and challenge from the actors of an institution, there are institutional constraints. In this chapter, we identify four areas, namely, resource allocation, formal curricula, informal curricula, and gate keeping of controversial issues, in which institutional constraints on the implementation of civic education are more salient.

Our primary aim is to examine the institutional constraints on the implementation of civic education in Hong Kong secondary schools on the basis of new data. We will also discuss how new institutionalism can bring us more insight in the understanding of our thesis.

DATA AND METHOD

Our data are compiled from interviews with principals, teachers, and students, conducted from January to April 1996.[7] These interview data are part of the Phase I data collection of the second International Educational Achievement (IEA) civic education study. Six schools were chosen for identifying school informants. The six schools were firstly recommended by the Educational Officers in the Education Department. Colleagues of the Department of Education of the University of Hong Kong and members of the National Expert Panel (Hong Kong) later endorsed this recommendation of the IEA study. The six schools represent three levels of students' academic achievement in Hong Kong, namely, "high level of achievement" (coded as H), "medium level of achievement" (coded as M), and "low level of achievement" (coded as L), as well as attitude in promoting civic education, one being "active" (coded as A) and another one "nonactive" (coded as N). In choosing these schools, we intended to include schools diversified in academic orientation (grammar, technical, and prevocational) and religious background (Taoist, Protestant, Catholic, Buddhist, and nonreligious). However, the major criteria of categorization are students' academic achievement and attitude in promoting civic education. Thus, a school that is active in promoting civic education (A) and with students of high academic achievement (H) is coded as AH.

Within each school, interviews were conducted with both the school practitioners as individuals (one principal and one teacher) and students in focus groups. The teachers interviewed were mainly those with assigned corresponding responsibilities for civic education. There were four students in one focus group. They were randomly selected from each form (or grade), from Form 1 to Form 4, in order to cover the age range of eleven to fifteen. In all, we interviewed six principals and six teachers as individuals and twenty-four students in six focus groups.

We adopted a structured questionnaire for the interview method because the IEA study is a comparative project, with most of the interview questions drawn from the core international framing questions I to IV of the study. In addition to the core questions, specific questions were also designed for each specific group of informants relevant to their particular categorizations. Moreover, questions for students in focus groups were adjusted to their level of understanding and concerns to enhance their responses. A typical interview, including focus group interview, lasted approximately forty-five minutes.

Questions were asked in relation to four major areas of citizenship: democracy, national identity, social cohesion and diversity, and the influence of mass media. The interviewers asked our informants both their ideal expectations in each of the four areas and their assessment of reality in the society and school. Another emphasis in our interviews was to ask questions on how those topics were taught in terms of curriculum, classroom teaching, extracurricular activities, and so on.

An initial report of the findings has already appeared as a chapter in the IEA Phase I report (Lee 1999). Here we attempt to employ the institutional perspective in understanding the implications of the data.

RESOURCE CONSTRAINT IN THE IMPLEMENTATION OF CIVIC EDUCATION

According to the *Guidelines,* schools are encouraged to adopt an interdisciplinary approach. That is to say, civic education should be taught in every subject. The suggestion sounds impressive. The implication is, however, very clear. The government would not earmark a sum of money for this educational project, or grant additional funding to secondary schools to set up an independent civic curriculum, or offer training courses for teachers teaching civic education. It is not an exaggeration to say that the proposed interdisciplinary approach simply passes the responsibility to secondary schools and sees how they can squeeze resources and staffing from already overloaded teaching routines. Consequently, only a minority of secondary schools in Hong Kong has an independent civic education subject. In our sample, none of the schools taught civic education as an independent subject. All of them mentioned social studies, economic and public affairs, religious education, government and public affairs, and so on, as their formal civic education subjects.

Without additional financial and staffing support from the government, we can hardly expect secondary schools to set civic education as their educational priority. As a matter of fact, distortion of top-down policies by lower-level practitioners is a normal phenomenon in big bureaucracy. This is exactly what Leung (1995) argues in his paper, "Trivialization of Civic Education in Secondary Schools." It is, therefore, not surprising to find that the principals of all six schools did not seem to have a clear idea of how civic education was implemented in their schools, not to say they could pay heed to the limited effect, if any, of their programs. In general, their answers to the question, "What is the school climate in carrying out civic education?" were rather short and without any elaboration: "We just started to set up a program by following the *Guidelines* issued by the Education Department. Because we are a school with religious background, we will add some religious element in the program" (NMP). "Our direction is to teach our students truth as well as knowledge. We have frequent joint activities with outside charity groups. These are also part of our civic education" (ALP). "From the viewpoint of school, we want our students to participate in our activities. Through these activities, they can think more about their rights and responsibilities" (AHP).

It is quite ironic that if the principals had answered the question in greater detail, one could easily cast doubt on the actual effect of their programs. AMP pointed out that their civic education had both moral and civic aspects. Students were not only educated to distinguish right from wrong, they could also gain knowledge about the Basic Law and the political transition of Hong Kong. The principal emphasized that the latter could not be found in current textbooks. However, it was the principal who told us that the school would only allow students to spend two to four periods every year to hold some special activities related to civic education in the school hall. Another principal, NHP, gave us the following answer: "We don't have any class, any textbook, nor any examination in civic education . . . but that does not mean we are not doing anything. In Form 1 and Form 2 we have special periods with lectures by form teachers every week. In this form period form teachers are allowed to do everything they like. It is, therefore, possible that they will teach students some civic topics. In Form 6 and Form 7, students have Ethics periods. They will at least do something related to civic education." NHP unmistakably comments that without resource support from the government, principals of secondary schools may pass the responsibility to teachers and expect, on a slippery ground, that they can fulfill what the *Guidelines* recommend.

The resource problem is real. Unless schools are instructed or forced to reallocate existing resources for the implementation of civic education, the normal response is to improvise or even to trivialize what is of low priority. Perhaps they are in the front line and they are not in a position that compels them to give socially desirable answers. Teachers' responses tell us more about the reality of the implementation of civic education in their schools. In replying to the question about whether they had consulted the *Guidelines,* most of them did not give positive answers. "I seldom follow all the suggestions listed in the *Guidelines.* Very often, we use teaching materials prepared by some interest groups or educational organizations" (AMT). "The *Guidelines* are principles only. In terms of practice, what we have to focus on are students. In my opinion, the suggestions of the *Guidelines* seem to be enough" (AHT). "We have to adopt the interdisciplinary approach because we don't have any single period. Senior form teachers, in particular, emphasize that they don't have enough time (for teaching). It is not good to add pressure on them" (NHT).

The answer of NHT gives us a clearer picture of how difficult it is to squeeze time from the originally overloaded teaching routine for the interdisciplinary teaching of civic education. Her spontaneous elaboration told us more about the impact of workload on the implementation of civic education: "Last year I took over this position from another teacher who left our school. The main task is to help students to understand what is happening outside the school. I am a Form Mistress. I have to teach language to students of two forms. It is really hard work. All I can do is to do my best. . . . If we know there are any activities related to civic education, we would recommend them to senior form teachers and let them decide whether to organize them or not. However, they would often say time is not enough, teaching is pressing, and students have a lot of exams. They may not do it. Even if they do, they would only introduce or talk about it a little bit in class."

To adopt the interdisciplinary approach does not mean that there will be no resource problem. The experience of NM demonstrates how tight the problem of time is: "Now we are planning to teach (civic education) through form period. . . . If a class is used for civic education in a particular day, then every class in that particular day has to be cut short by five minutes" (NMP).

On the one hand, ALT's answer is particularly informative. He told us that the *Guidelines* have no consideration of the special schools, which have a different schedule and curricula from normal grammar schools. He also pinpointed the problem of teachers' training. ". . . the *Guidelines* is based on five lessons per week. . . . We cannot have five periods. Time is our major problem. Besides, training of teachers is also a problem. Teachers teaching social studies have not received any training. For example, we have English teachers teaching social studies, but they have not been trained at all" (ALT).

Examining the transcripts of the principals' and the teachers' interviews simultaneously, we came to the conclusion that either the principals were giving us socially desirable answers or they really did not think carefully about the implementation of civic education. Interestingly, compared to the principals, the teachers were more aware of the resource problem in teaching civic education. They either have to improvise ways or let colleagues trivialize civic education in their schools. The resource problem is more salient if we come to formal and informal curricula, a problem that is totally neglected in the *Guidelines*.

CONSTRAINT OF FORMAL CURRICULUM DESIGN IN THE IMPLEMENTATION OF CIVIC EDUCATION

Adopting an interdisciplinary approach becomes a normal practice of all sampled schools. However, neither principals nor teachers mentioned the problem of differential accessibility to subjects, which are regarded as more appropriate for teaching civic education, such as social studies (SS), religious education (RE), economic and public affairs (EPA), and government and public affairs (GPA). The accessibility of students of our sample to these four subjects is reported in Table 15.1. We have additional information from other sources that findings reported in Table 15.1 are not a phenomenon unique to our sampled schools. As argued by Leung (1995, 289), ". . . science students are almost deprived of the opportunity of studying either EPA or GPA. According to our survey of classes of secondary students in 1988, among 883 science students, only 16.1 percent had taken EPA. Interestingly, even for arts students, the proportion of those taking EPA was only 37.4 percent of a total of 996. In fact, the number of enrollments for EPA in the Hong Kong Certificate of Education Examination dropped from 36,000 to 10,000 in 1988." If these subjects are not offered to all students, then an interdisciplinary approach simply means there will be a differential accessibility to civic education in secondary schools.

Table 14.1. Differential accessibility to civic education subjects

Code of Schools	SS	RE	EPA	GPA
AH	None	Form 1 to Form 3	Form 1 to Form 3 and Senior Form Arts students	None
NH	None	All forms	None	None
AM	None	Form 1 to Form 3	Form 1 to Form 3	Senior Form Arts students
NM	Form 1 to Form 3	None	None	None
AL	Form 1 to Form 3	None	None	None
NL	Form 1 to Form 2	None	Form 3	None

The interdisciplinary approach proposed by the *Guidelines* clearly does not take note of the peculiar schedule and curricula of some special schools. AL is one such special school. If normal grammar schools find difficulty in teaching civic education through formal curricula, then what AL has to do is to cut the Gordian knot. ALT gave us a vivid description of their difficulties: "The curriculum of social studies in our school is totally different from that in the *Guidelines*. Social studies described in the *Guidelines* is based on three to five periods per week but we used to have two periods per week, though we have managed to have three periods per week now. We have three semesters per year. Since it is a prevocational school, we can only offer Chinese history as an extra subject in the third semester. For Form 1 to Form 3 students, we add extra topics on current affairs, assigning significant weighting to the subject (social studies). . . . We do not have Chinese history. We need to insert Chinese history into our curricula. However, due to time constraints, we can only cover three-fifths of the original syllabus."

Even if all these subjects are offered to all students, there is still the problem of whether teachers really make use of these subjects to teach civic education. Without additional resources, to recommend that a teacher teach a subject as both an academic and a civic education subject is unrealistic in the real school context. As a consequence, problems of studying an academic subject will also become problems of studying civic education. First of all, teachers themselves would put much more emphasis on the academic purpose than on the civic education purpose of the subject. NMT's unconscious repetition during the interview indirectly informed us of what was really happening if the Education Department and the principals passed the responsibility to teachers by proposing the so-called interdisciplinary approach: "I believe that our colleagues are capable of transmitting knowledge of civic education to students. However, the attitude of teachers and their teaching strategies are very important. . . . We have a civic education committee. The attitude of committee members is very positive. We have regular meetings every Friday. The effectiveness of civic education greatly depends on the attitude of teachers. The more attention teachers pay to civic education, the greater the effectiveness (of our civic education). Attitude of teachers is our source of constraint."

The educational ethos in Hong Kong places an unreasonable emphasis on success in internal or open examinations. Both teachers and students consciously or unconsciously set this as their priority in teaching and learning. Thus, in replying to the question, "Do students need to memorize the facts about the system of government?" AMT told us that it was in Form 2 EPA subject that students needed to memorize the facts about the government for the examination. AHT echoed AMT's answers: "Interdisciplinary approach is and will be adopted. In EPA, the structure of the syllabus is examination oriented." NHT pinpointed the impact of this educational ethos on the teaching of civic education: "Students nowadays won't follow current affairs. They will only focus on their academic performance and individual interests. They don't have enough knowledge of society. If we don't have an independent (civic education) subject and invest much more time on teaching, they won't pay attention to current issues."

The long-term education ethos emphasizing success in examinations has led students to adopt rote learning as their learning strategy. Regardless of whether teachers treat the subject as an academic subject or as a civic education subject, students normally resort to rote learning. The answers of NL students are almost self-evident for this educational ethos. In replying to the question, "Do you need to memorize all the information about the system of government?" NLS F2 gave us an interesting answer reflecting his "growth" in the Hong Kong education system: "I remember I needed to [memorize textbooks] when I was in primary school. Now I am in secondary school, I will put all these into my mind without the 'push' of teachers. I think this kind of knowledge is useful to us for finding our jobs in future." NLS F1's answer was short and straightforward: "I memorize this information because I need to take the examination."

Resorting to rote learning by NL students could be explained by their lower academic performance. Among our sampled schools, AH and NH have students of Band 1 or Band 2.[8] However, students of AH gave us similar answers. A Form 3 student of AH told us that his way of studying EPA is to memorize all the facts about the government and political system (AH F3). A

Form 1 student admitted that in the first three months, every subject seemed difficult to him because they are in English (AH F1). A Form 2 student echoed this opinion (AH F2). A Form 4 student frankly said that he scarcely paid attention to civic education because preparation for the open examination was his major concern (AH F4). It seems rote learning and the emphasis on success in examinations is so popular that a NMS F3's answer is pretty informative. He told us that they had discussions, projects, and video programs as class activities of social studies. Moreover, they had to submit assignments and to take an examination for the subject. At last, when he was asked how he treated the projects, he answered, "For the exams."

Remy's (1972) comment in his study can help to summarize the constraint of formal curricula in the implementation of civic education in Hong Kong secondary schools:

> Improving civic and government instruction is a complex and multifaceted task. One important but too often neglected aspect of this task is the careful and systematic assessment of the ways in which students experience the efforts of schools to teach them about the political life of mankind. If we are to substantially improve school as agents of political learning we must move beyond "educated guess" and theoretically derived assumptions about students' needs, wants and perceptions. (621–622)

CONSTRAINT OF INFORMAL CURRICULUM DESIGN IN THE IMPLEMENTATION OF CIVIC EDUCATION

Both the principals and the teachers told us that they had a lot of extracurricular activities for civic education purposes. This is exactly what the *Guidelines* proposes. However, the problems of teaching civic education through formal curricula also become the problems of disseminating civic values through extracurricular activities. Because of the lack of resources, a great majority of secondary schools tend to encourage students to participate in normal extracurricular activities, for example, Boy Scouts, Girl Guides, Red Cross, various academic and sport clubs, and so forth. What they do not pay heed to is that these activities are not necessarily organized with civic education in mind. Just as with teaching civic education through academic subjects, the effect of these activities on civic education cannot be taken for granted. As Jones (1975) argues,

> Programs of student involvement cannot be implemented hastily or summarily. Nor can they be viewed as a salve for citizenship education. Unless involvement experiences carefully are tailored to the specific student community, they may be counterproductive. They also may function to increase rather than decrease the unequal impact of formal political education. (292)

The most salient example in point is the student union. Through participation in student unions, the principals and the teachers thought students could learn the practice of democracy. Most of the students interviewed by us did mention their student unions. However, with the exception of students of AM and AL, many of them criticized the nonfunctioning of student unions. Interestingly, they were quite outspoken and critical toward student unions. AHS F1 simply did not answer the question, "Do you think the student union is responsive to you?" to show his unhappy feeling toward the student unions. AHS F2 simply said, "I don't think so." NMS F3 replied in a satirical and negative way to the same question, "All students in our school need only to vote for the chairman of the student union . . . [The student union] suggests to install a drinking fountain in school campus. But till now no action has been taken." NHS F3 also gave us a similar answer: "No, I don't think so. For example, our student union said they would request our school to install a money exchange machine for the photocopier. This request has been raised for a long time but we do not see any follow-up."

NLS F4's answer is the most interesting. He seemed to have benefited, not from the participation in the activities organized by the student union, but from the reflection on the role of the student union.

INTERVIEWER: What is your opinion of the function of the student union?

NLS F4: The original purpose of setting up a student union is good. However, it seems to me that nothing has been done since its setting up.

INTERVIEWER: What do you mean by the original purpose?

NLS F4: It was suggested that we would have a representative responsible for general affairs from each class, but this suggestion seems to be a "blank check." Therefore, there is a discrepancy between the present performance of the student union and the ideal student union.

INTERVIEWER: What is your ideal student union?

NLS F4: An ideal student union should be able to represent the students' voices and reflect our opinion to the school. Students are able to express their view anytime and do not need to wait until teachers request us to do so.

INTERVIEWER: That means that the student union can act as a representative of the students and express their viewpoints to the school?

NLS F4: Yes.

INTERVIEWER: How was your student union formed?

NLS F4: There were two candidate cabinets and they pinned their platforms on the notice board. However, it seemed that we did not really know their understanding of our school nor their experiences. I felt the whole campaign was pretty "hard-sell," in a sense, the campaign was merely to enlist students' support. I saw an interesting phenomenon among junior form students. When they voted, they would not consider whether the welfare policy of the cabinet was realizable or not. I would say they did not think before they voted. They only had a scan of the welfare policy of the cabinet.

The democratization and socialization literature highlights the significance of participation for civic political learning (Pateman 1970; Almond and Verba 1972; Karvonen 1974; Jones 1974, 1975; Diamond 1994). However, according to our interview findings, the students were alienated from the student union, which was supposed to represent them. This helps to bring us to the underlying negative impact of resource problems in the implementation of civic education. The lack of resources implies the lack of priority given to civic education, and many civic education activities thus become trivialized. From policies to implementation, neither the principals nor the teachers would think carefully about what they really wanted their students to learn, or from what sort of curricula and activities. Under the pressure of the workload, they would only make use of what was already in hand. We can hardly expect them to anticipate the alienating effect of the student union. On the other hand, as students' discipline is a more pressing problem than their attitude toward and skills of participation, and because the principals and the teachers are in general very conservative in their political stance, they would emphasize the moral dimension but discard the political dimension of civic education. These two factors explain why, in their mind, many extracurricular activities are regarded as related to civic education. As a consequence, they become the frontline agents in depoliticizing civic education in schools.

CONSTRAINTS OF GATEKEEPING OF CONTROVERSIAL ISSUES IN THE IMPLEMENTATION OF CIVIC EDUCATION

Gupta and Rani (1984) argue that "teachers cannot play a vital role in inculcating democratic values unless they themselves develop these values" (149). A salient problem of implementing civic education in Hong Kong is the conservative political stance of both principals and teachers. They have a clear inclination to shut real-life politics out of the school campus.[9] This is perhaps the repercussion of the Hong Kong government's explicit ban on politics during the colonial era. Whereas Hong Kong society has been getting more and more politicized during the colonial transition and students can have greater and greater exposure to real-life politics through coverage of mass media, school practitioners decline to raise debates and controversies on politics in schools. In this way, it is very likely that students, especially those of senior forms, will find their civic education activities boring or even alienating. Also, through the mass media, students already know what is really going on. Most important of all, this inclination to shut real-life politics out of the school campus reflects a relatively autocratic attitude in school administration.[10] Consequently, there is a discrepancy between civic education activities ostensibly designed for transmitting democratic values in a school campus with an antidemocracy atmosphere.

Teachers' answers to the question on whether they would raise discussions on controversial issues in school are quite indicative of their political stance. A majority of the teachers did not give us a positive answer. AHT gave us a very straightforward reply: "Teachers should avoid talking about these issues in class. We should maintain objectivity in teaching. We should not speak of our subjective opinion." NHT's and ALT's replies were quite diplomatic: "I would study the issues from different points of view. If I find a standpoint is sound, I will support it. I won't be intimidated and I won't avoid discussing these issues" (NHT). "It depends on my understanding of the issues. I will raise the discussion of them if I am well prepared" (ALT).

The most interesting response is NLT. His answers to two consecutive questions smack of contradiction. From his answers, it is clear he takes a conservative stance:

INTERVIEWER: What concept of democracy do you think students should acquire?

NLT: From daily life, school, community, and society.

INTERVIEWER: Would you allow students to air their disagreements about the government in school?

NLT: There are many channels to air one's disagreement about the government. Students need not do this in school. We don't have this policy in our school. But I think it is acceptable for students to air their viewpoints provided that what they are talking about is based on facts and they are not incriminating others.

AMT is the only one who gave us an answer totally different from the others: "During the direct elections in 1995, I enthusiastically introduced the concept of voting to students. The information on candidates was posted on the notice board. I am not sure if this is sensitive or not. But I don't see anything wrong in this activity. I always promote citizen's rights, such as freedom of speech." In comparison with other teachers and principals, AMT openly declared her support for a democratic political system. She elaborated a lot on the democratization of Hong Kong during the transition and underscored the emergence of political parties. She seemed to follow closely what was happening in the political arena of transitional Hong Kong. She is clearly the most pro-democracy practitioner in our sample: "If the government is more determined to launch the system of one-person-one-vote, I think this will help to speed up the democratic development of Hong Kong."[11]

Two principals' replies in relation to the conception of democracy and the bringing of politically sensitive issues to school life are quite illuminating. AHP clearly tried to evade our questions about politics by declining to give us answers or by answering in an elusive way. To the question "Do you think schools should bring out the discussion of politically sensitive issues, for example, criticizing the government?" he answered, "Our school will give students different kind of opinions or references with respect to some politically sensitive issues. But we won't give our conclusion to students." To "What do you think is an ideal government?" the answer was, "I don't want to give any comment because the question itself is too abstract." To "What do you think is an ideal democracy?" the answer was, "I am a practical person. If it is not feasible in reality, it is difficult for me to give comment." And to "What do you think is the characteristics of the democracy of Hong Kong?" he answered, "Nowadays, it is a question we need to inquire more about and it is quite debatable." From his idea of civic education to his thinking of citizens' rights and responsibilities, AHP always emphasized students' and citizens' responsibilities rather than their rights.

NHP comes from a foreign country with a long history of democracy. In comparison with other principals, he had a much clearer concept of, and first hand experience with, democracy. He briefly outlined the obstacles to Hong Kong's democratization. He was the only one who underlined the importance of letting students experience democracy in daily life. However, he declined to bring politically sensitive issues into school life.

INTERVIEWER: Do you think the concept of democracy, government system, and citizen rights and responsibilities are essential elements for civic learners aged fourteen/fifteen?

NHP: I think it will be too difficult for them to absorb such abstract concepts. I think if they were given some opportunity to take some share in the decisions which affect their life in school and at home, and if they were introduced to a good course about history, then I think they would be able to accept that more abstract concept.

INTERVIEWER: Do you think their knowledge in this aspect is sufficient?

NHP: I fear their knowledge is not sufficient, because the school is good at teaching scientific subjects. And those students who are not able to do those subjects have lost interest in history, Chinese and Western history, and they are moving more toward the principle of accounts and computer studies. Though in economics they can learn about some participation and democracy, but the interest is either in scientific subjects or now more business and practically orientated subjects. So it is difficult to get across the ideas directly or indirectly in class anyway.

INTERVIEWER: Do you think schools should bring out the discussion of politically sensitive issues, for example, criticizing the government?

NHP: I think in general we have to ignore them.

INTERVIEWER: Why?

NHP: Maybe the students themselves quite resist criticism of the government, and of the authority. Even in school, the students are a bit slow to protest, even when they feel they were treated unjustly, as I am sure they are sometimes.

We are not sure why principals growing up in totally different political systems share a similar point of view toward bringing politically sensitive issues to school life. Their gatekeeping function is, however, pretty evident. We venture to suggest that even with additional resources for the implementation of civic education, principals and teachers of secondary schools may still earmark this resource to moral education, to enhancing students' discipline, and to organizing more activities that they think are conducive to a harmonious school life.

INSTITUTIONALIZATION CONSTRAINS ORGANIZATIONAL RATIONALITY: INSIGHTS FROM NEW INSTITUTIONALISM

The institutional constraints on the implementation of civic education in secondary schools seem to be salient in resource allocation, formal curricula, informal curricula, and gatekeeping of controversial issues. Adopting the theoretical logic of old institutionalism, we think these constraints come from the institutional norms and roles of secondary schools. However, in the light of the theoretical development of institutional analysis, a more powerful explanation of these constraints can be found in new institutionalism.

The development from old institutionalism to new institutionalism reflects a cognitive turn in social scientists' thinking about human motivation and behavior.[12] For old institutionalism, institutions implant a moral frame of reference into their participants; but for new institutionalism, "institutions inevitably involve normative obligations but often enter into social life primarily as *facts* which must be taken into account by actors" (Meyer and Rowan 1991, 42). That is to say, what is being institutionalized are taken-for-granted scripts, rules, and classifications. Thus, Douglas (1986) argues that institutions require a cognitive base that naturalizes and rationalizes the conventions that constitute the institution.

The most powerful consequence of institutionalization is that institutions can make morality become facts. Through institutionalization, actors of an institution are not being inculcated as to institutional norms and taking institutional roles, they are being led to adopt a cognitive schema to see things that are different from those outside the institutions. Whereas critics point out that by the depoliticization and trivialization of civic education in schools, teachers and principals may be emphasizing that they are doing their job, or complaining about the lack of resources and time, or underscoring the importance of open examination. In the light of this theoretical thinking of new institutionalism, we can make sense of a lot of the responses of principals and teachers, especially their reluctance to let controversial issues enter school life (the best example is NHP's response in the last section). In their eyes, they do not think there is anything wrong with or inadequate in their way of implementing civic education. By the same token, they do not think there is anything wrong with their emphasis on examinations. These are all facts in their organizational life. Unfortunately, because the data set forms part of the IEA comparative study of civic education project, the interview guideline is designed to follow a set of questions shared by participating countries. It prevents us from further exploring and substantiating this theoretical argument.

New institutionalism also differs from old institutionalism in explaining institutional irrationality. According to old institutionalism, institutional constraints on new policies and new programs introduced to the institution are explained by the "subversion of the organization's intended, rational mission by parochial interests" (DiMaggio and Powell 1991a, 13). According to new institutionalism, however, it is the formal organizational structure itself that brings forth institutional constraints. In his classic study of bureaucracy, Max Weber (1962) highlights the efficiency of a bureaucratic structure. In modern societies, organizations tend to adopt a bureaucratic structure not because it is efficient enough, but because such a structure can automatically bestow legitimacy to organizations. Meyer and Rowan (1991 put it succinctly:

> In modern societies, the myths generating formal organizational structure have two key properties. First, they are rationalized and impersonal prescriptions that identify various social purposes as technical ones and specify in a rulelike way the appropriate means to pursue these technical purposes rationally (Ellul, 1964). Second, they are highly institutionalized and thus in some measure beyond the discretion of any individual participant or organization. They must, therefore, be taken for granted as legitimate, apart from evaluations of their impact on work outcomes. (44)

To compete for resources and customers, political and institutional legitimacy, and social and economic fitness, organizations may copy the institutional structure of other organizations (DiMaggio and Powell 1991b). Institutional isomorphism is, therefore, common in modern societies.[13] To adopt a rationalized structure does not mean that the organizations are striving for the accomplishment of their organizational goals. In fact, this rationalized structure can be more ceremonial than functional. As DiMaggio and Powell argue:

> This [institutional isomorphism] can make it easier for organizations to transact with other organizations, to attract career-minded staff, to be acknowledged as legitimate and reputable, and to fit into administrative categories that define eligibility for public and private grants and contracts. None of this, however, ensures that conformist organizations do what they do more efficiently than do their more deviant peers. (73)

Meyer and Rowan (1991) further pinpoint that organization can absorb uncertainty (the implementation of civic education is a case in point) by assuming that everyone is acting in good faith. Critics point out that in this way teachers and principals do not face challenges in the implementation of civic education, but still think that they are doing their job properly. Or they can explain their failure, if any, by another fact: that they are doing a good job in preparing students for the open examinations.

The thesis of institutional isomorphism helps us to free the concept of institutional constraint from an intra-institutional context. In the light of institutional isomorphism, institutional constraint is an inter-institutional phenomenon. When organizations have a tendency to adopt rationalized structures without concomitant commitment to efficiency, goal attainment, and struggle for success, irrationality becomes a built-in mechanism in the formal structure itself. This explains why the halfhearted implementation of civic education is so common in Hong Kong secondary schools. Without qualification, our line of argument may smack of institutional determinism. This is not our theoretical stance. For us, the institution does place constraints on actors' values, cognizance, and behavior. On the other hand, we also believe that actors can transform institutional arrangements. Thelen and Steinmo (1992) posit a dual role of actors in institutions:

> To the extent that we take seriously notions of human agency as crucial to understanding political outcomes, we need to come to terms not just with political behavior as the dependent variable, influenced by these macrosocioeconomic structures, but as independent variable as well. (10–11)

To take notions of human agency seriously means to consider seriously the active part played by human agency in the social structure. This is the time-honored sociological tradition of interpretive sociology, of which ethnomethodological study of microinteractions in organizational settings has demonstrated that actors are highly sensitive to context in rule use. As argued by Friedland and Alford (1991), "Sometimes rules and symbols are internalized and result in almost universal conformity, but sometimes they are resources manipulated by individuals, groups, and organizations" (254).

In our study, we do have some interesting findings in this respect. Teachers, like AMT who has a predilection for democracy, can help to bring politically sensitive issues into school life. Schools like AL put a lot of effort into teaching civic education and launching a lot of civic education activities. During the interviews, ALT mentioned their different themes of activities in different periods. For example, they introduced to their students a three-tier system of Hong Kong political structure, issues on China and 1997, and the concept of "through train." Their motive seemed to be to give students updated knowledge on current affairs. They even invited legislative councilor Ms. Chan Yuen Hang to deliver a seminar on the problem of unemployment in Hong Kong. Perhaps it is because of its nature as a prevocational college that AL does not have to do everything to boost its students' academic standard as do dominant grammar schools.[14] In new institutionalism's perspective, AL does not have to adopt too much from the dominating grammar school structure. Paradoxically, more space can be found in AL than in other grammar schools for the development of civic education.

As we mentioned earlier, the comparative nature of our data defies us to do a thorough exploration of new institutionalism's line of thought. The present discussion, however, helps to locate several areas for further inquiry that we need to explore further:

1. Does the institutional isomorphism hinder not only the development of civic education, but also the introduction of new ideas and new programs in Hong Kong secondary schools?
2. Do principals and teachers view success in open examinations as so important that they reject any institutional change toward the development of other educational activities?
3. Can principals and teachers play an active agency role in the transformation of the institutional arrangement of schools? In what organizational setting are they more likely to take such a role?

NOTES

[1]Leung's (1997) work offers a chronological account of these disputes and confrontations and the concomitant of Hong Kong people's alienation.

[2]Chinese officials in Hong Kong were well aware of this problem. The Culture Committee of the Preliminary Working Committee also commented, "Accompanying China's resuming the exercise of sovereignty over Hong Kong from 1 July 1997, we

should pay particular attention to civic education. The main objectives include inculcating students' identity with the country and the nation and strengthening their knowledge of the Basic Law and 'one country, two systems' " (Tai Kung Pao, 13 September 1994).

[3]To revise the *Guidelines on Civic Education* in March 1995, the Education Department formally formed an ad hoc Working Group. The whole process of revision was deliberately made known to the public. Newspapers reported debates on the direction of the revision between the major camps. "The liberal camp called for strengthening of education for democratic education, legal education and human rights education. The patriotic camp called for strengthening of patriotic and nationalistic education, as well as knowledge of China" (Lee 1996, 319).

[4]The landslide victory of the liberal camps in the 1991 and 1995 direct elections of the Legislative Council can be explained by a predominant anti–Communist China sentiment among their supporters (Leung 1993, 1996).

[5]In the present institutional arrangement, simply issuing the *Guidelines on Civic Education in Schools* (1985) is doomed to failure. An institutional building, including institution variables like leadership, doctrines, programs, resources, and internal structure, and linkage variables like enabling linkages, functional linkages, normative linkages, and diffused linkages (Esman 1972), may be too ambitious. However, the government and the Education Department at least have to pay heed to these institutional constraints.

[6]For a detailed account, see Lee (1997, 3–7).

[7]The revised *Guidelines on Civic Education on Schools* were issued in 1996. The present interview data therefore reflects the implementation of the old guidelines published in 1995 rather than the latest revised version.

[8]In Hong Kong, students are classified into five bands, from Band 1 to Band 5. Secondary schools that can have students of mainly Band 1 and Band 2 are regarded as prestigious.

[9]In Hong Kong, the June 4 incident was perhaps the only one that could trigger hot discussions in school life (Leung 1997).

[10]A report by a Visiting Panel (1982) and another one by the Education and Manpower Branch and the Education Department (1991) have similar comments on the autocratic style of school administration.

[11]In the 1995 Legislative Council election, seats came from district constituencies with one-person-one-vote, and functional constituencies with individual or organizational voting. In this way, some Hong Kong voters can have two votes (one vote in their district constituency and one vote in their functional constituency) but some can only have one vote (in their district constituency only).

[12]"The current development represents a shift from Parsonian action theory, rooted in Freudian ego psychology, to a theory of practical action based in ethnomethodology and in psychology's 'cognitive revolution' " (DiMaggio and Powell 1991a, 15).

[13]Although the thesis of institutional isomorphism gives us insight, the new institutionalists "do not have the theoretical tools by which to understand the institutional content whose diffusion they do analyze, or the conditions under which particular forms are institutionalized or deinstitutionalized" (Friedland and Alford 1991, 224).

[14]In Hong Kong, the academic standard of prevocational schools is, in general, lower than that of grammar schools. Parents are very reluctant to have their children studying in the former.

REFERENCES

Almond, G. A., and S. Verba. (1972). *The civic culture: Political attitudes and democracy in five nations.* Princeton, NJ: Princeton University Press.
Cameron, N. (1978). *Hong Kong: The cultural pearl.* Hong Kong: Oxford University Press.
Curriculum Development Committee, Education Department. (1985). *Guidelines on civic education in schools.* Hong Kong: Government Printer.
Diamond, L. (1994). "Introduction: Political culture and democracy." In L. Diamond (ed.), *Political culture and democracy in developing countries.* Boulder, CO: Lynne Rienner.
DiMaggio, P. J., and W. W. Powell. (1991a). "Introduction." In W. W. Powell and P. J. DiMaggio (eds.), *The new institutionalism in organizational analysis.* Chicago: University of Chicago Press.
DiMaggio, P. J., and W. W. Powell. (1991b). "The iron cage revisited: Institutional isomorphism and collective rationality." In W. W. Powell and P. J. DiMaggio (eds.), *The new institutionalism in organizational analysis.* Chicago: University of Chicago Press.
Douglas, M. (1986). *How institutions think.* Syracuse, NY: Syracuse University Press.
Education and Manpower Branch and Education Department. (1991). *The school management initiative: Setting for framework for quality in Hong Kong schools.* Hong Kong: Government Printer.
Esman, M. J. (1972). "The elements of institution building." In J. W. Eaton (ed.), *Institution building and development: From concepts to application.* Beverly Hills, CA: Sage.
Friedland, R., and R. R. Alford. (1991). "Bringing society back in: Symbols, practices, and institutional contradictions." In W. W. Powell and P. J. DiMaggio (eds.), *The new institutionalism in organizational analysis.* Chicago: University of Chicago Press.
Gupta, S. K., and A. Rani. (1984). "Teachers' sense of political efficacy," *Eastern Anthropology* 37(2): 145–152.
Johnson, G. E. (1986). "1997 and after: Will Hong Kong survive? A personal view," *Pacific Affairs* 59(2): 237–254.
Jones, R. (1974). "Changing student attitudes: The impact of community participation," *Social Science Quarterly* 55: 439–450.
Jones, R. (1975). "Students' political involvement and attitude change," *Teaching Political Science* 2(3): 260–273.
Karvonen, J. (1974 June). "School democracy and social attitudes of students and teachers in Finnish schools," *Comparative Education Review*, pp. 207–216.
King, A. Y. C. (1981). "Administrative absorption of politics in Hong Kong: Emphasis on the grassroots level." In A. Y. C. King and R. P. L. Lee (eds.), *Social life and development in Hong Kong.* Hong Kong: Chinese University Press.

Knight, J. (1992). *Institutions and social conflict.* Cambridge: Cambridge University Press.

Lau, S. K. (1982). *Society and politics in Hong Kong.* Hong Kong: Chinese University Press.

Lee, W. O. (1996). "From depoliticization to politicization: The reform of civic education in Hong Kong in political transition." In Chinese Comparative Educational Society (eds.), *Educational reform—From tradition to postmodernity.* Taipei: Shih Ta Publishers.

Lee, W. O. (1997). "Civic education in Hong Kong in political transition: A case study report for the IEA civic education study (First Phase study)." Paper presented at the Fifth International Conference on Chinese Education Toward the 21st Century.

Lee, W. O. (1999). "Controversies of civic education in political transition: Hong Kong." In Judith Torney-Purta, John Schwille, and Jo-Ann Amadeo (eds.), *Civic education across countries: Twenty-four national case studies from the IEA civic Education Project.* Delft, Netherlands: Ecuron Publishers.

Leung, S. W. (1993). "The 'China Factor' in the 1991 Legislative Council election: The June 4th incident and anti-communist China syndrome." In S. K. Lau and K. S. Louie (eds.), *Hong Kong tried democracy: The 1991 elections in Hong Kong.* Hong Kong: Hong Kong Institute of Asia-Pacific Studies, Chinese University of Hong Kong.

Leung, S. W. (1995). "Depoliticization and trivialization of civic education in secondary schools: Institutional constraints on promoting civic education in transitional Hong Kong." In P. K. Siu and P. T. K. Tam (eds.), *Quality in education: Insights from different perspectives.* Hong Kong: Hong Kong Educational Research Association.

Leung, S. W. (1996). "The 'China Factor' and voters' choice in the 1995 Legislative Council election." In H. C. Kuan, S. K. Lau, K. S. Louie, and K. Y. Wong (eds.), *The 1995 Legislative Council elections in Hong Kong.* Hong Kong: Hong Kong Institute of Asia-Pacific Studies, Chinese University of Hong Kong.

Leung, S. W. (1997). *The making of an alienated generation: The political socialization of secondary school students in transitional Hong Kong.* London: Ashgate.

Meyer, J. W., and B. Rowan. (1991). "Institutionalized organizations: Formal structure as myth and ceremony." In W. W. Powell and P. J. DiMaggio (eds.), *The new institutionalism in organizational analysis.* Chicago: University of Chicago Press.

Pateman, C. (1970). *Participation and democratic theory.* Cambridge: Cambridge University Press.

Remy, R. C. (1972). "High school seniors' attitudes toward their civics and government instruction," *Social Education* 36:590–622.

Sigel, R. S. (1970). "Change, conflict and socialization." in R. S. Sigel (ed.), *Learning about politics: A reader in political socialization.* New York: Random House.

Stinchombe, A. L. (1975). "Merton's theory of social structure," in L. A. Coser and R. Nisbet (eds.), *The idea of social structure: Papers in honor of Robert K. Merton.* New York: Harcourt Brace Jovanovich.

Thelen, K., and S. Steinmo. (1992). "Historical institutionalism in comparative politics." In S. Steinmo, K. Thelen, and F. Longstreth (eds.), *Structuring politics:*

Historical institutionalism in comparative politics. Cambridge: Cambridge University Press.

Visiting Panel. (1982). *A perspective on education in Hong Kong.* Hong Kong: Government Printer.

Weber, Max, and Reinhard Bendix. (1962). *Max Weber: An intellectual portrait.* London: Methuen, 423–430.

DISCUSSION QUESTIONS

1. There are many stakeholders in formulating and implementing civic education. In the Hong Kong case, what role do these different stakeholders play in formulating, implementing, and perceiving civic education, and how do they interact with one another?

2. Define "old institutionalism" and "new institutionalism" according to what is discussed in this chapter. Summarize how institutionalism has played a constraining role in the formulation and implementation of civic education.

3. Do the institutional constraints only apply to Hong Kong? Can you apply the institutional-constraints perspective to another country in this book? Which country case will be the most illustrative of this method of analysis?

4. We have the concept of intended curriculum and unintended curriculum in curriculum studies. In terms of civic education in Hong Kong, are their any examples showing unintended outcomes for intended curriculum? If yes, what can this tell us in our teaching of civic education?

5. Schools in Hong Kong tend to adopt a conservative and apolitical perspective in civic education. Is this universal or exceptional? Can you discuss this in the context of your country?

About the Contributors

Ratna Ghosh is the dean of education, and a William C. Macdonald Professor of Education at McGill University in Montreal, Canada. She has been elected a fellow of the Royal Society of Canada and is a corresponding member of the European Academy of Arts, Sciences, and Humanities. Her publications in books, journals, encyclopedias, grants, and teaching address international and multicultural education, feminist pedagogy, and development studies. She has done research in Canada, Asia, Africa, and Latin America. Her most recent book is *Redefining Multicultural Education* (1996). She has held important administrative positions at McGill as director of Graduate Studies and Research for the Faculty of Education, and acting director of McGill International. She is active in the development and governance of the Shastri Indo-Canadian Institute (a consortium of Canadian universities involved in academic exchanges and programs between India and Canada) as its resident director in New Delhi, India, in 1982–1983 and as president of the Institute from 1988–1990. She has been on the board of directors (as well as the Education and International Committees) of the Canadian Human Rights Foundation. She is on the editorial board of several international journals and has been on the board of the Comparative and International Education Society of the United States.

Mark B. Ginsburg is a professor of comparative sociology of education, in the Departments of Administrative and Policy Studies and of Sociology at the University of Pittsburgh, Pennsylvania. He is also codirector of the Pitt's Institute for International Studies in Education. His book publications include *Contradiction in Teacher Education and Society: A Critical Analysis*, Falmer (1988); *Understanding Educational Reform in Global Context: Economy, Ideology, and the State*, Garland (1991); *The Political Dimension in Teacher Education: Comparative Perspectives on Policy Formation, Socialization,* *and Society,* Falmer (1995); *The Politics of Educators Work and Lives,* Garland (1995); and *Cuba in the Special Period: Cuban Perspectives,* Third World Studies (1997) and *Editorial de Ciencias Sociales de Cuba* (1998).

Aurora Elizondo Huerta holds the post of professor at the Universidad Pedagógica Nacional, Ajusco, and also serves as director of the Ph.D. program in education. She was director of a trinational research project on values in teacher education programs in Canada, the United States, and Mexico. She has played a major role in the development and implementation of binational teacher education programs in Mexico and California. Elizondo Huerta has published several books and written numerous articles and delivered many presentations on values in multicultural contexts, women's issues, education innovation, and educational supervision.

Yaacov Iram is a professor of comparative and international education at Bar Ilan University, Israel. He holds the Josef Burg Chair in Education for Human Values, Tolerance and Peace and is the immediate past president of the World Association for Educational Research. He has authored and edited several books, and has published extensively on a variety of educational issues in Israel from a comparative perspective, in Hebrew, English, German, Russian, French, and Italian scholarly journals, books, and encyclopedias. His most recent book is *The Educational System of Israel* (1998).

Lisa Laumann completed her Ph.D in education, specializing in comparative education, at the University of California, Los Angeles, where she was also assistant book review editor of the *Comparative Education Review* from 1999–2000. Her current research is on gender ideology and the nongovernmental sector in Pakistan. She has been a teacher in Morocco and has worked with a number of nongovernmental humanitarian organizations with relief and development programs. At present, she is working with a humanitarian organization in Pakistan.

Robert F. Lawson received his Ph.D. in education at the University of Michigan and is now a professor of comparative education in the School of Educational Policy and Leadership at Ohio State University. He has been head of the Department of Educational Foundations and dean of the Faculty of Education at the University of Calgary, and chair of the Department of Educational Policy and Leadership at Ohio State. He has spent extended research and teaching periods at the University of Hamburg, Freie Universitaet Berlin, University of Natal, University of Dar es Salaam, Edith Cowen University in Australia, Indiana University, and the University of California Los Angeles. He has been a member of the Comparative and International Education Society since 1963, and served as president in 1974–1975. His research interest is the political sociology of educational change in Central European, South African, and Commonwealth societies. Major published works include *Education and Social Concern,* with Susanne Shafer and Val Rust, *Changing Patterns of Secondary Education: An International Comparison,* and recently, "The Evolution of Democratic Education in South Africa," in E. Epstein and N. McGinn, *Comparative Perspectives on the Role of Education in Democratization.*

Lee Wing-on is professor and dean of the School of Foundations in Education and co-head of the Centre for Citizenship Education at the Hong Kong Institute of Education. He has previously served on the Faculty of Education at the University of Hong Kong as associate dean of Education and director of the Comparative Education Research Centre. He is also past president of the Comparative Education Society of Hong Kong. He has published widely in the areas of comparative education, focusing on values education and sociocultural perspectives.

Leung Sai-wing is associate professor of the Department of Public and Social Administration at the Hong Kong Polytechnic University. His research interests include voting behavior, popular culture, and social indicators.

Leslie J. Limage is a program specialist in education at the United Nations Educational, Scientific and Cultural Organization (UNESCO) and has worked for the Organization for Economic Cooperation and Development (OECD) on education for multicultural societies, and women and labor market issues. She holds graduate degrees in comparative education, sociology of education, and economics of education from the University of Paris and the University of London Institute of Education. She has taught at secondary, adult, and university levels in several countries. Her major research interests are in basic education, literacy, language, and gender issues, as well as European education and issues of democracy and civics responsibility. She has published widely as editor or contributor to collective scholarly volumes, international journals, and volumes she has edited through UNESCO, OECD, and other international organizations.

Hans Lingens is a professor and joined the faculty of the School of Education at California Lutheran University after a career as a high school science and foreign language teacher, and after working in the Research and Evaluation Branch in the Los Angeles Unified School District. His special research interests are in comparative and international education with emphasis on teacher education and higher education policy development. He is the editor of *European Education.* Teaching areas include multicultural education and methods of research. He received his Ed.D. from the University of Southern California.

Wolfgang Mitter holds a doctorate on the Russian historian Karamzin from the Free University of Berlin in 1954, and was a secondary school teacher until 1964. He then was professor of general and comparative education until his transfer to the position of emeritus professor in 1995. Between 1972 and 1995 he was head of the Department of General and Comparative Education at the German Institute for International Educational Research in Frankfurt am Main, and from 1978 to 1981 and from 1987 to 1995 was its director. Since 1974 he has been teaching at Frankfurt University. From 1991 to 1996 he was president of the World Council of Comparative Education Societies. He has published widely on general and comparative education, with special regard to Eastern and Central Europe and on comparisons in the global range.

David Phillips is a fellow of St. Edmund Hall and a reader in comparative education at the University of Oxford. His main research interest is in education in Germany, and he has published widely on aspects of education in the postwar and post-Unification periods. He is currently chair of the British Association for International and Comparative Education, editor of the *Oxford Review of Education,* and series editor of *Oxford Studies in Comparative Education.*

Val D. Rust is a professor of comparative and international education and the director of education abroad at the University of California, Los Angeles. His research interests include intercultural educational activities, the politics of school reform, institutional renewal and education in rapidly changing environments, and contemporary European education. He is a former president of the Comparative and International Education Society and has held many offices in other scholarly bodies. He is currently associate editor for book reviews of the *Comparative Education Review.*

Gerlind Schmidt holds a Ph.D for her thesis entitled *"Die polytechnische Bildung in der Sowjetunion und in der DDR"* (Polytechnical Education in the Soviet Union and in the German Democratic Republic) from the University of Bochum. From 1972 to 1998 she was a staff member of the Department for General and Comparative Education, chaired by Dr. Wolfgang Mitter, at the German Institute for International Educational Research (DIPF), Frankfurt. Since 1999, she has been attached to the working unit "Information on Education" of the DIPF. She has participated in many research projects in the field of comparative education primarily concerning Eastern and Western European countries, and in recent years, Russia and the Commonwealth of Independent States.

Nelly P. Stromquist is a professor of international development education at the University of Southern California. She specializes in gender issues, which she examines from a sociopolitical perspective. Her work has included studies of adult literacy, equity policies of states and international development agencies, and educational innovations. Her most recent books include *Literacy for Citizenship: Gender and Grassroots Dynamics in Brazil* (1997), *Gender Dimensions in Education in Latin America* (1996), and *Women in the Third World: An Encyclopedia of Contemporary Issues* (1999).

Margaret B. Sutherland is an emeritus professor of education, University of Leeds, Great Britain. She is a past editor of the *British Journal of Educational Studies* and an honorary fellow of the Scottish Council for Research in Education. She is past president of the Association *Francophone pour l'Éducation Comparée* and active in the World Council of Comparative Education Societies as well as other scholarly bodies. Her research interests are mainly in the field of comparative education, where she has published widely, especially with regard to the education of girls and women.

Elizabeth Sherman Swing, professor emerita of education at Saint Joseph's University in Philadelphia, is coeditor (with Juergen Schriewer and Francois Orivel) of the forthcoming *Problems and Prospects in European Education.* Much of her research has focused on languages in contact and on the education of minorities and immigrants in urban areas, in Europe as well as the United States. The Belgian government named her Ridder in de Kroonorde (Knight in the Order of the Crown) in 1990 for research on the educational implications of the Belgian language controversy. In 1992 (Prague) and 1996 (Sydney), she cochaired the European Commission of the World Congress of Comparative Education Societies with Raymond Ryba.

Norma Tarrow is a professor of education at California State University, Long Beach. She was director of California State Universities and Colleges International Programs in Mexico from 1994 to 1996. She was a visiting scholar at the Centre for Multicultural Education, Institute of Education, University of London in 1992 and has held Research Fellowships in Israel in 1973, in Columbia in 1985, and in Spain in 1982 and 1984, as well as holding a Fulbright fellowship in Catalonia and the Basque region in 1989. Her research interests include human rights and intercultural education, specializing in the education of indigenous minority groups. She is the coeditor of *Dimensions of the Community College: International, Intercultural, and Multicultural Perspectives* (1996) and editor of *Human Rights and Education* (1987). She has also authored chapters in several recent volumes, including *International Perspectives on Intercultural Educaton* (1998); *Education and Cultural Difference* (1992); *Socialization of School Children and Their Education for Democratic Values and Human Rights* (1991), as well as many journal articles.

For Product Safety Concerns and Information please contact our EU
representative GPSR@taylorandfrancis.com
Taylor & Francis Verlag GmbH, Kaufingerstraße 24, 80331 München, Germany